National G   ne

Parks
of the United States

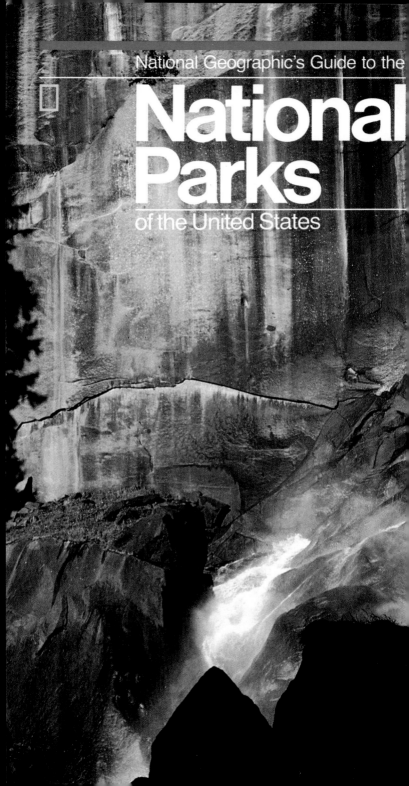

National Geographic's Guide to the

National
Parks

of the United States

Published by
The National
Geographic Society

Gilbert M. Grosvenor
President and
Chairman of the Board

Michela A. English
Senior Vice President

William R. Gray
Vice President and
Director, Book Division

Prepared by
National Geographic
Book Service

Charles O. Hyman
Director

Ross S. Bennett
Associate Director

Margaret Sedeen
Managing Editor

Susan C. Eckert
Director of Research

Guidebook Staff

Elizabeth L. Newhouse
Editor

Linda B. Meyerriecks
Illustrations Editor

David M. Seager
Art Director

Melanie Ann Patt-Corner
Research Editor

Thomas B. Allen
Carole Douglis
Writer-Editors

John L. Culliney
Kim Heacox
Catherine Herbert Howell
Gary Krist
Jeremy Schmidt
Gene S. Stuart
Scott Thybony
Writers

Paulette L. Claus
Mary Grady
Lise Swinson Sajewski
Anne E. Withers
Editorial Researchers

Mary Grady
Map Editor

Lise Swinson Sajewski
Style

Caroline Sheen
Picture Editor

Clare Wilson
Design Assistant

Jean Cantu
Laura E. Goodwin
Laurie Smith
Illustrations Assistants

T. Destry Jarvis
Chief Consultant

Karen F. Edwards
Traffic Manager

Richard S. Wain
Production Manager

Andrea Crosman
Assistant Production
Manager

Emily F. Gwynn
Production Assistant

Manufacturing &
Quality Management:
John T. Dunn
Director
David V. Evans
Manager

R. Gary Colbert
Senior Administrative
Assistant

Teresita Cóquia Sison
Editorial Assistant

Susan G. Zenel
Indexer

Michael S. Frost
Charlotte Golin
William H. Johns
Miranda Lescaze
Sandra F. Lotterman
Zoë Pagnamenta
Tibor Toth
Contributors

Preceding pages: Hikers sur-
veying falling water and granite
cliffs, two of Yosemite's main
attractions

First Edition 285,000 copies
Revised Edition (1992) 100,000 copies
429 Illustrations
72 Maps

Library of Congress
CIP Data: page 432

Contents

6	The Gift of the Parks
8	Using the Guide

The East   14   Map

18	Acadia
28	Biscayne
36	Everglades
48	Great Smoky Mountains
58	Hot Springs
64	Isle Royale
72	Mammoth Cave
80	Shenandoah
88	Virgin Islands
96	Voyageurs

The Southwest   106   Map

108	Big Bend
118	Carlsbad
126	Guadalupe

The Colorado Plateau   134   Map

136	Arches
142	Bryce Canyon
148	Canyonlands
158	Capitol Reef
164	Grand Canyon
176	Great Basin
184	Mesa Verde
192	Petrified Forest
198	Zion

The Pacific Southwest   208   Map

210	American Samoa
212	Channel Islands
218	Haleakala
226	Hawaii Volcanoes
234	Sequoia & Kings Canyon
242	Yosemite

The Rocky Mountains   254   Map

256	Badlands
262	Grand Teton
272	Rocky Mountain
282	Theodore Roosevelt
290	Waterton-Glacier
300	Wind Cave
306	Yellowstone

The Pacific Northwest   320   Map

322	Crater Lake
330	Lassen Volcanic
336	Mount Rainier
346	North Cascades
354	Olympic
364	Redwood

Alaska   374   Map

376	Denali
388	Gates of the Arctic
394	Glacier Bay
400	Katmai
406	Kenai Fjords
412	Kobuk Valley
418	Lake Clark
424	Wrangell-St. Elias

430	Acknowledgments
430	Illustrations Credits
431	Index of Excursions

Green River canyon in Canyonlands National Park

The Gift of the Parks

One of the things that distinguishes this guidebook is its conscience—its attention to the welfare of the parks it describes. As you read, you will find the travel information interspersed with news of some threat to a park, or the history of a threat that lost out. National parks have been battlegrounds of the conservation movement, and the battles continue.

But even the battles can offer inspiration and instruction, and both the parks and the ideals by which we manage them evolve continually. Indeed, it has been said that the establishment of a park is only the beginning; that if we do it right, we never stop establishing that park, because we never stop learning about it, and about ourselves.

There was a time when Congress set up national parks to protect a few specific things: the wildlife here, the geysers there, the scenery over there. Other parts of the park got less attention, or were even mistreated. Well into the 1930s managers killed predators in some parks to protect the "good" animals. In the early days of Yosemite National Park, woodpeckers were shot if their tapping disturbed the sleep of hotel guests. Yellowstone allowed commercial fishing until well after 1900.

Only as the science of ecology matured, and we began to realize that everything in the park was interrelated, did our view change. Slowly, we realized that what we had was not best measured in acres of meadow and that a park is not a zoo.

Instead, we seek to save the whole thing, the whole creeping, flying, grazing, preying, photosynthesizing, eroding, raining, erupting, evolving scene. Call it wildness, or natural-

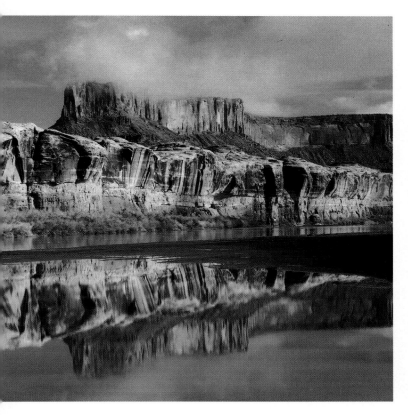

ness, or an ecosystem, or whatever you like, it is this entangled collection of processes that we must save.

That means many things, some of which haven't been easy to hear. It means that people like me, who love to fish, have to leave enough trout in the streams to feed the otters, pelicans, bears, and other wild fishermen. It means we don't pick flowers, or collect rocks, removing them from their place in the natural system. It means we stop feeding wildlife, and let the animals find their own way, in balance with their environment.

In short, it means a revolution in the way we appreciate nature. We as a nation have decided that here, in these precious, rare places, we shall give nature a little more room to make its choices. If that means we must be prepared to watch a bear half a mile away through binoculars rather than watch it eating aluminum foil right outside the car window, so be it; everybody knew all along which was best for the bear.

If that means we must respect the role naturally caused fire has played in regenerating forests for thousands of years, so be it.

Anyone who reads the papers knows that this doesn't always work smoothly. Nature isn't much for respecting our rules. Bears have a way of reminding us we're not always in charge. And, as Yellowstone showed us in 1988, fires can get a lot bigger than anybody expected. Nobody said this was going to be easy. But the more we try, the more we learn.

And so these great parks, which enchant us with their beauty and restore us with their peace, have yet another gift to give. They are laboratories of ideas, offering profound lessons in the natural way of things, and in what that way can mean to the human soul. The lessons don't always come easily, but they're always worth the trip.

Paul Schullery
Yellowstone National Park

Sightseers at Geyser Hill, Yellowstone

Using the Guide

Each of the 50 scenic parks offers you fun, adventure, and—usually—enthralling splendor. What you experience will depend on where you go and what you do. But exploring an unknown land is best done with a guide, a companion who has tested the trail and learned the lore.

Our coverage of each park begins with a portrait of its natural wonders, ecological setting, history, and, often, its struggles against pollution, erosion, development, and other environmental threats. You'll see why a single step off a trail can harm fragile plants, and why visitors are detoured from certain areas that shelter wildlife. The parks are not just for people; they conserve ecosystems that sustain plants and animals. Nine parks have been designated United Nations World Heritage sites for their outstanding scenic wonders; eighteen have International Bio-

sphere Reserve status, signaling the distinctive qualities of their natural environments.

Before starting off on your park exploration, use the *Guide* to preview the parks you may want to visit. You'll notice that each park introduction is followed by three how-and-when sections; below they give you general advice about visiting:

How to Get There

You may be able to include more than one park in your trip. The maps at the beginning of each regional section show the connecting highways. Base your itinerary not so much on mileage as on time, remembering that parks do not lie alongside interstates; park roads are usually rugged—and, in summer, crowded.

When to Go

Instead of going to a popular park in midsummer, avoid peak crowds by scheduling the trip for June or late August and timing your arrival early on a weekday. In many parks, fall is glorious, and autumn vistas coincide with a relative scarcity of visitors. Spring brings wildflowers to many parks and with winter comes snow-swept beauty, summoning skiers, snowshoe hikers, and ice skaters. Although parks are generally open year-round, off-season visitor facilities may be limited. Consult this heading for each park chapter as well as its **Information & Activities** section.

How to Visit

Examining nature in Waterton Lakes

Don't rush through a park. Give yourself time to savor the beauty. Incredibly, the average time the typical visitor spends in a park is half a day. Often, that blur of time flashes past a windshield. No matter how long you decide to stay, spend at least part of that time in the park, not in your car. Check bulletin boards or park newspapers for the activities schedule. Each park's **How to Visit** section recommends a plan for visits of $\frac{1}{2}$, 1, 2, or more days. *Guide* writers devised the plans and trekked every tour, but don't be afraid to explore on your own. And don't neglect the **Excursions** at the end of most park chapters; they take you to other natural areas nearby.

Other features of the *Guide:*

Maps The park maps and regional maps were prepared as an aid in planning your trip. For more detail on hiking trails and other facilities inside a park, contact the Park Service or the park itself. Always use a road map when traveling.

The maps note specially designated areas within park borders: *Wilderness Areas* are managed to retain their primeval quality. Roads, buildings, and vehicles are not allowed in them. *National Preserves* may allow hunting.

The following abbreviations are used for federal lands:
NP National Park
NRA National Recreation Area
NF National Forest
NM National Monument
NWR National Wildlife Refuge

Information & Activities

This section, which follows each park chapter, offers detailed visitor information. Call or write the park for

Exploring Big Bend's backcountry

anything else you need to know. Brochures are usually available free of charge from the parks or by writing to: National Park Service, US Dept. of the Interior, P.O. Box 37127, Washington, D. C. 20013-7127. Attention: Office of Public Affairs.

Entrance Fees. Some parks are free; others charge fees. Most remain free to those over 62 and under 16. For $25 you can buy a Golden Eagle Pass, which is good for a year and admits all occupants of a private vehicle to all national parks and other federal sites. The same entry rules cover people over 62 who have a lifetime Golden Age Passport, and disabled people carrying a Golden Access Passport, both of which are free. You can get these documents at any Park Service facility where entrance fees are charged.

Pets. Generally they're not allowed on trails, in buildings, or in the backcountry. Elsewhere, they must be leashed. Specific rules are noted.

Facilities for Disabled. This *Guide*

only touches on what each park can and cannot offer visitors with disabilities, but an excellent resource is the *Access America Guides to the National Parks*. They are available in libraries and bookstores or directly from the publisher: Northern Cartographic, Inc., P.O. Box 133, Burlington, Vermont 05402.

Special Advisories. □Don't take chances. People are killed or badly injured every year in national parks. Most casualties are caused by recklessness or inattention to clearly posted warnings.
□Stay away from wild animals. Don't feed them. Don't try to touch them. Not even raccoons or chipmunks (which can transmit diseases). Try not to surprise a bear

and don't let one approach you. If one does, scare it off by yelling, clapping your hands, or banging pots. Store all your food; keep it out of sight in your vehicle, with windows closed and doors locked. Or suspend it at least 15 feet above ground, and 10 feet out from a post or tree trunk.
□Guard your health. If you are not fit, don't overtax your body. Boil water that doesn't come from a park's drinking-water tap. Chemical treatment of water will not kill *Giardia*, a protozoan that causes severe diarrhea and lurks even in crystal clear streams. Heed park warnings about hypothermia and Lyme disease, carried by ticks.
□Expect RV detours. Check road regulations as you enter a park. Along

some stretches of many roads you will not be able to maneuver a large vehicle, especially a trailer.

Campgrounds. Most park campgrounds admit people first come, first served, with limits on length of stay and number of persons. A reservations system called MISTIX handles some campgrounds at the most heavily visited parks: Acadia, Grand Canyon, Great Smoky Mountains, Mammoth Cave, Rocky Mountain, Sequoia & Kings Canyon, Shenandoah, Yellowstone, and Yosemite. For a single campsite, reserve up to 8 weeks in advance by calling 1-800-365-2267 (up to 12 weeks in advance for groups of 8 or more). If a campground is booked, the reservations agent will recommend alternatives.

Pay by credit card over the phone, or by check or money order within 14 days. Or, write to MISTIX, P.O. Box 85705, San Diego, California 92138-5705. Mail reservation forms are available from MISTIX at the above address, from any park on the reservations system, or from the National Park Service at the address on page 9 under **Information & Activities.**

Hotels, Motels, & Inns. The *Guide* lists accommodations as a service to its readers. The lists are by no means comprehensive, and listing does not imply endorsement by the National Geographic Society. The information can change without notice. Most parks keep full lists of accommodations in their areas, which they will send you on request.

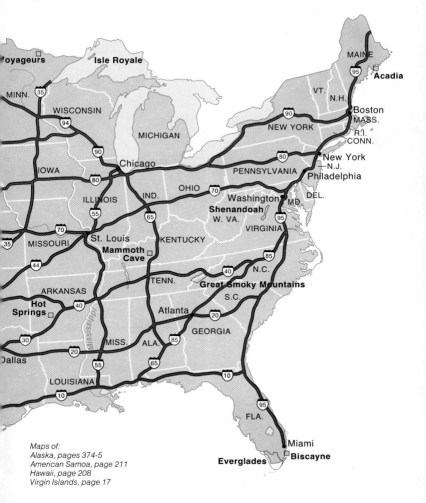

Maps of:
Alaska, pages 374-5
American Samoa, page 211
Hawaii, page 208
Virgin Islands, page 17

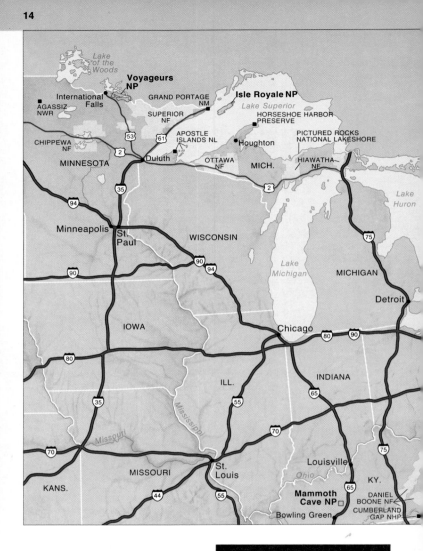

The East

Not until well into the 20th century, long after the idea of preserving the West's grand vistas had taken hold, did park planners turn their attention to the more subtle beauties of eastern scenery. The threats to nature from expanding cities and, after World War I, the surge in automobile travel and highway building boosted the movement to create eastern parks. Between 1919 and 1926, Congress authorized the first three in the crumpled belt of the Appalachian Mountains. Today these parks—Acadia, Great Smoky Moun-

Preceding pages: Along the Blue Ridge Parkway

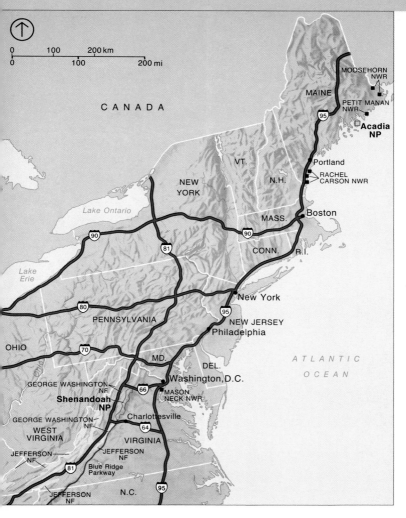

tains, and Shenandoah—rank among the most visited in the nation.

Acadia protects the plants and animals that inhabit the mountains, islands, sea, and tide pools along a stretch of wild New England coast. The hardwood forests and flowering meadows of Shenandoah, on land that had been logged, farmed, and grazed for 250 years, are studies in nature's power of recuperation. Great Smoky preserves large stands of virgin forest on 6,000-foot slopes and shelters more than a hundred species of trees.

Since the 1920s Congress has moved to safeguard other distinctive eastern biomes. Inside Mammoth Cave National Park lies the world's largest known cave network, with

Americans' love for the automobile led to the demand for highways to drive and helped spur the creation of national parks in the East. In 1935 the Blue Ridge Parkway was begun as a public works project; it became part of the Park Service the following year. The nation's most traveled federal parkway, the Blue Ridge links Shenandoah's Skyline Drive to Great Smoky Mountains National Park. Together, the drives create a spectacular 574-mile stretch of ridgetop road punctuated by wayside exhibits and trails.

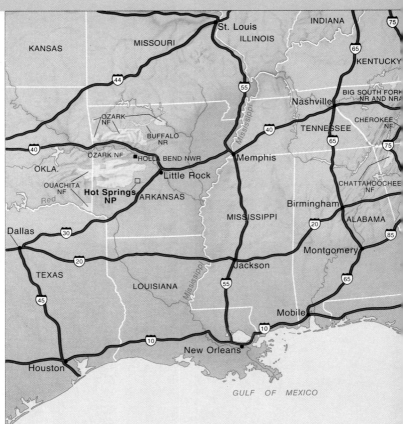

more than 330 miles of mapped passages. Isle Royale on the US-Canada border encompasses an entire island ecosystem. In and around its lakes, thick forest, and fjordlike coast live wolves and moose, their prey.

Not far away, dozens of lakes and uncountable streams lace the forests of Voyageurs National Park, named for the French-Canadian fur traders who for about a hundred years paddled these waters in canoes.

Other kinds of waters—those flowing from hot springs—inspired the creation of diminutive Hot Springs National Park. Most of the 47 hot springs lead into the plumbing of this former resort town's bathhouses.

Underwater wilderness awaits visitors to Florida's Biscayne National Park, home of the northernmost living coral reef in the continental United States. West of Biscayne lies Everglades National Park, established in 1947 less to preserve scenery than

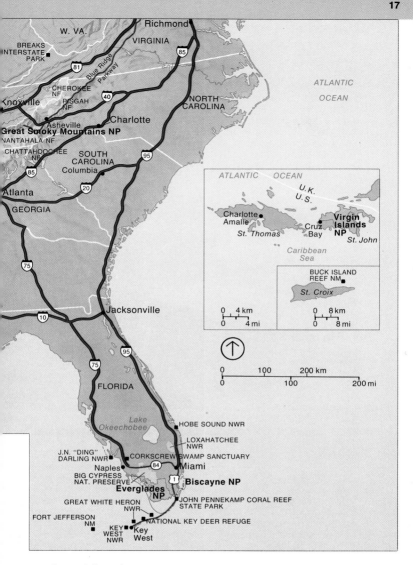

to safeguard the unique ecosystem created by a slow-moving river, inches deep and 50 miles wide. Itself endangered by the diversion of water to the growing towns and agribusinesses of south Florida, Everglades provides habitat for an enormous variety of wildlife, including numerous endangered species.

Offshore, the Virgin Islands National Park protects much of St. John, where hillsides, thick with bay rum, mango, and trumpet trees, slope to crescent beaches rimmed by turquoise water and coral reefs.

In the 1960s the National Park Service set a goal to create a park as a "vignette of primitive America" in every major natural community in the country.

The newer parks of the East—Virgin Islands, Biscayne, and Voyageurs—expanded the already considerable diversity of the region's parks.

Sunrise on Acadia's pink granite coast

Acadia

Maine

Established February 26, 1919

35,000 acres

Sea and mountain meet at Acadia, where, as one presumably ambidextrous visitor wrote, "you can fish with one hand and sample blueberries from a wind-stunted bush with the other."

Most of Acadia is on Mt. Desert Island, a patchwork of parkland, private property, and seaside villages that seasonally fill with what residents call "the summer people." Other bits of the park are scattered on smaller islands and a peninsula.

Mt. Desert Island once was continental mainland, a mountainous granite ridge on the edge of the ocean. Some 20,000 years ago, towering glacial ice sheets—sometimes a mile thick—flowed over the mountains, rounding their tops, cutting passes, gouging out lake beds, and widening valleys. As the glaciers melted, the sea rose, flooding valleys and drowning the coast. The preglacier ridge was transformed into today's lake-studded, mountainous island, which thrusts from the Atlantic like a lobster's claw.

Samuel de Champlain, who explored the coast in 1604, named the island L'Isle des Monts Déserts, sometimes translated as "the island of barren mountains." From his ship he probably could not see the mountains' forested slopes. The summer people rediscovered Mt. Desert in the mid-19th century, built mansions they called "cottages," anchored their yachts in rock-girt harbors, and cherished the wild. To preserve it, they donated the nucleus land for the park, the first east of the Mississippi.

When to Go

All-year park, but main visitor center is open from about May 1 to November 1. Expect traffic jams in July and August. Spectacular foliage also attracts crowds around the end of September. Snow and ice close most park roads from December through April, but parts of the park are open for cross-country skiing.

How to Visit

Allow at least a day for **Mt. Desert Island,** with a drive on the 20-mile **Park Loop Road** and the road to the summit of **Cadillac Mountain.** If fog comes, enjoy its gift: a softening of sights and sounds. On a second day, enjoy an uncrowded view of the rocky coast of Maine by visiting the **Schoodic Peninsula.** If you have more time, take your pick of one of the trails or smaller islands.

Mt. Desert Island

60 miles; at least a full day

To get the most from a tour of **Mt. Desert Island** on the **Park Loop Road** in summer, get up very early. (On most clear days, traffic is bumper-to-bumper between 10 a.m. and 3 p.m.) The day before, check the time of sunrise in a local newspaper or at the visitor center. About 30 minutes before dawn, take coffee and a blanket and drive from the visitor center to 1,530-foot **Cadillac Mountain.** The 3½-mile mountain road switchbacks up to a parking area.

The original name, Lafayette National Park, was changed in 1929.

Dependent on donated land since its inception, the park took what it could get, skirting around private property and growing piece by piece. Acadia's real estate was so patchy that not until 1986 did Congress set its official boundaries.

The fifth smallest national park, Acadia has the second highest visitation—more than five million people a year. Traffic jams often produce a phenomenon unknown to Mt. Desert's first summer people: gridlock.

How to Get There

From Ellsworth (about 18 miles north), take Hwy. 3 to Mt. Desert Island, where most of the park is located; the visitor center is about 3 miles north of Bar Harbor. Another section lies southeast of Ellsworth, on the Schoodic Peninsula, a 1½-hour drive from Bar Harbor. To get to the park's islands, see **The Islands.** Airports: Bangor and Bar Harbor.

Autumn on Cadillac Mountain

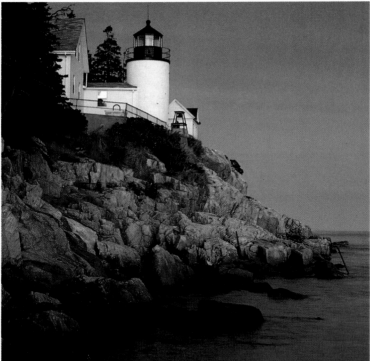

Bass Harbor Head lighthouse at dusk

From there walk to the **Summit Trail,** find an east-facing niche in the rocks, and settle in on the highest east coast mountain north of Brazil. Here is one of the places where dawn first touches the continental United States. After enjoying the dawn, use the new day's light to hunt for blueberries along the trails radiating from the summit. The blueberry season runs through July and August.

On the way down, stop at one of the eastern overlooks for a view of **Frenchman Bay,** a vast, island-dotted seascape; its name takes note of the area's early French settlers. (Another way to see the bay is on a 2-hour sea cruise; check schedules at the Municipal Pier in Bar Harbor.)

Return to the loop road and turn right. Less than ½ mile on, bear right again (here the road becomes one-way) and continue toward the ocean. Pass up **Sand Beach** for now. You may want to return to the beach later for sunbathing or swimming (though the summer water temperature is between 50° and 55°F).

Not quite a mile farther, a sign marks **Thunder Hole.** Park on the right and walk down the concrete steps to the cleft in the rocks, named for the roars produced when air, trapped and squeezed by incoming surf, explodes out of a cavern. A stop here may disappoint you, for you'll probably hear the thunder only at half tide with a rising sea, or after a storm. Other times, you may hear only gurgles and sloshes.

Continue to the 110-foot **Otter Cliffs.** Park, cross the road, and walk the shore path to **Otter Point.** Bobbing offshore are numerous brightly colored buoys marking lobster traps. Linger here to savor the essence of the Maine coast: rocks, gulls, the tang of salt air. At **Hunters Head** the loop road turns away from the sea and soon becomes two-way as you head back to where you started. You'll pass **Jordan Pond,** one of many glacier-carved ponds on the island.

Your drive has taken you around the eastern side of the island. To explore the western side, you must drive out of park property and back in again. Continue north on the loop

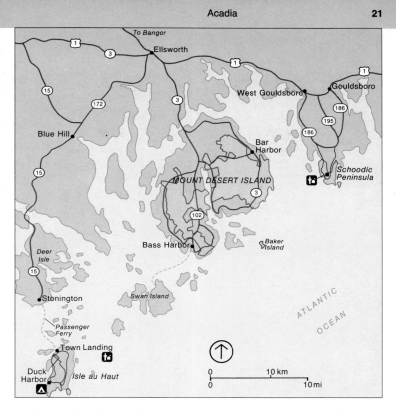

road, cross the bridge, and bear right to get on Maine Hwy. 233. Head west on 233 to Maine 198, then head south on Maine 102 toward Somesville. Continue south. On your left is **Somes Sound,** the only fjord on the US Atlantic coast. On your right is **Echo Lake,** a swimming spot with a small beach.

Maine 102 passes through Southwest Harbor. Just beyond, near Manset, bear left on Maine 102A, which takes you into a large patch of park property. You can picnic at **Seawall** and then stretch your legs on the nearby 1$\frac{1}{4}$-mile **Ship Harbor Nature Trail,** which gives you a lesson in how a forest shore is knit to the tidal sea.

A short detour off 102A takes you to **Bass Harbor Head,** site of a 19th-century lighthouse. Take 102A through **Bass Harbor** and bear left on 102 toward Tremont. Continue north for 7 miles to a tract of park called **Pretty Marsh,** a beautiful picnic spot. A short worn path leads to the rock-strewn shore. Continue on 102 and retrace your route from Somesville to the visitor center.

Schoodic Peninsula

100 miles; a full day

To drive the 45 miles from Bar Harbor to the park's outpost, the **Schoodic Peninsula,** take Maine 3 to US 1, south of Ellsworth, and head east to West Gouldsboro. Go south via Maine 186 to Winter Harbor, then follow signs to the park entrance.

From there, take the 6-mile one-way drive to **Schoodic Point.** The massive granite rocks here are laced by black diabase dikes, the product of magma that welled up into cracks. Schoodic's displays of thundering surf usually top those of Mt. Desert Island. And the audiences are much smaller; the peninsula does not draw crowds the way Mt. Desert does.

Continue on the drive and park opposite **Little Moose Island.** At low tide, take the short walk through the intertidal puddles and muck to the island. A meandering path leads you seaward for a panoramic view of the Atlantic. *Stay on the path* to avoid damaging the fragile plants.

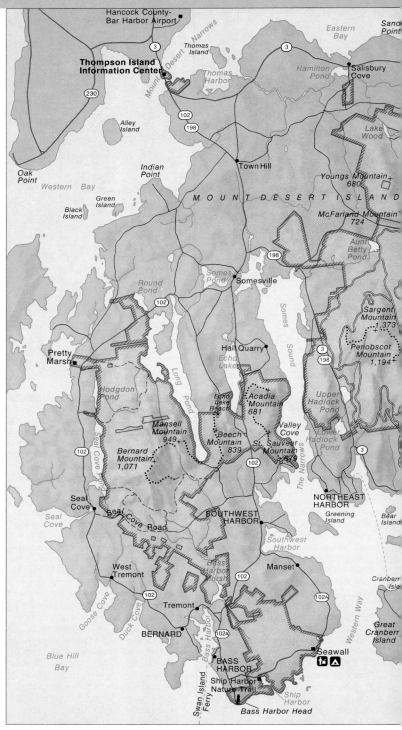

Hancock County-
Bar Harbor Airport

Thomas Narrows

Thomas Island

Eastern Bay

Sand Point

3

3

**Thompson Island
Information Center**

Thomas Harbor

Hamilton Pond

Salisbury
Cove

230

102

198

Alley Island

Lake Wood

Oak Point

Western Bay

Indian Point

Town Hill

M O U N T   D E S E R T   I S L A N D

Youngs Mountain
680

Green Island

Black Island

198

McFarland Mountain
724

Aunt Betty Pond

Round Pond

Somes Pond

Somesville

Somes Sound

*Sargent Mountain
1,373*

102

Penobscot
Mountain
1,194

Pretty
Marsh

Hall Quarry

Echo Lake

3

198

Hodgdon Pond

Long Pond

Echo Lake Beach

*Acadia Mountain
681*

Upper Hadlock Pond

*Mansell Mountain
949*

*Beech Mountain
839*

*St. Sauveur Mountain
679*

Valley Cove

Lower Hadlock Pond

3

*Bernard Mountain
1,071*

Seal Cove Pond

102

Seal Cove

Seal
Cove

Seal Cove Road

SOUTHWEST
HARBOR

NORTHEAST
HARBOR

Greening Island

Bear Island

Southwest Harbor

West
Tremont

Bass Harbor Marsh

Manset

102

Cranberry Isle

102

102A

Goose Cove

Duck Cove

Tremont

Bass Harbor

102A

Western Way

Great Cranberry Island

BERNARD

Blue Hill Bay

Swan Island Ferry

BASS
HARBOR

Seawall

Ship Harbor
Nature Trail

Ship Harbor

Bass Harbor Head

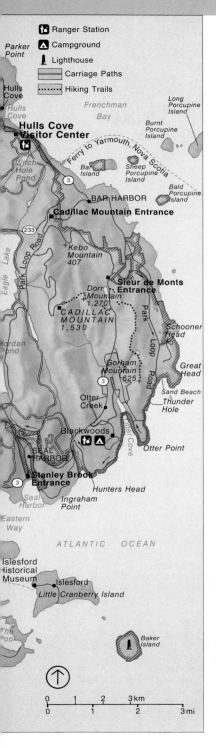

Map Legend

- **Ranger Station**
- **Campground**
- **Lighthouse**
- Carriage Paths
- Hiking Trails

Parker Point

Hulls Cove

Frenchman Bay

Long Porcupine Island

Burnt Porcupine Island

Hulls Cove Visitor Center

Ferry to Yarmouth, Nova Scotia

Witch Hole Pond

Bar Island

Sheep Porcupine Island

Bald Porcupine Island

BAR HARBOR

Cadillac Mountain Entrance

233

Eagle Lake

Kebo Mountain 407

Sieur de Monts Entrance

Dorr Mountain 1,270

CADILLAC MOUNTAIN 1,530

Park Loop Road

Schooner Head

Jordan Pond

Gorham Mountain 525

Great Head

Otter Creek

Sand Beach
Thunder Hole

Blackwoods

SEAL HARBOR

Otter Point

Stanley Brook Entrance

3

Seal Harbor

Hunters Head

Ingraham Point

Eastern Way

ATLANTIC OCEAN

Islesford Historical Museum

Islesford

Little Cranberry Island

The Pool

Baker Island

0 1 2 3 km
0 1 2 3 mi

The Islands

a full day each

Fragments of Acadia are on islands. Two worth visiting are **Isle au Haut**, about half of which is park property, and **Baker Island**, which is almost entirely park owned. Isle au Haut is served all year by mail boats, Baker Island in summer only by tour boats. Get boat schedules from the visitor center or from the boat operators.

The trip to Isle au Haut, or "high island," named by Samuel de Champlain, begins at Stonington, at the tip of **Deer Isle**, about 30 miles from Ellsworth. To make the boat on time from Mt. Desert Island, allot at least 2 hours for the drive and for finding a rare legal parking place near the harbor. Bring lunch. The mail boat takes passengers on a first-come, first-served basis. The 45-minute voyage ends at the Town Landing. In summer the boat also stops at **Duck Harbor**, a park campsite and trailhead.

American oystercatcher on nest

Blue mussels and a dog whelk with eggs

A grove of white birch, sunrise

For a fine hike, get off at the town landing and turn right. A short distance down the road is a ranger station. Here begins the 4-mile **Duck Harbor Trail,** which takes you through upland forest, along the shore, and past blueberry brambles (picking and eating allowed) to Duck Harbor. Spend the day here wandering the area's trails, enjoying woods-and-water scenery, and watching for ospreys and bald eagles. Get the late-afternoon boat back.

For Baker Island, round-trip tour boats leave daily in summer, weather permitting, from Northeast Harbor, a town at the tip of Mt. Desert Island. During the 45-minute trip, a park naturalist points out ospreys and seals and tells the story of the Gilley family, 19th-century inhabitants of Baker Island. The enterprising and self-sufficient pioneer family, which eventually included 12 children, lived on fish, duck, home-raised sheep, cattle, potatoes, and lobsters plucked from shallow waters.

When the boat reaches the island, you transfer to a dory and land on a rocky beach. With the naturalist, you tour the island, seeing a white brick lighthouse built in 1855, a beach piled high with boulders, and the island graveyard filled with Gilleys. Son John is not buried there. On a fall day in 1896, his boat capsized in heavy seas; his body was never found.

Carriage Paths & Hikes

In 1917 John D. Rockefeller, Jr., a summer resident of Mt. Desert Island, launched the building of a 57-mile network of wide gravel paths for horse-drawn carriages. Convinced that the newfangled automobile would destroy the tranquillity of the island, he banned it from the carriage paths. The paths were graced by 17 hand-built granite bridges, each a unique work of art. Rockefeller later donated the path network, along with 11,000 acres of his land, to the park. The carriage paths, still not open to cars, are a treasure prized by hikers, bikers, horseback riders, and cross-country skiers.

To introduce yourself to the carriage paths, try the $3^9/_{10}$-mile **Hadlock Brook Loop.** Park at the Maine Hwy. 198 parking area just north of **Upper Hadlock Pond** and walk to the trailhead. Take the left fork east toward **Hemlock Bridge,** a gem of hand-hewn stone. Follow the rising road to an-

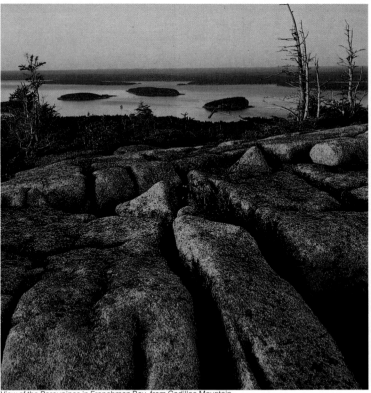

View of the Porcupines in Frenchman Bay, from Cadillac Mountain

Herring gull in Schoodic fog

other handsome span, **Waterfall Bridge,** site of a 40-foot fall. (You can turn around here, cutting your hike to about 2 miles round-trip.) Cross the bridge and walk south for a mile to one of the network's well-marked intersections. Turn right at intersection 19 and right again at intersection 18 and continue along the pond. Watch—and listen—for loons. The road crosses **Hadlock Brook Bridge** and loops back to the trailhead.

The park also has 120 miles of hiking trails, which range from easy strolls along the ocean or around ponds to steep climbs up Cadillac and other mountains. For a jaunt into history try the **Gorge Path,** which, like several other trails, has stone steps to ease your way up slopes. The steps, flat stones imbedded in rising ground, were built by turn-of-the-century summer people who wanted to rough it, but not too much. The path begins at a parking spot on the Park Loop Road, near 407-foot **Kebo Mountain,** and leads to a wood trail. Cairns mark the trail when it follows a rocky, brook-washed ravine. About a mile into the woods is an intersection. Depending upon your time and stamina, you can turn and retrace your steps or push on to Cadillac or **Dorr Mountain,** each a steep hike of more than $1\frac{1}{2}$ miles.

Information & Activities

Headquarters
P.O. Box 177, Bar Harbor, Maine 04609. Phone (207) 288-3338.

Seasons & Accessibility
Park open all year, but in winter the visitor facilities close and much of the Park Loop Road remains unplowed. For recorded weather information call (207) 667-8910. For boats to Isle au Haut call (207) 367-5193; for Baker Island call (207) 276-3717.

Visitor & Information Centers
Visitor center on Maine Hwy. 3 just south of Hull's Cove, open daily May through October. Also, Thompson Island Information Center on Hwy. 3, just before crossing onto Mt. Desert Island. Off season, information available at headquarters $2\frac{1}{2}$ miles west of Bar Harbor on Hwy. 233.

Entrance Fee
$5 per car per week, collected from about May 1 to November 1.

Pets
Permitted on leashes except on swimming beaches, in public buildings, on a few hiking trails, and at Isle au Haut campsite.

Facilities for Disabled
Visitor center, some rest rooms and carriage paths are wheelchair accessible. Free brochure available.

Things to Do
Free naturalist-led activities: nature walks, photography workshops, stargazing, films, slide shows. Also available, bus tours (call 207-288-3327), bay and island cruises, carriage rides, hayrides, auto tape tour, hiking, bicycling, horseback riding, swimming, fishing, cross-country skiing, snowshoeing, ice-skating and ice fishing, snowmobiling.

Special Advisories
☐ Be careful on ledges and rocks along shore; algae are slippery.
☐ In spring and fall, watch out for strong storm waves.

Overnight Backpacking
Not allowed.

Campgrounds
Two campgrounds, both with 14-day limit. **Blackwoods** open all year. Reservations—through MISTIX (see page 11)—recommended June 15-Sept. 15; other times first come, first served. **Seawall** open late May to Sept. 30. First come, first served. Fees $7-$12 per night. (**Blackwoods** free mid-Oct. to mid-May.) Private showers outside park. Tent and RV sites; no hookups. Two group campgrounds; reservations needed; contact headquarters. Food services in park.

Hotels, Motels, & Inns
(unless otherwise noted, rates are for 2 persons in a double room, high season)
In Bar Harbor, Maine 04609:
Bar Harbor Inn (on Newport Drive) P.O. Box 7. (800) 248-3351. 130 units. $95-$195. Pool, rest. **Bar Harbor Regency Holiday Inn** 123 Eden St. (207) 288-9723 or (800) 234-6835. 224 units. $109-$139. AC, pool, rest. Open mid-May to mid-Oct. **Bayview Hotel and Inn** 111 Eden St. (800) 356-3585. 38 units, some with kitchens. $85-$425. Pool, rest. **Best Western Inn** (on Hwy. 3) Route 1, Box 1127. (800) 528-1234 or (207) 288-5823. 64 units. $92-$99. AC, pool, rest. Open May to late Oct. **Cleftstone Manor** 92 Eden Street. (207) 288-4951. 16 units. $95-$180, includes breakfast. Open mid-April to Oct. 30. **Cromwell Harbor Motel** 359 Main Street. (207) 288-3201. 19 units. $76. Open mid-May to mid-Oct. **Wonder View Motor Lodge** (Eden Street) P.O. Box 25. (800) 341-1553 or (207) 288-3358. 80 units. $60-$100. Pool, rest. Open May through Oct.
In Northeast Harbor, Maine 04662:
Asticou Inn (on Hwy. 3). (207) 276-3344. 50 units. $200-$260, includes 2 meals. Pool, restaurant. Open mid-June to mid-Sept. **Kimball Terrace Inn** Huntington Road. (207) 276-3383. 70 units. $63-$104. Pool, restaurant.
In Southwest Harbor, Maine 04679:
Moorings Motor Sail Inn (on Shore Road, Manset) P.O. Box 744. (207) 244-5523. 19 units, some kitchens. $55-$90. Rest. Open May to Nov.

For additional accommodations, call the Chambers of Commerce of Bar Harbor (207) 288-5103, Northeast Harbor (207) 276-5040, and Southwest Harbor (207) 244-9264.

Excursions

Moosehorn
National Wildlife Refuge
Calais, Maine

At dawn and dusk in spring, the male woodcock soars into the air to begin his mating ritual. The refuge's two units protect the essential habitat of the American woodcock as well as other waterfowl and forest wildlife species. Contains two wilderness areas. 22,745 acres. Facilities: hiking, boating, bicycling, fishing, hunting, winter sports. Open all year, dawn to dusk. Headquarters at the Baring Unit, off US 1, about 75 miles from Acadia NP. (207) 454-3521.

Petit Manan
National Wildlife Refuge
Steuben, Maine

Migrating waterfowl and shorebirds take rest on Petit Manan Peninsula and three offshore islands. The peninsula's two hiking trails lead visitors through spruce and jack pine, blueberry barrens, peat lands, and salt and freshwater marshes. Petit Manan Island features one of the largest tern and laughing gull colonies in Maine and a 123-foot lighthouse; contact refuge manager before attempting a visit. 3,335 acres. Hiking trails. Peninsula open all year, dawn to dusk. Accessible from US 1 in Steuben, about 35 miles from Schoodic Unit of Acadia NP. (207) 546-2124.

Rachel Carson
National Wildlife Refuge
Wells, Maine

Stretching along Maine's southern coast from Kittery to Cape Elizabeth, this refuge's ten units offer closeup looks at the fragile and dynamic world of the tidal estuary. The unit at Wells contains the 1-mile-long self-guided Carson Trail. Breeding and migrating shorebirds, wading birds, waterfowl, and raptors also featured. 3,500 acres. Facilities include hiking, canoeing, bicycling, fishing, hunting, picnic areas, scenic drives, cross-country skiing, handicapped access. Open all year, dawn to dusk. Headquarters at Wells, on Maine 9, off US 1, about 160 miles from Acadia NP. (207) 646-9226.

A school of blue-striped grunts in the underwater splendor of Biscayne Bay

Biscayne

Florida

Established June 28, 1980

181,500 acres

Biscayne, a seascape in watercolor, offers vistas ashore and beneath the sea. Standing on the park's narrow shore, you look out upon a bay that is tranquil on the surface and teeming with life below. Aboard a glass-bottom boat, you look down and see some of that life—dazzlingly colored fish, fantastically shaped corals, gently waving fronds of sea grass.

Biscayne is an underwater wilderness. Only 4 percent of the park is land—about 45 small barrier islands and a mangrove shoreline, the longest such undeveloped shore on the East Coast. Park wildlife musters under water in the form of minuscule, unusual, or rarely seen animals. The most extensive life-form is a community known as the coral reef—colonies of tiny polyps that secrete limestone and live within ever growing rocky crannies. Biscayne's coral reefs are part of the only living ones in the continental United States.

The park reprieved a living system condemned to die under the pressure of progress. The threat came in the 1960s, when developers were making plans to build resorts and subdivisions on Florida's northern keys, from Key Biscayne to Key Largo. Conservationists campaigned to preserve Biscayne Bay; it became a national monument in 1968. When Biscayne National Park was established, boundaries were expanded to encompass several more of the bay's keys and reefs.

Biscayne embraces a complex ecosystem that extends from the mangrove shoreline to the Gulf Stream.

park entrance. Airport: Miami.

When to Go
All-year park. The best time to visit
is from mid-December to mid-April,
subtropical Florida's dry season. In
summer, you face the perils of mosquitoes and fast-moving thunderstorms. Hurricanes are rare.

How to Visit
Unless you have your own boat, plan
to see Biscayne on a concessioner-
run cruise. You can look underwater
on a **reef cruise** aboard a glass-bottom
boat or swim the shallow waters on a
snorkeling cruise (snorkels for rent).
There are also scuba cruises to the
outer reef for qualified divers. You
should make reservations in advance. Cruises may be canceled if
there are too few passengers or the
weather is inclement. Although this
is a water park, a walk around the
mangrove shore will give you a
chance to examine the coastal edges
of the bay's ecosystem.

Reef Cruise
a half day

Sign up for a cruise well ahead (see
Information & Activities for details).
Schedules vary by season. At **Convoy
Point**, the glass-bottom boat's home
port and site of park headquarters,
you can get an orientation to the
bay's unique flora and fauna before
setting out. A cruise takes about 3
hours. Cruises for snorkel and scuba
divers last longer and cost more.

Besides the mangrove coast and living reef, the ecosystem includes two
other biological realms found on the
small islands and the shallow bay's
marine nursery. The realms are in-
terwoven, and each sustains still other webs of life.

Guarding all this are the northernmost Florida Keys, barrier islands
that keep ocean waves from batter-
ing the bay. Thus shielded, the bay
offers sanctuary to the life within it
and beauty to those who come to look
beneath the surface.

How to Get There
From Miami, take US 1 south about
25 miles. South of Cutler Ridge, at
Goulds, watch for a park billboard;
continue a short distance to another
park sign. Take a left here onto SW
137th Ave. (Tallahassee Road) and
continue to SW 328th St. (North Canal Drive). Turn left to the park entrance at Convoy Point. From
Homestead (about 15 miles), take SW
328th St. (North Canal Drive) to the

Diver and sea fans near Elliott Key

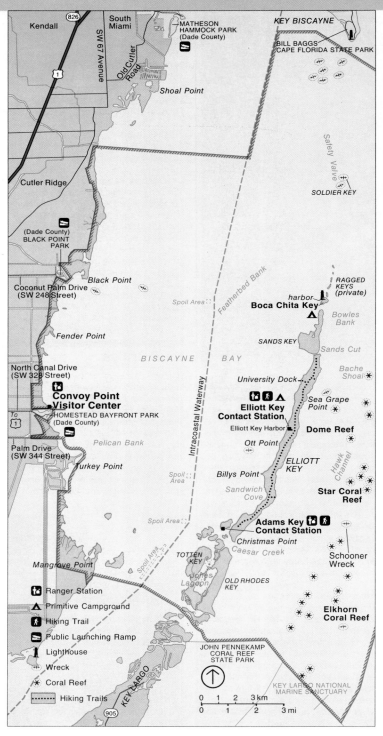

826

Kendall

South Miami

MATHESON HAMMOCK PARK
(Dade County)

KEY BISCAYNE

BILL BAGGS
CAPE FLORIDA STATE PARK

SW 67 Avenue

Old Cutler Road

1

Shoal Point

Safety Valve

Cutler Ridge

SOLDIER KEY

(Dade County)
BLACK POINT PARK

Black Point

Featherbed Bank

RAGGED KEYS
(private)

harbor

Boca Chita Key

Coconut Palm Drive
(SW 248 Street)

Spoil Area

Bowles Bank

Fender Point

SANDS KEY

Sands Cut

BISCAYNE BAY

Bache Shoal

North Canal Drive
(SW 328 Street)

University Dock

Convoy Point
Visitor Center

Sea Grape Point

To
1

HOMESTEAD BAYFRONT PARK
(Dade County)

Elliott Key
Contact Station

Dome Reef

Elliott Key Harbor

Pelican Bank

Ott Point

ELLIOTT KEY

Palm Drive
(SW 344 Street)

Hawk Channel

Turkey Point

Spoil Area

Billys Point

Sandwich Cove

Star Coral Reef

Spoil Area

Adams Key
Contact Station

Christmas Point

Caesar Creek

Schooner Wreck

Mangrove Point

Spoil Area

TOTTEN KEY

Jones Lagoon

OLD RHODES KEY

Elkhorn Coral Reef

Intracoastal Waterway

Ranger Station

Primitive Campground

Hiking Trail

Public Launching Ramp

Lighthouse

Wreck

Coral Reef

Hiking Trails

JOHN PENNEKAMP
CORAL REEF
STATE PARK

KEY LARGO

KEY LARGO NATIONAL
MARINE SANCTUARY

0   1   2   3 km
0   1   2   3 mi

905

Tropical hardwood edging Elliott Key's shoreline

The center of the boat's deck is a rectangular viewing chamber. Its floor is made up of rows of broad, angled windows; beneath them are spotlights trained on the seabed. Passengers line rails around the chamber and peer down at the constantly changing, green-tinted scene.

As the boat crosses the bay, a park ranger prepares the audience by passing out pieces of hard coral and previewing the sights that will be seen in the reefs. A ruffled seabed and waving strands of turtle grass pass under the windows. Vast beds of turtle grass and water only 4 to 10 feet deep make Biscayne Bay a nursery for a host of young marine animals, including shrimp, spiny lobsters, sponges, and crabs. You can see some of these animals through the windows. More than 200 types of fish swim in park waters. You may also see large, graceful sea turtles.

If you walk to the outer edge of the deck, you can watch boats skimming the bay and brown pelicans flapping by. When they spot fish, they dive headfirst into the sea to scoop them up in their huge bills. Among the many other birds you will

Nursing manatee with mother

see are cormorants and herons; together, their calls can be deafening.

Through the bay runs the Intracoastal Waterway, marked by posts whose signs bear numbers keyed to navigational charts. In one short, shallow stretch near the waterway are natural mud banks rising near the surface and visible at low tide. Bonefish, prized by sportfishermen for their speed and strength, inhabit the mud banks.

The boat slips through the keys toward the reefs beyond. The boat

Spiny lobsters in the sea grass of Biscayne Bay

lingers here for the floor show: the multicolored flash of a parrotfish, the sinuous glide of an angelfish, the little jungles of coral. Slowly the boat moves to another vantage point, and a new seabed show begins to roll by. Giant brain coral and mountainous star coral dominate the reefs, many so high that the glass bottom seems close enough to graze them. Sea fans and other soft corals ripple in the calm, clear water. The ranger helps viewers identify the vibrantly colored fish flitting around the massive coral formations. Before reaching the outer reefs the boat turns for home.

Some of the cruises stop at **Adams Key,** 7 miles out, where rangers, aided by exhibits, point out another resource guarded by the park: the remains of sunken ships. The key overlooks **Caesar Creek,** named for Black Caesar, a legendary pirate said to have lurked here in the 1600s. More than 50 shipwrecks have been cataloged within park boundaries. Federal law protects them from salvagers or souvenir collectors. Visitors in their own boats can also dock at Adams Key for picnics.

Elliott Key has primitive campsites, rest rooms, a nature trail, a swimming area, a seasonal visitor center, and what conservationists label a "road scar"—a bulldozer's legacy and a reminder of how close devastation came to these keys. To the north is **Boca Chita Key,** which has a boat dock, primitive campsites, and rest rooms, but no drinking water.

Mangrove Shore
¹/₄ mile; at least an hour

If you have little time, no boat, and some curiosity, walk the shore around Convoy Point, a fine place for a picnic. If you have more time, inquire about ranger-led canoe trips into mangrove tidal creeks. You can also rent a canoe and explore on your own.

The mangroves stabilize the shore, trapping their own fallen leaves and other organic material in tangles of stilt-like roots. The trees attract many birds—including, on rare occasions, the peregrine falcon and bald eagle, 2 of the 13 endangered animal species monitored by park naturalists. Barnacles, fish, and other sea creatures cluster at the trees' half-submerged roots. The decaying mangrove leaves, rich in protein, feed tiny animals at the bottom of a food chain that ends with the fisherman who eats the gray snapper he caught in the bay.

The mangroves also filter pollutants from the freshwater runoff into the bay. Whether you walk or paddle, watch carefully for the bay animals that find food and refuge in the mangrove waterways. On a winter's day the creatures may include a manatee, a huge, grass-chewing "cow of the sea." The scene keeps changing as each outgoing tide carries nutrients out to sea and each incoming tide brings in new inhabitants for the sheltering mangroves.

Life on the Coral Reef

Tunneling through a school of fish

Queen angelfish

Filefish on soft coral

Porcupinefish

Nassau grouper

Information & Activities

Headquarters
P.O. Box 1369, Homestead, Florida 33090. Phone (305) 247-7275.

Seasons & Accessibility
Open year-round. Keys (islands) can be reached by boat only. Private concessioners operate daily, though underbooked cruises may be canceled in the off-season. Private boats allowed; free boat docks on Elliott, Adams, and Boca Chita Keys.

Visitor & Boat Information
Convoy Point Visitor Center open daily all year. Elliott Key Contact Station staffed by rangers intermittently. Adams Key Contact Station not staffed. For park information, call (305) 247-PARK.

For information and reservations for concessioner-run glass-bottom boat, snorkeling, scuba diving, island and canoe trips, write Biscayne Aqua Center, Inc. P.O. Box 1270, Homestead, Fla. 33090, or call (305) 247-2400. Rentals available. Tours leave from Convoy Point.

Entrance Fees
None; fees charged by concessioner for boat trips.

Pets
Allowed on leashes (6-ft. maximum length) in parking, picnic, and boat launching areas. Not permitted on trails or boat tours.

Facilities for Disabled
Elliott Key and Convoy Point centers and rest rooms are accessible to wheelchairs, as are all concessioner boat tours.

Things to Do
Naturalist-led activities: canoe trips, Elliott Key nature tours, interpretive exhibits. Also available, swimming, snorkeling, glass-bottom boat trips, scuba diving, water skiing, boating, canoe rentals, fishing, lobstering, hiking, birdwatching.

Special Advisories
☐Do not touch coral or other living things on the reef. They are easily damaged; they can also inflict deep cuts and cause serious infections.

☐Mosquitoes and other insects can be a problem on the islands, particularly from April to December; carry plenty of repellent.

Backpacking
Permits required for backcountry hiking on Elliott Key; they are available free from the visitor center or from a park ranger. No permit needed for hiking on Boca Chita Key.

Campgrounds
Two boat-in campgrounds, both with 14-day limit. **Elliott Key** and **Boca Chita Key** open all year first come, first served. No fees. Cold showers at **Elliott Key**. Tent sites only. Group Campground at **Elliott Key**; reservations required; contact park headquarters.

Hotels, Motels, & Inns
(unless otherwise noted, rates are for 2 persons in a double room, high season)
In Florida City, Florida 33034:
Coral Roc Motel 1100 N. Krome Ave. (305) 247-4010. 16 units, 4 with kitchenettes. $58. AC, pool. **Knights Inn** 401 US Hwy. 1. (305) 245-2800. 108 units, 11 with kitchenettes. $53-$65. AC, pool. **Seaglaze Motel** 1223 NE First Ave., US 1. (305) 247-6621. 49 units, 10 kitchenettes. $58. AC, pool.
In Homestead, Florida 33030:
Days Inn 51 S. Homestead Blvd. (305) 245-1260. 100 units. $78. AC, pool, restaurant. **Everglades Motel** 605 S. Krome Ave. (305) 247-4117. 19 units, 6 with kitchenettes. $52. AC, pool.

For other area accommodations, write or call the Homestead/Florida City Chamber of Commerce, 160 US Hwy. 1, Florida City, Florida 33034. (305) 247-2332.

Excursions

John Pennekamp Coral Reef State Park
Key Largo, Florida

In the world's first undersea park, a living coral reef may be viewed through a diver's mask or a glass-bottom boat. 55,000 acres. Facilities: visitor center, 47 campsites, hiking, boating, boat ramps, fishing, picnic areas, water sports, handicapped access. Open all year during daylight. Off US 1 in Key Largo, about 40 miles from Biscayne NP and 35 from Everglades NP. (305) 451-1202.

National Key Deer Refuge
Big Pine Key, Florida

The key deer—a diminutive subspecies of the white-tailed deer—struggle to survive in this shrinking mangrove and pine-palm habitat. *Don't feed them!* 3,500 acres. Facilities include hiking, boating, fishing, scenic drives, swimming. Open year-round, dawn to dusk. Off US 1 on Big Pine Key, about 100 miles south of Biscayne NP. (305) 872-2239.

Great White Heron National Wildlife Refuge
Big Pine Key, Florida

Dedicated to the protection of the great white heron, this site partly overlaps the National Key Deer Refuge. These mangrove islands also shelter the rare white-crowned pigeon and the roseate spoonbill. 7,600 acres. No facilities. Access by boat only. Open all year, dawn to dusk. Information at National Key Deer Refuge; see above. (305) 872-2239.

Key West National Wildlife Refuge
Big Pine Key, Florida

Encompassing nearly all the islands west of Key West, this refuge offers protection to terns, frigatebirds, ospreys, herons, and roseate spoonbills. 2,019 acres. No camping or other facilities. Access by boat only. Open year-round, dawn to dusk. Information at National Key Deer Refuge; see above. (305) 872-2239.

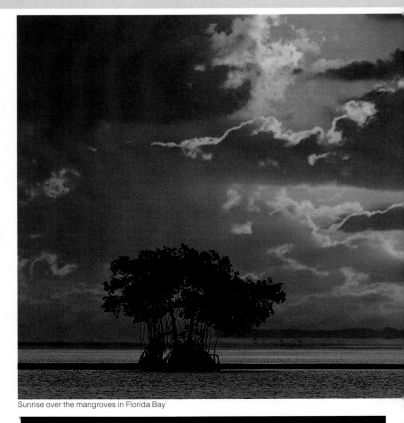

Sunrise over the mangroves in Florida Bay

Everglades

Florida

Established December 6, 1947

1,506,539 acres

A short parade of visitors follows a ranger on an Everglades nature walk. For more than an hour she has shown them the living wonders around them—butterflies and snails, alligators and fish, and bird after bird. Near the end of the walk, she gathers the visitors around her. She points to a string of nine white ibis coursing a cloudless sky.

"Imagine seeing ibis in the 1930s," she says. "That would have been a flight of about 90 birds. We are seeing only about 10 percent of the wading birds that were here then. When you get home, write your congressmen and tell them we have to save Everglades." In this threatened national park, lobbying happens on nature walks and appears in official literature.

The park is at the southern tip of the Everglades, a hundred-mile-long subtropical wilderness of saw-grass prairie, junglelike hammock, and mangrove swamp, running from Lake Okeechobee to Florida Bay. Water, essential to the survival of this ecosystem, once flowed south from the lake unhindered. But as the buildup of southern Florida has intensified, canals, levees, and dikes have increasingly diverted the water to land developments and agribusinesses. Vast irrigated farmlands have spread to the park's gates. The waning of the ibis carries a warning: Watery habitats in the park are shrinking because not enough water is getting to Everglades.

The park's special mission inspires the crusade to save it. Unlike early

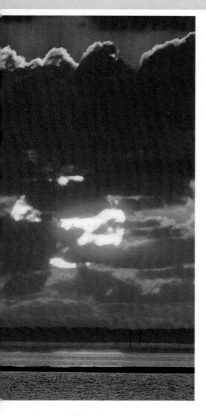

The plants and animals are a part of this rhythm. When humans change it, they put Everglades life at risk.

How to Get There
South from Miami, take US 1 to Florida City, then west on Fla. Hwy. 9336 (formerly Fla. Hwy. 27) to the Main Visitor Center, about 50 miles from Miami. West from Miami, take US 41 (the Tamiami Trail) to Shark Valley Information Center. From Naples, head east on US 41 to Fla. Hwy. 29, then south to Everglades City. Airports: Miami and Naples.

When to Go
Everglades has two seasons: dry (mid-December through mid-April) and wet (the rest of the year). The park schedules most of its activities in the dry season; hot, humid weather and clouds of mosquitoes make park visitors extremely uncomfortable during the wet season.

How to Visit
If you can stay only a day for a drive-in visit, get out of your car and learn about Everglades ecology by taking self-guided walks at road turnoffs on the drive from the **Main Visitor Center** to **Flamingo.** For a longer stay, pick either Flamingo or **Everglades City** as your base and time your travels to the schedules of concession boat tours. In wet or dry season, only a boat or canoe gives you access to the backcountry. Because of mosquitoes, the dry season is best for canoeing. (Near park entrances you'll see signs advertising airboat rides; airboats, which disturb wildlife and tear up saw grass, are banned in the park.)

parks established to protect scenery, Everglades was created to preserve a portion of this vast ecosystem as a wildlife habitat. The park's unique mix of tropical and temperate plants and animals—including more than 700 plant and 300 bird species, as well as the endangered manatee, crocodile, and Florida panther—has earned it International Biosphere Reserve and United Nations World Heritage site designations.

Everglades crusaders urge the purchase of privately owned wetlands east of the park. This would expand protection of the ecosystem and give the park a larger claim to the water that Everglades shares with its thirsty neighbors.

The diverse life of Everglades National Park, from algae to alligators, depends upon a rhythm of abundance and drought. In the wet season, a river inches deep and miles wide flows, almost invisibly, to the Gulf of Mexico. In the dry season, the park rests, awaiting the water's return.

Royal Palm to Flamingo
76 miles round-trip; a full day

The main **park road** connects the main entrance, southwest of Florida City, with **Flamingo** on **Florida Bay.** Make the drive an exploration, not a 55-mph dash. Stops at the sites suggested can be made on the way to or from Flamingo, depending upon when you want to board a concession boat there. Check on that day's cruises by calling the concessioner (see **Information & Activities**).

At the **Main Visitor Center,** get oriented to this complex park. A short

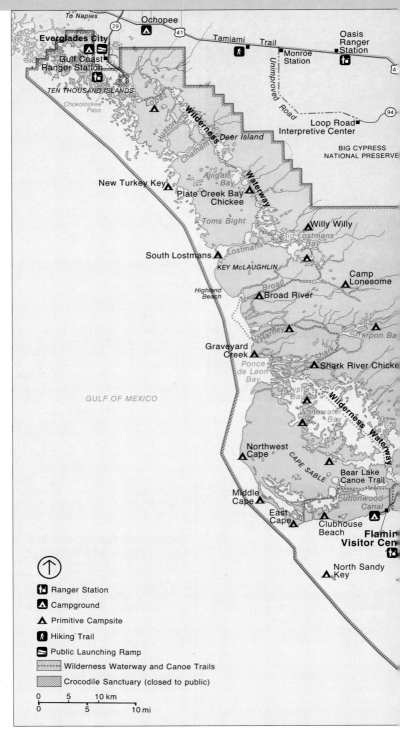

To Naples
Ochopee
29
41
Tamiami Trail
Oasis Ranger Station
Everglades City
Gulf Coast Ranger Station
Monroe Station
TEN THOUSAND ISLANDS
Chokoloskee Pass
4
Unimproved Road
Lopez
Huston
Wilderness
Deer Island
94
Loop Road Interpretive Center
BIG CYPRESS NATIONAL PRESERVE
Chatham
Alligator Bay
Waterway
New Turkey Key
Plate Creek Bay Chickee
Toms Bight
Willy Willy
Big Lostmans Bay
South Lostmans
Lostmans
KEY McLAUGHLIN
Camp Lonesome
Highland Beach
Broad
Broad River
Graveyard Creek
Harney
Tarpon Ba
Ponce de Leon Bay
Shark
Shark River Chicke
GULF OF MEXICO
Oyster Bay
Whitewater Bay
Wilderness Waterway
Northwest Cape
Joe
CAPE SABLE
Bear Lake Canoe Trail
Buttonwood Canal
Middle Cape
East Cape
Clubhouse Beach
Flamin Visitor Cen
North Sandy Key

Ranger Station
Campground
Primitive Campsite
Hiking Trail
Public Launching Ramp
Wilderness Waterway and Canoe Trails
Crocodile Sanctuary (closed to public)

0   5   10 km
0   5   10 mi

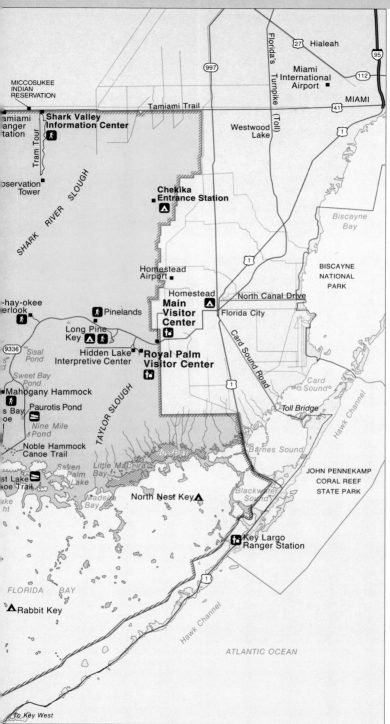

MICCOSUKEE
INDIAN
RESERVATION

Tamiami Trail

**Shark Valley
Information Center**

Florida's Turnpike

27 Hialeah

95

997

Miami
International
Airport

112

41 MIAMI

1

amiami
anger
tation

Tram Tour

Westwood
Lake

servation
Tower

SHARK   RIVER   SLOUGH

**Chekika
Entrance Station**

Biscayne
Bay

1

Homestead
Airport

BISCAYNE
NATIONAL
PARK

-hay-okee
erlook

Pinelands

Long Pine
Key

**Main
Visitor
Center**

Homestead

North Canal Drive

Florida City

9336

Sisal
Pond

Hidden Lake
Interpretive Center

**Royal Palm
Visitor Center**

Card Sound Road

Card
Sound

Sweet Bay
Pond

Mahogany Hammock

Paurotis Pond

s Bay
oe
l

Nine Mile
Pond

TAYLOR   SLOUGH

1

Toll Bridge

Hawk Channel

Noble Hammock
Canoe Trail

Seven
Palm
Lake

Little Madeira
Bay

Joe Bay

Barnes Sound

JOHN PENNEKAMP
CORAL REEF
STATE PARK

st Lake
oe Trail

Wadeira
Bay

North Nest Key▲

Blackwater
Sound

ake
ht

**Key Largo
Ranger Station**

FLORIDA   BAY

▲Rabbit Key

1

Hawk Channel

ATLANTIC OCEAN

To Key West

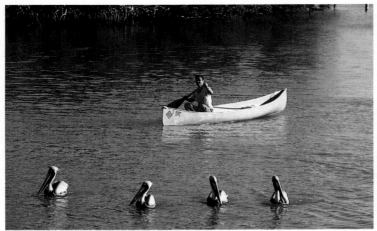
Paddling on a channel into Florida Bay

A snail kite in search of food

An American alligator

film stresses environmental threats to the park and alerts you to the subtle, imperiled beauty you will be seeing. Check the center's posted daily schedule for ranger-led hikes at the **Royal Palm Visitor Center**, just ahead, and for that day's cruises at Flamingo, 38 miles away. Time your road travel each way by adjusting to the day's schedules.

Egrets, herons, and other species dot the saw grass and roadside trees. On the road, use a passenger as a bird spotter; simultaneous driving and birdwatching can be dangerous. At 4 miles, turn off to **Royal Palm**. If you have time while waiting for a ranger-led walk on the **Anhinga Trail**, take your own plunge into the canopied shadows of the 1/2-mile **Gumbo Limbo Trail**, named for a tree whose peeling red bark gives it another name: tourist tree.

The trail takes you to a hammock, an elevated island of tropical hardwood—including gumbo limbos and some magnificent examples of strangler figs—in a sea of saw grass. The slight elevation keeps the ground drier, permitting the hardwoods to flourish and creating a shaded habitat for many creatures, from snakes to deer, foxes, and raccoon.

Watch for "solution holes," limestone depressions that hold moisture and become miniature ecosystems in the dry season. Filled with organic material and seeded by winds or bird droppings, some solution holes evolve into hammocks.

You can also walk the 1/2-mile An-

Watching the alligators at Shark Valley

hinga Trail on your own. But you have a better chance of spotting wildlife if a ranger is available to guide you. The boardwalk trail skirts a shallow, freshwater slough (pronounced slew). You almost certainly will see alligators and some fascinating birds, including the long-necked, long-beaked fish-spearer for which the trail is named.

The ranger adds lore to what you see: That beautiful zebra butterfly tastes terrible; a predatory bird never tries for second helpings. Those white egg sacs on that branch will hatch apple snails, the prime food of the endangered snail kite. The hawklike kite has a bill adapted to extracting the snail from its shell. That slim, long-snouted fish gliding through the clear water is a gar; in the dry season it can survive in a mudhole because a primitive lung allows it to breathe air. That alligator loosens the muck in water-filled solution holes and sweeps it away with its tail; in the dry season the gator-made oasis keeps fish, frogs, snails, and birds alive—as long as they are wary of the major resident. In Everglades, unusual adaptations and delicate balances sustain the park's astonishing variety of animals and plants.

Back on the road, visit the roadside exhibits. Stop-and-walk lessons begin on the $\frac{3}{4}$-mile **Pineland Trail**, 7 miles along the road. Slash pines grow on high ground, so pinelands were wiped out to develop Miami and other towns. What you see here are remnants of the pines that once covered southeastern Florida.

At 9 miles, a short boardwalk stroll takes you to **Pinnacle Rock**, a sample of the porous limestone that is south Florida's bedrock. At 12 miles, stop again to see dwarf cypress, trees stunted by shallow soil.

Half a mile farther is an overlook called **Pa-hay-okee**, or "grassy waters," the Indian name for the Everglades. A boardwalk takes you to a shaded observation stage where you can look out on a seemingly endless prairie of grassy waters. At $19\frac{1}{2}$ miles is **Mahogany Hammock**, where a boardwalk leads to the largest living mahogany tree in the United States.

If you want to picnic, there are fine spots at **Paroutis Pond** (at $24\frac{1}{2}$ miles), **Nine Mile Pond** (at $26\frac{1}{2}$ miles), and **West Lake** (at $30\frac{1}{2}$ miles).

At Flamingo, sign up for a boat tour in the marina ticket office near the visitor center. While you are waiting, take the self-guided, $\frac{1}{2}$-mile walk around the waterfront to see Florida Bay, a marine nursery protected by the park. The 2-hour backcountry cruise begins in the marina and enters **Buttonwood Canal**, built in 1957. Among the spidery roots of the three species of mangrove you will see along the waterway, watch for shy crocodiles, sometimes seen sunning on the banks of the canal. The cruise crosses **Coot Bay** and enters **Whitewater Bay**, where backcountry canoeists camp on chickees, tent-size platforms raised on poles. Don't expect to see flamingos; they rarely appear at their namesake town.

White ibis, herons, pelicans, and spoonbills on mangrove islands

A raccoon hiding in mangrove roots

Shark Valley to Everglades City

49 miles one way; a full day

The **Tamiami Trail** (US 41) forms part of the park's northeastern border. Near the eastern park entrance, stop at the **Shark Valley Information Center.** Here is a 15-mile loop road accessible only on foot, on bike, or, year-round, on a 2-hour, narrated tour aboard an open-sided concessioner tram.

You will not see sharks. The valley gets its name from the **Shark River;** sharks gather at its mouth in the Gulf of Mexico. But you will see alligator trails leading to hammocks in the saw grass—and you will almost certainly see alligators and wading birds. The trail leads to a 65-foot tower looking down on the vista that became a name: glades that seem to go on forever.

About $\frac{1}{2}$ mile from the end of the tour, the tram sometimes stops to give passengers the choice of walking back along a stretch of road used as a nature trail. A walk here can be rewarding to alligator seekers. Alligators nest nearby, and mothers and their progeny can often be seen alongside the road.

Return to US 41, which veers

Slash pines and saw-palmettos, remnants of Florida's flatwoods

Bull thistle in Shark Valley

northward into Big Cypress National Preserve, part of the Everglades ecosystem. Most of the water flowing into the park comes through four floodgates that you can see north of the highway along the park boundary. At Fla. Hwy. 29, turn south for **Everglades City.** Follow the highway through the town to the waterfront. Sign up for one of the regularly scheduled, round-trip, narrated concessioner boat tours.

The **Ten Thousand Island** trip explores mangrove islands along the Gulf of Mexico. On the way to and from the islands, protected sea mammals—sleek bottlenose dolphins and lumbering manatees—often pop up to look at the boat. You can usually see ospreys, pelicans, and cormorants. From a distance, the islands look like a solid stretch of low-lying green land. Close up, you see a labyrinth of thousands of waterways.

There are far fewer than 10,000 islands, but the number is unknown and ever changing. Islands form from the buildup of leaves and other organic material among the stilt-rooted mangroves. As an island grows, storms and tidal forces may break it into fragments, which continue to grow and spread. The islands, ranging in size from a couple of trees to several hundred acres, provide shelter and food for many creatures in the gulf web of life.

The boat crosses **Chokoloskee Bay,** which shares its name with an island of shells, 15 feet high and 147 acres, built by Indians long before the first white men appeared here. The bay is the northern end of the 99-mile, Everglades City-to-Flamingo **Wilderness Waterway,** a system of backcountry canoe trails through the estuarine fringes of the park.

Birds of Everglades

White ibis taking flight near Flamingo

Green-backed heron striking at fish

Roseate spoonbill tending chicks

A great egret preening

An anhinga drying its wings

Information & Activities

Headquarters
P.O. Box 279, Homestead, Florida 33030. Phone (305) 242-7700.

Seasons & Accessibility
Park open daily, year-round; some facilities and services limited or un-available during off-season, May 1 to mid-December.

Visitor & Information Centers
Main Visitor Center on Hwy. 9336 at park entrance. Royal Palm Visitor Center off main park road a few miles inside park entrance. Flamingo Visitor Center on main park road at Florida Bay. Shark Valley Information Center at north end of park on US 41. Gulf Coast Ranger Station at Everglades City on Hwy. 29 at northwest entrance. Main Visitor Center open daily all year; others may close temporarily in off-season.

Entrance Fees
$5 per car per week at main entrance; $3 at Shark Valley and Chekika.

Pets
Permitted on leashes except on trails and in backcountry. Permitted on private boats in backcountry.

Facilities for Disabled
Main Visitor Center, Shark Valley Information Center, and tram tours are wheelchair accessible. Several trails at least partly accessible. Free pamphlet available.

Things to Do
Free naturalist-led activities: nature walks and talks, hikes, exhibits, evening programs. Also available, day-time and moonlight tram tours; sight-seeing boat rides; canoe, houseboat, motorboat, and bicycle rentals; fishing (license required); crabbing; shrimping (ask at park for regulations). During winter season and on holidays, call ahead to reserve space on guided tours and activities.

Rentals and boat and tram tours in Flamingo: (813) 695-3101 or (305) 253-2241. Tram tour at Shark Valley: (305) 221-8455. Boat tour and rentals at Everglades City: (800) 445-7724 in Fla. or (800) 233-1821 out of state.

Special Advisories
☐You'll need insect repellent year-round, but especially April to Dec.
☐Swimming not advised; alligators and snakes live in ponds, sharks and barracuda in saltwater areas.

Overnight Backpacking
Permits required; they are obtainable free in person, no more than 24 hours before trip, at Flamingo and Everglades City. No reservations; first come, first served; limits on number of people and length of stay.

Campgrounds
Three campgrounds, 14-day limit Nov. to May; otherwise 30-day limit. **Flamingo, Long Pine Key,** and **Chekika** open all year first come, first served. Fees $4-$8 per night. Cold showers at **Flamingo.** Tent and RV sites; no hookups. Three group campgrounds; reservations required; contact head-quarters. Food services in park.

Hotels, Motels, & Inns
(unless otherwise noted, rates are for 2 persons in a double room, high season)
INSIDE THE PARK:
Flamingo Lodge, Marina & Outpost Resort (end of main park road) P.O. Box 428, Flamingo, Fla. 33090. (305) 253-2241 or (813) 695-3101. 127 units. Lodge rooms $81; cottages with kitchens $95. AC, pool, restaurant.
OUTSIDE THE PARK:
In Florida City, Florida 33034:
Coral Roc Motel 1100 N. Krome Ave. (305) 247-4010. 16 units, 4 kitchenettes. $58. AC, pool. **Knights Inn** 401 US Hwy. 1. (305) 245-2800. 108 units, 11 kitchenettes. $53-$65. AC, pool. **Seaglaze Motel** 1223 NE First Ave., US Hwy. 1. (305) 247-6621. 49 units, 10 kitchenettes. $58. AC, pool.
In Homestead, Florida 33030:
Days Inn 51 S. Homestead Blvd. (305) 245-1260. 100 units. $78. AC, pool, restaurant. **Everglades Motel** 605 S. Krome Ave. (305) 247-4117. 19 units, 6 with kitchenettes. $52. AC, pool.

For other accommodations, write or call the Homestead/Florida City Chamber of Commerce, 160 US Hwy. 1, Florida City, Fla. 33034. (305) 247-2332.

Excursions

Big Cypress National Preserve
Ochopee, Florida

Dispensing life-giving fresh water to the Everglades and coastal estuaries, Big Cypress is more than a grassy swamp: Marshes, wet and dry prairies, hardwood hammocks, pinelands, and mangrove forests flourish here, as do wading birds and alligators. The endangered Florida panther roams the area. 570,000 acres. Facilities: 75 primitive campsites, hiking, fishing, hunting, canoeing, off-road vehicles (permits required), picnic areas, scenic drives. On US 41 (Tamiami Trail); adjoins Everglades NP. (813) 695-4111.

Corkscrew Swamp Sanctuary
Naples, Florida

A 2-mile-long boardwalk takes visitors on a self-guided tour through this Audubon Society site featuring the country's largest stand of virgin cypress forest and varied wildlife, including swallow-tailed kites, wintering painted buntings, nesting wood storks, and alligators. 10,560 acres. Hiking and picnic areas. Open year-round 9 a.m. to 5 p.m. Off Florida Hwy. 846, about 50 miles northwest of Everglades NP. (813) 657-3771.

J. N. "Ding" Darling National Wildlife Refuge
Sanibel, Florida

Migratory songbirds and a large population of roseate spoonbills feature among the 291 bird species on this island refuge named for Pulitzer Prize-winning political cartoonist and refuge system pioneer Jay Norwood Darling. 5,030 acres. Facilities: hiking, boating, bicycling, fishing, scenic drive. Open all year, dawn to dusk. Visitor center off Florida Hwy. 80, about 100 miles northwest of Everglades NP. (813) 472-1100.

Hobe Sound
National Wildlife Refuge
Hobe Sound, Florida
Endangered sea turtles nest on this 3½-mile Atlantic beach near the Intracoastal Waterway. Thousands of migrating birds also find haven among the dunes, mangroves, and sand pine-scrub oak habitats. 965 acres. Facilities include hiking, boating, fishing, handicapped access. Open all year during daylight hours. Off US 1, about 115 miles northeast of Everglades NP. (407) 546-6141.

Loxahatchee
National Wildlife Refuge
Boynton Beach, Florida
Freshwater marshes and cypress swamps surrounded by levees provide essential habitat for more than 250 bird species including the rare snail kite and its namesake diet, the apple snail. 145,636 acres. Facilities: hiking, boating, boat ramp, fishing, hunting, handicapped access. Open all year, sunrise to sunset. Headquarters on US 441, about 80 miles northeast of Everglades National Park. (407) 734-8303.

Fort Jefferson
National Monument
Dry Tortugas, Florida
An abandoned 19th-century fort is the focus of this site that includes the islands, shoals, and surrounding waters of the Dry Tortugas—seven coral keys strategically located at the entrance to the Gulf of Mexico. Marine life and birds abound. 64,657 acres. Facilities: primitive camping (no fresh water available), boating, fishing, picnic areas, water sports. Open year-round. Access by boat or seaplane from Marathon, Key West, or Naples, Florida. About 180 miles from Everglades NP. (305) 247-6211.

Mist-shrouded autumn view from Clingmans Dome

Great Smoky Mountains

North Carolina and Tennessee

Established June 15, 1934

520,004 acres

The fact invariably stated about Great Smoky is this: It is the nation's busiest park, drawing some ten million visitors a year, more than twice the number of any other national park. Most of the millions see the park from a mountain-skimming scenic highway that, on a typical weekend day during the summer, draws 60,000 people, bumper-to-bumper.

Luckily, there is plenty of park, thinly laced by 270 miles of mountain roads. And you can pull off the road, park the car, and stroll one of Great Smoky's many Quiet Walkways, $^{1}/_{4}$-mile paths into what the signs call a "little bit of the world as it once was." Nine hundred miles of hiking trails, from $^{1}/_{2}$ mile to 70 miles long,

also give you that world. Relatively few visitors walk the trails, for most people prefer to stay in their cars.

The park, which covers 800 square miles of mountainous terrain, preserves the world's best examples of deciduous forest and a matchless variety of plants and animals. Because it contains so many types of eastern forest vegetation—much of it virgin—the park has been designated an International Biosphere Reserve.

The Smoky Mountains are among the oldest on earth. Ice Age glaciers stopped their southward journey just short of these mountains, which became a junction of southern and northern flora. Rhododendron and mountain-laurel thrust from the weathered rocks. Amid the woodland and craggy peaks bloom more than 1,500 species of flowering plants, some found only here. Shrubs

How to Get There

From Knoxville, Tenn. (about 25 miles away), take I-40 to Tenn. Hwy. 66, then US 441 to Gatlinburg entrance. From Asheville, N.C. (about 40 miles away), take I-40 west to US 23, then US 441, to park's southern entrance near Cherokee, N.C. For a scenic, low-speed approach, take the 469-mile Blue Ridge Parkway that connects Virginia's Shenandoah National Park with Great Smoky. Airports: Knoxville and Asheville.

When to Go

All-year park. In summer and in fall (when spectacular foliage draws huge crowds), time your visit to mid-week, and arrive early. Some visitor centers close November to April.

How to Visit

On a 1-day visit, take the **Newfound Gap Road** to **Clingmans Dome** and get the best overview of the park by seeing it from the highest point. The best second-day activity is the **Cades Cove Loop Road**, a chance to drive or cycle through pioneer history. For a longer stay, focus on the self-guided nature trails and drives, which get you away from the crowds and show you the flora and fauna.

take over in places, creating tree-free zones called heath balds, laurel slicks (because of the shiny leaves), or just plain hells (because they are so hard to get through).

The tangle of brush and trees forms a close-packed array of air-breathing leaves. The water and hydrocarbons exuded by the leaves produce the filmy "smoke" that gives the mountains their name. Air pollution in recent years has added microscopic sulfate particles to the haze, cutting visibility back about 30 percent since the 1950s. The pollution has also affected the park's red spruce stand—the southern Appalachians' largest. And insects are destroying the Fraser fir, the spruce's high-altitude companion.

The park also preserves the humble churches, cabins, farmhouses, and barns of the mountain people who began settling here in the late 1700s. When the park was founded, most people left. But some chose to stay and live out their lives here.

Newfound Gap Road to Clingmans Dome

40-45 miles; a half to full day'

Newfound Gap Road, which begins at 2,000 feet and ascends to 5,048 feet, connects the park's major visitor centers, **Sugarlands** and **Oconaluftee.** The road, passing from lowland hardwood timber to high-altitude spruce-fir forests, gives you a vertical trip that is ecologically equivalent to a journey from Georgia to Canada. Be prepared for rain on almost any day. A clear day below can be a day of mist and fog on high. From Sugarlands (for an Oconaluftee start, reverse the order below), stop after 5 miles at **Chimneys**, a fine picnic spot. Stretch your legs on the $^3/_4$-mile self-

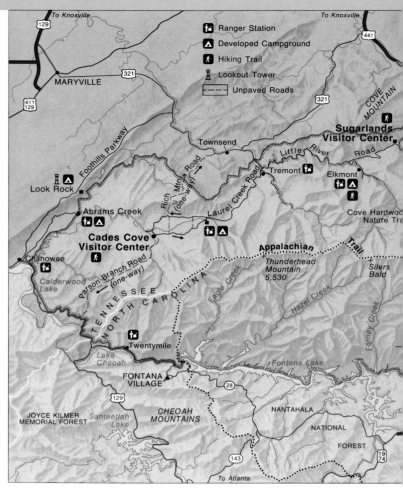

Ranger Station
Developed Campground
Hiking Trail
Lookout Tower
Unpaved Roads

To Knoxville
To Knoxville
MARYVILLE
Townsend
Sugarlands Visitor Center
COVE MOUNTAIN
Little River Road
Tremont
Elkmont
Foothills Parkway
Look Rock
Rich Mtn Road (one-way)
Laurel Creek Road
Cove Hardwood Nature Tra
Abrams Creek
Cades Cove Visitor Center
Appalachian Trail
Chilhowee
Thunderhead Mountain 5,530
Silers Bald
Calderwood Lake
Parson Branch Road (one-way)
TENNESSEE
NORTH CAROLINA
Eagle Creek
Hazel Creek
Forney Creek
Twentymile
Lake Cheoah
Fontana Lake
FONTANA VILLAGE
JOYCE KILMER MEMORIAL FOREST
Santeetlah Lake
CHEOAH MOUNTAINS
NANTAHALA
NATIONAL
FOREST
To Atlanta

guided **Cove Hardwood Nature Trail**. Then return to the car for a short drive to the **Chimney Tops Overlooks**, which offer views of the double summits the Cherokee called Duniskwalguni ("forked antlers").

Here you can extend your stop with a hike on the steep **Chimney Tops Trail** (4-mile round-trip) through a virgin forest and up 1,335 feet to the sheer cliffs named the Chimneys. Depending on your time and stamina, you can also get out of the car and hike at the next overlook, where a trailhead leads to a steep climb to **Alum Cave Bluffs**, site of a 19th-century commercial alum mine and reputedly a source of saltpeter for Civil War gunpowder. The trail begins with an easy 2½-mile loop trail along

a tree-bordered creek to **Arch Rock**, a tunnel made by eons of erosion. The trees include towering 200-year-old eastern hemlocks. This is a magnificent spot for a spring wildflower hike graced by the songs of nesting warblers. You can loop back to your car or continue on a steep offshoot trail for a ¾-mile ascent to the bluffs.

Back in the car continue on to **Newfound Gap** (5,048 feet), through which runs the Tennessee-North Carolina state line and a long leg of the Appalachian Trail. From the overlook here, on a clear day, you can see **Mt. LeConte** (6,593 feet) and your next stop, **Clingmans Dome**. The 7-mile **Clingmans Dome Road** veers sharply off here and winds through a spruce-fir forest to a parking lot.

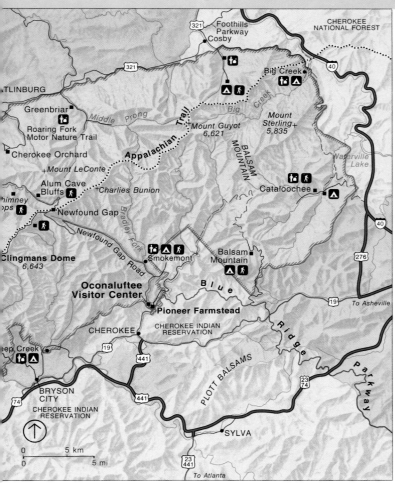

Foothills
Parkway
Cosby

321

CHEROKEE
NATIONAL FOREST

40

Big Creek

TLINBURG

321

Greenbriar
Roaring Fork
Motor Nature Trail

Cherokee Orchard

Middle *Prong*

Appalachian Trail

Big *Creek*

Mount Guyot
6,621

Mount
Sterling
5,835

BALSAM MOUNTAIN

Mount LeConte

Alum Cave
Bluffs

Charlies Bunion

Waterville
Lake

Cataloochee

himney
ops

Newfound Gap

Bradley *Fork*

40

276

Clingmans Dome
6,643

Newfound Gap Road

Smokemont

Balsam
Mountain

19

To Asheville

**Oconaluftee
Visitor Center**

Blue

Pioneer Farmstead

CHEROKEE

CHEROKEE INDIAN
RESERVATION

Ridge

eep Creek

19

441

PLOTT BALSAMS

Parkway

74

BRYSON
CITY

441

23
74

CHEROKEE INDIAN
RESERVATION

SYLVA

0   5 km
0   5 mi

23
441

To Atlanta

Carter Shields Cabin in Cades Cove

Summer sunlight on a Smokies creek

There begins a steep ½-mile trail ending at a spiral ramp. It leads to a lookout tower at the top of the 6,643-foot dome, the highest point in the park, where you get either a panoramic view or a sense of floating on a sea of churning clouds. From here retrace the route to Sugarlands or, depending on time and destination, continue on to Oconaluftee Visitor Center. (Between May and October, at **Mingus Mill**, a miller produces cornmeal and flour on an ingenious water-run turbine.) From Oconaluftee walk to **Pioneer Farmstead**, a cluster of farm buildings gathered from their original locations within the park. Pioneer-costumed park employees, playing farmstead roles, give demonstrations spring through October.

Cades Cove Loop Road

11 miles; at least a half day

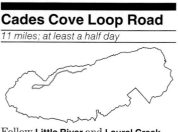

Follow **Little River** and **Laurel Creek Roads** from Sugarlands Visitor

Center to the **Cades Cove** loop road. Cades Cove traces its history to 1819, when, under a treaty with the Cherokee Indians, settlers cleared the broad, high valley. By 1850 more than 680 people were living there. They left behind structures that evolved into an open-air museum whose galleries are sites along the paved, 11-mile one-way loop road. Official sites are well marked. But you may find yourself making unofficial stops to admire the quietude, to watch white-tailed deer bounding across the valley, or to spot curious woodchucks popping out of their burrows along the road.

The first stop is **John Oliver Place**, site 3. The cabin was built with hand-hewn logs. Stand on the porch and look down the long, green-carpeted valley that drew the family to this place, the edge of the American world in 1826. **Primitive Baptist Church**, site 4, is skipped by some visitors because it lies on a two-way dirt road off the loop road. Don't miss it. The plain church guards a small graveyard. Time has made many stones nameless, but the past still can be read on them. The church shut down during the Civil War because, a letter says, "we was Union people and the Rebels was too strong here in Cades Cove." **Methodist Church,** site 5, had a door for men and another for women and children. During services, the separation was enforced in the pews by a barrier.

Just past the church is **Hyatt Lane,** an old road out of Cades Cove and to-day a shortcut that slices off a big piece of the tour. Stay on the loop road and continue to **Missionary Baptist Church,** site 7, formed in 1839 by expelled members of the Primitive Baptist Church. Because the congregation split between Union and Confederacy sympathizers, this church also closed during the Civil War.

Continue on the road, past **Rich Mountain Road,** site 8. Save this for another day. The gravel road, laid over an Indian trail, goes up **Rich Mountain** and provides a spectacular backward glance at Cades Cove before exiting the park. Also skip **Cooper Road Trail,** site 9, a onetime wag-on road that is now a 13-mile hiking trail ending outside the park. Ahead on the right is a short, two-way road to the next stops, **Abrams Falls,** site 10, and **Elijah Oliver Place,** site 11.

If you take the offshoot road, you come to a parking lot and a choice: a 2-hour, 2½-mile hike up to stunning Abrams Falls, or a ½-mile hike to another farmstead. Or continue your drive along the loop road to the next offshoot, which leads to **Cable Mill,** site 12. At the **Cades Cove Visitor Center** you can meet some of the pioneers in their photos on the rough-plank walls. Here is Mike Tipton in his World War I uniform and white-bearded Dan Myers in his high-laced boots. Mary Abbot clutches the hand of Samuel Tipton with one hand; in her other she holds a bunch of wild-flowers. Now leave the center and wander about, reliving the life that centered on the old mill.

Other buildings—a blacksmith shop, a large cantilever barn, a smokehouse—were imported from elsewhere in the park. Check at the visitor center for schedules of farm-life demonstrations; they include the making of sorghum molasses: a horse-powered mill squeezes juice from the stalks, which is then boiled down in an open-air vat. Just beyond the Cable Mill area is **Parson Branch Road,** which can take you out of the park—and the 20th century. The narrow winding one-way dirt road

Rhododendron along Clingmans Dome

Raccoon in a yellow poplar

(sometimes closed by weather) was carved out of wilderness about 1838. The 8-mile trip to US 129 can take an hour. If prudence keeps you on the loop road, your next stop will be **Tipton Place,** site 17. Built by Hamp Tipton shortly after the Civil War, it later became the home of a blacksmith, who put up his shop nearby.

Drive on to the last stop, **Carter Shields Cabin,** site 18. Log cabins like this would be succeeded by board houses, which arrived with lumbering in the early 1900s.

Hikes & Drives

Self-guided nature trails begin with an honor system document rack. You drop in a quarter and pluck out a leaflet keyed to numbered stops. **Balsam Mountain Trail** is the easiest climbing trail in the park, a 1½-mile loop from Balsam Mountain Campground. The trail gives you a short lesson in the identification of trees and, especially in spring, wild-flowers. **Laurel Falls Trail** is paved. The 2½-mile round-trip trail, which starts on Little River Road near Elkmont, winds through thickets of mountain-laurel and rhododendron to one of the park's many waterfalls.

Two of at least 400 black bears living in the park

White-tailed buck, often seen at dawn and dusk

Slimy salamander, one of park's 23 kinds

For a longer stay in the park, try some of the more rugged trails. The most rewarding hike is to Mt. LeConte, at 6,593 feet the park's third highest peak. The shortest (though steepest) way up is via **Alum Cave Bluffs Trail,** which starts at the trail to the Alum Cave Bluffs (see Newfound Gap Road tour). Here begins a steep $2\frac{1}{2}$-mile climb to the summit of LeConte. At one point the trail skirts a cliff face so sheer that climbers must grasp a cable to make their way up. Do not attempt a climb at this height, with its oxygen-thin air, unless you have good weather, good health—and good sense.

For the motorist, there are also self-guided nature trails using roads. The **Roaring Fork Motor Nature Trail,** 4 miles from Gatlinburg off **Cherokee Orchard Road,** is a 5-mile curvy, one-way road with a well-warranted 10 mph speed limit. About a mile before the trail begins, you will see the **Noah "Bud" Ogle Place** on your right. A $\frac{3}{4}$-mile path takes you around the remains of a farm—a mill, a barn, and the house where the big Ogle family lived after the Civil War.

At the Roaring Fork trail, avail yourself of the self-guiding booklet that suggests scenic stops. The road climbs a hill that provides, on clear days, a splendid view of **Sugarland** and **Cove Mountains.** Along the roadside is a virgin hemlock forest. Here and there are moldering chestnut logs, reminders of the blight that struck down the onetime forest king.

Information & Activities

Headquarters
Gatlinburg, Tennessee 37738. Phone (615) 436-1200.

Seasons & Accessibility
Park open year-round. The road to Clingmans Dome and some unpaved roads closed in winter.

Visitor & Information Centers
Open daily all year: Sugarlands, on US 441 south of Gatlinburg, Tenn., entrance; Oconaluftee, on US 441 north of Cherokee, N.C., entrance. Open April to November: Cades Cove Visitor Center, near Townsend, Tenn., entrance; enter off US 321, east of Townsend. Call park headquarters for information.

Facilities for Disabled
Visitor centers and rest rooms are wheelchair accessible. Clingmans Dome and Laurel Falls Trails are paved but steep; negotiable with assistance only. Free brochure.

Things to Do
Free naturalist-led activities: nature walks (day and evening), children's and campfire programs, pioneer exhibits and demonstrations, slide talks. Also, annual festivals, auto tape tour, hiking, bicycling, fishing (permit needed), horseback riding (several stables in park).

Overnight Backpacking
Permit required; available free from visitor centers and ranger stations. You can reserve up to 30 days in advance; write Backcountry Permit c/o park, or call (615) 436-1231.

Campgrounds
Ten campgrounds, most with a 7-day limit. **Cades Cove, Elkmont,** and **Smokemont** open all year; 7-day limit mid-May to Oct. 31; other times 14-day limit; reservations recommended May 1 to Oct. 31; available through MISTIX (see page 11). Other campgrounds open mid-May to Oct. 31, first come, first served. Fees $6-$11 per night. No showers. Tent and RV sites; no hookups. Seven group campgrounds; reservations recommended; contact park headquarters. Can reserve for **Cades Cove, Elkmont,** and **Smokemont Group Campgrounds** through MISTIX. Food services available in park.

Hotels, Motels, & Inns
(unless otherwise noted, rates are for 2 persons in a double room, high season)
INSIDE THE PARK:
LeConte Lodge (atop Mt. LeConte; access by hiking trail) 250 Apple Valley Rd., Sevierville, Tenn. 37862. (615) 429-5704. 10 cabins, no electricity, shared bathrooms. $56 per person, includes 2 meals. Open late March to mid-Nov. **Wonderland Hotel** Rte. 2, Box 205, Gatlinburg, Tenn. 37738. (615) 436-5490. 27 units, 16 private baths. $42-$76. Rest. Open mid-April to mid-Nov.

OUTSIDE THE PARK:
In Bryson City, N.C. 28713:
Hemlock Inn (On Galbraith Creek Rd., off Hwy. 19) P.O. Drawer EE. (704) 488-2885. 22 rooms, 2 cottages. $110-$150, with 2 meals. Cabin, $850 2-week min. Rest. Open April-Dec.
In Cherokee, N.C. 28719:
Best Western Great Smokies Inn (Hwy. 441 and Acquoni Rd.) P.O. Box 1309A. (800) 528-1234 or (704) 497-2020. 112 units. $65. AC, pool, rest. Open April to Nov. 30. **Holiday Inn Cherokee** (Hwy. 19 West) P.O. Box 648. (704) 497-9181. 154 units. $74. AC, pool, restaurant.
In Fontana Dam, N.C. 28733:
Peppertree Fontana Village P.O. Box 68, Hwy. 28. (800) 849-2258. 94 rooms, 150 cottages with kitchens. $76-$145. AC, pool, restaurant.
In Gatlinburg, Tenn. 37738:
Buckhorn Inn (on Tudor Mt. Rd. off Buckhorn Rd.) Route 3, Box 393. (615) 436-4668. 6 rooms, 5 cottages, 3 kitchenettes. $105-$150, includes breakfast. AC, rest. **Gillette Motel** (172 Airport Rd.) P.O. Box 231. (615) 436-5601. 80 units. $55-$90. AC, pool. **Holiday Inn of Gatlinburg** (333 Airport Rd.) P.O. Box 1130. (800) 435-9201; in Tenn. (615) 436-9201. 402 units. $70-$100. AC, pool, rest. **Park Vista Hotel** (Airport Rd.) P.O. Box 30. (800) 421-7275; in Tenn. (800) 526-1235. 315 units. $110-$120. AC, pool, rest.

For other accommodations in Gatlinburg, call the Chamber of Commerce at (800) 822-1998 or (615) 436-4178.

Excursions

Pisgah National Forest
Asheville, North Carolina

The Blue Ridge Parkway traverses this mountainous forest with slopes of mixed hardwoods, azaleas, and rhododendrons, rocky gorges, and delicate waterfalls. Outstanding in spring and fall. Contains three wilderness areas and Mt. Mitchell, the highest peak east of the Mississippi. 495,712 acres. Facilities include 482 campsites, hiking, fishing, horseback riding, hunting, picnic areas, scenic drives, swimming. Open all year; most campsites open spring to late fall. Visitor center on US 276, about 50 miles from Great Smoky Mountains NP. (704) 257-4200.

Nantahala National Forest
Asheville, North Carolina

The hardwood-covered mountains here contain deep, narrow valleys, canyons, and waterfalls. Noted for azaleas, rhododendrons. Contains three wilderness areas. 515,492 acres. Facilities include 365 campsites, hiking, boating, boat ramps, fishing, horseback riding, hunting, picnic areas, scenic drives, handicapped access. Open all year; most campsites open spring to late fall. Adjoins Great Smoky Mountains NP on the south. (704) 253-2352.

Breaks Interstate Park
Breaks, Virginia

Russell Fork cuts through the Pine Mountains here, creating Breaks Canyon, the "Grand Canyon of the South." Features class VI white water. Two rhododendron species provide long blooming season, mid-May through June; fall leaves peak mid-October. Gospel music festival Labor Day weekend. 4,600 acres. Facilities include 138 campsites, cottages and motel units, visitor center, food service, hiking, boating, boat ramp, fishing, picnic areas, scenic drives, swimming, handicapped access. Open all year; most facilities available April 1-October 31. On Va. Hwy. 80, about 190 miles from Great Smoky Mountains NP. (703) 865-4413.

Big South Fork
National River & Recreation Area
Oneida, Tennessee
The Big South Fork of the Cumberland River bisects the Cumberland Plateau, yielding white water as well as calm stretches, sandstone cliffs, waterfalls, and natural arches. 101,000 acres, part in Ky. Facilities: 235 campsites, hiking, horseback riding, boating, boat ramp, fishing, swimming, hunting, picnic areas. Open all year. Off US 27, about 100 miles northwest of Great Smoky Mountains NP. (615) 879-4890.

Cherokee National Forest
Cleveland, Tennessee
This rugged mountain backcountry is densely wooded with mixed pines and hardwoods, azaleas, mountain-laurels. 625,000 acres. Facilities include 686 campsites, hiking, boating, boat ramp, fishing, hunting, picnic areas, scenic drives, swimming. Open all year; most campsites open May-October. Adjoins Great Smoky Mountains NP on northeast and southwest. (615) 476-9700.

Chattahoochee National Forest
Gainesville, Georgia
This hardwood forest encompasses a mix of terrain—lakes, streams, valleys, mountains, and piedmont plateau. Contains five wilderness areas and a stretch of the Chattooga Wild and Scenic River with Tallullah Gorge. Also, Brasstown Bald, the state's highest mountain at 4,784 feet. 748,060 acres. Facilities include 547 campsites, food service, hiking, sailing, boat ramp, fishing, hunting, picnic areas, scenic drives, swimming, handicapped access. Open year-round; most campsites open May-September. On US 441, about 65 miles from Great Smoky Mountains NP. (404) 536-0541.

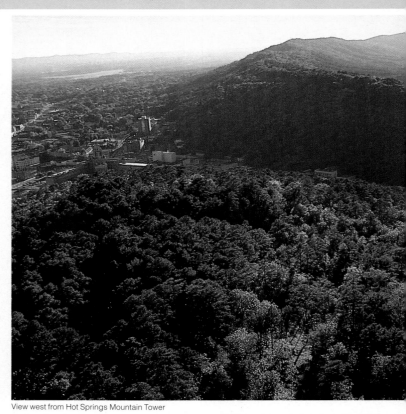

View west from Hot Springs Mountain Tower

Hot Springs

Arkansas

Established March 4, 1921

4,837 acres

Most national parks cover hundreds of thousands of acres, are far from city streets, and keep natural resources away from commercial users. . . . But not Hot Springs. This smallest of national parks is centered in a city that has made an industry out of tapping and dispensing the park's major resource: mineral-rich waters of hot springs.

The heart of this peculiar park is Central Avenue, the main street of Hot Springs, Arkansas. Rising above Central Avenue is Hot Springs Mountain, from which the waters flow. The mountain's lower western side once was coated with tufa, a milky-colored, porous rock formed of minerals deposited from

the hot springs' constant cascade.

When Hot Springs prospered as a health spa in the mid-19th century, promoters covered, piped, and diverted the springs into Central Avenue bathhouses. The entrepreneurs also prettified the slope by covering it with tons of dirt and planting grass and shrubs. "Ever since then," a longtime Hot Springs resident says, "it's been afflicted by eastern landscape architects who can't stand the sight of rocks."

The park calls itself the "oldest area in the national park system" because in 1832, 40 years before Yellowstone became the first national park, President Andrew Jackson set aside the hot springs as a special reservation. The federal land became a national park in 1921. By then Hot Springs had long been famous as a spa where people "took the waters,"

when mountains around Hot Springs produce spectacular foliage. Winter is usually short and mild; four-petaled bluets, the first of many wildflowers, appear in February.

How to Visit
Walk **Central Avenue**'s **Bathhouse Row,** then continue north to explore **Hot Springs** on the genteel trails of an urban hillside. To see a more rugged side of the park, hike the woodland trails of **Gulpha Gorge.**

Bathhouse Row
4 city blocks; 2 hours

In the early years of this century, elegant buildings lined a stretch of **Central Avenue** dubbed **Bathhouse Row.** In later years, as medical science's faith in hot springs faded, so did the bathhouses. But you can still enjoy the mystique of taking the waters. First visit the **Fordyce Bathhouse Visitor Center,** a restored "temple of health and beauty" adorned with stained-glass windows and statuary. In rooms full of gleaming plumbing and luxurious tubs, you walk through a museum of the ritual, which in its full form involved three weeks of daily baths and massage. The **Buckstaff** is the Row's only bathhouse still offering a traditional bath. (Some hotels also have baths; ask for information at the visitor center.)

seeking relief from bunions, rheumatism, and other afflictions.

The park preserves the mountain's "recharge zone," slopes where rain and snow soak into the ground, and the "discharge zone," which contains 47 springs belonging to the park. Each day about 850,000 gallons of water—at 143°F—flow from the springs into a complex piping and reservoir system. This supplies water to commercial baths and to park-maintained "jug fountains," where people flock daily to fill containers. The devotees have faith in the water's powers, but the park makes no healing claims.

How to Get There
From Little Rock, about 55 miles west on US 70 to Ark. Hwy. 7; from the south, Hwy. 7; from the west, US 70 or 270. Airport: Little Rock.

When to Go
All-year park. Summers are hot and July is crowded. Try the late fall,

Springs flowing over Tufa Terrace

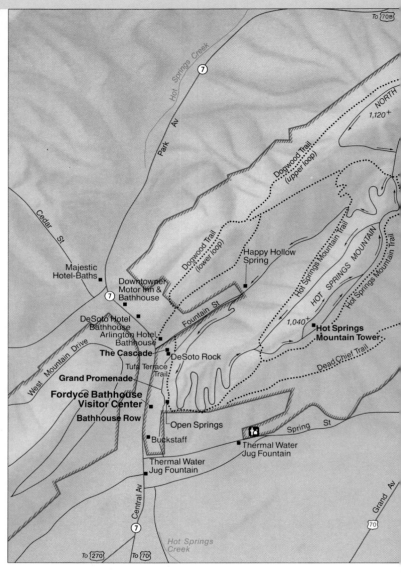

Hot Springs

a half mile; 2 hours

At the foot of the mountain (the corner of Central Avenue and Fountain Street) look for **DeSoto Rock,** a huge boulder that commemorates both the Indians who named this "place of the hot waters" and the explorer Hernando De Soto. He and his party are supposed to have bathed in the waters in 1541, beginning a tourist tra-

dition. Head up the trail to **The Cascade,** created in 1982 when decades of turf were cleared away so that a hot spring could again be seen. The water flowing here began its journey as long as 4,000 years ago when it fell as rain and seeped through fractures. Heated deep in the earth, the water returns through the faults in the rock of the mountain in a year or two, hardly enough time to cool off.

The tufa created by The Cascade's splashing waters is building up at the

A tiled tub in Fordyce Bathhouse

heat exchanger cools it to 100° F.

The springs are sealed off—and thus kept sterile—by locked green bunkers that jut out of the lawns carpeting the slope. When some of the hillside springs were open, men and women discreetly took turns soaking their feet at one of them; at another, people cooked eggs. To see more of the famous hot water bubbling out of the earth, follow the trail to **Open Springs** behind the **Maurice Bathhouse.** The two springs flow into a collecting pool, where you can safely touch the water.

Go up the stairs and finish your trek on the Grand Promenade. The walkway, which took 30 years to build and landscape, serves as a pleasant transition between the formal architecture of the bathhouses and the trails of the wooded hillside.

Gulpha Gorge

1³/₅ miles round-trip; 2 hours

To find the more traditional terrain of a national park, leave **Hot Springs** on Ark. Hwy. 7 heading north and turn right onto US 70B for Gulpha Gorge Campground, about 3 miles from downtown Hot Springs. Near the amphitheater pick up the **Gulpha Gorge Trail**, which crosses **Gulpha Creek** on stepping-stones and courses a woodland rich in dogwood and redbud; in spring and early summer wildflowers flank the trail. In less than a mile the trail intersects with another up to **Goat Rock**, a fine overlook for viewing the mountains around the city. In summer, rangers lead hikes to nearby quarries, where Indians mined novaculite for making arrowheads and spearpoints; under the name Arkansas Stone it is used today as a whetstone.

rate of ¹/₈ inch a year. The brilliant blue-green algae is the only plant species that can survive in the hot waters. So can ostracods, a crustacean about the size of a sand grain found in some of the other springs.

Near The Cascade is the **Tufa Terrace Trail**, which takes you by many concealed springs. To get there, cross the **Grand Promenade**, a landscaped brick walkway that runs behind the bathhouses. Taste the water at the drinking fountain there. A

Information & Activities

Headquarters
P.O. Box 1860, Hot Springs, Arkansas 71902. Phone (501) 624-3383.

Seasons & Accessibility
Park open year-round. Bathing facilities open generally Monday through Saturday all year.

Visitor & Information Centers
Fordyce Bathhouse Visitor Center, in the middle of Bathhouse Row. Open daily except Christmas and New Year's Day. For information call (501) 623-1433.

Entrance Fee
None, but fees charged for the concessioner-operated thermal baths.

Pets
Not allowed in buildings; otherwise permitted on leashes.

Facilities for Disabled
Visitor center is fully accessible to wheelchairs; the Thermal Feature and the Bathhouse Row Tours are partially accessible.

Things to Do
Free naturalist-led activities: hikes and bathhouse tours, campfire programs at Gulpha Gorge Campground. Also available, audiovisual and interpretive exhibits, hiking, horseback riding (horses for rent nearby); six bathing facilities offering thermal baths, whirlpools, steam cabinets, hot packs, massages.

Special Advisory
□Bathing in thermal waters not recommended for people with certain ailments; consult your doctor if in doubt.

Overnight Backpacking
Permitted in campground only; see below.

Campground
One campground, **Gulpha Gorge**, with 14-day limit from April 1 to October 31; other times 30-day limit. Open all year on first-come, first-served basis. Fees $6 per night. No showers. Tent and RV sites; no hookups.

Hotels, Motels, & Inns
(unless otherwise noted, rates are for 2 persons in a double room, high season)

Arlington Resort Hotel & Spa Central and Fountain St., Hot Springs, Arkansas 71901. (800) 643-1502 or 1503. 488 units. $50-$275. AC, 2 pools, 3 restaurants.

Best Western Hot Springs Inn (US Hwy. 70) P.O. Box CC, Hot Springs, Ark. 71902. (800) 528-1234 or (501) 624-4436. 50 units. $29-$39; with hot tub $60. AC, pool, restaurant.

Buena Vista Resort (Off Ark. Hwy. 7) Rte. 3, Box 175, Hot Springs, Ark. 71913. (800) 255-9030 or (501) 525-1321. 40 units with kitchenettes. Rooms $64-$74; cottages $70-$94. AC, pool.

Hot Springs Hilton 305 Malvern Ave., Hot Springs, Ark. 71901. (800) 445-8667 or (501) 623-6600. 200 units. $60-$94. AC, pool, restaurant.

Lake Hamilton Resort 3501 Albert Pike, Hot Springs, Ark. 71914. (800) 426-3184 or (501) 767-5511. 104 units. $89-$150. AC, pool, restaurant.

Stillmeadow Farm 111 Stillmeadow Lane, Hot Springs, Ark. 71913. (501) 525-9994. 4 rooms. $50-$85, includes breakfast. AC.

SunBay Resort Hotel 6110 Central Ave., Hot Springs, Ark. 71913. (501) 525-4691. 30 rooms; 80 condos, all with kitchens. Rooms $69-$89; condos $110-$175. AC, pool, restaurant.

Williams House Bed & Breakfast Inn 420 Quapaw, Hot Springs, Ark. 71901. (501) 624-4275. 6 rooms, 2 share a bath. $50-$80, includes breakfast. AC.

For additional accommodations, write or call the Hot Springs Convention and Visitors Bureau, P.O. Box K, Hot Springs, Ark. 71902. (800) 543-2284.

Excursions

Ouachita National Forest
Hot Springs, Arkansas
Pine-hardwood forest blankets the Ouachita Mountains, and water abounds in lakes, springs, waterfalls, and the Ouachita River. Contains seven wilderness areas. 1,601,146 acres, part in Oklahoma. Facilities: 556 campsites, hiking, boating, boat ramp, fishing, horseback riding, hunting, picnic areas, water sports, handicapped access. Open all year, including many campsites. Entrance on US 70, about 5 miles west of Hot Springs NP. (501) 321-5202.

Holla Bend
National Wildlife Refuge
Russellville, Arkansas
Wintering bald eagles and immense flocks of migratory waterfowl share this site along the Arkansas River. 4,083 acres. Facilities include hiking, boating, boat ramp, fishing, hunting, scenic drives. Open year-round, dawn to dusk. Off Arkansas Hwy. 7, about 60 miles from Hot Springs NP. (501) 968-2800.

Ozark National Forest
Russellville, Arkansas
Oak, hickory, and pine cover the high Ozark Mountain bluffs. Many streams and lakes offer excellent fishing. Features Blanchard Springs Caverns and five wilderness areas. 1,119,000 acres. Facilities: 278 campsites, 3 cabins, hiking, boating, boat ramp, fishing, hunting, horseback riding, picnic areas, scenic drives, water sports, handicapped access. Open year-round, including some campsites. Information in Russellville on US 64, about 80 miles from Hot Springs NP. (501) 968-2354.

Buffalo National River
Harrison, Arkansas
This park preserves 132 miles of the wild Buffalo River and adjacent lands. White water on upper river, more benign stretches on lower. 95,700 acres. Facilities include 200 campsites, food services, boating, fishing, hunting, picnic areas, swimming. Open all year, including most campsites. Headquarters at Harrison on Ark. 7, about 110 miles from Hot Springs NP. (501) 741-5443.

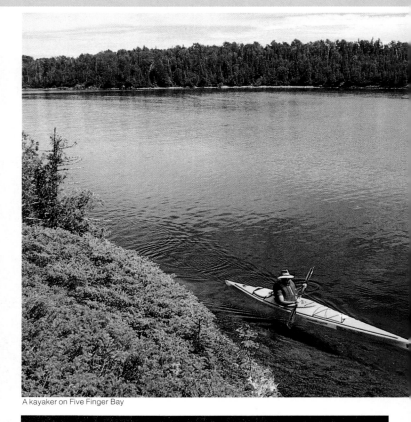

A kayaker on Five Finger Bay

Isle Royale

Michigan

Authorized March 3, 1931

134,400 acres

Out of the vastness of Lake Superior rises an island known more for its immigrant wolves and moose than for its splendors as a park. But the people who discover Isle Royale treat this isolated realm like no other park: Isle Royale visitors typically stay there $3\frac{1}{2}$ days, while the average visit to a national park is about 4 hours.

Most people get to the 37-mile-long island aboard a commercial or Park Service boat. As soon as they touch land in this wilderness park, they are on their own. They must pack in what they need and carry out their refuse.

This is rough, untamed country. Trails may be fogbound and muddy. Blackflies and mosquitoes may descend upon hikers in swarms. And, because campsites cannot be reserved, a backpacker is never certain where the day's trek may end.

"It's not like deciding to drive into Yellowstone, see Old Faithful, and drive out," a ranger says. In an entire year Isle Royale gets fewer people than Yellowstone sees in a day.

Everyone who lands on Isle Royale—even day-trippers—must stop near dockside to hear a ranger's brisk summary of rules and regulations. The most important: Water must be boiled for 2 minutes or filtered; chemical purifiers will not wipe out disease carriers.

Human hikers share trails with wolves and moose, the island's most famous inhabitants. They are descendants of the mainlanders that made Isle Royale an unexpected

Airports: Houghton, Michigan; Duluth, Minnesota.

When to Go
Late June to September; park closes from November 1 to mid-April. Mosquitoes, blackflies, and gnats are most pesky in June and July. Summer can be cool (40°F at night). Blueberries ripen in late July and Aug.

How to Visit
Although 1-day visits are feasible at **Rock Harbor** or **Windigo**, you need a longer stay to appreciate the wild beauty of **Isle Royale**. A 1-day visitor must sandwich a couple of hours of sightseeing between boat arrival and departure. Voyages take 2½ to 6½ hours, depending on the starting point. The best way to see the park is to backpack to campgrounds strung along the park's 165 miles of trails. Noncampers who plan well ahead can reserve lodgings at Rock Harbor and explore on tour boats and on foot.

Windigo
a full day

Take the **Wenonah**, a concessioner passenger boat, from Grand Portage, Minn. The 2½-hour trip is the shortest from any port serving Isle Royale. On the way into fjordlike **Washington Harbor**, watch for the buoy marking the resting place of the *America*, a 183-foot lake steamer that went down in 1928; the wreck

ark—moose by swimming to it in the early 1900s; wolves by walking across the ice in 1949. Scientists have been studying the interplay of predator and prey ever since 1958.

On the trails, all you can expect to see are the animals' tracks and droppings, although moose do surprise hikers by suddenly appearing, particularly in lush meadows. On beaver ponds you may spot the rippling Vs of the ponds' creators. In campgrounds watch for a fox looking for a handout. And remember another rule: Don't feed any of the animals.

How to Get There
Make reservations well in advance for passenger boats from Houghton or Copper Harbor, Mich., or Grand Portage, Minn. The port you pick will determine the length of your visit. For information about boats and charter seaplane service, see **Information & Activities**. Isle Royale is 56 miles from the Michigan mainland, 18 miles from Minnesota's shore.

Backpacking along Greenstone Ridge Trail

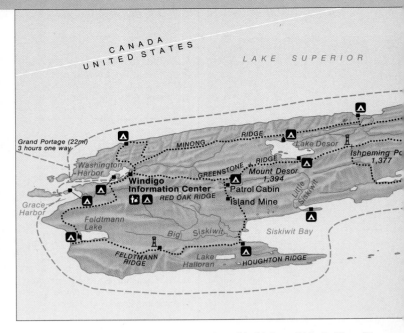

rests at a sharp angle, its ghostly bow about 2 feet below the surface. Scuba divers, with permits, frequently prowl this and the other nine major wrecks around **Isle Royale.**

As soon as you land, check at the dockside ranger station for the next **Windigo Nature Walk,** a 1-hour ramble around this western entrance to the park. You'll learn how the island was born: As glacial ice retreated some 10,000 years ago, Isle Royale rose above what would become Lake Superior. Gouges in the barren rocks became lakes. Early migrants—lichens, mosses, birdborne seeds—drifted into cracks and crannies, beginning the long work of building soil. Animals also found their way onto Isle Royale, and an ecosystem emerged. It still evolves, with some animals appearing, as did the wolves and moose, and some animals disappearing, as did caribou and coyotes.

If you miss the ranger-guided walk, try the **Windigo Nature Trail,** a 1¼-mile loop that identifies plants and shows where animals dine. Be sure to take the short side trip to the fenced-in **Moose Exclosure,** which shows how differently a forest grows when moose don't munch on it. Within the moose-free zone is a small **Hare Exclosure,** which demonstrates what

the ankle-high world looks like without hungry snowshoe hares. Remember to close the gate!

Your stay—about 3 hours—will depend on your boat's schedule. So you may have time to stroll westward a while along **Feldtmann Lake Trail.** This shoreline stretch gives you a view of **Beaver Island** and the harbor's forested northern shore.

Rock Harbor

1 or more days

A 1-day visit to **Rock Harbor,** the park's eastern gateway, can be tight. The voyage aboard *Isle Royale Queen III* from Copper Harbor takes about 4½ hours. You'll have little more than enough time for the 1-hour, ranger-led jaunt aptly named "At a Glance." You get a quick glimpse of the Rock Harbor area while looking over your shoulder to make sure the *Queen* is still at dock.

If you can stay longer and aren't a backpacker, Rock Harbor offers many relatively easy sojourns. But make advance reservations at the Rock Harbor Lodge (see **Information & Activities**). From there you can set out for a choice of adventures.

Begin with a walk along **Stoll Trail,**

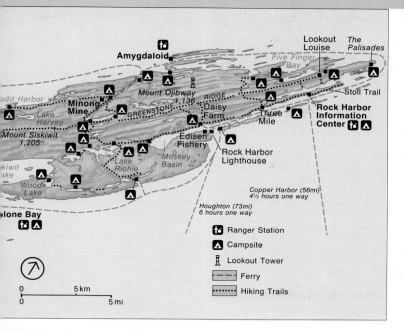

Bull moose feeding on water plants

a 4-mile loop that starts at Rock Harbor Lodge and winds through forest and plank-pathed bog. After about ½ mile you'll come to shallow mining pits, where Indians chipped away, stone on stone, to extract outcrops of copper. Mining here began around 2500 BC and continued for at least 1,500 years. The copper, traded along the upper Mississippi Valley, was formed into fishhooks, knives, and awls. Over a thousand mining pits have been found on Isle Royale.

Continue another 1½ miles, mostly along a rocky shore, to craggy **Scoville Point,** a fine spot for viewing some of the roughly 200 rocky islets that form the Isle Royale archipelago. On the way back you can switch to a branch trail that clings to the forested shore of **Tobin Harbor.** As the trail nears the lodge, you can see traces of **Smithwick Mine,** one of many relics of 19th-century mining ventures.

For a small round-trip fee you can

take a shuttle boat from Rock Harbor across ½ mile of usually calm water to **Raspberry Island**, where a 1-mile trail introduces you to a boreal forest—white spruce, balsam fir, paper birch, aspen—and a bog. You'll also see a pit dug in 1848 in a vain search for copper. Bring a picnic.

For another fee a boat takes you on a ½-day, guided tour into history. First stop is **Edisen Fishery**, which belonged to Pete Edisen. One of the last commercial fishermen on the island, Pete died in 1983. The Park Service is restoring his jumble of moss-chinked log cabins and shacks made of such odds and ends as a cabin door from a wrecked passenger boat. A short trail leads to the handsome **Rock Harbor Lighthouse**, erected in 1855 to guide ore ships. That same year marked the closing of the mine that was expected to fill those ships.

Into the Backcountry

3 to 5 days

To savor Isle Royale's isolated grandeur you must venture into the island's great beyond. Plan your 3- or 5-day stay around passenger boat arrivals and departures.

A sample 5-day itinerary: Arrive at Rock Harbor on Monday aboard the *Isle Royale Queen III* and hike southwest along the **Rock Harbor Trail** that courses forest, bog, and smooth shore rocks. At not quite 2 miles, look for a sign to **Suzy's Cave**, about 80 yards up a side trail. The cave is an unusual, water-carved arch. At 3 miles is Three Mile Campground. Stay here and head out next morning on the 4½-mile shore trail to **Daisy Farm**; in this spot daisies have flourished where vegetables never would.

You can camp here for 3 days and start back early Friday to meet the returning *Queen*. Or you can split the hike into 2 days by spending Thursday night at Three Mile.

While at Daisy Farm, climb **Mount Ojibway Trail**, an easy 1¾-mile ascent up the 1,136-foot mountain, which is topped by a lookout tower. You're welcome to climb as far as the cabin, which houses a solar-powered air monitoring station. The Park Service runs a network of such monitors to check air quality in 65 national park areas. From the tower take the **Greenstone Ridge Trail**, which runs about 40 miles along the backbone of the island. About 1½ miles west of the tower look for the wooden post marking the **Daisy Farm Trail**, which winds back to the campground.

The Wolves of Isle Royale

Visitors to Isle Royale probably will never see a gray wolf. Wolves avoid people, but live in packs as social animals. Only the dominant male and female—the alpha pair—mate and produce young. Others help protect and feed the pups born each spring.

Hundreds of thousands of wolves once roamed North America. But early settlers killed or drove away most of them. Today North America has only about 60,000 gray wolves, principally in Canada and Alaska.

When Isle Royale's first wolves crossed frozen Lake Superior in 1949, they found a growing moose herd with no natural predators. The wolves hunted the old, the young, and the sickly, preventing overpopulation. Both species prospered, the wolves increasing to 50 in 4 packs.

By 1980 a smaller moose herd provided few easy targets, and the wolf population began to fall. As moose

Gray wolf

numbers rose, the wolves' decline mysteriously continued. By the winter of 1990-91 only 11 wolves survived. Park scientists, trying to solve the mystery, are monitoring six wolves fitted with radio collars.

Information & Activities

Headquarters
87 North Ripley Street, Houghton, Mich. 49931. Phone (906) 482-0984.

Seasons & Accessibility
Park open mid-April to October 31; can be reached by boat or seaplane only; full services available mid-June to August 31. Weather and rough waters may delay departures; allow extra time and be flexible. Mainland headquarters open year-round.

Boat & Seaplane Information
Reservations required (a month in advance suggested).

Write or call headquarters for boat schedule from Houghton to Rock Harbor. (The Park Service's boat, *Ranger III*, will transport boats under 20 feet between those points.)

For boats from Copper Harbor to Rock Harbor, write to Isle Royale Queen, Copper Harbor, Mich., 49918, or call (906) 289-4437 in summer or (906) 482-4950 in winter. For boats from Grand Portage to Windigo and Rock Harbor write to GPIR Transport Lines, 1507 N. First St., Superior, Wis. 54880, or call (715) 392-2100. For seaplane information, write to Isle Royale Seaplane Serv., Box 371, Houghton, Mich. 49931, or call (906) 482-8850 in summer.

Visitor & Information Centers
Windigo Information Center at west end of island, Rock Harbor Information Center at east end. Both open daily all season. Phone park headquarters for information.

Pets
Not allowed in park or on boats.

Facilities for Disabled
Park headquarters at Houghton, Rock Harbor Lodge, both information centers, and a campsite at Daisy Farm are wheelchair accessible. Boats to island require assistance.

Things to Do
Free naturalist-led activities: nature and history walks and talks, canoe tour, lighthouse and copper mine tours, films, evening interpretive programs. Also, boating (motorized crafts permitted on Lake Superior only), canoeing (rentals at Windigo and Rock Harbor; permit required), hiking, scuba diving, fishing (license required for Lake Superior only), boat cruises to the outer islands.

Special Advisories
☐ Expect sudden squalls and rough seas on Lake Superior; do not attempt to take boats under 20 feet across it. See above.
☐ No public phone service available in the park.

Camping
Thirty-six backcountry camping areas; 1-day to 5-day limit. Camping allowed from mid-April through October. First come, first served. No fees. Permit required; available at ranger stations. Seventeen of the areas permit group camping; contact park headquarters for information.

Hotels, Motels, & Inns
(unless otherwise noted, rates are for 2 persons in a double room, high season)

INSIDE THE PARK:
Rock Harbor Lodge P.O. Box 405, Houghton, Mich. 49931. (906) 337-4993. From Oct. to April write c/o Mammoth Cave, Ky. 42259. (502) 773-2191. 80 units. Cottages, kitchenettes $98; rooms with meals $162. Rest. Open mid-June to mid-Sept.

OUTSIDE THE PARK:
In Copper Harbor, Mich. 49918:
Bella Vista Motel P.O. Box 26. (906) 289-4213. 29 units. Rooms $42; cottages with kitchenettes $35-$50. Pool. Open early May to mid-Oct.
Keweenaw Mountain Lodge US 41. (906) 289-4403. 42 units. Rooms $42; cottages $45-$52. Rest. Open May to mid-Oct. **Lake Fanny Hooe Resort & Campground** (off US 41) (906) 289-4451. 14 rooms, kitchens. $50-$54.

In Grand Portage, Minn. 55605:
Grand Portage Lodge P.O. Box 307. (800) 232-1384 or (218) 475-2401. 100 rooms. $64. Pool, restaurant, casino.

In Houghton, Mich. 49931:
Best Western King's Inn 215 Shelden Ave. (800) 528-1234 or (906) 482-5000. 68 units. $64. AC, pool. **Best Western-Franklin Square Inn** 820 Shelden Ave. (800) 228-2828 or (906) 487-1700. 77 units, 2 with kitchenettes. $84-$90. AC, pool, restaurant.

Excursions

Grand Portage National Monument
Grand Portage, Minnesota

In the 18th and 19th centuries, fur traders called voyageurs converged at this central supply depot of the North West Company. Visitors can tour the reconstructed stockade, great hall, kitchen, and canoe warehouse. Open late May to mid-October. The Grand Portage Trail, open all year, follows the route used by voyageurs who portaged their equipment almost 9 miles to avoid the rapids and falls of the Pigeon River. 707 acres. Facilities: hiking, cross-country skiing, historic exhibits, handicapped access. On US 61, about 22 miles from Isle Royale NP by boat to Grand Portage. (218) 475-2202.

Horseshoe Harbor Preserve
Copper Harbor, Michigan

This remote Lake Superior harbor is nearly land's end on Michigan's Upper Peninsula. Superb birdwatching includes nesting wood warblers, ravens, herring gulls, and great hawk migrations in the spring. Four-wheel drive needed on road leading to this Nature Conservancy site; RVs prohibited; other vehicles can approach to within $1\frac{1}{2}$ miles. 500 acres. Hiking. No camping. Off US 41, about 60 miles from Isle Royale NP by ferry to Copper Harbor. (517) 332-1741.

Hiawatha National Forest
Escanaba, Michigan

In two units, this mixed evergreen-and-hardwood forest dotted with lakes descends to the shores of Lake Superior, Lake Michigan, and Lake Huron. Contains six wilderness areas and a section of the North Country National Scenic Trail. 860,000 acres. Facilities include 709 campsites, hiking, boating, boat ramp, fishing, horseback riding, hunting, picnic areas, scenic drives, winter sports, water sports, handicapped access. Open all year; most campsites open May 15-October. Info. at Rapid River, Manistique, Munising, and other locations. More than 300 miles from Isle Royale NP (via Michigan-side ferry). (906) 786-4062.

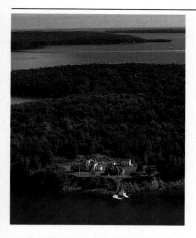

Apostle Islands
National Lakeshore

Bayfield, Wisconsin

The national lakeshore encompasses 21 of the 22 remote, berry-covered Apostle Islands and 11 miles of Lake Superior shoreline. Access to islands by boat; commercial and charter boats, charter fishing trips available. 42,009 acres. Facilities include primitive camping (permits required), hiking, boating, fishing, picnic areas, winter sports, water sports, handicapped access. Open year-round, including campsites. Visitor center in Bayfield on Wisconsin Hwy. 13, about 250 miles from Isle Royale National Park (Michigan-side ferry). (715) 779-3397.

Pictured Rocks
National Lakeshore

Munising, Michigan

Sandstone cliffs sculptured by nature into formations resembling castles and palisades give this first national lakeshore (1966) its name. The site also features extensive dunes and banks, sand beaches, forests, inland lakes, streams, and waterfalls. 71,400 acres. Facilities include 67 campsites, hiking, boating, boat ramps, fishing, hunting, picnic areas, winter sports, water sports, handicapped access. Open year-round; campsites open May-November. Visitor center at Munising on Michigan Hwy. 28, about 335 miles from Isle Royale NP (via Michigan-side ferry). (906) 387-3700 or 2607.

Ottawa National Forest

Ironwood, Michigan

Lakes, streams, rivers, and waterfalls abound in this isolated ski-country forest. Also features three wilderness areas, Black River Harbor Recreation Area, and the North Country National Scenic Trail. 958,000 acres. Facilities include more than 500 campsites, hiking, canoeing and kayaking, boat ramp, fishing, hunting, picnic areas, winter sports, handicapped access. Open all year, campsites included. Visitor center in Watersmeet on US 2, about 140 miles from Isle Royale NP (via Michigan-side ferry). (906) 932-1330.

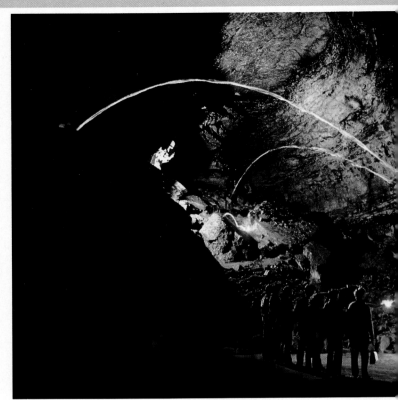

Torch tossing—no longer done—to demonstrate 19th-century way of lighting caves

Mammoth Cave

Kentucky

Established July 1, 1941

52,714 acres

Under a swath of Kentucky hills and hollows is a limestone labyrinth that became the heartland of a national park. The surface of Mammoth Cave National Park encompasses about 80 square miles. No one knows how big the underside is. More than 330 miles of the five-level cave system have been mapped, and new caves are continually being discovered. Two layers of stone underlie Mammoth's hilly woodlands. A sandstone and shale cap, as thick as 50 feet in places, acts as an umbrella over limestone ridges. The umbrella leaks at places called sinkholes, from which surface water makes its way underground, eroding the limestone into a honeycomb of caverns.

Mammoth, the world's largest known cave system, a United Nations World Heritage site and the core area of an International Biosphere Reserve, still is as "grand, gloomy, and peculiar" as it was when Stephen Bishop, a young slave and early guide, described it. By a flickering lard-oil lamp he found and mapped some of Mammoth's passages. Bishop died in 1857. His grave, like his life, is part of Mammoth; it lies in the Guides Cemetery near the entrance.

Most visitors see the eerie beauty of the caverns on some of the 12 miles of passages available for tours. Rangers dispense geological lore and tell tales about real and imagined happenings 200 or 300 feet down. The tours are hikes inside the earth; uphill stretches can be hard going for some visitors. Few seem frightened;

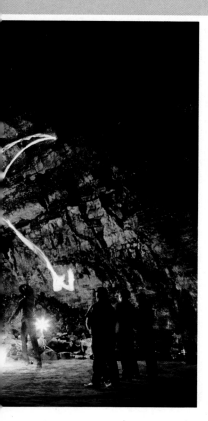

Cave City and head northwest on Ky. 70 to the park. Don't be misled by signs proclaiming commercial "mammoth" caves. Airports: Nashville and Louisville.

When to Go
All-year park. Underground, all days are about the same; temperatures in interior passages fluctuate from the mid-50s to the low 60s. Summer brings the most people, and frequent tours are offered. Though there are fewer tours the rest of the year, they are less crowded.

How to Visit
The tours vary greatly; pick ones to fit your time and stamina. All of them require you to buy a ticket. Reservations are strongly advised in summer, on holidays, and on spring and fall weekends. For a ½-day visit, you might take the **Historic Tour**, which combines geology with Mammoth's rich history. If you plan to stay longer, consider the fairly strenuous **Half Day Tour** (there are three steep hills, each nearly 90 feet high) or the **Echo River Tour**. To enjoy the caves safely and comfortably, wear shoes with nonskid soles and take a jacket. Top off your underground trips with a river trip or a walk on the **Cave Island Nature Trail**.

The least arduous cave tour (¼ mile, 75 minutes) is the **Travertine Tour**. A modified version of the **Frozen Niagara Tour**, it has only 18 steps each way (plus an optional 49) and is designed for visitors who want a short and easy trip. The toughest challenge is the 5-mile, 6-hour, belly-crawling **Wild Cave Tour**, offered in summer, by reservation.

people terrified by darkness or tight spots naturally avoid caves. Rangers say they rarely have problems guiding the 600,000 men, women, and children who venture below yearly.

Mammoth does not glamorize the underworld with garish lighting. You never forget that you are deep in the earth. And nowhere else can you get a better lesson in the totality of darkness and the miracle of light. Sometimes on a tour a ranger gathers everyone and, after a warning, switches off the lights. The darkness is sudden, absolute. Then the ranger lights a match and the tiny dot of light magically spreads, illuminating a circle of astonished faces.

How to Get There
Mammoth Cave, 9 miles northwest of I-65, is nearly equidistant (about 85 miles) between Louisville and Nashville, Tenn. From the south, take Exit 48 at Park City and head northwest on Ky. Hwy. 255 to the park; from the north, take Exit 53 at

Historic Tour
2 miles; 2 hours

You leave daylight and walk into dimly lit gloom at the **Historic Entrance**, discovered by pioneers in the 1790s and by Indians thousands of years before. Near the entrance, at the **Rotunda**, 140 feet down, are relics of the cave's use as a nitrate mine during the War of 1812. Slaves hauled in logs, built leaching vats, and filled them with cave dirt. Water, poured into the vats, trickled into a trough as brine. Two pipelines of hollowed-out logs carried water in and brine out. The residue, nitrate crystals, was used to make much of the gunpowder used in the war.

Broadway, an underground avenue, leads to a spot called **Methodist Church,** where services may have been conducted in the 1800s. Farther on, **Booth's Amphitheater** recalls the visit of actor Edwin Booth. Here, Edwin, brother of assassin John Wilkes Booth, recited Hamlet's famous Soliloquy.

The **Bottomless Pit** looked that way to early visitors; it's 105 feet deep; looking up, you see its dome 38 feet above. (The top of a shaft is a dome, the bottom a pit.) On your way back toward the entrance you pass through **Fat Man's Misery,** a passage polished smooth by generations of squirming spelunkers. You emerge into **Great Relief Hall,** a large chamber with rest rooms and benches. Then back on the trail for the final spectacles: **Mammoth Dome**—192 feet from floor to ceiling—carved by water dripping through a sinkhole, and the **Ruins of Karnak,** a cluster of gleaming limestone pillars that look like an Egyptian temple.

Half Day Tour

4 miles; 4¹⁄₂ hours

The tour (likely to be very crowded in summer) begins with a 2-mile bus ride from the visitor center to the **Carmichael Entrance,** a concrete bunker and stairway that leads down to **Cleaveland Avenue,** a long tubular chamber tunneled out by a river. Its walls sparkle with flowery patches of gypsum. The white mineral crystallizes below the surface of the limestone from seeping moisture, then bursts out in blossomlike designs.

About a mile beyond is the **Snowball Dining Room,** a restaurant where the tour stops for lunch. The once beautiful snowball-like features on the roof are now dull gray from a black fungus that grows from deposits of lint on visitors' clothing. Lint that has a residue of phosphate from certain laundry detergents encourages the fungus's growth on the cave

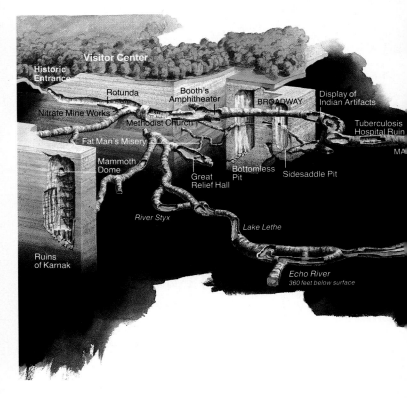

Visitor Center

Historic Entrance

Rotunda

Booth's Amphitheater

BROADWAY

Display of Indian Artifacts

Nitrate Mine Works

Methodist Church

Tuberculosis Hospital Ruin

MA

Fat Man's Misery

Mammoth Dome

Great Relief Hall

Bottomless Pit

Sidesaddle Pit

River Styx

Lake Lethe

Ruins of Karnak

Echo River
360 feet below surface

Crawling through a stretch of the Wild Cave Tour

Eyeless, colorless cave shrimp

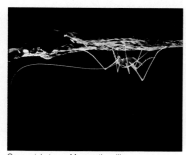

Cave cricket on a Mammoth ceiling

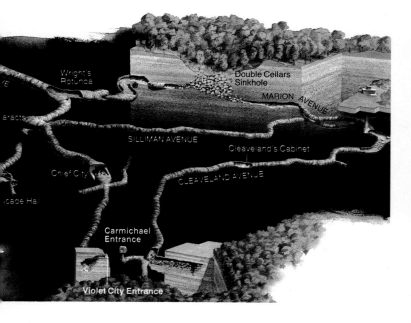

Wright's Rotunda

Double Cellars Sinkhole

MARION AVENUE

aracts

SILLIMAN AVENUE

Cleaveland's Cabinet

Chief City

CLEAVELAND AVENUE

cade Hall

Carmichael Entrance

Violet City Entrance

Crystal Lake beneath Moonlight Dome

of flowstone—the legacy of mineral-laden water that seeped here, vanished, and left behind the shimmering stalactites and stalagmites. Such formations build up at the rate of about a cubic inch every 200 years.

Echo River Tour

3 miles; about a half day

This tour (offered June to September) adds to the Historic Tour a look at some of Mammoth's subterranean waterways: the **River Styx, Lake Lethe,** and **Echo River.** Here you don life jackets and climb into a boat that a ranger paddles for a 10-minute trip. You are not likely to see the river's blindfish, one of about 30 species of animals in a class called troglobites—permanent cave dwellers. These animals have so thoroughly adapted to cave conditions that they could never survive above ground. Many have been isolated from related species in other caves for about a million years. But on this and other tours watch for tan, long-antennaed crickets, known as troglophiles (cave lovers); they live in the cave but commute to the outside for food.

Along with food for the troglobites, cave rivers sometimes carry pollutants into the park from the outside—waste from septic systems, pesticides and fertilizers from farms. When these pollutants enter the park's underworld, they damage the

formations. Environmentalists have long been lobbying for the restaurant's removal.

Another river canyon, **Boone Avenue,** takes you 300 feet into the earth along a passage so narrow you can touch both walls. The tour ends at **Frozen Niagara,** a massive cascade

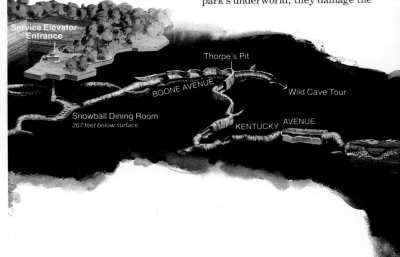

Service Elevator Entrance

Thorpe's Pit

BOONE AVENUE

Wild Cave Tour

Snowball Dining Room
267 feet below surface

KENTUCKY AVENUE

Scenic boat cruise on Green River

fragile and unique cave ecosystem. One loss could be Kentucky cave shrimp, which are now endangered.

Boat Trips & Hikes

To explore the **Green River,** which winds through the park, you can buy tickets at the visitor center for a sedate, 1-hour scenic boat cruise aboard the *Miss Green River II.* Or you can walk the **Cave Island Nature Trail,** part of which passes along the river. The trail, which begins and ends near the visitor center, shows you the interplay between surface features and Mammoth's underworld. At **River Styx Spring** you can see water emerging from the cave and flowing into the Green River.

Farther along the shore, you see **Cave Island,** formed of waterborne logs, silt, and other materials.

Most of the park's 70 miles of trails are in the backcountry across the Green River. Within the park, there are no bridges over the river. You can drive onto the Green River Ferry at a crossing southwest of the visitor center, or Houchen's Ferry at the western edge of the park; ferries have carried people and their vehicles across the river since the 1800s. Head north on **Mammoth Cave Ferry Road** to Maple Spring Group Campground. A gravel road there leads to **Good Spring Church,** founded in 1842. From here you can walk 10 miles on a trail that winds through forests slowly reclaiming land once cleared by farming and logging.

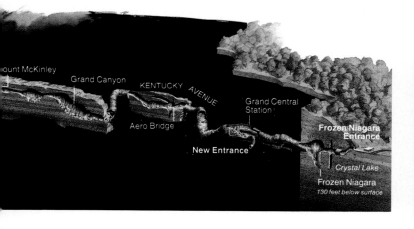

Mount McKinley
Grand Canyon
KENTUCKY AVENUE
Aero Bridge
New Entrance
Grand Central Station
Frozen Niagara Entrance
Crystal Lake
Frozen Niagara
130 feet below surface

Information & Activities

Headquarters
Mammoth Cave, Kentucky 42259.
Phone (502) 758-2328.

Seasons & Accessibility
Park open year-round. Visitors must join a tour to view the caves; tours offered every day but Christmas.

Visitor & Information Centers
Visitor Center open daily all year except Christmas. If space is available, you can buy tickets there on the day, or 1 day in advance, for all tours except Wild Cave, for which advance reservations are essential. But tours sell out quickly—especially in summer, on holidays, and on spring and fall weekends—so if at all possible, buy tickets in advance through MISTIX (see page 11).

For more information on ranger-led activities, call (502) 758-2328.

Entrance Fees
None. Fees required for tours, however; charges range from $3.50 to $10 for adults and youths; free for children under 6. Higher fees for special tours; the Wild Cave Tour is $25 per person. Prices subject to change.

Pets
Permitted on leashes except in caves and Visitor Center. Kennel facilities through the Mammoth Cave Hotel.

Facilities for Disabled
Visitor Center, some sites at Headquarters Campground, and rest rooms are wheelchair accessible. Also, cave tour available for persons in wheelchairs; $1/2$-mile Heritage Trail on surface is fully accessible.

Things to Do
Naturalist-led activities: cave tours, (12 types offered in summer, 5 the rest of the year), children's exploration program, nature walks, evening programs. Also, nature trails, fishing (no license required), horseback riding, Green River boat trip, bicycling, occasional special events.

Special Advisory
☐Cave tours are strenuous; talk with a ranger before selecting one if you have difficulty walking or trouble with your heart or lungs. Wear sturdy shoes and bring a jacket.

Overnight Backpacking
Permits required. They are free and available from ticket office at Visitor Center.

Campgrounds
Three campgrounds, all with a 14-day limit. Open all year first come, first served. Fees: None to $6 per night. Showers near **Headquarters** for a fee. Tent and RV sites at **Headquarters** and **Houchins Ferry**; no hookups. Tent sites only at **Dennison Ferry**. Water unavailable at **Dennison Ferry**. Reservations required at **Maple Spring Group Campgrounds**; contact headquarters. Food services in park.

Hotels, Motels, & Inns
(unless otherwise noted, rates are for 2 persons in a double room, high season)
INSIDE THE PARK:
Mammoth Cave Hotel Mammoth Cave, Ky. 42259. (502) 758-2225. 107 units. Hotel $65; motor lodge $68; cottages $36-$51. AC, restaurant.
OUTSIDE THE PARK:
In Cave City, Kentucky 42127:
Best Western Kentucky Inn P.O. Box 356. (800) 528-1234 or (502) 773-3161. 50 units. $49. AC, pool. **Days Inn & Oasis Restaurant** P.O. Box 2009. (800) 325-2525 or (502) 773-2151. 110 units. $45. AC, pool, restaurant. **Interstate Inns** P.O. Box 397. (502) 773-3101. 140 units. $48; includes breakfast. AC, pool. **Quality Inn** P.O. Box 547. (800) 221-2222 or (502) 773-2181. 101 units. $48-$56. AC, pool, restaurant.
In Park City, Kentucky 42160:
Best Western Park Mammoth Resort I-65 & 31 West. (800) 528-1234 or (502) 749-4101. 93 units. $54. AC, pool, restaurant.
In Bowling Green, Kentucky 42104:
Bowling Green Bed & Breakfast 1415 Beddington Way. (502) 781-3861. 2 rooms, 1 private bath. $45; includes breakfast. AC. **New's Friendship Inn** 3160 Scottsville Rd. (502) 781-3460. 51 units. $36-$39. AC, pool.

For additional accommodations, call the Chambers of Commerce of Cave City (502) 773-3131 and Bowling Green (502) 781-3200.

Excursions

Daniel Boone National Forest
Winchester, Kentucky

Impressed with eastern Kentucky's vegetative bounty, Daniel Boone called this land Eden. The region's geologic wonders also attracted the 18th-century pioneer: more than 80 natural sandstone arches in the Red River Gorge Geological Area, left by 70 million years of wind and water. One of these arches, Sky Bridge, offers a panoramic view of the gorge. The Sheltowee Trace National Recreation Trail, linking many of the forest's recreation sites, memorializes Boone's Indian name, Sheltowee, or "Big Turtle." Also contains two wilderness areas. 661,000 acres. Facilities include 118 campsites, hiking, boating, boat ramp, marinas, fishing, hunting, off-road vehicle routes, picnic areas, scenic drives, water sports, cross-country skiing, handicapped access. Open all year; most campsites open April-November. Information at London off I-75, about 125 miles from Mammoth Cave NP. (606) 745-3100.

Cumberland Gap National Historical Park
Middlesboro, Kentucky

Following the path trod by bison and deer, Indian hunters breached the great wall of the Appalachians long before westering pioneers "discovered" the gap in the mid-18th century. In 1775, Daniel Boone and his band of axmen forged the Wilderness Trail into Kentucky, opening the West to its first wave of expansion. Some 50 miles of hiking trails lead visitors to the Pinnacle Overlook, White Rocks, Sand Cave, and to the Hensley Settlement atop Brush Mountain—an early 20th-century effort at self-sufficient living. 20,281 acres, part in Virginia and Tennessee. Facilities include 160 campsites, hiking, fishing, picnic areas, scenic drives, handicapped access. Open all year, including campsites. Visitor center at Middlesboro on US 25E, about 190 miles from Mammoth Cave NP. (606) 248-2817.

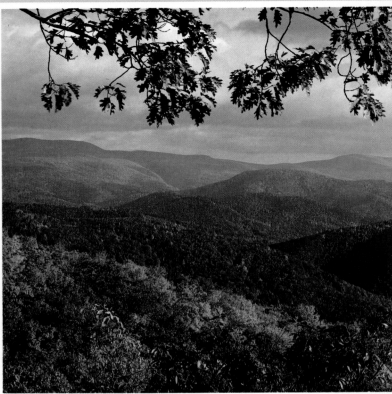

October morning at Buck Hollow Overlook

Shenandoah

Virginia

Established December 26, 1935

194,630 acres

The Skyline Drive, which runs for 105 miles along the crest of the Blue Ridge Mountains, is flanked by a rumpled panorama of forests and mountains. To many who travel the drive, the highway itself is a park. But the cars are passing the real Shenandoah. Nearly 500 miles of trails crisscross Skyline Drive, and the Appalachian Trail roughly parallels it for its entire length.

The long, narrow park flows outward, upward, and downward from the highway that splits it. The drive, following ridge trails walked by Indians and early settlers, transports visitors to a park built on a frontier that lingered into modern times.

Unlike most national parks, Shenandoah is a place where people lived for a long time. To create the park, Virginia state officials acquired 3,870 privately owned tracts and donated the land to the nation. Never before had a large, populated expanse of private land been converted into a national park. And never before had planners made a park of land so worn by human use.

In the decade before the park opened, some 2,000 mountain people moved or were moved from their cabins and resettled outside the proposed park boundaries. A few mountaineers, though, lived out their lives in the park and were buried in the secluded graveyards of Shenandoah's vanished settlements.

Much of Shenandoah consisted of scrabbly farmland, eroded hillsides, and second- or third-growth forests logged since the early 1700s. Today

in October to see the foliage. To avoid fall traffic jams, arrive early (preferably on a weekday), park at an overlook, and walk a trail. Snowstorms sometimes close the Skyline Drive, the park's north-south highway. Most concession-operated facilities close in winter. Campgrounds fill on summer weekends, but day trippers still have plenty of park. Wildflowers bloom from early spring to late fall.

How to Visit

On a day's drive-in visit, whatever entrance you use, get out and walk a trail. Even if you venture only a few hundred feet from an overlook, you will be in the real park and not on a scenic highway. For a longer stay, make a base at one place, such as **Big Meadows** or **Skyland**, and explore from there.

Skyline Drive from Front Royal to Big Meadows

51 miles; a full day

Not quite 5 miles south of the **Front Royal Entrance Station** is the **Dickey Ridge Visitor Center,** where exhibits introduce you to the park and its facilities along **Skyline Drive.** To walk a path of mountain life, cross the drive at the visitor center and start the self-guided, 1⅓-mile **Fox Hollow Trail,** named for the family that first settled this hollow, as tenant farmers, in 1837. Their houses have disappeared, but you can see relics of their toil: large, well-stacked piles of rock cleared from farmland. Other stones—rough and dimly lettered— jut from the family graveyard.

Along the drive, stop at overlooks for views of the **Shenandoah Valley** and the peaks looming above it. The views are magnificent except on days when pollution levels mar visibility. At many overlooks are signposts for well-marked trails. Daubs of paint identify them: white, the **Appalachian Trail;** blue, a park hiking trail; yellow, a horse trail (hiking also allowed).

At Mathews Arm Campground, 22 miles from Front Royal, the easily accessible, self-guided, 1¾-mile **Traces Nature Trail** takes you back through an oak forest to the time of the earliest white settlers. The traces are faint: an old road, trees,

the marks of lumbering, grazing, and farming are disappearing as forests make a slow, steady comeback.

Spring arrives first in the park valleys and then moves upward. Walking a valley trail, a visitor can follow spring's path and see, in a single day, a variety of flowers that bloom elsewhere over a span of weeks.

How to Get There

From Washington, D.C. (about 70 miles away), take I-66 west to US 340, then head south to the park's Front Royal (North) Entrance. From Charlottesville, take I-64 to the Rockfish (South) Entrance. From the west, take US 211 through Luray to the Thornton Gap Entrance or head east on US 33 to the Swift Run Gap Entrance. Airports: Dulles International, near Washington, and Charlottesville.

When to Go

Of the nearly 2,000,000 people who visit the park each year, 400,000 go

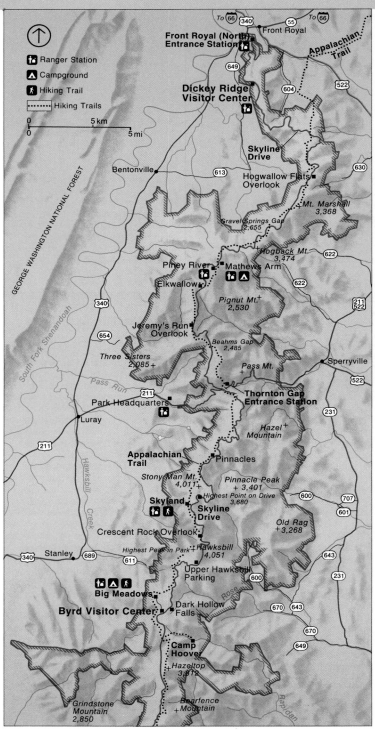

Ranger Station
Campground
Hiking Trail
Hiking Trails

0 — 5 km
0 — 5 mi

GEORGE WASHINGTON NATIONAL FOREST

To 66 — 340 — 55 — To 66
Front Royal
Front Royal (North)
Entrance Station
Appalachian Trail
649
604
522
Dickey Ridge
Visitor Center
Skyline
Drive
613
Bentonville
Hogwallow Flats
Overlook
630
Mt. Marshall
3,368
Gravel Springs Gap
2,655
Hogback Mt.
3,474
622
Piney River
Mathews Arm
622
Elkwallow
Pignut Mt.
2,530
340
654
Jeremy's Run
Overlook
Beahms Gap
2,485
Three Sisters
2,085
Pass Mt.
Sperryville
211
522
Pass Run
211
522
Park Headquarters
Thornton Gap
Entrance Station
231
Luray
Hazel
Mountain
211
Appalachian
Trail
Pinnacles
Stony Man Mt.
4,011
Pinnacle Peak
3,401
600
707
Skyland
Highest Point on Drive
3,680
601
Skyline
Drive
Old Rag
3,268
Crescent Rock Overlook
Hawksbill Creek
Highest Peak in Park
Hawksbill
4,051
340
Stanley
689
611
Upper Hawksbill
Parking
643
600
231
Big Meadows
Byrd Visitor Center
Dark Hollow
Falls
Rose
670
643
670
649
Camp
Hoover
Hazeltop
3,812
Grindstone
Mountain
2,850
Bearfence
Mountain
Rapidan

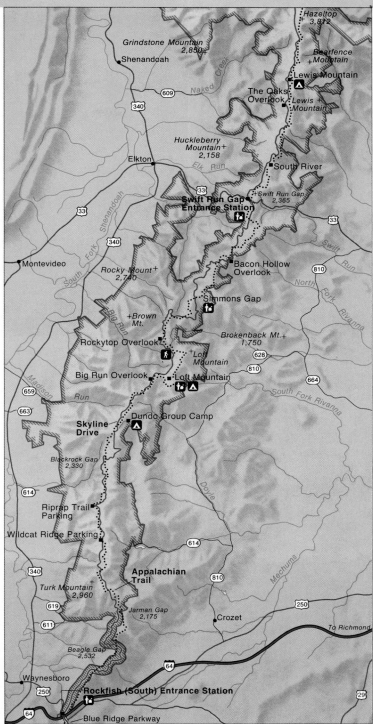

Hazeltop
+ *3,812*

Grindstone Mountain
2,850+

● Shenandoah

Bearfence
+ *Mountain*

▲ Lewis Mountain

609

The Oaks
Overlook

Lewis +
Mountain

340

Huckleberry
Mountain+
2,158

● South River

Elk Run

33

Swift Run Gap
Entrance Station

+ *Swift Run Gap*
2,365

33

33

340

● Montevideo

Rocky Mount +
2,740

● Bacon Hollow
Overlook

810

Shenandoah

Simmons Gap

South *Fork*

+ *Brown*
Mt.

Brokenback Mt. +
1,750

North Fork Rivanna

Swift Run

Rockytop Overlook

Big Run

+ *Loft*
Mountain

628

810

664

Big Run Overlook

▲ Loft Mountain

659

Run

Skyline
Drive

Madison

Dundo Group Camp ▲

South Fork Rivanna

663

Blackrock Gap
2,330

614

Riprap Trail
Parking

Wildcat Ridge Parking

614

810

Mechums

340

Appalachian
Trail

Turk Mountain +
2,960

619

611

Jarman Gap
2,175

● Crozet

250

To Richmond

Beagle Gap
2,532

64

● Waynesboro

250

29

64

Rockfish (South) Entrance Station

Blue Ridge Parkway

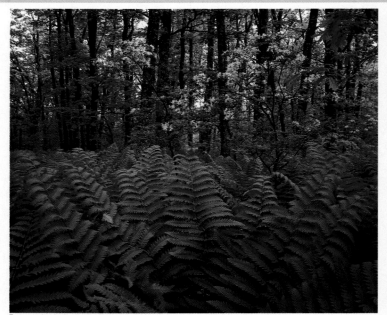

Ferns on forest floor near Swift Run Gap

tumbling stone walls. For a more rugged hike into the past, stop at the parking area past milepost 37 and take the **Corbin Cabin Cutoff Trail.** The steep trip (1½ miles each way) ends at **Corbin Cabin,** the only typical mountain residence in the park. In 1909, George Corbin cut and hewed logs, and, with the help of neighbors, built this cabin. The Corbin family, like many others, lived on what they grew or made, including brandy from peaches and apples. The Potomac Appalachian Trail Club maintains the cabin for rent to members and the public, along with other rustic cabins of recent vintage scattered through the park's backcountry.

Skyland (near milepost 42) dates to the 1890s. The resort, which includes a lodge, dining room, and cabins, is open from April to December. The 1½-mile **Stony Man Nature Trail** begins near the parking area and, climbing about 340 feet, reaches the cliffs of **Stony Man**'s summit (4,011 feet, second highest point in the park). From an outcrop on the cliffs you get a sweeping view of the mountains. The trail loops back to the start.

Stop at **Crescent Rock Overlook** (near milepost 44) for a look at **Hawksbill Mountain** (4,051 feet, highest point in park). Then, 6 miles far-

ther, stop at the parking area for **Dark Hollow Falls Trail,** a 1½-mile round-trip to waterfalls, the shortest route to any falls in the park. The steep trail takes you past clusters of ferns, mosses, and liverworts. Split-log benches offer a rest en route.

Big Meadows (milepost 51) is many places in one. It has trails, a campground, a lodge, a complex of facilities for visitors, and the **Byrd Visitor Center,** where exhibits tell the story of the people who lived in these mountains from prehistoric times to 1936. Part of the story is the saga of the chestnut tree. Once the source of food and rot-resistant wood, the chestnut began to disappear during the last century, when farmers and stockmen began to "deaden" the trees by girdling. Deadening killed the leaves, allowing sunlight to spur the growth of grasses for grazing. By 1930 the killing was unnecessary; blight had wiped out the chestnuts. They never returned.

Today the defoliated trees you see, especially in this northern section, attest to the presence of another natural phenomenon—the gypsy moth. If the annual assault of these insects persists, many trees (mainly oak) will die. But, unlike the chestnut blight, the moths will not wipe out

Corbin Cabin, relic of a mountaineer past

Scarlet tanager in summer plumage

an entire species. Healthy trees will renew the forest in future decades.

You can end your day at Big Meadows with a wildflower walk or a ride in a horse-drawn wagon.

Camp Hoover to Rockfish

54 miles; a full day

Park at the west side of the Skyline Drive at **Milam Gap** (mile 52.8). Cross the drive to a trail marker to begin the 4-mile round-trip to **Camp Hoover.** You walk a short distance on the Appalachian Trail, then turn left onto the **Mill Prong Trail**, which passes through a wooded tract, descends to a small waterfall, crosses three streams, and meets a road. Turn right and continue toward the cabins of **Camp Hoover,** a National Historic Landmark. The camp satisfied President Herbert Hoover's three requirements for a hideaway: It had to be within 100 miles of Washington,

have a trout stream, and be high enough to discourage mosquitoes. You can walk around and look at the outside of the cabins; they are sometimes occupied by US government officials. President Hoover's cabin is open to the public on the weekend nearest his birthday, August 10.

A $4/5$-mile, $1\frac{1}{2}$-hour hike to **Bearfence Mountain** starts at mile 56.4 before the Lewis Mountain Campground. It demands some scrambling over rocks but finally rewards you with a spectacular, 360-degree view. The 2-mile loop hike to the **Pocosin Mission**, which starts past milepost 59, takes you to the ruins of a missionary church and graveyard.

The **Swift Run Gap Entrance** (near milepost 65) is an old Blue Ridge crossing now paved by US 33. In May, wildflower seekers climb the nearby **Hightop Summit Trail** (3 miles round-trip) to see painted trillium.

Loft Mountain (near milepost 79), with campground and ranger station, is a southern base for exploring the park. Near a service complex along Skyline Drive, look for the trailhead to the **Deadening Trail,** a $1\frac{1}{2}$-mile loop hike that demonstrates how pasture is evolving back into forest. After the demise of the chestnut trees, other trees and shrubs began repopulating the land. You can see it happening here, and from a rocky vantage point on the trail you can also see it happening on a grand scale throughout the park.

At **Rockfish Gap,** near the **Rockfish Entrance Station,** a buffalo path evolved into a colonial road, and later a modern highway. Here, at the southern end of the park, begins the **Blue Ridge Parkway,** a National Park Service highway that connects Shenandoah and Great Smoky Mountains National Parks.

Information & Activities

Headquarters
P.O. Box 348, Luray, Virginia 22835.
Phone (703) 999-2243.

Seasons & Accessibility
Park open year-round. For recorded
information call (703) 999-2266. Skyline Drive may close temporarily
during heavy snow or hazardous ice
conditions. For weather and road information, call (703) 999-2229.

Visitor & Information Centers
Dickey Ridge Visitor Center, near
North Entrance, open daily late
March through mid-November. Byrd
Visitor Center at Big Meadows, near
center of park, open daily March
through December, and Friday
through Sunday in January and
February.

Entrance Fee
$5 per car allows 7 days' access.

Pets
Must be kept on leash; not allowed
on posted trails or in park buildings.

Facilities for Disabled
Visitor centers, amphitheaters, picnic areas, campgrounds, and a self-
guided nature trail at Big Meadows
are accessible to wheelchairs. Some
exhibits and most rest rooms accessible, too. Free brochure available.

Things to Do
Free naturalist-led activities: nature
walks, evening programs and campfire talks. Limited winter schedule.
Also available, self-guided nature
trails, auto tours, fishing, horseback
riding, bicycling, cross-country skiing (some groomed trails in Big
Meadows area).

Special Advisories
☐Rocks around waterfalls are very
slippery and dangerous.
☐Pull off the road completely when
stopping for a view.

Overnight Backpacking
Permits required and available free
of charge from visitor centers and
campgrounds.

Campgrounds
Five campgrounds, all with 14-day
limit. **Mathews Arm, Lewis Mountain,
Loft Mountain,** and **Dundo Group
Campground** open May through October, first come, first served. **Big
Meadows** open March through December; reservations recommended
from Memorial Day weekend
through October; available through
MISTIX (see page 11); other times,
first come, first served. Fees $9-$17
per night. Showers except at **Mathews Arm** and **Dundo Group Campground.** Tent and RV sites; no hookups. Reserve for **Dundo Group
Campground**; contact park; no RV
sites. Food services in park.

Hotels, Motels, & Inns
*(unless otherwise noted, rates are for 2
persons in a double room, high season)*
INSIDE THE PARK:
Big Meadows Lodge (milepost 51) P.O.
Box 727, Luray, Va. 22835. (800)
999-4714 or (703) 743-5108. 102 units.
Lodge $42-$56; motel $71-$73; cabins
$58; suites $96. Restaurant. Open
mid-May through October.
Lewis Mountain (mile 57.6) P.O. Box
727, Luray, Va. 22835. (800) 999-
4714 or (703) 743-5108. 10 cabins,
outdoor grills. $47-$72. Open May
through October. **Skyland Lodge**
(miles 41.7 & 42.5) P.O. Box 727, Luray, Va. 22835. (800) 999-4714 or
(703) 743-5108. 186 units, including
10 rustic cabins. Cabins $37-$49; motel $71-$75; suites $98. Restaurant.
Open April through Nov.
OUTSIDE THE PARK:
In Front Royal, Virginia 22630:
Constant Spring Inn 413 S. Royal Ave.
(703) 635-7010. 9 units. $58, includes
breakfast. AC. **Quality Inn** 10 Commerce Ave. (703) 635-3161. 107 units.
$62. AC, pool, restaurant.
In Sperryville, Virginia 22740:
The Conyers House Slate Mills Road.
(703) 987-8025. 8 units. $100-$195, includes breakfast. AC, restaurant.
In Stanley, Virginia 22851:
Jordan Hollow Farm Inn Rte. 2, Box
375. (703) 778-2209. 21 rooms. $78-
$130. AC, restaurant.
In Waynesboro, Virginia 22980:
Holiday Inn P.O. Box 849. (703) 942-
5201. 118 units. $50-$55. AC, pool,
rest.

Excursions

George Washington National Forest
Harrisonburg, Virginia

This mountain forest flanks the Shenandoah Valley, rich in Civil War history. Excellent fishing and fall color. Contains many hot springs, four wilderness areas, and 57 miles of Appalachian Trail. 1,054,922 acres in three sections, part in W.Va. Facilities include 807 campsites, food services, boating, boat ramp, fishing, hiking, horseback riding, hunting, picnic areas, water sports, winter sports, handicapped access. Open all year, including many campsites. Visitor center at Massanutten on US 33, about 8 miles from Shenandoah NP. (703) 433-2491.

Jefferson National Forest
Roanoke, Virginia

Some 300 miles of the Appalachian Trail traverse mountains blanketed in hardwood, pine, and rhododendron. Streams and waterfalls abound. Contains 11 wilderness areas and Mount Rogers National Recreation Area. More than 700,000 acres, part in W.Va. and Ky. Facilities include 670 campsites, hiking, boating, boat ramp, fishing, horseback riding, hunting, picnic areas, water sports, handicapped access. Open all year, including some campsites. Information at USFS Roanoke headquarters, about 120 miles south of Shenandoah NP. (703) 982-6270.

Mason Neck National Wildlife Refuge
Lorton, Virginia

The nation's first refuge dedicated to the protection of the bald eagle lies on a peninsula in the Potomac River, near Washington, D.C. Timberland and marsh combine to form ideal habitat for the eagles and for numerous other wildlife species such as great blue herons, wood ducks, bluebirds, beavers, and deer. 2,277 acres. Facilities include hiking, photo blind (reservations required). Open year-round during daylight hours. On Va. 242, about 75 miles from Shenandoah NP. (703) 690-1297.

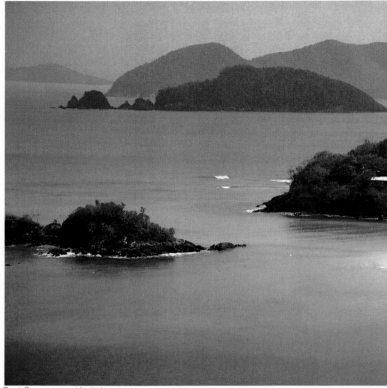

Trunk Bay, renowned for its beauty

Virgin Islands

United States Virgin Islands

Established August 2, 1956

12,909 acres

High green hills dropping down to turquoise bays, white powdery beaches, coral reefs, and ruins that evoke an era of sugar and slavery all find protection on St. John, one of about a hundred specks of Caribbean land known as the Virgin Islands.

Despite its small size—19 square miles—St. John's wide range of rainfall and exposure give it surprising variety. More than 800 subtropical plant species grow in areas from moist, high-elevation forests to desert-like terrain to mangrove swamps, among them mangoes, soursops, and teyer palms, turpentine trees and wild tamarind, century plants and seagrapes. Around the island live the fringing coral reefs—

beautiful, complex, and exceedingly fragile communities of plants and animals on which the existence of St. John's famous beaches depend.

In 1493, Columbus sighted the large assemblage of islands and cays and named it after St. Ursula's legendary 11,000 virgins. Since then, Spain, France, Holland, England, Denmark, and the United States have controlled various islands at different times. The Danes began to colonize them in the 17th century, and in 1717, planters arrived on St. John. By mid-century 88 plantations had been established there; slaves stripped the steep hillsides of virgin growth and cultivated the cane. When the Danes abolished slavery in 1848, the sugar industry was doomed. A fallow, century-long period known as the "subsistence era" followed.

How to Get There

By plane to Charlotte Amalie, St. Thomas, then taxi or bus to Red Hook, then ferry across Pillsbury Sound to Cruz Bay, a 20-minute ride. Or, try to catch one of the less frequently scheduled ferries from Charlotte Amalie—the boat takes 45 minutes, but the dock is much nearer the airport. Seaplanes fly directly into Cruz Bay from Charlotte Amalie, Christiansted, St. Croix, and San Juan, Puerto Rico.

How to Visit

If you have only 1 day, drive the **North Shore Road** as far as the **Annaberg Sugar Mill Ruins,** taking time to stretch your legs along some seaside trails—and perhaps do a little snorkeling. Return via **Centerline Road,** stopping at the ruins of **Herman Farm.** On a second day, consider hiking the **Reef Bay Trail,** explore the island's **East End,** visit **Saltpond Bay,** and walk to **Ram Head.** With more time, sign up for some of the excellent ranger-led tours and activities.

If you're driving yourself, be prepared for steep, often potholed roads with blind curves, and *stay on the left.* The speed limit is 20 mph. An alternative is to hire a taxi and guide.

Fearful that the Germans might capture the islands during World War I, the United States bought St. John, St. Croix, St. Thomas, and about 50 smaller islands from Denmark for $25,000,000. In 1956, conservationist Laurance S. Rockefeller bought more than 5,000 acres for a national park on St. John; in 1962, the park acquired 5,650 undersea acres off the northern and southern coasts. Today, though its boundary includes three-quarters of St. John, the park owns only slightly more than half the island. Of increasing concern is the escalating pace of development on private inholdings inside its borders. It also feels pressure from the many cruise ships that disgorge large numbers of visitors at once, badly straining park resources.

When to Go

All-year park. High season is mid-December to mid-April, but year-round temperatures vary little from the average of 79°F.

North Shore Road-Centerline Road Loop

15 miles; 3 hours to a full day

Begin your visit with a stop at the park visitor center in **Cruz Bay** to pick up a map, a trail brochure, and a guide leaflet to the **Annaberg Sugar Mill,** and to find out what ranger-led activities are scheduled. Head east out of town along the **North Shore Road** (Route 20). This road is in good condition but very steep in places. Near the top of the hill, pull off at the overlook for a bird's-eye view of the picturesque town and harbor, the many small adjacent islands, and the big island of **St. Thomas** across the sound. For an even better view of **St. John's West End,** climb **Caneel Hill;** the ⅘-mile moderately strenuous trail begins a short distance ahead on the right, across the road from the Park Service sign. (Or save this hike for sunset, when it's cooler and the view from the hilltop spectacular.)

Stop at the next overlook ½ mile

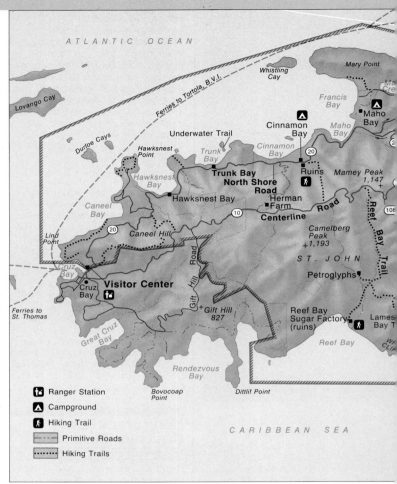

Ranger Station
Campground
Hiking Trail
Primitive Roads
Hiking Trails

farther along the road for a view of **Caneel Bay** and, to the northeast, the big island of **Jost van Dyke**, one of the British Virgins. Since the 1930s the site of a famous resort, Caneel Bay was a sugar plantation for most of the 18th and 19th centuries. Its name, both Dutch and Danish for "cinnamon," comes from the cinnamony leaves of the bay tree, a member of the myrtle family. (From the 1860s to the 1930s, oil from the leaves was used to make St. John Bay Rum cologne.)

The entrance to the Caneel Bay resort is down the hill on the left, just past road marker 1.5. The land belongs to the park but is leased to the resort, owned until recently by the Rockefellers. To get a look at its

lovely beaches and bays—and palm-studded grounds flowered with bougainvillea and pink oleander—walk the mostly level **Turtle Point Trail** around **Hawksnest Point,** which takes about an hour. The resort management asks only that you register as a day guest at the front desk; ask there for directions to the trailhead.

From Caneel Bay the road climbs steeply and descends to **Hawksnest Beach,** where you can swim, snorkel, and picnic. Visitors tend to bypass this beach, so it might be less crowded than those farther on. Exhibits describe the damage being done to the island's fragile reefs by pollutants, swimmers, snorkelers, and the anchors of careless boaters—and strongly urge you not to touch,

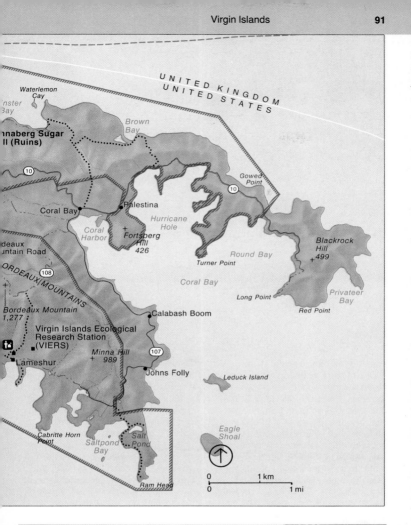

Waterlemon Cay

nster Bay

Brown Bay

UNITED KINGDOM
UNITED STATES

nnaberg Sugar
ll (Ruins)

10

Gowed Point

10

Coral Bay

Palestina

Coral Harbor

Hurricane Hole

Fortsberg Hill 426

deaux untain Road

BORDEAUX MOUNTAINS

108

Turner Point

Round Bay

Blackrock Hill +499

Coral Bay

Long Point

Privateer Bay

Bordeaux Mountain 1,277

Red Point

Virgin Islands Ecological Research Station (VIERS)

Calabash Boom

Minna Hill + 989

107

Lameshur

Johns Folly

Leduck Island

Cabritte Horn Point

Saltpond Bay

Salt Pond

Eagle Shoal

Ram Head

0   1 km
0   1 mi

The partly restored Annaberg Sugar Mill, built in the 18th century

Snorkelers bobbing toward a coral reef off Caneel Bay resort

stand, or sit on the reefs.

One of the Caribbean's premier vistas awaits you a mile farther up the road. From the overlook, **Trunk Bay** with its lush palm-fringed crescent beach and dozens of bobbing sailboats lies before you. Off a point in the middle distance is **Whistling Cay,** where in the 19th century a customs shed stopped boats plying the passage between the Danish and British Virgins. Trunk Bay's beauty draws many visitors, especially on days when cruise ships are in. The park has set up an underwater nature trail for snorkelers here; some 16 plaques identify the reef's plants and animals. If you're a serious snorkeler, however, you might want to skip this reef for a less traveled one farther along.

Beyond Trunk Bay's entrance be prepared for the road to sharply steepen. Near the top of the hill is the multimillion-dollar development at **Peter Bay,** a private inholding. Such developments distress park officials and environmentalists, who say that sediments run off the steep hillsides into the ocean, badly damaging the reefs and sea grass beds.

At **Cinnamon Bay** (road marker 4.5) are the only park-run campground and, across the road, the ruins of the Danish (first Dutch) Cinnamon Bay sugar factory, one of the island's oldest. Plaques along the 1-mile trail tell you its history and point out native trees such as bay, lime, teyer palm, and calabash, which produces a gourd-like fruit that's carved into bowls. If you're lucky enough to be there for a tour led by one of the Virgin Islanders on the park staff, you'll learn some colorful local lore as well.

Continue down the road ½ mile to yet another stunning, sweeping view—**Maho Bay, Francis Bay,** where sea turtles come to feed, and **Mary Point.** You'll see diving pelicans and frigatebirds, which, to avoid waterlogging their own enormous wings, harass other seabirds for food. The red roofs visible in the trees belong to a house built in 1952 by an American eccentric named Ethel McCully, who swam ashore from a boat and stayed. Since no paved roads or automobiles existed on St. John then, donkeys hauled the materials from Cruz Bay—a 4-hour trip.

Down the hill, the road flattens, passing a stretch of beach on the left. Continue on for a mile to the road's end and then turn right toward **Annaberg.** On the right, you'll see a thick mangrove swamp, one of many on the island. Its large, tangled roots

Sea horse, a seldom seen Caribbean creature

help protect the shoreline and provide a breeding ground for fish.

On the left, about 100 yards from the turnoff, look for the marker identifying one of the toxic manchineel trees common to the Caribbean; Columbus called their green fruit "death apples." Do not stand under this tree in the rain: runoff can raise painful blisters on your skin.

Just ahead is **Mary Creek** with a view of **Mary Point.** An important marine community inhabits the shallow reefs and sea grass beds of the creek, site of a weekly naturalist-led seashore walk. If you wade out (be sure to wear something on your feet), you can find brilliantly colored conchs, spiny black sea urchins, and brittle stars that regenerate their tentacles. Coral rocks host many tiny animals. Pick up and examine the rocks, but put them back as you found them.

From here consider an easy walk along the $^4/_5$-mile **Leinster Bay Trail**, which follows the seashore east to **Waterlemon Bay** and some of the best snorkeling in the park. Or drive the trail, an old Danish road, if your car has high clearance.

You can swim and snorkel off the sandy beach at the trail's end. Better yet if you have the stamina, walk out to the point and swim across the narrow channel to snorkel around little **Waterlemon Cay.**

Back at the Leinster Bay trailhead, park in the small lot and walk up the hill to the partially restored ruins of the **Annaberg Sugar Mill.** A $^1/_4$-mile self-guided walk introduces you to the workers' quarters, windmill, horse mill, oven, cistern, and factory that for much of two centuries produced raw sugar, molasses, and rum for Denmark. Native stone, ballast brick, and coral went into building the thick walls.

From the overlook you can see a number of other Virgin Islands across the narrows, including **Tortola**, largest of the British Virgins, and the dinosaur shape of Britain's **Great Thatch** on the left. In winter, humpback whales sometimes cruise by. Annaberg slaves reportedly tried to swim to Great Thatch after the British freed their slaves in 1833, 15 years ahead of the Danes. Before leaving the overlook, treat yourself to the scent of a frangipani blossom from the nearby tree.

To return to Cruz Bay, drive the more level **Centerline Road** (Route 10), watching out for blind curves. Slowness should be no hardship, however: The views of the island's **East End** are spectacular. If you have time, look for the **Catherineberg Road** on the right after about 3 miles. A short way up that are the ruins of the 18th-century **Herman Farm.** The outer shell of the windmill has been restored, and there are 4-foot stone walls, handsome archways, a massive stone pillar, and some original beams to see.

East End: Coral Bay & Saltpond Bay

26 miles round-trip; at least a half day

Take Centerline Road (Route 10) out of Cruz Bay, stopping after nearly 3 miles at the Herman Farm (see above), if you haven't already been there. About ½ mile farther is the **Konge Vey Overlook,** where a wayside exhibit points out Jost van Dyke, Great Thatch, and other islands and bays to the north.

The popular **Reef Bay Trail** begins after another 1¼ miles. It descends into a steep V-shaped valley through moist, subtropical forest to dry forest to acacia scrub near the coast. Ruins of sugar estates can be seen along its 2½ miles and nearby are some mysterious petroglyphs. Walk this trail at least partway to experience the lush forest, or even better, save it for the ranger-led trip, when a boat meets you at the coast and spares you the hike back up.

Back in your car, continue on to the overlook near **Mamey Peak** for a lovely view of **Coral Bay** and the island's East End. The name of the bay comes not from the island's abundant coral but from an 18th-century Dutch corral (*kraal*) here. The Danes established their first plantations at this end of the island, among them the vast Estate Carolina, once the property of the king. They built a

fort—called **Fort Frederik**—on **Fortsberg Hill** on the bay's eastern shore. In 1733 a bloody slave uprising took place here, reputedly the first in the New World. It would have succeeded—1,087 of the island's 1,295 inhabitants were slaves—had the French not sailed in to quell it.

Continue on Route 10 as it winds eastward outside the park to the village of **Coral Bay,** about 2 miles away. You may well see a mongoose scuttering across the road. Introduced a century ago to kill rats, the mongoose has multiplied explosively, to the detriment of some native island fauna. At Coral Bay stop to see the handsome pink-roofed **Emmaus Church,** built by Moravian missionaries in the 1780s. If you continued on, you'd be rewarded with magnificent views of **Hurricane Hole, Round Bay,** and the British Virgins. But for now backtrack a short distance and turn left at the intersection of Route 108. Drive 4 miles along the coast to the trailhead for **Saltpond Bay** and a wilder part of the island.

About ⅕ mile beyond the parking area, the horseshoe bay is fringed by a wide, sandy beach, gently lapped by transparent waters. Continue around the beach and onto the rocky ⁹⁄₁₀-mile **Ram Head Trail** that winds up the promontory and down the other side. There a blue pebbly beach and an arid environment await you. Plants include several kinds of cactuses and the century plant, which takes ten years to bloom, then dies.

Continue to the crest of the hill for a grand Caribbean view. Watch your footing and hold onto any children you've brought on this windswept point 200 feet above the sea. Here at **Ram Head** you'll be standing on rock that emerged some 108 million years ago, the oldest land on St. John.

Information & Activities

Headquarters
10 Estate Nazareth, St. Thomas, US Virgin Islands 00802. Phone (809) 775-6238.

Seasons & Accessibility
Park open year-round. Access by boat or seaplane. The weather is stable all year.

Visitor & Information Centers
Cruz Bay Visitor Center, at west end of St. John, open daily all year. Call (809) 776-6201 for visitor information.

Pets
Not allowed on public beaches, in picnic areas, or in campgrounds. Permitted elsewhere on leashes.

Facilities for Disabled
Some ferries to St. John are accessible to wheelchairs, with assistance. The visitor center, several Cinnamon Bay campsites, and rest rooms there and at Trunk Bay and Hawksnest Bay are also accessible.

Things to Do
Free naturalist-led activities: interpretive talks and exhibits, nature and history walks, hikes, snorkel tours, cultural demonstrations, evening programs. Also available, self-guided nature and underwater trails, swimming, snorkeling, boating, fishing (no license needed), historic bus tour.

Overnight Backpacking
Not allowed in park.

Campgrounds
One park campground, **Cinnamon Bay;** 14-day limit Dec. to mid-May; other times 21-day limit. Open all year. Reservations required; contact Rockresorts Inc., 30 Rockefeller Plaza, Suite 5400, New York, N.Y. 10112, (800) 223-7637, or Cinnamon Bay Campground, P.O. Box 720, Cruz Bay, St. John, USVI 00831, (809) 776-6330. Nightly for 2 persons: $14 for bare sites; $62 for equipped tents; $79 for equipped screened rooms. Cold showers. Groups contact Rockresorts. Food services.

Also, **Maho Bay;** Maho Bay Camp, 17-A East 73rd St., New York, N.Y. 10021. (800) 392-9004 or (212) 472-9453. 114 equipped tent-cottages, central baths. $75 per night. Rest. Reserve early for Dec. to May.

Hotels, Motels, & Inns
(unless otherwise noted, rates are for 2 persons in a double room, high season)
On St. John, USVI 00831:
Battery Hill P.O. Box 458. (800) 338-0987. 8 units, kitchens. $195. Pool. **Caneel Bay** Rockresorts, Inc., 30 Rockefeller Plaza, Suite 5400, New York, N.Y. 10112. (800) 223-7637. 171 units. $200-$535. Pool, rest. **Cruz Inn** P.O. Box 566. (809) 776-7688. 9 rooms, shared baths, $50, includes breakfast; 5 apartments, kitchens, $65-$85. **Gallows Point** P.O. Box 58. (800) 323-7229 or (809) 776-6434. 48 units, kitchens. $225-$275. Pool, restaurant. **Raintree Inn** P.O. Box 566. (809) 776-7449. 11 units, 3 kitchens. $70-$95. Restaurant. **Virgin Grand Beach Hotel** P.O. Box 8310. (800) 323-7249 or (809) 776-7171. 285 units. $295-$475. AC, pool, restaurant.

Excursion

Buck Island Reef National Monument
St. Croix, US Virgin Islands
A coral reef nearly encircles this small island, and two marked underwater trails guide snorkelers or passengers of glass-bottom boats through the exquisite and dynamic reef ecosystem. Breathtaking views of St. Croix and the reef can be had from Buck Island's summit. 850 acres. Facilities include hiking, picnic areas, water sports. Open year-round. Access by charter boat from Christiansted, St. Croix (charter operators supply snorkeling equipment). (809) 773-1460.

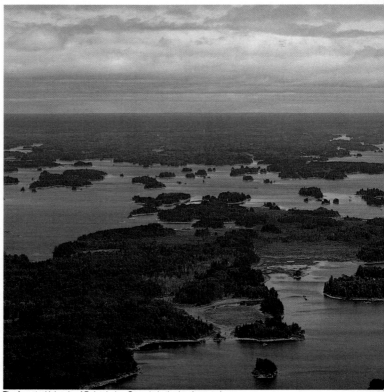

The forested islands of Rainy Lake; Canada in the background

Voyageurs

Minnesota

Established April 8, 1975

218,054 acres

From the air, the forest areas of Voyageurs look like green pieces of a jigsaw puzzle scattered on a huge mirror. A north woods realm of more than 30 lakes and more than 900 islands, Voyageurs spans a watery stretch of the US-Canada border.

A third of the park's area is water, most of it in four large lakes—Rainy, Kabetogama, Namakan, and Sand Point—linked by narrow waterways. Smaller lakes gleam in the forests and bogs of Voyageurs' terra firma, which consists of small islands, a strip of mainland shore, and the Kabetogama Peninsula, a long, bay-fringed landmass that forms an opposite shore for Kabetogama Lake.

The splendors of this 55-mile-long park can be reached only by water. Motorboats (banned in the adjacent Boundary Waters Canoe Area Wilderness) churn the lakes. Canoes glide the narrow waterways. Fishermen sit at the rails of anchored houseboats, hoping to hook walleye, smallmouth bass, and northern pike. Nearly every lake is haunted by the cry of the loon. And probably in no other national park in the lower 48 states is there a better chance to see bald eagles on the nest and on the wing or hear wolves howl at night.

The park is named for the voyageurs, French Canadians who paddled birch-bark canoes for fur trading companies in the late 18th and early 19th centuries. The voyageurs were famous for stamina—paddling up to 16 hours a day—and roisterous songs. Their canoe route between Canada's northwest and Montreal is

turn east at Orr and drive 25 miles on County Roads 23 and 24. For Ash River, stay on US 53 for 25 more miles, turn right at the Ash River Trail sign, and continue for 9 miles. For Kabetogama Lake Visitor Center, stay on US 53 for 3 more miles, turn right onto County Road 122, and drive to the lakeshore. For Rainy Lake, stay on US 53 to International Falls, then head east for 12 miles on Minn. Hwy. 11 to Island View and turn right to the visitor center. Airports: Duluth, International Falls, and Fort Frances, Ontario.

When to Go

All-year park, but most accessible from spring through early fall. Water travel is curtailed by freeze-up in late fall and ice break-up in early spring. Winter opens the park to cross-country skiing, snowshoeing, snowmobiling, and ice fishing. And the 7-mile ice road at Rainy Lake provides a unique entry into the park: You drive your car on the ice to places that in other seasons you can reach only by boat or floatplane.

How to Visit

The only way to the heart of this park is by water. **Kabetogama Lake, Rainy Lake, Crane Lake,** and **Ash River** are private resort areas, which, though not within the park, serve as entrances. Begin your trip planning by choosing an entrance; each of them is widely spaced and offers a different experience. You can make motel or lodge reservations at one of the area's resorts on a park list (see **Information & Activities**), or stay in a car campground, and use the resort as a base for park activities, particularly fishing. Or you can rent a houseboat or camp out by boat.

cited as part of the US-Canada border in the treaty that ended the American Revolution.

In a boat in the labyrinth of waterways and islands, you can unwittingly cross this border. It's marked by US and Canadian buoys; sometimes the only way to tell which country you're in is by spotting one of them.

How to Get There

From Duluth, drive north about 110 miles on US 53. For Crane Lake,

Modern voyageurs on Kabetogama Lake

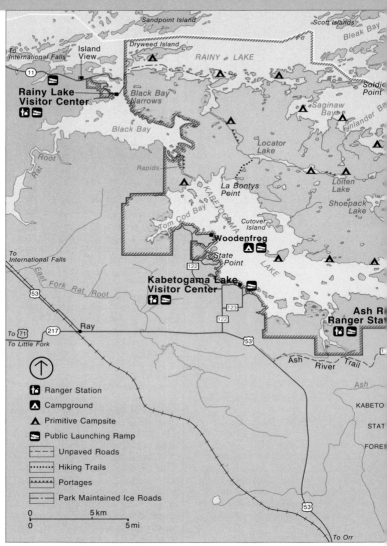

Ranger Station

Campground

Primitive Campsite

Public Launching Ramp

--- --- Unpaved Roads

·········· Hiking Trails

▪▪▪▪▪▪ Portages

—·—·— Park Maintained Ice Roads

0   5 km
0   5 mi

Guides, canoes, houseboats, and motorboats are for hire at all places. Or you can tow in your own craft.

Concessioner-run boats, with park naturalists aboard, also operate out of visitor centers. Even if you have your own boat, you may want to take a commercial cruise and rely on experienced navigators; the lakes are broad with submerged rocks in shallow areas, and they're sometimes brushed by stiff winds.

If your time is limited, Kabetogama Lake is a good place for exploring and understanding the park.

Kabetogama Lake

at least a full day

Make reservations for the weekly, naturalist-led trip from **Kabetogama Lake Visitor Center** to **Locator Lake.** You go across the lake to a dock east of **La Bontys Point.** You leave the boat there and at the trailhead start on a 2-mile hike along a spruce bog and past a beaver pond, dam, and lodge. Watch for the rippling V that marks a swimming beaver. The trail climbs to a ridge and drops to the lakeshore.

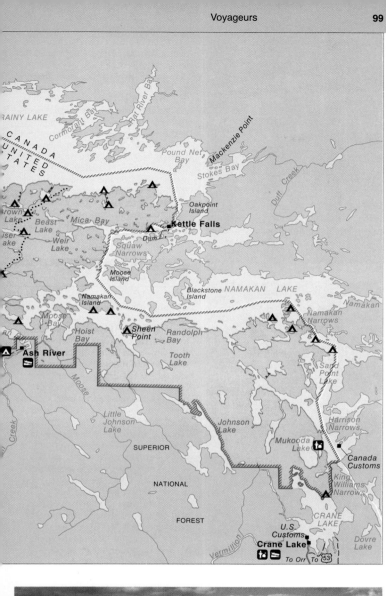

RAINY LAKE

Cormorant Bay

Rat River Bay

CANADA
UNITED
STATES

Pound Net Bay

Mackenzie Point

Stokes Bay

Duff Creek

rown
Lake

Beast
Lake

Mica Bay

Oakpoint
Island

Kettle Falls

Weir
Lake

Dam

iser
ake

Squaw
Narrows

Moose
Island

Namakan
Island

Blackstone
Island

NAMAKAN   LAKE

Namakan

Moose
Bay

Hoist
Bay

**Sheen
Point**

Randolph
Bay

Namakan
Narrows

Ash River

Tooth
Lake

Sand
Point
Lake

Moose

Little
Johnson
Lake

Johnson
Lake

Harrison
Narrows

SUPERIOR

Mukooda
Lake

**Canada
Customs**

NATIONAL

King
Williams
Narrows

Creek

FOREST

**CRANE
LAKE**

Dovre
Lake

**U.S.
Customs**

Crane Lake

Vermilion

To Orr   To (53)

Autumn forest and cattails on Rainy Lake

Showy lady's slipper

American white pelican

There you board a cached canoe and paddle around the lake, watching for muskrat, bald eagles, ospreys, common loons, blue-winged teal, and great blue herons. You can also get free use of one of the park's cached canoes at Locator Lake by making reservations and picking up the key to the storage rack at the visitor centers at **Kabetogama Lake** or **Rainy Lake.** If you do this, you must get to the Locator Lake trailhead by your own or a rented boat. Ask for information at a visitor center. If you cannot time your visit to the weekly lake trip, an alternative is an all-day cruise to **Kettle Falls.** For details, see **Crane Lake & Ash River** below.

Rainy Lake

at least a half day

Although this lake is large—60 miles long, 12 miles wide—you can safely explore it in your own or a rented motorboat, houseboat, or canoe. At the **Rainy Lake Visitor Center** get weather and navigation information and take a self-guided waterborne excursion. About $1\frac{1}{2}$ miles northwest is **Little American Island,** where the discovery of gold set off a short-lived gold rush a hundred years ago. About 2 miles east is **Bushyhead Island,** where you can see a mine shaft carved into the rock and a pile of tailings. Nearby is **Dryweed Island,** site of an idyllic primitive campsite, typical of many on park islands.

Lacking your own boat, you can still explore. The park offers free trips aboard a 26-foot replica of a voyageurs canoe. From late spring through summer, a concessioner's 49-passenger tour boat also frequently cruises the lake, with a naturalist usually leading the tour.

Crane Lake & Ash River

at least 1 to 2 days each

Near the Ash River resort area is a visitor center (open only in summer). Here you can get information about obtaining charts for navigating the lakes. Be alert to warning buoys and numbered channel markers. These are hazardous waters; if you're new to them, *don't fail to use charts.*

If you want a good exploratory

Sphagnum moss on a pine forest floor

voyage, go to Kettle Falls, a water-ways hub used by Indians, voyageurs, loggers, fishermen, and, during Prohibition, bootleggers smuggling liquor from Canada.

From Crane Lake you travel north through **King Williams Narrows**, across **Sand Point Lake** and through **Namakan Narrows**, then west across **Namakan Lake** along the US-Canada border, which veers northward here.

From Ash River you go the length of **Sullivan Bay** to the mouth of the river, then weave through a string of islands into **Moose Bay**. For a scenic voyage, pass through the channel on the south side of **Williams Island** (site of a primitive campsite) into **Hoist Bay**, named for the hoisting of logs that were loaded onto a train. You can still see pilings that supported a train track, which ran from the middle of the bay to a white-pine sawmill on the mainland. Head north toward **Namakan Island**, site of other campsites, and go around the western side of the island.

Both courses take you to the southern end of **Squaw Narrows.** Pass through the narrows, then head east along the border through **Squirrel Narrows** to Kettle Falls. Near the dock is a dam that serves a regional system regulating water flow for electric power and flood control. At the dock is a gravel road, which is a portage trail. Walk the woodland-edged road for about $1/4$ mile to a red-roofed, white clapboard building with a long front porch—the **Kettle Falls Hotel.**

Built in 1910, the hotel welcomed lumberjacks and their money, which they left in the bar and in little rooms upstairs. Today the hotel welcomes more genteel patrons: park visitors who make reservations well ahead.

Another way to get to Kettle Falls: Take a cruise boat. Trips are run several times a week out of visitor centers at both Rainy Lake and Kabetogama Lake. The all-day trip is timed for you to eat lunch at the hotel before the return voyage.

Information & Activities

Headquarters
HCR 9, Box 600, International Falls, Minn. 56649. Phone (218) 283-9821.

Seasons & Accessibility
Park open year-round. Travel within it is by boat, floatplane, and foot in summer; snowmobile, snowshoes, cross-country skis, and ski-plane in winter. Limited access during lake freeze-up (mid-November to mid-December) and thaw-out (April). In winter, weather permitting, an ice road on Rainy Lake connects the visitor center to Cranberry Bay, 7 miles into the park.

Visitor & Information Centers
Rainy Lake on Hwy. 11 at northwest edge of park open daily May 1 to Oct. 15, reduced hours from October 16 to April 30. Call (218) 286-5258. Kabetogama Lake on County Road 122 at southwest edge of lake open daily mid-May to Labor Day. Call (218) 875-2111. Ash River on southeast edge of Kabetogama Lake open mid-May to Labor Day.

Entrance Fee
None.

Pets
Permitted on leashes in developed areas and on major lakes. Not allowed on park trails, in backcountry, or on interior lakes.

Facilities for Disabled
Kabetogama Lake and Rainy Lake Visitor Centers are wheelchair accessible; also, guided boat trips, with assistance. Fact sheet available.

Things to Do
Free naturalist-led activities: nature walks, canoe trips (reserve at visitor centers), children's and campfire programs, films, exhibits, cross-country ski trips. Also, hiking, park canoes and rowboats (free of charge), boat tours, rental boats, fishing and ice fishing (guides available, ask park for list; license required) swimming, waterskiing, snowmobiling, cross-country skiing, and snowshoeing.

Special Advisory
☐Practice safe boating: Use navigational maps; be aware of weather conditions; make sure your boat is well equipped; do not overload it.

Camping
Backcountry boat-in campsites, some hike-in campsites, 14-day limit. Open all year (though mostly inaccessible during fall freeze-up and spring thaw); first come, first served. No permit needed. No fees. No showers. Tent sites only. Two group campsites. In winter, access mainly by snowmobile, cross-country skiing, or snowshoeing. Private campgrounds with tent and RV sites near park.

Hotels, Motels, & Inns
(unless otherwise noted, rates are for 2 persons in a double room, high season)
INSIDE THE PARK:
Kettle Falls Hotel (17 miles by water from the Ash River Trail) Ash River Trail, Orr, Minn. 55771. (800) 322-0886. 12 hotel rooms, shared baths, $60 per person with 2 meals; single units and suites nearby, with baths and kitchens, $120-$170. Open mid-May to September 30.

OUTSIDE THE PARK:
In International Falls, Minn. 56649:
Holiday Inn (US Hwy. 71) P.O. Box 272. (218) 283-4451. 126 units. $67. AC, pool, rest. **Island View Lodge** (on Rainy Lake) HCR 8, Box 411. (218) 286-3511. 9 rooms $60-$65; 11 cabins with kitchens, $95-$195. AC, rest. **Thunderbird Lodge** (on Rainy Lake) Rte. 8, Box 407. (218) 286-3151. 15 rooms $50-$68; 10 cabins with kitchens, $90-$175. AC, restaurant.
In Ray, Minn. (on Lake Kabetogama):
North Star Resort 56669. (218) 875-2175. 7 cabins with kitchens. $410-$680 per week. Open mid-May to Labor Day. **Rocky Point Resort** Box 183, 56669. (218) 875-2411. 8 cabins with kitchens, $180-$600 per week; 2 lodge rooms, $15 per person. Rest. **Voyageur Park Lodge** Box 160A, 56669. (800) 331-5694. 11 cabins with kitchens (summer only), $267-$1,135 per week; 5 rooms with shared bath (winter only), $60-$76 per person.

For a full listing of accommodations in the four resort communities adjacent to the park, contact park headquarters.

Excursions

Superior National Forest
Duluth, Minnesota

Here the northern lights preside over stands of pine, spruce, fir, alder, and birch, and loons bob on the more than 1,000 portage-linked lakes of the famous Boundary Waters Canoe Area Wilderness. Overnight reservations required for this very popular site adjoining Canada's Quetico Provincial Park. 3,800,000 acres. Facilities include some 2,000 campsites, food services, hiking, boating, boat ramp, fishing, hunting, picnic areas, winter sports, water sports. Open all year; campsites open May-October. Visitor center east of Ely on Minn. 169, about 100 miles from Voyageurs NP. (218) 720-5324.

Chippewa National Forest
Cass Lake, Minnesota

This lake-country forest boasts one of the largest breeding bald eagle populations outside Alaska and offers a variety of water-based recreation, including the chance to explore the Mississippi's headwaters by canoe. 661,161 acres. Facilities: 683 campsites, hiking, boating, boat ramps, fishing, hunting, picnic areas, scenic drives, historic sites with summer interpretive programs, winter sports, handicapped access. Open all year; campsites generally open mid-May to mid-Sept. Information at Cass Lake on US 2, about 85 miles from Voyageurs NP. (218) 335-2226.

Agassiz National Wildlife Refuge
Middle River, Minnesota

More than 265 species of migratory and upland game birds utilize the many resources of this wetlands refuge on the Mississippi Flyway. They share the site with some 250 moose and a resident pack of eastern gray wolves—the only such pack in any national refuge outside Alaska. 61,449 acres. Facilities include hiking, hunting, scenic drives. Open May 1-October 31, dawn to dusk. Headquarters on Route 7, 11 miles east of Holt, about 185 miles from Voyageurs NP. (218) 449-4115.

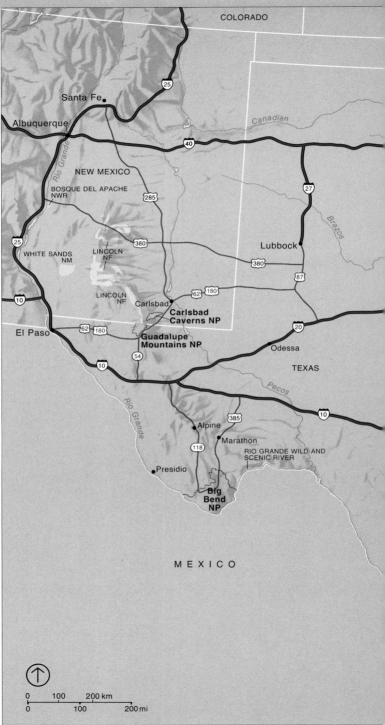

COLORADO

Santa Fe

Albuquerque

Rio Grande

NEW MEXICO

BOSQUE DEL APACHE
NWR

WHITE SANDS
NM

LINCOLN
NF

LINCOLN
NF

Carlsbad

**Carlsbad
Caverns NP**

**Guadalupe
Mountains NP**

El Paso

Lubbock

Canadian

Brazos

Odessa

TEXAS

Pecos

Rio Grande

Alpine

Marathon

RIO GRANDE WILD AND
SCENIC RIVER

Presidio

**Big
Bend
NP**

M E X I C O

0   100   200 km
0   100   200 mi

Preceding pages: Dunes, Guadalupe Mountains

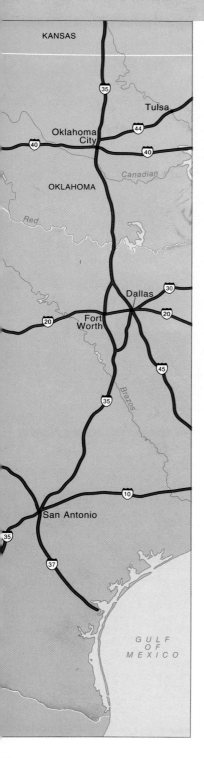

The Southwest

The national parks of the Southwest, all set in the Chihuahuan Desert, offer scenery ranging from underground caves to high and rugged mountain peaks. Sparse vegetation opens the spectacular vistas up to visitors without their having to go above tree line.

Water sculptured these landscapes. A reef from an ancient sea forms the 50-mile-long Guadalupe mountain chain. The seeping of water over millions of years created the cool, dark world of Carlsbad Caverns. Rivers etched out the dramatic canyons of Big Bend, and flash floods still tumble boulders from the steep Chisos mountaintops, continuing to rearrange the scenery.

The vagaries of yearly precipitation also determine whether the visitor beholds a land of blossoms—Texas bluebonnets, brilliant red and orange cactus flowers, heavy stalks of white yucca blooms—or, more often, a parched terrain dominated by creosote bush, prickly pear, and dagger-sharp lechuguilla. Where water flows year-round, oases produce gardens that resonate with birdsong.

Visitors to the Southwest parks have a chance to view wildlife as diverse as multicolored lizards and snakes, the elusive mountain lion, deer, hundreds of species of birds, and, in Big Bend, pig look-alikes called javelinas. Archaeologists have found fossils of many other creatures, including giant crocodiles and the Big Bend pterosaur, the largest animal ever to fly.

Hikers may take their own trip back in time by climbing up to the pine-fir forests that cloak the cooler, moister mountaintops in the Guadalupes and Big Bend. This type of forest probably covered the region at the end of the last ice age, when early peoples hunted camels, mammoths, and four-horned antelope.

Carlsbad Caverns and Guadalupe Mountains National Parks are linked by the Lincoln National Forest; proposals would unite the three areas into one large park encompassing the Guadalupe range. Base yourself at Carlsbad or, even closer, in White's City to visit these areas. Allow a day to drive the 250 miles from Guadalupe to Big Bend.

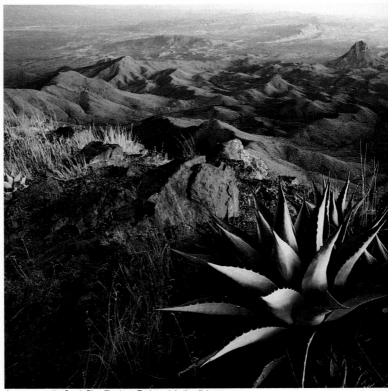

An agave on the South Rim; Elephant Tusk peak in the distance

Big Bend

Texas

Established June 12, 1944

801,146 acres

As the Rio Grande winds south along the Texas-Mexico border, it suddenly veers northward in a great horseshoe curve before continuing its journey. Inside the horseshoe lies the region of Texas known as the Big Bend; Big Bend National Park flanks the river at the southerly tip of the curve. A wild and surprising land, the park remains remote enough that only the dedicated reach it.

Chihuahuan Desert vegetation—bunchgrasses, creosote bushes, cactuses, lechuguillas, yuccas, and sotols—covers most of the terrain. But the Rio Grande and its lush floodplains and steep, narrow canyons almost form a park of their own. So do the Chisos Mountains; up to 20 de-

grees cooler than the desert floor, they harbor pine, juniper, and oak, as well as deer, mountain lions, and other wildlife. A heavy rain transforms the very desert: Normally dry creek beds roar with water, and seeds long dormant burst into fields of wildflowers.

The rocks of Big Bend are a complex lot. Two seas, one after another, flowed and subsided in the region hundreds of millions of years ago, leaving thick deposits of limestone and shale. The present mountains, except the Chisos, uplifted along with the Rockies, roughly 75 million years ago. Around the same time, a 40-mile-wide trough—most of the present-day park—sank along fault lines, leaving the cliffs of Santa Elena Canyon to the west and the Sierra del Carmen to the east rising 1,500 feet above the desert floor. In

from Alpine leads to the west entrance; Ranch Road 170, from Presidio, joins Hwy. 118 shortly before the west entrance. Nearest airports: El Paso (325 miles) and Midland-Odessa (230 miles).

When to Go

All-year park, though fall and winter may be the best seasons. Deciduous leaves turn color in the mountains in autumn; winters are mild. Summer temperatures in the desert can exceed 110°F; the Chisos Mountains remain cooler. If enough rain falls, the desert blooms stunningly in March through May, and again in August and September. Birdwatching is good all year, but especially in March, April, and May.

How to Visit

Allow several days, especially if you plan to hike. Explore the **Chisos Mountains Basin** and the **Ross Maxwell Scenic Drive,** engineered to take you past many of the park's geological and scenic highlights. Ideally, devote the better part of a day to each area. With extra time on the second afternoon, or on a third day, drive out to **Rio Grande Village** and the **Boquillas Canyon Overlook** to experience the river environment and enjoy views of the **Sierra del Carmen,** particularly spectacular at sunset. On your way in or out, view the landscape and exhibits along US 385 between **Panther Junction** and **Persimmon Gap.** For an extended visit, try more of the many rewarding hikes, drive some dirt roads, and consider a leisurely float trip along the **Rio Grande** through one of the park's three major canyons.

the center, volcanic activity spewed layer upon layer of ash into the air and squeezed molten rock up through the ground to form the Chisos Mountains some 35 million years ago. Molten rock also cooled and hardened underground later to be exposed by erosion.

Big Bend's topographic variety supports a remarkable diversity of life, including a thousand plant species—some found nowhere else in the world. More species of birds—over 400—have been counted here than in any other US national park.

People have passed through this terrain for at least 10,000 years. The human pageant in historical times has included Apaches, Spanish conquistadores, Commanches, US soldiers, miners, ranchers and farmers, Mexican revolutionaries, and international outlaws and bandits.

How to Get There

US 385 leads from Marathon to the north entrance; Texas Hwy. 118

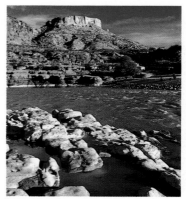

Rocks at the entrance to Santa Elena Canyon

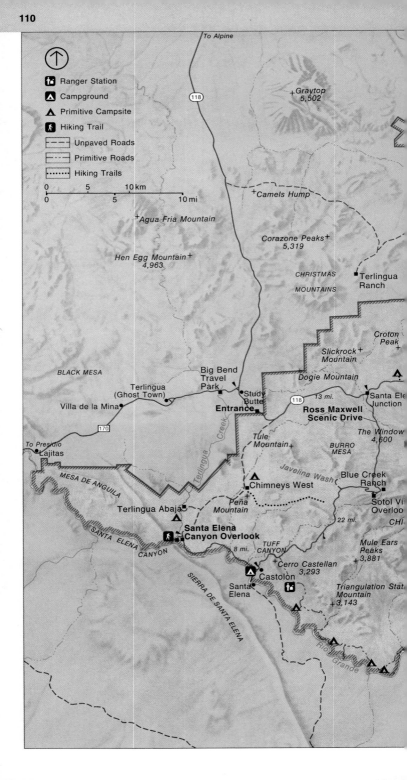

Legend

⬆ (North arrow)

🚻 Ranger Station
🏕 Campground
▲ Primitive Campsite
🥾 Hiking Trail
– – – Unpaved Roads
–·–·– Primitive Roads
········· Hiking Trails

0   5   10 km
0   5   10 mi

To Alpine

118

Graytop
5,502

Camels Hump

Corazone Peaks
5,319

Agua Fria Mountain

Hen Egg Mountain
4,963

CHRISTMAS

MOUNTAINS

■ Terlingua
Ranch

Croton
Peak

Slickrock
Mountain

BLACK MESA

Big Bend
Travel
Park

Dogie Mountain

Terlingua
(Ghost Town)

Study
Butte

Santa Ele
Junction

Villa de la Mina

Entrance

118   13 mi.

**Ross Maxwell
Scenic Drive**

170

The Window
4,600

To Presidio
Lajitas

*Tule
Mountain*

BURRO
MESA

Javelina Wash

Blue Creek
Ranch

MESA DE ANGUILA

Chimneys West

Sotol Vi
Overloo

Terlingua Abaja

*Pena
Mountain*

22 mi.

CHÍ

**Santa Elena
Canyon Overlook**

SANTA ELENA

8 mi.

*Mule Ears
Peaks*
+*3,881*

TUFF
CANYON

CANYON

Cerro Castellan
3,293

Castolon

Santa
Elena

*Triangulation Stat.
Mountain*
+*3,143*

SIERRA DE SANTA ELENA

Rio Grande

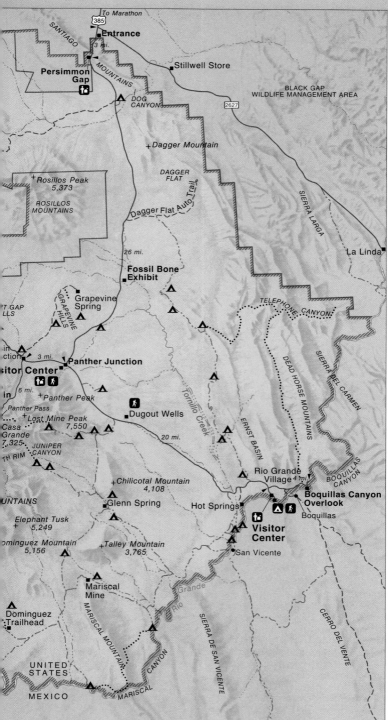

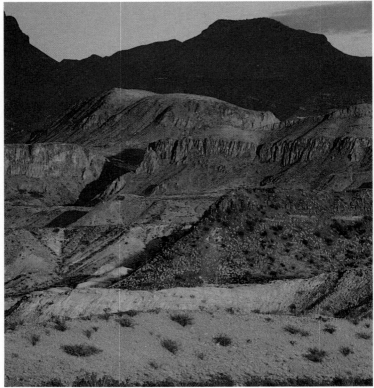

Sunset on the Maverick Badlands

Panther Junction to the Chisos Basin

9 miles one way; at least a half day

Start your tour at the visitor center at **Panther Junction**. Collect maps, information on hiking, and safety tips on avoiding encounters with rattlesnakes, mountain lions, and flash floods. Don't miss **Panther Path**—the 50-yard nature trail near the visitor center entrance whose self-guiding pamphlet provides an excellent introduction to the plants you'll see on much of your trip. Behind the visitor center lie the **Chisos Mountains**, the

southernmost range in the continental United States, and your destination. When ready, return to your car and turn left out of the visitor center, then left at **Basin Junction** in 3 miles. Ahead on the right looms **Pulliam Bluff**. Look closely and you might see in the mountain the profile of a man's face, reclining. Legend relates that the man is Alsate, an important Apache chief whose ghost lives on in the high Chisos Mountains, and whose campfire can occasionally be seen at night. At 2.5 miles, the jagged summit to your left is **Lost Mine Peak**. Spanish explorers, it is told, discovered a rich silver mine near the summit and enslaved Indians to work it. The miners rebelled, killed their overlords, and sealed the entrance to the mine so that it might remain lost forever. As you drive on, the castle-like summit of **Casa Grande**—"the big house"—will be straight ahead, a landmark for much of the park.

The road climbs higher into the

Riding the slopes of the Chisos Basin

mountains through a canyon called **Green Gulch:** Watch the vegetation change from desert shrub to sotol grasslands, then to pinyon pine, juniper, and oak woodland. The Chisos form a cooler, moister island in the surrounding desert. Some 10,000 years ago, pinyon-juniper forests extended down to the desert floor, but the trees withdrew to higher altitudes as the climate gradually warmed at the end of the Ice Age. In about 5 miles the road hits its highest point at **Panther Pass** (5,770 feet), named for the mountain lions that still roam these hills. Only the lucky few ever see one. If you have time, park at the nearby trailhead for the **Lost Mine Trail**, a self-guided nature trail with an informative booklet. The panorama from the top, one of the grandest in the park, makes the moderately strenuous $4\frac{4}{5}$-mile round-trip well worth the trek. But if you're short of time, just hike the 2-mile round-trip to the **Juniper Canyon Overlook**, for good vistas of wooded **Juniper Canyon** to the south and Pulliam Bluff to the northwest.

After Panther Pass, the road descends in hairpin curves to the basin, a 3-mile-wide depression in the mountains, chiseled by wind and water. Many of the park's choice hikes start from the basin trailhead, west of the ranger station. At the least, make sure to stroll the easy $\frac{3}{10}$-mile round-trip **Window View Trail**. Particularly photogenic at sunset, the **Window** is a V-shaped opening, or pour off, in the mountains, through

Claret cup cactus abloom in the high Chisos

which all rain and meltwater from the basin drains. A more challenging trail descends through desert and shady canyon to the Window itself, offering classic afternoon views of Casa Grande framed by oaks and pines. In summer, take this and other lower elevation hikes in early morning or late afternoon.

The literal high point of many visitors' trips to the park is a hike to the **South Rim** (7,400 feet), a moderately steep 13-mile round-trip that provides unforgettable vistas of much of the park. At **Boot Canyon**, $4\frac{1}{2}$ miles up the trail to the South Rim, lives an oasis of bigtooth maple, Douglas-fir, and Arizona pine. The gray-and-yellow Colima warbler nests on the canyon floor, its only US home.

Before you hike, check at the ranger station for maps and hiking tips, and make sure you carry plenty of water. At the ranger station, ask also about the peregrine falcons. Several of these endangered birds nest in the Chisos.

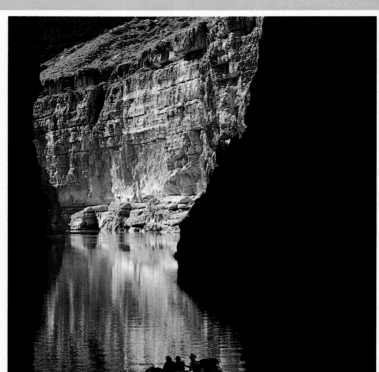

Rafting the Rio Grande through Santa Elena Canyon

Ross Maxwell Scenic Drive: Santa Elena Junction to Santa Elena Canyon

30 miles one way; a half to full day

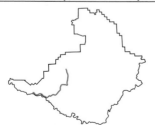

Heading south from **Santa Elena Junction, Burro Mesa**—named for the burros that once grazed the top—will be to your right, and the Chisos to your left. After 2 miles, stop at the exhibit on the left for a fine view of the Window framing Casa Grande. Drive on a little over a mile, then park at the old **Sam Nail Ranch** and stroll the short path to the remains of windmills and a ranch house. The shade of the pecan and willow trees the Nails planted makes a fine resting and birdwatching spot. Walk back to your car and motor on. In about a mile, long walls of rock traverse the landscape. They are dikes, created by molten rock that squeezed up into underground cracks before hardening. The softer rock layers above them eventually eroded away, leaving the erosion-resistant dikes.

Stop next at the **Blue Creek Ranch** overlook. A century ago most of Big Bend was cloaked in grasses. But ranchers grazed thousands of cattle, sheep, and goats, destroying the grass and exposing the topsoil to erosion. Creosote, mesquite, allthorn, and other spiny shrubs moved into the damaged areas. Here, and elsewhere in the park, grasses are slowly returning.

Go back to the road and take a quick left onto the **Sotol Vista** spur road, named for the ridge's rich growth of sotol, the bright green plant with sawlike teeth on the edges of the leaves. Indians roasted and ate the heart of the sotol and fermented it to yield an alcoholic drink. The parking lot at the top provides vistas of the surrounding mountains, and a plaque at the end of the loop identifies what's what.

Return to the main road; an exhibit on the left in about $6\frac{1}{2}$ miles describes how volcanism shaped this striking landscape. Take the next spur road on the left, for an excellent view of the peaks known as **Mule Ears**, a name explained at a glance. During the 1930s, Army Air Corps pilots drilled by flying planes between the twin peaks. Stop again after $4\frac{1}{2}$ miles to see **Tuff Canyon**, carved by **Blue Creek** through layers of lava flows, boulders, and compressed volcanic ash called tuff. Stroll the short trail to the right to view the canyon. The trail at the left of the parking lot provides a moderately steep hike down into the canyon, a $\frac{3}{4}$-mile round-trip.

Back in your car, you'll be approaching **Cerro Castellan**, another important landmark, rising 1,000 feet above its surroundings. Turn left into **Castolon** to stroll around the old army post that protected residents from bandits during the 1914-18 border troubles with Mexico. The main building, originally the barracks, was converted to a frontier trading post around 1920. Today you can buy cold drinks and picnic there, as well as pick up a free pamphlet on the history of **Castolon Valley**. After Castolon the road parallels the **Rio Grande**, passing adobe houses dating back to the turn of the century. The occupants once grew food crops and cotton in the fertile floodplain.

Be sure to stop about 8 miles from Castolon, at the parking area for the **Santa Elena Canyon Overlook.** Laden with abrasive silt and gravel, the Rio Grande sculptured the canyon 1,500 feet deep, through the cliffs that tower above the geological trough that forms the bulk of the park. Drive on to the end of the road, put on some old shoes and, if the water is low, wade across **Terlingua Creek** to reach the **Santa Elena Canyon Trail.** The moderate $1\frac{7}{10}$-mile round-trip trail amply rewards the hiker with striking views of the canyon.

Mule Ears Peaks and prickly pear cactus

Cerro Castellan looming over an old army post

Panther Junction to Rio Grande Village & Boquillas Canyon Overlook

24 miles one way; a half to full day

Before starting this tour, check at the visitor center for the condition of the **Hot Springs** road. The main road, heading southeast, descends nearly 2,000 feet through desert shrub, terminating near the willows and cottonwoods on the banks of the Rio Grande. After about $6\frac{1}{2}$ miles, turn left onto the unpaved road to see the spring at **Dugout Wells**, formerly the site of a ranch and schoolhouse, and now a fine place to picnic and look for wildlife. Return to the main road. As you continue, the peak aptly named **Elephant Tusk** will be on your right in the distance, and **Chilicotal Mountain** closer to the road. Far ahead looms the **Sierra del Carmen** in Mexico. Its striated rock formations are the

Greater roadrunner speeding across the desert

same limestone and shale as in the cliffs at **Santa Elena Canyon**.

If you're up to a somewhat rough ride, be sure to take the turnoff to Hot Springs, whose mineral waters were valued for centuries. Look for Indian pictographs on the cliffs along the trail to the springs, just beyond the old motel. After returning to the main road, pull over at the **Rio Grande Overlook** just past the tunnel on the right, and stroll a 50-yard trail for superb views of the Sierra del Carmen, the river floodplain, and part of **Boquillas** village in Mexico. Big Bend bluebonnets bloom profusely here during a well-watered springtime. Back on the road, continue straight for ½ mile, then turn left and continue another 3 miles to the unpaved spur road to **Boquillas Canyon Overlook**. Then double back; if you wish to see a Mexican village, take the dirt road on your left in about a mile. At the riverbank, a ferryman should be waiting to row you across the Rio Grande for a small fee. The middle of the river forms the international border. Then pay for a donkey ride or walk the ¾ mile into Boquillas. When you're back, turn left onto the main road, then left again to visit **Rio Grande Village**, an excellent place to watch birds. Don't miss the nature trail starting across from site #18 in the campground. This easy ¾-mile loop leads through jungle-like floodplain vegetation before climbing onto a ridge that provides terrific views of the river and the Sierra del Carmen.

Javelina, a cactus-loving herbivore

Panther Junction to Persimmon Gap

26 miles one way; 2 hours

This road follows an ancient trail used by the Commanches on their annual raiding forays into Mexico, and by army expeditions, settlers, and miners of silver and lead. For an excellent self-guided auto tour, pick up a pamphlet at either end of the road and, if traveling in springtime, ask whether the giant dagger yuccas are in bloom. (If so, be sure to take the unpaved **Dagger Flat Auto Trail** to see stalkfuls of white blooms weighing up to 70 pounds; if not, skip the detour.) Much of the road traverses **Tornillo Flat**, one of the most overgrazed and poorly recovered areas of the park. Highlights of the drive include a view of **Dog Canyon**, through which camels once lumbered in a 19th-century US Army experiment, and the exhibit of fossil mammal bones found in the park.

Information & Activities

Headquarters
Panther Junction, Big Bend National Park, Texas 79834. Phone (915) 477-2251.

Seasons & Accessibility
Open all year. Check current conditions before driving dirt roads.

Visitor & Information Centers
Panther Junction and Chisos Basin Visitor Centers open daily all year. Rio Grande Village Visitor Center open Nov. through mid-May. Information station also at Persimmon Gap. Call headquarters for visitor information.

Entrance Fee
$5 per car allows 7 days' access.

Facilities for Disabled
Visitor center facilities and two nature trails are wheelchair accessible.

Things to Do
Free naturalist-led activities: nature walks, raft trips, workshops, evening programs. Also, hiking, fishing, river-running (permit required), horseback riding, nature seminars.

Overnight Backpacking
Free permits required. Obtain in person at visitor centers or ranger stations within 24 hours of trip.

Campgrounds
Four campgrounds with 14-day limit. Open all year, first come, first served. Fees $3-$11 per night. Tent and RV sites. At **Rio Grande Village Trailer Park,** full hookups only available. Three group campgrounds; reservations through headquarters.

Hotels, Motels, & Inns
(unless otherwise noted, rates are for 2 persons in a double room, high season)
Chisos Mountains Lodge National Park Concessions, Inc., Basin Rural Station, Big Bend NP, Tex. 79834. (915) 477-2291. 66 rooms, $48.50-$60.50; 6 cottages, $65.50. AC, restaurant.
Big Bend Motor Inn (Junct. of Tex. 118 and Rte. 170) P.O. Box 336, Terlingua, Tex. 79852. (915) 371-2218. 48 rooms, 10 with kitchenettes, $60-$70; 12 tent-cabins, $18.50; 4 cottages with kitchens, $119.95. AC, pool, rest. **Gage Hotel** (Junct. of US 90 and US 385) P.O. Box 46, Marathon, Tex. 79842. (915) 386-4205. 20 units, 7 private baths. $38-$52. AC, rest. **Lajitas on the Rio Grande** (on Rte. 170) Star Rte. 70, Box 400, Terlingua, Tex. 79852. (800) 527-4078 or (915) 424-3471. 81 rooms; 12 condos, kitchenettes. $62-$239. AC, pool, rest.

Excursion

Rio Grande Wild and Scenic River
Big Bend National Park, Texas
Floating the Rio Grande is an experience not to be missed. Big Bend NP administers both the section along its border and the Wild and Scenic stretches downstream. Easy floats include the Mariscal and Boquillas Canyons; Santa Elena and the Lower Canyons are more difficult. Boating permits required. Main access point to Lower Canyons in Mexico; most take-out points fall on private land in Texas (permission required). 191 Wild and Scenic miles. Facilities also include primitive camping, hiking, fishing; inner-tubing and swimming *not* recommended. Info. about outfitters offering 1-day to 2-week trips at Panther Junction. (915) 477-2251.

Hall of Giants in the Big Room

Carlsbad Caverns

New Mexico

Established May 14, 1930

46,766 acres

The Chihuahuan Desert, studded with spiky plants and lizards, offers little hint that what Will Rogers called the "Grand Canyon with a roof on it" waits underground. Yet, at the northern reaches of this great desert, underneath a mountain range called the Guadalupes, lies one of the deepest, largest, and most ornate caverns ever found.

Water molded this underworld. Some 250 million years ago, the region lay underneath the inland arm of an ancient sea. Near the shore grew a limestone reef. By the time the sea withdrew, the reef stood hundreds of feet high, later to be buried under thousands of feet of soil. Some 20 to 40 million years ago,

the ground uplifted. Slightly acidic groundwater seeped into cracks in the limestone, gradually enlarging them to form a honeycomb of chambers. Millions of more years passed before the cave decoration began. Then, drop by drop, limestone-laden moisture built an extraordinary variety of glistening formations. Today, some of these are six stories tall; others tiny, delicate confections.

Cave scientists have explored more than 20 miles of passageways of the main cavern of Carlsbad, and investigation continues. Visitors may tour 3 of these miles on a paved trail. Another cavern, New Cave, provides the hardy an opportunity to play spelunker, albeit with a guide. The park has more than 70 other caves open primarily to specialists.

Some visitors think the park's most spectacular sight is the one

When to Go

All-year park. The weather underground remains a constant 56°F. The main cavern gets crowded, especially in summer and on major holiday weekends. Either spring or fall, when the desert's in bloom, is an excellent time to go. You'll see the bats fly from April or early May through October, sometimes later.

How to Visit

One full day allows you time to tour the main cavern and take a nature walk or a drive before watching the bats fly at sunset. For a second day's activity, reserve space on a tour of **New Cave**, if you're ready for a more rugged caving experience.

At the visitor center, select either the **Blue Tour** (a 3-mile, 3-hour walk) or the **Red Tour** ($1\frac{1}{4}$ miles and at least an hour.) Try the Blue unless you have walking, breathing, or heart problems. It starts at the natural entrance and is mostly downhill or level, except for one stretch where you climb 83 feet; an elevator whisks you back to ground level. The **Main Corridor** and **Scenic Rooms** are more intimate and may be less crowded than the **Big Room**, which both tours visit. The Scenic Rooms feature a stunning concentration of formations.

The Red Tour begins with an elevator ride directly to the Big Room, in which you can see most of the types of formations visible in the other sections. If after the Red Tour you want to see more cave, simply return to ground level and proceed with the first half of the Blue.

seen at the cave's mouth. More than a half million Mexican free-tailed bats summer in a section of the cave, and around sunset they spiral up from the entrance to hunt for insects. The nightly exodus led to the discovery of the cave in modern times. Around the turn of the century, miners began to excavate bat guano—a potent fertilizer—for shipment to the citrus groves of southern California. One of the guano miners, James Larkin White, became the first to explore and publicize the caverns beyond the Bat Cave.

How to Get There

The park is off US 62/180, 20 miles southwest of Carlsbad and 164 miles east of El Paso, Texas. For the visitor center, turn west at White's City and drive 7 miles. For New Cave, turn west on County Rd. 418, 5 miles south of White's City; drive another 11 miles, some unpaved, to the parking lot. Airports: Carlsbad and El Paso, Texas.

Main Corridor & Scenic Rooms (Blue Tour)

$1\frac{3}{4}$ miles; about $1\frac{1}{2}$ hours

At the visitor center, rent a receiver for an audio tour, if you wish, and exit to the right, following the path to the cavern's natural entrance. The opening formed when part of the cave's ceiling collapsed thousands of years ago. Once in the mouth of the cave, glance right to spot 1,000-year-old red and black pictographs high on the wall. Indians knew of the cavern and used the entrance for shelter. But without dependable lighting they could not have gone very far past the small sunlit area. You are

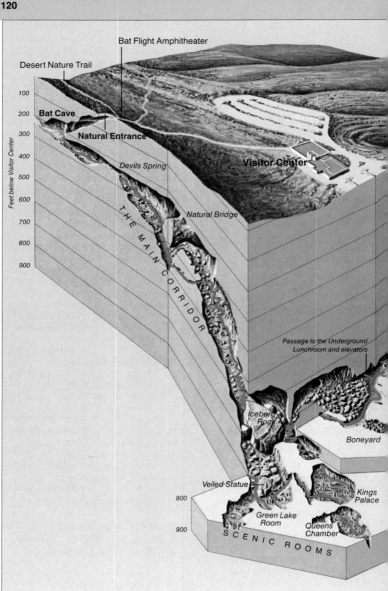

Bat Flight Amphitheater

Desert Nature Trail

100
200
300
400
500
600
700
800
900

Feet below Visitor Center

Bat Cave

Natural Entrance

Devils Spring

THE MAIN CORRIDOR

Natural Bridge

Visitor Center

Passage to the Underground Lunchroom and elevators

Iceberg Rock

Boneyard

Veiled Statue

Kings Palace

800

Green Lake Room

Queens Chamber

900

SCENIC ROOMS

descending the **Main Corridor,** which, if you keep looking around and up, conveys some of the cavern's enormity: The ceiling at times rises more than 200 feet above the path.

The trail soon passes **Devils Spring**. Here cave decoration continues. As water from rain and snow percolates through the ancient reef, it picks up calcite crystals from the limestone. The water then releases the crystals with each drop, splattering them onto the floor as the water drips— producing a stalagmite—or leaving them on the ceiling as the water discharges carbon dioxide into the cave air—creating a stalactite. (Park rangers like to repeat the mnemonic that stalactites "hang tight" to the ceiling, while stalagmites "might grow off your head.") You would have heard a lot more dripping

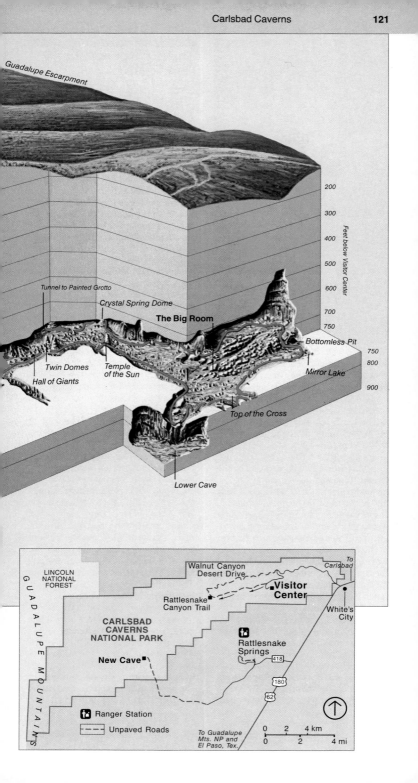

Guadalupe Escarpment

Feet below Visitor Center

200
300
400
500
600
700
750

Tunnel to Painted Grotto
Crystal Spring Dome
The Big Room
Bottomless Pit
750
800
900
Twin Domes
Temple of the Sun
Hall of Giants
Mirror Lake
Top of the Cross
Lower Cave

LINCOLN NATIONAL FOREST

G U A D A L U P E   M O U N T A I N S

Walnut Canyon Desert Drive

To Carlsbad

Visitor Center

Rattlesnake Canyon Trail

White's City

CARLSBAD CAVERNS NATIONAL PARK

Rattlesnake Springs

418

New Cave

180

62

Ranger Station
Unpaved Roads

To Guadalupe Mts. NP and El Paso, Tex.

0   2   4 km
0   2   4 mi

Twin Domes in the Hall of Giants

The Big Room (Blue & Red Tours)

1 1/4 mile; 1 to 1 1/2 hours

After a minute's elevator ride, you'll be 755 feet, or about 75 stories, underground. (Compare your entrance to that of visitors of the early 1920s: They entered by "bucket elevator," as a pulley lowered them into the Bat Cave in a guano bucket.) **Blue Tour** participants will have walked this far and need only exit the lunchroom. Follow the signs for the **Big Room:** For the next hour or so, you'll be circling one gigantic chamber. The Big Room is the largest single room most visitors will ever see (unless they go to Borneo, where there is a cave with a larger, undecorated chamber), 1,800 feet long at its longest point, and 1,100 feet at its widest. It could encompass 14 football fields.

To best enjoy the tour, linger, look, listen, and above all let loose your imagination. What do the various formations look like to you? Layer cakes? Chinese friezes? Fossilized bonsai? In recent years the Park Service removed labels from many of the formations, so now you can name the fantasyscape yourself.

Near the beginning of the walk, the **Hall of Giants** sports some of the largest formations in the cave, many of them about six stories tall. Appearances are deceptive here because of the immensity of the chamber. The trail continues along the periphery of the room (resist the call of the shortcut) and leads past a view of the **Lower Cave,** one of the many explored passages inaccessible to the public. Farther along, at **Top of the Cross,** rangers sometimes give talks at an amphitheater. Glance up: The ceiling here soars to 255 feet, its highest point above the trail.

The footpath continues through a less ornate area that was once a bat cave. The so-called **Bottomless Pit** has been measured at about 140 feet in depth; it does not lead to other passages. As you proceed, take a good look at sparkling **Crystal Spring Dome,** the cave's largest active stalagmite: Each drop of water adds crystals that make it infinitesimally bigger. Iron carried in the water delicately stains the formations of the **Painted Grotto.** Just a few minutes past the

10,000 years ago, when the climate was wetter. Now the Guadalupes receive only about 14 to 19 inches of precipitation a year, and most of the formations are no longer growing.

The trail soon skirts **Iceberg Rock,** a 200,000-ton boulder that crashed down from the ceiling thousands of years ago. Resist the temptation to take the shortcut, and proceed to the **Scenic Rooms.** Many consider the **Veiled Statue,** in the **Green Lake Room,** one of the most beautiful columns in the cavern. A column develops when a stalagmite and a stalactite grow together. The **Kings Palace** may be one of the most ornate cave rooms in the world. In the **Queens Chamber,** look for the rare helictites, small, twisted formations that are governed as much by capillary action as by gravity. More obvious are the giant draperies, formed when water trickles down a slanted ceiling. The **Papoose Room** grew a forest of soda-straw stalactites. Water drips down the center of these soda straws, elongating them. After climbing **Appetite Hill,** stroll on past the **Boneyard,** which probably resembles the cavern of 40 million years ago, when water filled the chambers. Follow the signs to the Underground Lunchroom to relax before continuing the tour.

Mexican free-tailed bats emerging from their cave

grotto, you'll reach the elevator and ascend to daylight.

In the visitor center, don't miss the exhibits on cave restoration or the historical photographs of guano mining and early tourism. Then climb the stairs to the **Observation Tower.** Standing above the ancient reef, you see a striking vista of the reef's seaward side (the slope past the parking lot) and the ancient sea-bed, called the Delaware Basin. On clear days, the panorama before you extends 100 miles into Texas.

Other Trails & Sights

The easy ½-mile loop **Desert Nature Trail** makes an interesting diversion before the evening bat flight program. The trail's interpretive plaques describe how Indians made use of virtually every plant in sight. The trail starts to the right of the cave's natural entrance.

Walnut Canyon Desert Drive is an alternative introduction to the area's natural history. A booklet available at the start guides you along this 9½-mile gravel loop off the main park road, just before the visitor center.

Bat Flight: Don't miss the evening cyclone of bats; at its peak, more

Immature bats in Bat Cave

than 5,000 bats per minute speed out of the cave on their way to consume some three tons of insects. From the visitor center, walk to the amphitheater, at the natural entrance, or drive there by turning right onto the main road, then right again.

New Cave: Be prepared to slip and slide as you explore an "unimproved" cave for 2 hours by flashlight. Accompanied by rangers, you'll see several types of formations not found in the public passages of the main cave, after a steep ½-mile climb up to the cave's entrance from the parking lot in **Slaughter Canyon.** New Cave is open daily in summer; weekends only in winter. Reservations are required; you can make them at the visitor center or by calling the park.

Information & Activities

Headquarters
3225 National Parks Highway, Carlsbad, New Mexico 88220. Phone (505) 785-2232.

Seasons & Accessibility
Park open year-round, except Christmas Day.

Visitor & Information Centers
The Visitor Center is 7 miles from White's City; open daily all year, except Christmas. Call headquarters for information.

Entrance Fees
No entrance fee for park. Fees to enter the cavern: adults $5; children ages 6-15, $3; children under 6 free. No charge for bat flight program. To tour New Cave: adults $6, children under age 16, $3; children under 6 not permitted.

Pets
Not allowed in caves or backcountry. Kennel at the Visitor Center.

Facilities for Disabled
The Visitor Center and Bat Flight Amphitheater are wheelchair accessible, as is a portion of the cave tour. Picnic area and rest rooms accessible at Rattlesnake Springs.

Things to Do
Ranger-led activities: tours of the main cavern (call park for details), cavern talks, dusk bat flight programs, flashlight trip into New Cave (reservations required, see page 123). Also available, self-guided Desert Nature Trail, self-guided Walnut Canyon Desert Drive, backcountry trails.

Special Advisories
☐Wear low-heeled, non-skid shoes in the caverns, and bring a jacket.
☐Intense summer thunderstorms may cause floods in low-lying areas, lightning strikes in higher areas.
☐Watch out for rattlesnakes when hiking.
☐Cactuses and other spiny desert plants can inflict painful injuries.

Overnight Backpacking
Permits required. Available free at the Visitor Center.

Campgrounds
None; backcountry camping only. Food services in park.

Hotels, Motels, & Inns
(unless otherwise noted, rates are for 2 persons in a double room, high season)
In White's City, N. Mex. 88268:
Best Western Cavern Inn (12 Carlsbad Cavern Hwy.) P.O. Box 128. (800) 228-3767; in N. Mex. (800) 843-2283; or (505) 785-2291. 131 units. $52-$65. AC, pool, restaurant.
In Carlsbad, N. Mex. 88220:
Best Western Motel Stevens (1829 S. Canal St.) P.O. Box 580. (505) 887-2851. 202 units, 39 with kitchenettes. $45-$65. AC, pool, restaurant.
Carlsbad Travelodge South Motel 3817 National Parks Hwy. (800) 255-3050 or (505) 887-8888. 60 units. $52, includes breakfast. AC, pool.
Continental Inn 3820 National Parks Hwy. (505) 887-0341. 63 units, 3 with kitchenettes. $40-$55. AC, pool.
Park Inn International 3706 National Parks Hwy. (800) 437-7275 or (505) 887-2861. 126 units. $39-$70. AC, pool, restaurant.
Rodeway Inn 3804 National Parks Hwy. (800) 228-2000 or (505) 887-5535. 107 units, 50 with kitchenettes. $59. AC, pool, restaurant.

Contact the Carlsbad Chamber of Commerce for a full list of accommodations: P.O. Box 910, Dept. BM, Carlsbad, N. Mex. 88221. (800) 221-1224; in N. Mex. (505) 887-6516.

Excursions

Lincoln National Forest
Alamogordo, New Mexico

In 1950, a game warden here made history by rescuing a badly burned black bear cub from a forest fire and naming him Smokey. Lincoln is also noted for life zones ranging from desert to subalpine forest and for unexplored limestone caves. 1,103,441 acres. Facilities include 368 campsites, climbing, fishing, horseback riding, hunting, picnic areas, winter sports. Open all year; most campsites open May-September. Adjoins Carlsbad Caverns NP on west. Information at Carlsbad on US 285, about 20 miles from park. (505) 437-6030.

White Sands National Monument
Alamogordo, New Mexico

Undulating waves of gypsum sand, some 50 feet high, offer an ever changing vista here in the Tularosa Basin. Weathered rock from surrounding highlands settles in Lake Lucero and adjacent alkali flats; scouring southwest winds create the dunes. Features 16-mile-long Heart of Sands Loop. 144,420 acres. Facilities include primitive camping (registration required), food services, hiking, picnic areas. Open daily except Christmas. Visitor center on US 70, about 120 miles from Carlsbad Caverns NP. (505) 479-6124.

Bosque del Apache National Wildlife Refuge
Socorro, New Mexico

The Rio Grande bisects this refuge, where carefully maintained ponds and marshes shelter wintering snow geese and other waterfowl, as well as sandhill cranes and endangered whooping cranes, bald eagles, and peregrine falcons. 57,191 acres. Facilities include hiking, fishing (in summer), hunting, scenic drives. Open year-round, from 1 hour before sunrise to 1 hour after sunset. Visitor center on New Mexico 1, off I-25, about 270 miles from Carlsbad Caverns NP. (505) 835-1828.

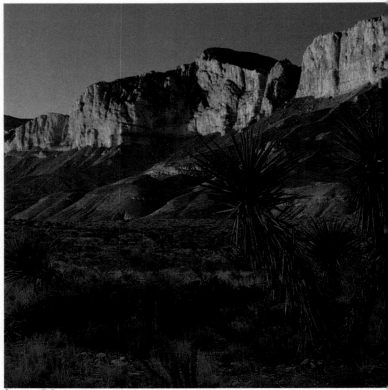

Sunset on El Capitan, beacon of the Guadalupes

Guadalupe Mountains

Texas

Established September 30, 1972

86,416 acres

In west Texas, only about 40 miles southwest of Carlsbad Caverns, lies a gem of a park that few people outside the state have ever heard of, let alone visited. Guadalupe Mountains National Park contains the southernmost, highest part of the 50-mile-long Guadalupe range. From the highway, the mountains resemble a nearly monolithic wall through the desert. But drive into one of the park entrances, take even a short stroll, and surprises crop up: dramatically contoured canyons, shady glades surrounded by desert scrub, a profusion of wildlife and birds.

Some 80 miles of trails can lead the more energetic hiker to Guadalupe Peak, the highest point in Texas (8,749 feet), and to mountaintops with scattered but thick conifer forests typical of the Rockies hundreds of miles to the north. The range's origins may be surprising too: The Guadalupe Mountains were once a reef growing beneath the waters of an ancient inland sea. That same vanished sea spawned the honeycomb of the Carlsbad Caverns.

Pottery, baskets, and spear tips found in the mountains suggest that people first visited the Guadalupes about 12,000 years ago, hunting the camels, mammoths, and other animals that flourished in the wetter climate of the waning Ice Age. When the Spaniards arrived in the Southwest in the mid-16th century, Mescalero Apaches were periodically camping near the springs at the base of the mountains and climbing to the highlands to hunt and forage. Both

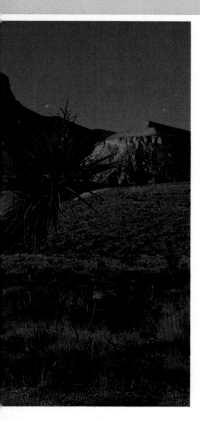

trick Canyon, turn off US 62/180 about 7 miles northeast of the main visitor center, then continue 4 miles to the parking lot. For Dog Canyon, either hike 12 miles from Pine Springs Campground or drive north on 62/180, then west on County Road 408, and south on N. Mex. 137, about 115 miles total from Pine Springs. Airports: Carlsbad and El Paso.

When to Go
All-year park, but spring and fall are best. In spring, the foliage is fresh and, with enough rain, the blossoms abundant. In late October to mid-November, changing leaves provide splashes of red, yellow, burgundy.

How to Visit
On a day trip, head to the visitor center and **Pine Springs;** take at least a short hike. On a second day, visit **McKittrick Canyon** for a stroll through a hidden oasis. To visit a wilder, more isolated area, where trails take you quickly into the high country, drive about 3 hours to reenter the park at **Dog Canyon** in the north.

Pine Springs-Frijole Area
a half to full day

Pick up maps and trail information at the **Headquarters Visitor Center,** where you can also enjoy audiovisual programs on the park's ecology and history. Fill your water bottles before leaving. Then stroll to **The Pinery** or drive back to the highway, turn left in about $\frac{1}{10}$ mile, and park. The stone walls remain from the 1858 Pinery Station of the Butterfield Overland Mail Line—forerunner of the Pony Express. Buy a self-guiding leaflet to learn about the colorful local history. Back in your car, return to the highway and turn left, then left again in about a mile onto a dirt road. Park at the end, near the **Frijole Ranch.** The 1870s ranch house is now a cultural history center, preserving artifacts of frontier life.

Be sure to walk the easy $2\frac{3}{10}$-mile loop trail to **Smith** and **Manzanita Springs,** an excellent introduction to the striking contrasts the Chihuahuan Desert presents. Bear right at the trailhead. The thorny plants may seem forbidding, but the Mescalero Apaches used a great majority of the

the Apaches and Europeans spun legends of fabulous caches of gold in these mountains.

As American prospectors, settlers, and cavalry pushed west, the Apaches made the mountaintops their bases and fought to ward off encroachers. By the late 1880s, however, virtually all the Indians had been killed or forced onto a reservation. Donations of ranchlands eventually gave impetus to the park.

In 1988, more land became available to the park: 10,000 acres to the west of its boundary, including some 2,000 acres of white gypsum sand dunes and dunes of brick red quartzose, both deposits left by the ancient sea. The park is in the process of acquiring these new lands.

How to Get There
The main visitor center and most visitor activities are located in the Pine Springs-Frijole area, off US 62/180, 55 miles southwest of Carlsbad and 110 miles east of El Paso. For McKit-

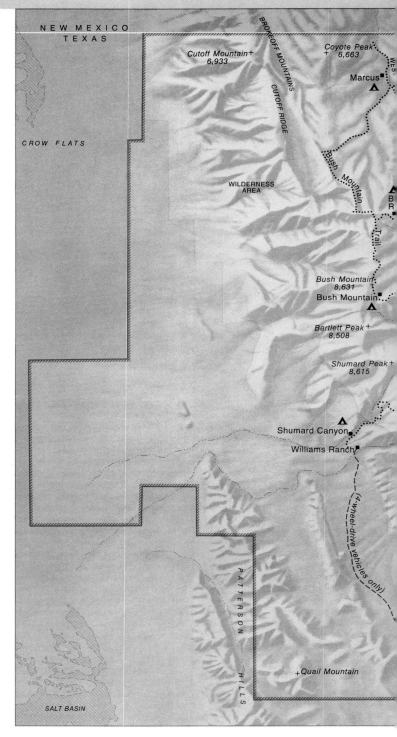

NEW MEXICO
TEXAS

Cutoff Mountain +
6,933

BROKEOFF MOUNTAINS

Coyote Peak
+ 6,663

Marcus ■

CUTOFF RIDGE

CROW FLATS

WILDERNESS
AREA

Bush Mountain Trail

BR

Bush Mountain
8,631 +
Bush Mountain ■

Bartlett Peak +
8,508

Shumard Peak +
8,615

Shumard Canyon ■
Williams Ranch ■

(4-wheel-drive vehicles only)

PATTERSON

HILLS

+ Quail Mountain

SALT BASIN

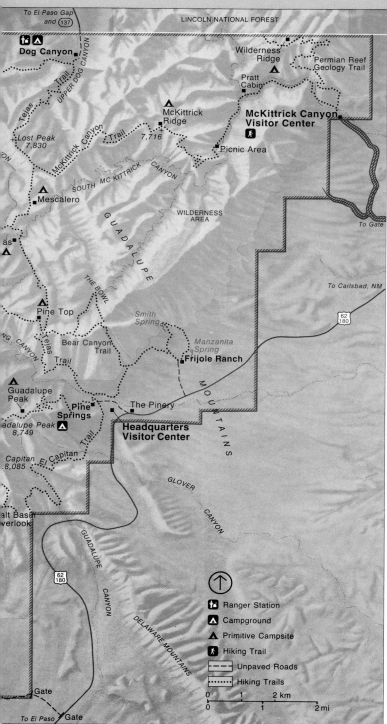

To El Paso Gap
and (137)

LINCOLN NATIONAL FOREST

Dog Canyon

Wilderness
Ridge

Permian Reef
Geology Trail

Pratt
Cabin

Trail

UPPER DOG CANYON

McKittrick
Ridge

McKittrick Canyon
Visitor Center

Tejas

McKittrick Canyon

Trail   7,716

Picnic Area

Lost Peak
7,830

SOUTH MC KITTRICK CANYON

Mescalero

G
U
A
D
A
L
U
P
E

WILDERNESS
AREA

To Gate

THE BOWL

To Carlsbad, NM

Pine Top

62
180

Tejas

Bear Canyon
Trail

Smith
Spring

ING CANYON

Trail

Manzanita
Spring

Frijole Ranch

Guadalupe
Peak

M
O
U
N
T
A
I
N
S

Pine
Springs

The Pinery

adalupe Peak
8,749

Headquarters
Visitor Center

Capitan
8,085

El Capitan

Trail

GLOVER

CANYON

alt Basin
verlook

GUADALUPE

62
180

CANYON

DELAWARE MOUNTAINS

Ranger Station

Campground

Primitive Campsite

Hiking Trail

Unpaved Roads

Hiking Trails

0   1   2 km

0   1   2 mi

Gate

Gate

To El Paso

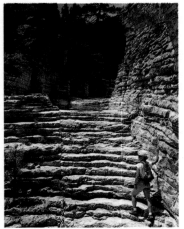
Hiker's Staircase, in Pine Spring Canyon

plants in sight for food or fiber. Their diet consisted largely of mescal—the heart of the agave plant, one of the succulents with spikes at the tips of the leaves—hence the culture's name. You'll soon approach Manzanita Spring, a place to spot wildlife.

Continue on to Smith Spring, a veritable garden of maidenhair ferns, Texas madrone trees (the ones shedding layers of paper-thin bark), alligator juniper (named for its distinctively textured bark), oak, and maple. As you loop back to your car, bear left at the fork.

Return to the highway and drive west-southwest about 2 miles, or at least as far as the first pullover, for a superb view of **El Capitan** (8,085 feet), the southernmost bluff of the **Guadalupes.** Late afternoon light shows off this imposing symbol of the region, once the beacon for conquistador, stagecoach driver, and homesteader.

McKittrick Canyon

foot tour; a half to full day

The walls of **McKittrick Canyon** shelter the only year-round stream in the park; the water creates a 3-mile-long oasis of oak and juniper, madrone and maple. The canyon itself is nearly 5 miles long. Pick up a self-guiding booklet on the area's human and natural history at the **McKittrick Canyon Visitor Center** near the trailheads. For an easy hike (although the trail is rocky and best negotiated in hiking boots), walk the $2\frac{3}{10}$ miles to the

Pratt Cabin. If you have time, continue another mile through the woods that border the intermittent stream to the **Grotto** picnic area. Because the canyon plants are fragile, *be sure to stay on the trail.*

McKittrick Canyon exposes millions of years of geological events. During the Permian era, about 250 million years ago, an inland sea covered parts of west Texas and southeast New Mexico. Along the shore of the sea grew a reef of lime-secreting algae, sponges, other marine organisms, and calcium carbonate precipitated from the water. After millions of years, the climate changed and the ocean dried up; the Capitan Reef loomed hundreds of feet high in a horseshoe 400 miles long. Sediments and mineral salts buried both basin and reef over the next eons. Later, the region began to rise, and erosion slowly reexposed the seabed with part of the fossil reef—today's Guadalupe range—towering above.

As you walk into McKittrick Canyon, you are entering the Capitan Reef from the seaward side. To best observe the reef's varied formation and fossils, try the **Permian Reef Geology Trail.** You'll see layers of the ancient reef exposed by centuries of cutting by McKittrick Creek. The trail—$4\frac{1}{2}$ miles one way—climbs the 2,000-foot ridge to a ponderosa forest on the top.

Dog Canyon

a half to full day

Accessibility to the forested high country and its spectacular scenery make **Dog Canyon** well worth the drive. Ask a ranger to point out Apache mescal-roasting pits, still visible among the hip-high grasses, creosote bushes, and succulents. Then picnic and hike; the trails begin past the stables. Popular hikes include the **Bush Mountain Trail,** which, in about 3 miles, leads through open pinyon-juniper woodland to splendid views of the Guadalupes and the **Cornudas Mountains,** 55 miles to the west. The **Tejas Trail** offers similar views and in about 4 miles climbs into a temperate woodland of Gambel oak, Douglas-fir, and limber and ponderosa pine. This forest is a relict of the plant communities that cloaked the region in the last ice age. It survives because of the particular, unusual combination of temperature and humidity at this high-altitude site.

Other Hikes

Hikers may find the following three treks rewarding. They all begin from Pine Springs Campground; ask a ranger for information:

Guadalupe Peak, 9⅓ miles round-trip. Because lightning storms can quickly gather on hot summer afternoons, it's best to begin your ascent by 8 a.m. and your descent by 1 p.m. *Watch the weather. If you see a storm coming, start down immediately.*
The Bowl, a lush area of relict ice age conifer forest. The 9½-mile loop is comprised of the Tejas, **Bowl,** and **Bear Canyon Trails.**
Devils Hall, a steep, narrow canyon; 5 miles round-trip, mostly level.

Information & Activities

Headquarters
HC 60, Box 400, Salt Flat, Texas 79847. Phone (915) 828-3251.

Seasons & Accessibility
Open year-round but may be inaccessible for brief periods in winter due to snowstorms. Best to phone park.

Visitor & Information Centers
Headquarters Visitor Center, ¹⁄₁₀ mile off US 62/180 at Guadalupe Pass, open all year except Christmas and New Year's Day. McKittrick Canyon Visitor Center off US 62/180 on eastern edge of park and Dog Canyon Ranger Station in the north open intermittently. Call park for details.

Entrance Fee
None.

Pets
Not permitted on trails or in buildings; elsewhere must be leashed.

Facilities for Disabled
The visitor centers, rest rooms, and Pine Springs Campground and amphitheater are wheelchair accessible.

Things to Do
Free naturalist-led activities (summer only): hikes, horseback trail rides (no rentals), evening and children's programs. Also, hiking.

Special Advisories
☐Rattlesnakes and other potentially harmful desert animals live here; watch out!
☐Bring maps with you if planning to hike; park is managed as wilderness, so trail signs are minimal.

Overnight Backpacking
Allowed at designated sites only; permits required; they are free and may be obtained at the visitor centers. Backcountry Use permits required to bring a horse into the park, available from Main Visitor Center or Dog Canyon. Horses are not allowed in the backcountry overnight; they can be stabled in Pine Springs and Dog Canyon corrals (reserve space by calling 915-828-3251).

Campgrounds
Two campgrounds, both with 14-day limit. Open all year, first come, first served. $6 per night at **Dog Canyon** and **Pine Springs.** No showers. Tent and RV sites; no hookups. Two group campgrounds; reservations required through headquarters.

Hotels, Motels, & Inns
(unless otherwise noted, rates are for 2 persons in a double room, high season)
In White's City, New Mexico 88268:
Best Western Cavern Inn (12 Carlsbad Cavern Hwy.) P.O. Box 128. (800) 228-3767 or (505) 785-2291. 131 units. $52-$65. AC, pool, restaurant.
In Van Horn, Texas 79855:
Best Western American Inn 1309 W. Broadway, Box 626. (800) 528-1234 or (915) 283-2030. 33 units. $40. AC, pool.
Plaza Inn of Van Horn P.O. Box 776. (800) 543-8831 or (915) 283-2780. 98 units.$42. AC, pool, restaurant.

See also Carlsbad Caverns NP listings.

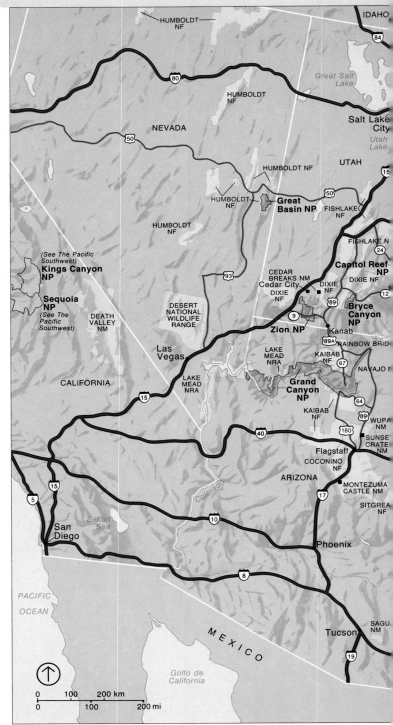

Preceding pages: Grand Canyon

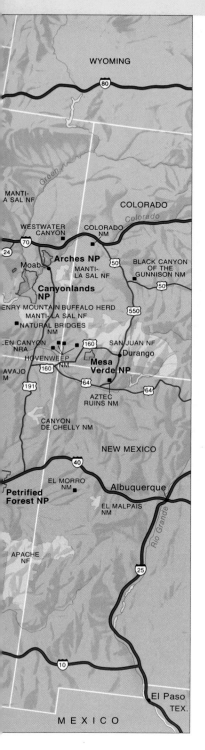

The Colorado Plateau

Theodore Roosevelt called Grand Canyon "the one great sight . . . every American should see." Although Grand Canyon remains the most famous sight on the Colorado Plateau, this high desert drained by the Colorado River and its tributaries teems with scenic treasures. Numerous gorges slice the colorfully layered rock; stairstep terraces, buttes, and spires embellish it. The region contains the nation's largest concentration of national parks; some people contend that the entire Colorado Plateau merits national park status.

The striated cliffs of the canyon parks collectively encompass nearly two billion years of earth's history, divulging tales of ancient seas and volcanoes, deserts and dinosaurs. The rush of rivers sculptured the colossal gorges and side canyons of Grand Canyon, Zion, and Canyonlands. Grit-bearing winds and the freeze and thaw of water droplets in tiny cracks chiseled multihued rock into the hoodoos, arches, balanced rocks, and pinnacles visible in Arches and Bryce Canyon.

Although one of the most sparsely populated regions of the United States today, the plateau features some of the country's richest remains of early Indian civilizations. Archaeological highlights range from petroglyphs in Canyonlands and Capitol Reef to pueblos and solstice markers in Petrified Forest to spectacular cliff dwellings in Mesa Verde.

Thanks to abrupt changes in elevation, the canyon parks shelter a wide diversity of plants and animals. Desert or semidesert at canyon bottom gives way to pinyon-juniper woodland and then ponderosa pine forest. Spruce-fir forest caps the higher elevations. Visitors can encounter lizards and deer, desert cottontails, and bighorn sheep in the same park.

Flagstaff, Arizona, makes a convenient base for the South Rim of the Grand Canyon and for Petrified Forest. From Kanab, Utah, you can visit Grand Canyon's forested North Rim, Bryce, Capitol Reef, and Zion. Just west of the plateau, a 5-hour drive from Kanab, lie the glacier-carved peaks of Great Basin. For Arches and Canyonlands, Moab, Utah, is the place to stop.

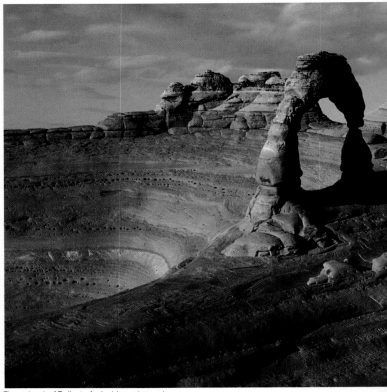

The red rock of Delicate Arch ablaze at sunset

Arches

Utah

Established November 12, 1971

77,379 acres

This park contains more than 950 natural arches—the greatest concentration in the world. But numbers have no significance beside the grandeur of the landscape—the arches, the giant balanced rocks, spires, pinnacles, and slickrock domes against the enormous sky.

Perched high above the Colorado River, the park is part of southern Utah's extended area of canyonlands, carved and shaped by eons of weathering and erosion. Most of the formations at Arches are made of soft red sandstone deposited 150 million years ago in a vast desert. As underlying salt deposits dissolved, the sandstone collapsed and weathered into a maze of vertical rock slabs called "fins." Sections of these slender walls eventually wore through, creating the spectacular rock sculptures.

The land has a timeless, indestructible look that is misleading. More than a half million visitors each year threaten the fragile high desert ecosystem. One concern is a dark crust called cryptogamic soil composed of algae, fungi, and lichens that grow in sandy areas in the park. Footprints tracked across this living community may remain visible for years. In fact, the aridity helps preserve traces of past activity for centuries.

Well-preserved petroglyphs carved into a low cliff near a pioneer cabin add to the evidence that Indians roamed this land. Pictures of riders on horseback date the carvings to historic times, after the Spaniards introduced horses to the Southwest.

How to Get There

From Moab, take US 191 north 5 miles to the park entrance. From I-70, exit at Crescent Junction and follow Utah Hwy. 191 south for 25 miles to the entrance. Airport at Grand Junction, Colo., about 120 miles away.

When to Go

All-year park, but spring and fall are best; moderate temperatures are ideal for hiking in the high desert. Summers are hot and winters mild. Wildflowers peak in April and May.

How to Visit

Take the **Arches Scenic Drive** at least as far as **The Windows Section**. Allow time for hiking one of the park's spectacular trails. If it's spring or summer (and you're not bothered by heights), consider joining a naturalist-led 2-hour hike through **Fiery Furnace**. It's strenuous, but you'll appreciate the shadiness in summer's heat. Check at the visitor center for times.

Arches Scenic Drive

18 miles one way; a half to full day

The scenic drive climbs from the floor of **Moab Canyon** to **Devils Garden** passing through the heart of the park with spur roads leading to **The Windows Section** and **Wolfe Ranch**. Numerous pull-offs allow leisurely viewing of the park's major features.

From the visitor center the road winds up the canyon wall. Pull off after 2 miles at the **South Park Avenue Trailhead** for a view down an open canyon flanked by sandstone skyscrapers. If you have a willing driver—or don't mind the 320-foot return climb—walk the easy $\frac{7}{10}$-mile path to the **Courthouse Towers** parking area, where you can be picked up. Here interpretive signs draw your attention to nearby rock formations that show the birth and death of an arch.

Continue your drive to the beautiful slickrock expanse known as the **Petrified Dunes.** Here you skirt knolls—ancient dunes turned to stone—as the **La Sal Mountains** rise nearly 13,000 feet in the far distance. Farther along, stop at the **Balanced Rock** pull-off where a $\frac{3}{10}$-mile trail loops past this classic hoodoo, a strangely eroded rock spire 128 feet high. Edward Abbey wrote his classic *Desert Solitaire* after living in a trailer here as a park ranger. Just beyond, turn onto the paved road leading to The Windows.

The road passes a cluster of pinnacles and monoliths called **Garden of Eden** and ends at a parking area fronted by a sandstone wall perforated by several arches. Short trails lead to closeup views of these colossal gateways. The $\frac{3}{10}$-mile walk to **South Window**, 105 feet wide, also gives you good views of **North Window** and **Turret Arch.** If time allows walk the $\frac{1}{5}$-mile trail for a dramatic closeup look at **Double Arch.**

Retrace your route back to the main road. A graded dirt road leaves the scenic drive and leads $1\frac{4}{5}$ miles to historic Wolfe Ranch, where a Civil War veteran raised cattle around the turn of the century, and the **Delicate Arch Viewpoint**, $1\frac{1}{5}$ miles farther (closed to trailers). The distant view of **Delicate Arch** is disappointing, so if you have the stamina and at least 2 extra hours return to

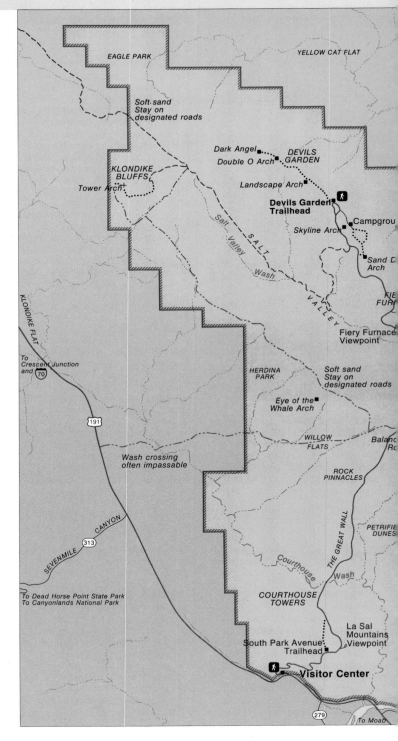

EAGLE PARK

YELLOW CAT FLAT

*Soft sand
Stay on
designated roads*

Dark Angel ■ ···· **DEVILS
GARDEN**
Double O Arch ■

*KLONDIKE
BLUFFS*

Landscape Arch ■

Tower Arch

**Devils Garden
Trailhead**

Skyline Arch ■

Campgrou

Sand D
Arch

*Salt
Valley
Wash*

S A L T

V A L L E Y

FIE
FUR

Fiery Furnace
Viewpoint

KLONDIKE FLAT

*To
Crescent Junction
and* (70)

HERDINA
PARK

*Soft sand
Stay on
designated roads*

*Eye of the
Whale Arch* ■

191

WILLOW
FLATS

Balan
Ro

*Wash crossing
often impassable*

ROCK
PINNACLES

THE GREAT WALL

PETRIFIE
DUNES

SEVENMILE CANYON

313

*Courthouse
Wash*

*To Dead Horse Point State Park
To Canyonlands National Park*

**COURTHOUSE
TOWERS**

La Sal
Mountains
Viewpoint

South Park Avenue
Trailhead ■

Visitor Center

(279)

To Moab

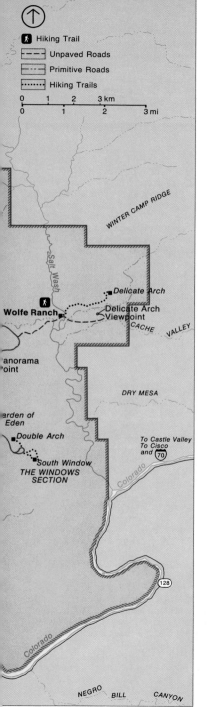

Wolfe Cabin and hike to the foot of the arch. The magnificent views make this one of the most rewarding hikes in canyon country, but you're better off saving it for a second day if you plan to take the full drive and other walks.

The trail to Delicate Arch gains 500 feet in elevation as it traverses 1½ miles across slickrock as smooth and cambered as the back of a whale. Near the trail, juniper trees grow from cracks so small the trunks seem to emerge from solid rock. Keep your eye out for the rock cairns that mark the trail; they're easy to miss. The arch perches on the edge of a bowl, framing white-capped mountains; the suddenness of your encounter with it at trail's end adds to its drama.

Return to the main road. Skip the **Salt Valley Overlook** but pull off at **Fiery Furnace,** a dense array of red fins that appear to ignite when the sun is low in the west. Here you see a world standing on end—hoodoos, spires, and slabs 200 feet high. It's easy to get lost in the maze of deeply grooved slots and dead-end passageways, so rangers encourage hikers to join the 2-hour guided tours.

Continue your drive. Take the short ⅕-mile walk to the cool shade of **Sand Dune Arch,** tucked between two fins, but save **Broken Arch** for another time. Farther down the road **Skyline Arch** comes into view. In 1940 a great rock mass broke from the arch, doubling the size of the opening to 45 by 69 feet.

The road ends at the Devils Garden campground and trailhead beyond. The **Devils Garden Trail** leads to seven major arches, each with its own character. The 2¼-mile trail takes about 5 hours to hike round-trip. Be sure to save enough time to walk at least as far as **Landscape**

Landscape Arch framing pinyon pines

Arch, $\frac{4}{5}$ of a mile. Here a narrow ribbon of stone 306 feet long appears to defy gravity as it floats in a graceful span above a steep dune. It's one of the world's longest free-standing natural arches. Take the trail that leads behind it for a wide-open vista of slickrock desert framed in stone.

If you walk the trail early in the morning, watch for the white flowers of the evening primrose. As the sunlight grows stronger, the flowers wilt, turning the petals pink. Though primitive beyond Landscape Arch, the trail continues on another $1\frac{1}{4}$ miles to **Double O Arch** where a circular arch, 160 feet wide, hangs above a smaller bore. From here you can walk about $\frac{1}{2}$ mile to the rock spire known as the **Dark Angel.**

Information & Activities

Headquarters
P.O. Box 907, Moab, Utah 84532. Phone (801) 259-8161.

Seasons & Accessibility
Park open year-round. Some unpaved roads may become temporarily impassable after heavy rains. Call headquarters for current weather and road information.

Visitor & Information Centers
Visitor Center, on US 191 at park entrance, open daily all year except Christmas. Call headquarters number for visitor information.

Entrance Fees
$3 per car per week. Yearly fee of $10 is also good at Canyonlands.

Pets
Not allowed on any trails.

Facilities for Disabled
Visitor Center and one of its rest rooms are wheelchair accessible. Rest room and one campsite accessible in Devils Garden Campground. Park Avenue Trail is self-guided and accessible to wheelchairs.

Things to Do
Free naturalist-led activities: nature hikes and talks, evening programs. Also available, geological and historical exhibits, self-guided auto tour, hiking, jeep tours, horseback trail rides (call Park Creek Ranch 801-259-5505), sight-seeing flights. Contact park headquarters for list of concessioners offering rental and guide services.

Special Advisories
□Always carry water on hikes—at least a gallon a day per person in summer.
□Stay on trails to protect fragile desert soils and plant life.
□Sandstone slickrock crumbles easily and can make climbing dangerous. Consult a ranger before going out.

Overnight Backpacking
Permits required. They are free and available at Visitor Center.

Campgrounds
One campground, **Devils Garden,** with a 7-day limit. Open all year on a first-come, first-served basis. Fees $7 per night. No showers. Tent and RV sites; no hookups. Reservations required for **Devils Garden Group Campgrounds**; tent sites only; contact park headquarters.

Hotels, Motels, & Inns
(unless otherwise noted, rates are for 2 persons in a double room, high season)
In Moab, Utah 84532:
Best Western Green Well Motel 105 S. Main Street. (800) 528-1234 or (801) 259-6151. 72 units. $82. AC, pool, restaurant. **Cedar Breaks Condos** Center and Fourth East. (801) 259-7830. 6 2-bedroom units, all with full kitchens. $60. AC. **Moab Travelodge** 550 S. Main Street. (800) 255-3050 or (801) 259-6171. 56 units. $62-$66. AC, pool, restaurant. **Pack Creek Ranch** (15 mi. SE of Moab, off LaSal Mountain Loop Rd.) P.O. Box 1270. (801) 259-5505. Cabins, houses, bunkhouses. $80-$125 per person. Includes all meals, trail rides. Pool. **Ramada Inn—Moab** 182 S. Main Street. (800) 228-2828 or (801) 259-7141. 84 units. $79. AC, pool, restaurant.

For other accommodations in the area, contact Utah's Canyonlands Region, P.O. Box 550-R9, Moab, Utah 84532. (800) 635-MOAB or (801) 259-8825.

Excursions

Manti-LaSal National Forest
Price, Utah
Mountains densely wooded with aspen, pine, fir, and spruce and rugged grassland-covered plateaus provide cool contrast here in red-rock country. Contains Dark Canyon Wilderness Area. 1,265,254 acres, part in Colorado. Facilities include 136 campsites, hiking, boating, boat ramp, climbing, bicycling, fishing, horseback riding, hunting, picnic areas, winter sports, water sports. Open year-round; campsites open May/June-October. Information at Moab on US 191, about 5 miles southeast of Arches National Park. (801) 259-7155.

Colorado National Monument
Fruita, Colorado
The 23-mile-long Rim Rock Drive and well-maintained trails with gentle switchbacks provide easy access to this monument's small, sheer-walled canyons and sandstone monoliths. Contains ancient Fremont rock carvings and many dinosaur fossils and shelters mule deer, elk, bighorn sheep, and mountain lions. 20,450 acres. Facilities include 81 campsites, hiking, climbing, bicycling, horseback riding, picnic areas, scenic drives, winter sports, handicapped access. Open year-round. Located on Colorado Hwy. 340, about 100 miles from Arches NP. (303) 858-3617.

Black Canyon of the Gunnison National Monument
Montrose, Colorado
Masked in shadows most of the day, the 2,000-foot-deep gorge carved by the Gunnison River is a wild, awesome place. North and South Rim Drives (not connected) take visitors to the brink of the canyon; extremely fit hikers can descend unmarked trails to the canyon's bottom. Sheer, steep walls challenge experienced climbers. 20,766 acres. Facilities include 102 campsites, hiking, climbing, fishing, picnic areas, scenic drives. South Rim open to traffic all year; North Rim closed in winter. Campsites open May 1-October 1. Off Colo. Hwy. 347, about 135 miles from Arches NP. (303) 249-7036.

Bryce Amphitheater, seen from Bryce Point

Bryce Canyon

Utah

Established September 15, 1928

35,835 acres

Perhaps nowhere are the forces of natural erosion more tangible than at Bryce Canyon. Its wilderness of phantom-like rock spires, or hoodoos, attracts more than a million visitors a year. Many descend on trails that give hikers and horseback riders a close look at the fluted walls and sculptured pinnacles.

The park follows the edge of the Paunsaugunt Plateau. On the west are heavily forested tablelands more than 9,000 feet high; on the east are the intricately carved breaks where the country drops 2,000 feet to the Paria Valley. Many ephemeral streams have eaten into the plateau, forming horseshoe-shaped amphitheaters. The largest and most striking is Bryce Amphitheater. Encompassing 6 square miles, it is the scenic heart of the park.

Water has been helping carve Bryce's rugged landscape for millions of years and is still at work. Water may split rock as it freezes and expands in cracks—a cyclic process that occurs some 200 times a year. In summer, runoff from violent cloudbursts etches into the softer limestones and sluices through the deep runnels. In about half a century the present rim will be cut back into the plateau another foot. But there is more here than spectacular erosion.

In the early morning you can stand for long moments on the rim, held by the amphitheater's mysterious blend of rock and color. Warm yellows and oranges radiate from the deeply pigmented walls as scatterings of light illuminate the pale rock spires.

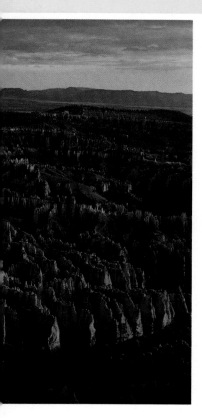

There is a sense of place here that goes beyond rocks. Local Paiute Indians explained it with a story. Once there lived animal-like creatures that changed themselves into people. But they were bad, so Coyote turned them into rocks of various configurations. The spellbound creatures still huddle together here with faces painted just as they were before being turned to stone.

How to Get There

From Zion National Park (about 80 miles west), take Utah Hwy. 9 east, turn north onto Utah Hwy. 89, then east on Utah Hwy. 12 to Utah Hwy. 63, the park entrance road. From Capitol Reef National Park (about 65 miles away), take Utah 12 southward to Utah 63. Airport: Cedar City, 86 miles away.

When to Go

All-year park. Wildflowers are at their peak in spring and early summer; the greatest variety of the park's 170 bird species appears between May and October. Winter lasts from November through March; snow highlights the brilliantly colored cliffs and provides fine cross-country skiing.

How to Visit

On a 1-day visit, tour the **Bryce Amphitheater,** beginning, if possible, with sunrise at **Bryce Point.** If limited time requires choosing between the scenic drive or a walk beneath the rim, take the walk. On a longer stay, drive to **Rainbow Point;** consider a moonlight stroll among the hoodoos.

Bryce Amphitheater

8 miles; 2 hours to a full day

Watch sunrise from **Bryce Point,** one of the highest overlooks along the rim of the amphitheater. Drive about 4 miles south of the visitor center, then walk a short distance from the parking lot to the viewpoint.

Colors begin to glow even before the sun breaks over the **Aquarius Plateau,** at over 10,000 feet the highest plateau in North America. First light catches the rim of the amphitheater, then drops into the basin, igniting the crowded pillars of rock. From this vantage point you see shallow caves along the rim called the **Grottoes.** Look for the **Alligator,** a sharply incised butte that appears reptilian from above, and the **Sinking Ship,** which resembles a vanishing prow.

Drive back to **Inspiration Point,** bypassing the **Paria View** turnoff. From the parking lot walk up a short but steep trail to upper Inspiration Point. If the trail looks too ambitious, stay below at the lower viewpoint. Both look over the head of the amphitheater and place you close to the rock formations. No matter what time of day, they provide excellent all-around views.

In the valley below is the small town of **Tropic.** Scottish emigrant Ebenezer Bryce and his wife Mary homesteaded nearby in 1875. They grazed cattle in **Bryce Canyon** but moved away 5 years later, leaving behind little more than their name.

Continue on to **Sunset Point.** The name is misleading since the viewpoint faces east, limiting sundown views. But the mix of shadows and

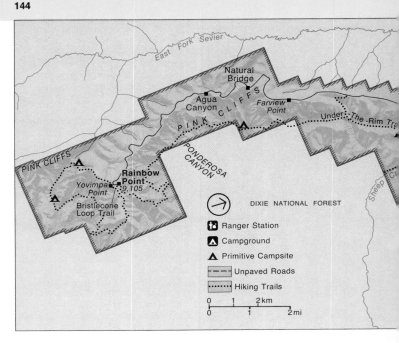

Thor's Hammer at sunrise

deep-hued colors makes this an excellent viewpoint in the low-angled light of later afternoon. To the left is **Thor's Hammer;** to the right is the **Silent City**—a gridwork of deep ravines that divide turreted walls suggesting the ruins of an ancient metropolis.

Those with time and stamina can follow the **Navajo Loop Trail,** a fairly strenuous 1½-mile loop into the canyon. The trail drops steeply in a series of tight switchbacks before entering a narrow, steep-walled gorge called **Wall Street.** Several Douglasfirs, two of them 700 years old, grow between the towering cliffs.

Continue down the trail to the junction with **Queen's Garden Trail,** the least strenuous trail below the rim. It winds along the bottom of the amphitheater to **Queen's Garden,** then climbs to the rim at **Sunrise Point,** passing weird rock formations and occasional bristlecone pines. From Sunrise Point follow the **Rim Trail** ½ mile back to your car at Sunset Point.

The Drive to Rainbow Point

17 miles; 3 hours to a half day

Following the edge of the gently tilted plateau, a scenic drive ascends over 1,000 feet to **Rainbow Point,** the plateau's southernmost reach. Before beginning the drive, be sure to see **Fairyland Point.**

Just after you enter the park boundaries, but before the entrance station, is a mile-long spur road leading to the Fairyland overlook. The temptation is to leave this for later, but here you see one of the finest vistas in the park. In colorful array, spires and monoliths rise close at

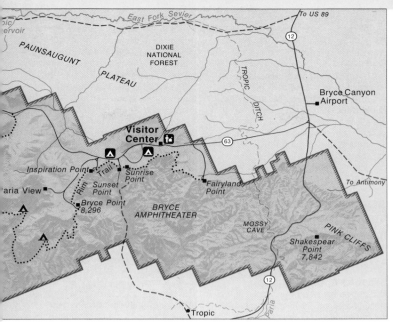

Exploring Bryce Canyon on horseback

hand. Some stand isolated like chess pieces; others group together like a Greek chorus. A short hike down the trail takes you right among them—a quick immersion course in the effects of erosion.

When you return to your car, drive past the Sunset Point turnoff (trailers are not allowed beyond here) and on past the Bryce Point turnoff. You leave the ponderosa pine forest behind and quickly find yourself among the high-elevation Douglas-fir and blue spruce.

Pull in at **Farview Point** for a panoramic view of **Table Cliffs** and a series of broad platforms stairstepping southeast to the **Kaibab Plateau** at the North Rim of the **Grand Canyon.**

Continue south to **Natural Bridge** pull-off. Here you have a closeup view of a natural arch 85 feet long and 125 feet high. Its bright rusty red contrasts with the deep green of the trees below and the deep blue of the sky above.

The next pull-off is **Agua Canyon,** one of the finest vistas in the park. Massive hoodoos stand close to the rim; farther off are the vividly colored **Pink Cliffs;** and on the far horizon is the domed profile of **Navajo Mountain,** over 10,000 feet high.

Continue to the end of the road at **Rainbow Point.** Stop here for a picnic among the thick stands of fir on the park's highest elevation, 9,105 feet. A pleasant mile walk follows the **Bristlecone Loop Trail** to expansive views. A spur trail leads to more views at **Yovimpa Point;** the cliffs that descend from there in stairsteps are named for their rock colors—pink, gray, white, vermilion, and chocolate. A stand of ancient bristlecone pines grows on the exposed edge of the plateau; the oldest in the park has been alive for more than 1,500 years.

Acoustic studies have found that the natural silence here equals the quality of a sound studio. Park air is superb, too. But rangers worry that this purity will be threatened by possible development on adjacent lands.

Information & Activities

Headquarters
Bryce Canyon, Utah 84717. Phone (801) 834-5322.

Seasons & Accessibility
Park open year-round. Roads may be closed for short periods during and immediately after snowstorms. Some spur roads closed in winter to permit cross-country skiing. Phone headquarters for information.

Visitor & Information Centers
Visitor Center on main road, 1 mile inside park boundary, open all year except Christmas. Call headquarters number for visitor information.

Entrance Fees
$5 per car per week, $2 per person on foot or bus, multiple entries.

Facilities for Disabled
Visitor Center partially accessible to wheelchairs; all viewpoints and a ½-mile stretch of trail between Sunset and Sunrise Points also accessible.

Things to Do
Free naturalist-led activities (summer): prairie dog and other nature walks, history and geology talks, evening programs, night sky programs, moonlight walks. Also, hiking, horseback trail rides (inquire at Bryce Lodge or call 801-834-5219), cross-country skiing, snowshoeing.

Overnight Backpacking
Allowed only on the Under-the-Rim Trail near Bryce Point. Free permits available from Visitor Center or from Nature Center in summer.

Campgrounds
Two campgrounds; 14-day limit. Part of **North** open all year. **Sunset** open May to Sept. 30. Both first come, first served. Fees $6 per night. Showers nearby. Tent and RV sites; no hookups. **Sunset Group Campground;** reservations suggested; contact park. Food services in park.

Hotels, Motels, & Inns
(unless otherwise noted, rates are for 2 persons in a double room, high season)
INSIDE THE PARK:
Bryce Canyon Lodge (south of Utah Hwy. 12 on Utah 63) TW Services, Inc., P.O. Box 400, Cedar City, Utah 84720. (801) 586-7686 or (801) 834-5361. Cabins, rooms, suites. $63-$100. Rest. Open April through Oct.
OUTSIDE THE PARK:
In Bryce, Utah 84764:
Best Western Ruby's Inn (on Utah 63). (800) 528-1234 or (801) 834-5341. 216 units, 2 kitchenettes. $68. AC, pool, rest. **Bryce Canyon Pines Motel** (on Utah 12) P.O. Box 43. (801) 834-5441. 45 rooms; 7 cabins, 2 kitchenettes. $60-$75. AC, pool, rest. **Bryce Village Resort** (on Utah 12) P.O. Box 6. (801) 834-5303. 20 cabins; 56 rooms. $45-$65. AC, pool, restaurant.
In Panguitch, Utah 84759:
Best Western New Western Motel (180 East Center St.) P.O. Box 73. (800) 528-1234 or (801) 676-8876. 37 units. $55-$58. AC, pool. **Color Country Motel** (526 N. Main St.) P.O. Box 163. (801) 676-2386. 26 units. $35-$48. AC, pool. Open all year. **Sands Motel** (390 N. Main St.) P.O. Box 593. (801) 676-8874. 32 units. $52-$80. AC, pool. Open May 1 to Nov. 1.

Excursions

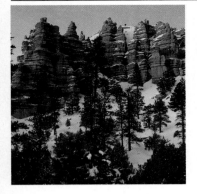

Dixie National Forest
Cedar City, Utah
Four sections of this canyon-country forest fan out across southwestern Utah, featuring unusual rock formations, "stands" of petrified forest, and sections of the historic Spanish Trail. 1,967,129 acres. Facilities include 555 campsites, hiking, boating, boat ramp, fishing, horseback riding, hunting, picnic areas, scenic drives, winter sports, water sports. Open year-round; most campsites open May-October. Information at Cedar City on I-15, about 70 miles from Bryce Canyon NP. (801) 586-2421.

Cedar Breaks National Monument
Cedar City, Utah
Erosion carved an immense amphitheater in a 10,000-foot southern Utah plateau; in it are extraordinary rock shapes colored red, purple, and yellow by iron and manganese. 6,155 acres. Facilities include 30 campsites, hiking, picnic areas, scenic drives, winter sports, handicapped access. Services, roads, closed late fall and winter. Visitor center on Utah 143, about 60 miles from Bryce Canyon NP. (801) 586-9451.

Fishlake National Forest
Richfield, Utah
Fish Lake, hopping with splake and trout (including 35-pound Mackinaw) is only one attraction of this region of dense forests, mountains, and plateaus. The Skyline Trail winds through its 12,000-foot peaks and the largest known village of the prehistoric Fremont people lies within its boundaries. 1,424,524 acres. Facilities include 300 campsites, food services, hiking, boating, boat ramp, bicycling, fishing, horseback riding, hunting, scenic drives, winter sports, handicapped access. Open year-round; most campsites open May-October. Information at Richfield on US 89, about 80 miles from Bryce Canyon NP. (801) 896-4491.

Monument Basin from Grand View Point, Island in the Sky

Canyonlands

Utah

Established September 12, 1964

337,570 acres

From the rim you glimpse only segments of the Green River and the Colorado River, which flow together at the heart of Canyonlands. But everywhere you see the water's work: canyon mazes, unbroken scarps, sandstone pillars.

The paths of the merging rivers divide the park into three districts. The high mesa known as the Island in the Sky rises as a headland 2,000 feet above the confluence. Below to the east is The Needles, where red and white banded pinnacles tower 400 feet over grassy parks and sheer-walled valleys. A fine confusion of clefts and spires across the river to the west marks The Maze, a remote region of pristine solitude.

On every side the ground drops in great stairsteps. Flat benchlands end abruptly in rock walls on one side and sheer drops on the other. It is a right-angled country of standing rock, and only a few paved roads probe the edges of the park's 527 square miles.

Sandstone layers of varying hardness comprise Canyonland's visible rock. But the character of the land is largely shaped by underlying salt deposits, which, under tremendous pressure from the rock above, push upward, forming domes that fracture the surface. Because salt domes are easy to mine and seal, a dome just outside the park has been studied as a possible nuclear waste repository.

Yearly rainfall averages 8 inches but varies greatly from year to year. Trees that grow here have to be tough and resilient. In drought

How to Visit
The park's isolation and preponderance of backcountry make visiting a spectacular experience, but not for everyone; there are few visitor facilities and paved roads. A four-wheel-drive vehicle will let you explore. If you have only 1 day, visit the **Island in the Sky** for an overview. On another day, go to **The Needles** for a chance to explore classic canyon country. With more time, focus on the trails and four-wheel-drive routes to **The Maze** and other remote areas.

Island in the Sky
40 miles; a half to full day

The road enters the park just before you cross **The Neck,** a rock span not much wider than the road that connects the mesa to the rimlands.

For a sweeping view of the park's narrow, interlocked canyons and its wide skies, drive right to the end of the road at **Grand View Point Overlook** (6,080 feet). Directly below in **Monument Basin,** stone columns rise more than 300 feet from the canyon floor.

years, junipers survive by limiting growth to a few branches, letting the others die. Gnarled juniper and pinyon pine take root in the rimlands wherever soil collects, including slickrock cracks and potholes.

How to Get There
Island in the Sky District. From Moab (30 miles away), take US 191 north to Utah 313 to The Neck entrance road.

Needles District. From Moab (80 miles away), take US 191 south to Utah Hwy. 211 and then west for 34 miles to entrance at Squaw Flat.

Maze District. From Green River, take I-70 west to Utah Hwy. 24, then south to a dirt road leading 46 miles to Hans Flat Ranger Station.

Airport at Grand Junction, Colo., about 160 miles from The Neck.

When to Go
Spring and fall are ideal for exploring by foot or vehicle. Summer is hot, but humidity low. Snow and cold can make it hard to get around in winter.

Snakeweed tussocks along the Colorado

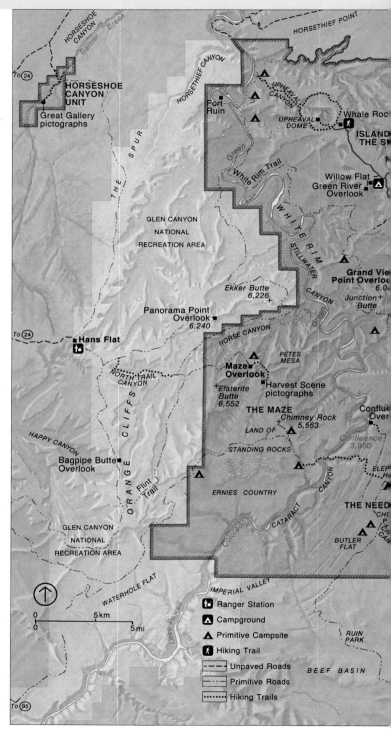

HORSESHOE CANYON

Barrier Creek

To (24)

HORSESHOE CANYON UNIT

Great Gallery pictographs

HORSETHIEF POINT

HORSETHIEF CANYON

T H E   S P U R

UPHEAVAL CANYON

Fort Ruin

UPHEAVAL DOME

Whale Roc

ISLAND THE SK

White Rim Trail

W H I T E   R I M

Willow Flat
Green River Overlook

GLEN CANYON
NATIONAL
RECREATION AREA

Green

STILLWATER

Ekker Butte
6,226 +

Panorama Point Overlook
6,240

HORSE CANYON

Grand Vie Point Overlo
6,0

Junction +
Butte

To (24)

Hans Flat

NORTH TRAIL CANYON

Maze
Overlook

PETES MESA

+ Elaterite Butte
6,552

Harvest Scene pictographs

THE MAZE

LAND OF

STANDING ROCKS

Chimney Rock
5,563

Conflu
Over

Confluence
3,950

HAPPY CANYON

Bagpipe Butte
Overlook

Flint Trail

O R A N G E   C L I F F S

ERNIES COUNTRY

CATARACT

Green

CANYON

ELEP
H

THE NEED

CHE
P
C

GLEN CANYON
NATIONAL
RECREATION AREA

Colorado

BUTLER FLAT

WATERHOLE FLAT

IMPERIAL VALLEY

Lake Powell

RUIN PARK

BEEF BASIN

To (95)

0   5km
0   5mi

 Ranger Station

Campground

Primitive Campsite

Hiking Trail

--- Unpaved Roads

—·— Primitive Roads

······ Hiking Trails

Hidden in deep gorges to the south, the **Green River** joins the **Colorado River**. During his exploration of the Colorado in 1869, John Wesley Powell scaled the canyon walls at the confluence and discovered a strangely carved landscape. "Wherever we looked," he wrote, "there was a wilderness of rocks."

Drive back the way you came, bypassing **Buck Canyon** and **Murphy Point Overlooks**. Turn onto the road leading to **Upheaval Dome,** then follow the graded spur road past Willow Flat Campground to **Green River Overlook.** Here you view a wide expanse of canyon country: Below, a quiet stretch of the Green River runs through **Stillwater Canyon,** with **The Maze** beyond and the **Henry Mountains** topping the distant horizon.

Continue on to Upheaval Dome, where the road ends at a good picnic spot shaded by junipers and pinyon pines. Stretch your legs on the 500-yard trail to the lip of this unusual geological feature. Here the surface drops into a mile-wide crater enclosed by rock strata upturned in concentric circles, with a rock spire at the center. Some geologists believe that a meteorite collided with Earth here. Return to the main road.

Be sure to pull off at the **Mesa Arch Trailhead.** An easy $\frac{1}{2}$-mile loop takes you through a pinyon-juniper woodland to a small natural arch carved from the rim. The curve of the arch frames a magnificent view of the **Washer Woman Arch** and the **La Sal Mountains,** snowy in winter.

Just before leaving the park, pull off at the **Shafer Canyon Overlook.** The short **Shafer Trail** leads along a promontory above canyons gouged from miles of layered stone. In late afternoon, the rocks seem to ignite in the low angle of the setting sun.

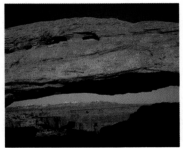

La Sal Mountains through Mesa Arch

The Needles, weathered spires of sandstone

The Needles

18 miles; most of a day

Unless you're camping, you'll probably be driving from Moab, 1½ hours away, or Monticello, an hour away. Utah 211 enters at **Squaw Flat,** a grassy park studded with juniper and pinyon pines. Bring a picnic. **The Needles** area covers a lattice of canyons, flat-bottomed valleys called grabens, arches, and spectacular sandstone walls notched by spires and columns. To the north, **Island in the Sky** and **Junction Butte** stand silhouetted against the horizon.

At the ranger station a dirt road heads north to the **Colorado River Overlook.** Don't take it unless you have a four-wheel-drive vehicle.

Continue on the paved road to the **Roadside Ruin** pull-off. Stretch your legs on a ⅓-mile self-guided nature trail that leads to a small but well-preserved granary used by Indians to store corn more than 700 years ago. These ancient farmers were related to the Anasazi of Mesa Verde and Chaco Canyon. Pick up a booklet at the trailhead to learn how they used the trailside plants.

Your next stop will be **Pothole Point** where a ⅗-mile trail leads past

Unusual pictograph called the All-American Man

Pothole Point, in The Needles

an important canyon-country water source. These depressions fill with water after a rain, and although the water looks as still as the rock, they often teem with life. Snails, fairy shrimp, and horsehair worms lay eggs that survive the summer encased in dried mud. When the rains come, they hatch in days.

The road ends at **Big Spring Canyon Overlook,** where squat columns of sandstone rise from barren bedrock. Here the $5\frac{1}{2}$-mile **Confluence Overlook Trail** climbs the far side of the canyon by a ladder and ends at a point 930 feet above the junction of the rivers. This is a popular trail but less scenic than the $2\frac{3}{5}$-mile **Slickrock Trail,** which begins just before the road ends at the overlook. If time allows, stop here on your return drive for a moderate hike across slickrock balds of Cedar Mesa sandstone.

The Needles' "Molar Rock" and Angel Arch

Turn on the **Elephant Hill** spur, a graded dirt road that leads to the base of a notorious climb for four-wheel drivers. Along the road are great views of The Needles. You see tall fingers of rock arrayed along the skyline, their red and white bands created by the interlayering of ancient river deposits with sand dunes. A shaded area at the end of the graded road makes a good place to picnic.

The Chocolate Drops, shale and sandstone formations in The Maze

Hikes & Four-Wheel-Drive Routes

To really explore Canyonlands—85 percent of which is backcountry—you must leave your car and proceed on foot, mountain bike, horseback, or four-wheel-drive vehicle.

In The Needles, **Chesler Park Trail** leads 2$\frac{9}{10}$ miles to a grassland sunk in a wide rock pocket rimmed by colorful spires. **Druid Arch Trail** branches off at **Elephant Canyon** and leads another 2$\frac{2}{5}$ miles with a short ladder climb to the great arch that resembles a megalithic ceremonial site.

Elephant Hill Trail, a route only for rugged four-wheel-drive vehicles, runs 9 miles to the **Confluence Overlook.** It begins by climbing Elephant Hill's jaw-clenching switchbacks and 40 percent grade and ends with a $\frac{1}{2}$-mile walk to the overlook.

White Rim Trail in Island in the Sky is one of the most popular jeep roads. From The Neck, the **Shafer Trail** will take you to it. It follows a broad bench, lunar white along the edge where the red talus has been stripped to bedrock. For more than 80 miles it stays above the inner gorge, 1,200 feet below the Island, as it meanders through prime desert bighorn sheep country.

Northwest of The Maze lies a detached section of the park, the **Horseshoe Canyon Unit,** entered by a 3$\frac{1}{2}$-mile trail. You follow an old road into the canyon, then walk up **Barrier Creek** past some of the continent's finest prehistoric rock art. At the **Great Gallery,** ghostly figures painted in red ocher stare through hollow eyes as the centuries pass. Archaeologists believe these life-size pictographs may be more than 3,000, perhaps as much as 6,000, years old.

The **Maze Overlook** can be reached by a 14-mile hike beginning at **North Trail Canyon,** 3$\frac{1}{2}$ rough miles past **Hans Flat Ranger Station.** Reaching the trailhead can be an adventure, but the views from the rim of this isolated wedge of canyon country make it worth the effort. And the quiet is as expansive as the vistas. The trail passes north of **Elaterite Butte** for a tantalizing view into the twists and blind alleys of The Maze.

With a high-clearance four-wheel-drive vehicle you can drive the 34 miles from **Hans Flat** to the overlook. This is one of the park's classic jeep routes. Negotiating steep switchbacks allows the driver little chance to sightsee, and the route becomes impassable in snow.

Information & Activities

Headquarters
125 W. 200 South, Moab, Utah
84532. Phone (801) 259-7164.

Seasons & Accessibility
Park open year-round. Flash floods
from July through September can
temporarily close dirt and gravel
roads. Call headquarters for information about road conditions.

Visitor & Information Centers
Visitor centers just inside entrances
to Island in the Sky and The Needles, and at the Hans Flat Ranger
Station, just outside the park near
the Maze—all open all year. Headquarters in Moab is about 30 miles
northeast of park. Call headquarters
number for visitor information.

Entrance Fees
$3 per vehicle good for 7 days, multi-
ple entries. Yearly permit $10, also
good at Arches National Park.

Pets
Must be leashed at all times. Not allowed on hiking trails or in river corridors or Horseshoe Canyon.

Facilities for Disabled
The visitor centers and Moab headquarters are wheelchair accessible.

Things to Do
Free naturalist-led activities: nature
walks, interpretive exhibits. Also
available, hiking, boating, rafting
(permit needed for Cataract Canyon), bicycling on designated roads,
horseback riding, fishing (license required). Write or phone park for list
of concessioners offering four-wheel-
drive, mountain bike, hiking, and
river-running trips; and trail rides.

Special Advisories
☐Always carry water when hiking—
at least a gallon per person per day.
Drinking water available near
Squaw Flat Campground in The
Needles and sometimes at springs.
☐Use care near cliff edges and on
slickrock surfaces; falls here are of-
ten fatal.
☐Do not walk on microbiotic crust; it
is a fragile, crunchy, black soil
that is composed of living plants.

Overnight Backpacking
Permits required. They are free and
can be obtained in person at visitor
centers, ranger stations, and park
headquarters. Campsites along the
White Rim Trail, in Island in the
Sky, are available to mountain bikers
and campers in four-wheel-drive
high-clearance vehicles; limits on
group size and length of stay; reserve by writing park, Attention:
White Rim Reservations.

Campgrounds
Two campgrounds, **Squaw Flat** and
Willow Flat, both with 14-day limit.
Open all year, first come, first
served; May to October filled by mid-
day. Fees: None to $6 per night. No
showers. Tent and RV sites; no hookups. Three group campsites in The
Needles; reservations required; contact park headquarters. No food services inside park.

Hotels, Motels, & Inns
*(unless otherwise noted, rates are for 2
persons in a double room, high season)*
In Moab, Utah 84532:
Best Western Green Well Motel 105 S.
Main Street. (800) 528-1234 or (801)
259-6151. 72 units. $82. AC, pool,
restaurant. **Cedar Breaks Condos**
Center and Fourth East. (801) 259-
7830. 6 2-bedroom units, all with full
kitchens. $60. AC. **Moab Travelodge**
550 S. Main Street. (800) 255-3050.
56 units. $62-$66. AC, pool, restaurant. **Pack Creek Ranch** (15 mi. SE of
Moab, off LaSal Mountain Loop Rd.)
P.O. Box 1270. (801) 259-5505. Cabins, houses, bunkhouses. $80-$125
per person. Includes all meals, trail
rides. Pool. **Ramada Inn—Moab** 182 S.
Main Street. (800) 228-2828 or (801)
259-7141. 84 units. $79. AC, pool,
restaurant.
In Monticello, Utah 84535:
Best Western Wayside Inn P.O. Box
699. (800) 528-1234 or (801) 587-2261.
35 units. $55-$59. AC, pool.
Triangle H Motel P.O. Box 876. (800)
657-6622 or (801) 587-2274. 26 units.
$36-$52. AC, rest. Open all year.

*For other area accommodations, con-
tact Utah's Canyonlands Region, P.O.
Box 550-R9, Moab, Utah 84532. (800)
635-MOAB or (801) 259-8825.*

Excursions

Westwater Canyon
Moab, Utah

The names of the white-water rapids on this 17-mile section of the Colorado River tell all: Funnel Falls, Skull, Sock-it-to-Me, Last Chance. Only experienced boaters should attempt them; permits and reservations required. Sights include natural arches, mining ruins, a desperadoes' hideout, and many bird species. Facilities: primitive camping, hiking, boating, boat ramp, fishing, picnic areas, swimming. Open all year. Info. (mid-April to Sept. 30) at Westwater, about 80 miles NE of Canyonlands NP. (801) 259-8193.

Henry Mountains Buffalo Herd
Hanksville, Utah

Normally plains animals, the 400 or so bison of this herd roam to 11,000 feet in summer. 150,000 acres. Facilities include 3 campgrounds, many primitive campsites, hiking, climbing, horseback riding, hunting, picnic areas, rockhounding, scenic drives. Open all year. Info. at Hanksville BLM, junct. of Hwys. 24 and 95, about 110 miles west of Canyonlands NP. (801) 542-3461.

Natural Bridges National Monument
Lake Powell, Utah

Three natural bridges here represent different states of development: youth, maturity, and old age. First discovered by white men in 1883, the three bridges bear Hopi names: Sipapu, Kachina, and Owachomo. Site also features Anasazi ruins and the world's largest photovoltaic power system. 7,779 acres. Facilities: 1 campground, primitive campsites, picnic areas, scenic drives. Trails closed in winter; campsites open all year, but snow covered in winter. Visitor center on Utah 275, 5 miles off US 95, about 95 miles from Canyonlands NP. (801) 259-5174.

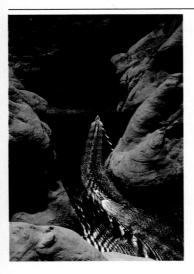

Glen Canyon
National Recreation Area ·

Page, Arizona

The centerpiece of Glen Canyon NRA is Lake Powell, 186 miles of the Colorado River backed up behind one of the world's highest dams. The lake and the desert and canyons around it offer memorable experiences for boaters, anglers, hikers, and campers. Fishing for bass, black crappie, catfish, walleye available; trout thrive below the dam. Free dam tours. 1,245,855 acres, most in Utah. Facilities: tent and RV campsites, 6 marinas, lodging, food services, boating (rentals available), boat ramp, fishing, hunting, picnic areas, water sports, handicapped access. Area and campsites open all year. Adjoins Canyonlands NP on south. (602) 645-2471.

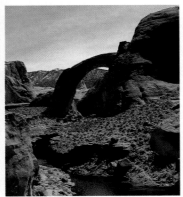

Rainbow Bridge
National Monument

Page, Arizona

To the Navajo this 290-foot-high pink sandstone bridge is a sacred "rainbow of stone." Rough foot- or horse-trails lead to it through the Navajo reservation (permits required)—a vigorous trip for the fit only. Most visitors to the world's largest natural bridge boat in from Lake Powell in Glen Canyon NRA (see above), via Halls Crossing, Bullfrog or Wahweap Marinas. 160 acres. Facilities: boat dock, rest rooms. No water. Trailheads off Arizona Hwy. 98, about 135 miles from Canyonlands NP. (602) 645-2471.

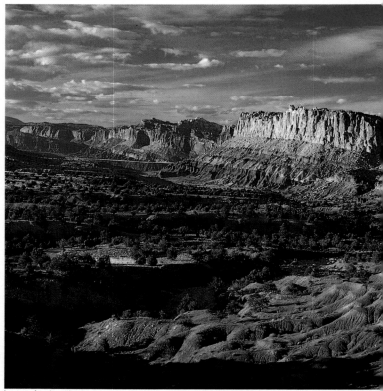

Layers of rock uplifted and exposed on the west face of Waterpocket Fold

Capitol Reef

Utah

Established December 18, 1971

241,904 acres

The unifying geographic feature of Capitol Reef is the Waterpocket Fold. For a hundred miles its parallel ridges rise from the desert like the swell of giant waves rolling toward shore. Exposed edges of the uplift have eroded into a slickrock wilderness of massive domes, cliffs, and a maze of twisting canyons.

Geologists know the fold as one of the largest and best exposed monoclines in North America. Travelers know it as a place of dramatic beauty so remote that the nearest traffic light is 78 miles away. Although its 378 square miles are off the beaten track, the park attracts 700,000 visitors a year.

Capitol Reef is named for a partic-ularly colorful section of the fold near the Fremont River where sheer cliffs formed a barrier to travel for early pioneers. It reminded them of an ocean reef. Although a highway now crosses the "reef," travel is still challenging for those wishing to see the park's more remote regions.

The southern end of the fold offers fine wilderness backpacking in Lower Muley Twist Canyon and Halls Creek Narrows. Along the park's northern border lies Cathedral Valley, a repository of quiet solitude where jagged monoliths rise hundreds of feet.

The middle region is best known. Here the raw beauty of the towering cliffs contrasts with the green oasis that 19th-century Mormon pioneers created along the Fremont River, establishing the village of Fruita. Their irrigation ditches still water fruit

When to Go
All-year park. Spring and fall are mild and ideal for hiking. Winter is cold but brief. Back roads can become impassable during spring thaw, summer rains, and winter snows at higher elevations.

How to Visit
On a 1-day visit, take Utah 24 along the **Fremont River** and then the **Scenic Drive** through the heart of the park. This section offers fine hiking on nearly 40 miles of developed trails. The best second-day activity is a drive along portions of the **Burr Trail Loop** with a walk to **Strike Valley Overlook.** For a longer stay, drive the **Cathedral Valley Loop** or hike in one of the more remote canyons of the **Waterpocket Fold.**

Fremont River & Scenic Drive
35 miles; a half to full day

Drive east on Utah Hwy. 24 as you enter the park from the west. Ahead of you rises the eroded west face of the **Waterpocket Fold,** a massive line of cliffs running north and south. After the first few miles, the highway follows the course cut through the rock wilderness by the swift **Fremont River,** named for frontier explorer John C. Fremont.

Take the unpaved spur road to the **Goosenecks Overlook.** From the parking area an easy $\frac{1}{10}$-mile trail ends above the deeply entrenched mean-

trees in fields abandoned by Fremont Indians 700 years ago. Mule deer now graze on orchard grasses and alfalfa, and park visitors harvest the apples, peaches, and apricots.

The most striking reminder of the Fremont culture is fine rock art. Figures resembling bighorn sheep crowd many petroglyph panels. The last sighting in the park of a native desert bighorn, a subspecies, occurred in 1948. Their disappearance is attributed to hunting and diseases caught from domestic sheep. The Park Service reintroduced desert bighorn in 1984, and the transplanted herd has survived.

How to Get There
From Green River (about 85 miles away), take I-70 to Utah Hwy. 24, which leads to the east entrance. For a scenic approach, start at Bryce Canyon National Park. Take Utah Hwy. 12 over Boulder Mountain to Utah 24, just outside the park's west entrance. Airport: Salt Lake City.

Imposing Chimney Rock

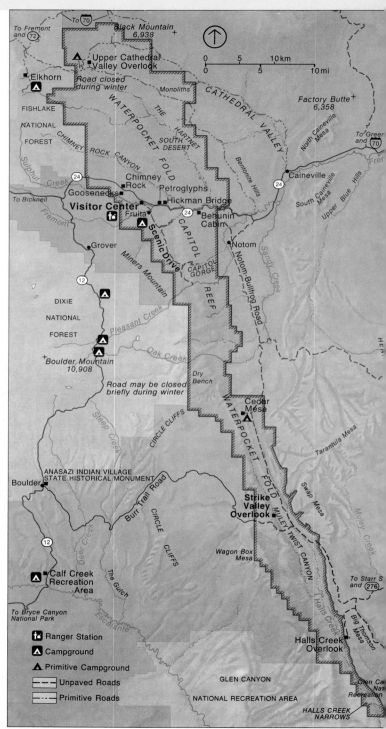

To Fremont and 72

To 70

Black Mountain 6,938

↑

0   5   10km
0   5   10mi

▲ Upper Cathedral Valley Overlook

■ Elkhorn
▲

Road closed during winter

Monoliths

CATHEDRAL VALLEY

Factory Butte 6,358

FISHLAKE

NATIONAL

FOREST

CHIMNEY ROCK CANYON

WATERPOCKET FOLD

THE HARTNET

SOUTH DESERT

Bentonite Hills

North Caineville Mesa

To Greer and 70

Sulphur Creek

24

Chimney Rock

Goosenecks

Visitor Center
🏛

Fruita
▲

Petroglyphs

Hickman Bridge

24

Behunin Cabin

Caineville

South Caineville Mesa

Upper Blue Hills

To Bicknell

Fremont

Grover

Scenic Drive

CAPITOL REEF

CAPITOL GORGE

Notom

Sandy Creek

Notom-Bullfrog Road

12

Miners Mountain

DIXIE

NATIONAL

FOREST

▲

Pleasant Creek

Oak Creek

Boulder Mountain 10,908

▲
▲

Road may be closed briefly during winter

Dry Bench

WATERPOCKET FOLD

Cedar Mesa
▲

Tarantula Mesa

HEN

Steep Creek

CIRCLE CLIFFS

Boulder

ANASAZI INDIAN VILLAGE STATE HISTORICAL MONUMENT

Burr Trail Road

CIRCLE CLIFFS

Strike Valley Overlook

MULEY TWIST CANYON

Swap Mesa

Muley Creek

12

Deer Creek

Wagon Box Mesa

Halls Creek

To Starr S and 276

Calf Creek Recreation Area
▲

The Gulch

Escalante

To Bryce Canyon National Park

🏛 Ranger Station

▲ Campground

▲ Primitive Campground

- - - Unpaved Roads

-·-·- Primitive Roads

Big Thomson Mesa

Halls Creek Overlook

GLEN CANYON

NATIONAL RECREATION AREA

Glen Ca Nati Recreation

HALLS CREEK NARROWS

ders of **Sulphur Creek.** Another short walk takes you to **Sunset Point** for a sweeping view of the **Capitol Reef** section of the Waterpocket Fold.

Bypass the **Chimney Rock** turnoff unless you plan to walk the 3½-mile Chimney Rock loop trail or the more ambitious 9-mile **Chimney Rock Canyon** route. This follows a deep gorge cutting through fine exposures of Wingate and Navajo sandstones and ends with a ford at the Fremont River to rejoin Hwy. 24. (Check on river levels and trail conditions before setting out.)

Stop at the visitor center on the edge of **Fruita,** the remnants of the Mormon frontier community settled in the 1880s and now part of the national park. Be sure to see the 10-minute slide show—the view of the red sandstone cliffs from the theater window is itself worth the stop.

Take the 25-mile round-trip **Scenic Drive** along the rugged face of Capitol Reef. Graded and graveled, it follows a century-old wagonway known as the Blue Dugway. The old road was used by Indians, outlaws, gypsies, and once even the devil himself, according to an early pioneer who chased him off by brandishing the *Book of Mormon.* Take the short spur road into **Grand Wash.** Look high on the cliff rim for **Cassidy Arch** named for outlaw Butch Cassidy, who reportedly used the canyon as a hideout. A 2¼-mile trail from the parking area leads down Grand Wash through spectacular narrows to the Fremont River. Another trail climbs 1¾ miles to Cassidy Arch. The Scenic Drive ends with a winding 2-mile spur road into **Capitol Gorge.** This was the main road through the reef prior to 1962. It now ends at a parking area where an easy 1-mile trail continues down canyon to historic inscriptions and a series of natural waterpockets.

Return by the same road to Fruita, then go east on Utah 24, passing well-maintained orchards. Turn in at the **Petroglyphs** pull-off. Here Fremont Indians pecked into the cliff large human figures in headdresses. Since you can view this cliff art only at a distance, binoculars come in handy.

The origin of these Indian farmers about AD 600 and their disappearance six centuries later are still mys-

Fruita orchards along the Fremont River

Desert bighorn sheep, recently reintroduced

teries. Early settlers found what appeared to be remnants of their irrigation ditches, granaries, and pithouses. One unusual discovery was a brick of tule sugar, grass seeds, and pulverized grasshoppers—thought to have been emergency food.

Continue down the highway a short distance to the **Hickman Bridge** parking area. Stretch your legs with a 1-mile hike up a self-guided nature trail that leads under the natural bridge, 125 feet above. For a longer and more arduous hike, take the 2¼-mile **Rim Overlook Trail** along the cliff tops. It ends at a 1,000-foot drop to the Fremont River, providing a good vantage point to view the green pocket of Fruita enclosed in a landscape of tilted rock.

Farther along the road, pull off at the **Behunin Cabin.** This one-room stone cabin was once home to a family of ten. The parents and two youngest children slept inside, the girls in a wagon box outside, and the boys in a nearby rock alcove.

The Temple of the Sun, a butte

Claret cup cactus

Burr Trail Loop

125 miles; at least a full day

The drive begins at the visitor center. Go east on Utah Hwy. 24 to the **Notom-Bullfrog Road.** This dirt road heads south skirting the uplift where rock has pushed skyward at 70-degree angles. The road crosses a number of washes that turn into slot canyons where they cut into the east flank of the fold.

At the junction with the **Burr Trail Road,** decide whether to return to the visitor center ($\frac{1}{2}$-day trip) or take a full day to complete the loop. To continue, turn west and climb a series of spectacular switchbacks to the high rim of the fold. Views of the **Henry Mountains** to the east, and **Burr Canyon** straight below, are dramatic.

One of the finest vistas in the park is the **Strike Valley Overlook** in **Upper**

Muley Twist Canyon. Many visitors walk the $2\frac{1}{2}$ miles from the hikers' parking area through a beautiful canyon with double arches and a large rock window in the rim. Four-wheel-drive vehicles can follow the canyon floor most of the way to the overlook. The trail continues up canyon another $6\frac{1}{2}$ miles, passing several large arches.

Those looking for solitude can backpack into **Lower Muley Twist Canyon** and its miles of fine slickrock wilderness. Bends in the canyon are so tight, early teamsters said, a mule had to twist itself to get through.

Burr Trail Road becomes paved as it leaves the park and continues west to the town of Boulder. Turn north on paved Utah Hwy. 12, which winds over **Boulder Mountain** through a high alpine forest. You join Utah Hwy. 24 about 10 miles west of the visitor center.

Cathedral Valley Loop

70 miles; a half to full day

A high-clearance or four-wheel-drive vehicle is recommended for this scenic back roads trip; check unpaved road conditions before setting out. Follow Utah Hwy. 24 for 11 miles east of the visitor center. At a marked crossing, you turn off 24 and ford the Fremont River. If the river is too high or your vehicle too low, use the Caineville access to reach the valley.

As the road heads north, it passes through colorful badlands of the **Bentonite Hills** and follows a mesa called **The Hartnet** to the edge of a 400-foot escarpment overlooking **South Desert.** On the opposite side of the mesa is a spectacular view into **Upper Cathedral Valley.**

Eroded spires and monoliths of Entrada sandstone jut 500 feet from the valley floor like enormous weathered teeth. The road loops back to the south and drops among the unusual formations, following the valley past the **Walls of Jericho,** the **Gypsum Sinkhole,** and the **Temples of the Sun** and **Moon.** It ends at Utah Hwy. 24 near the community of Caineville.

Information & Activities

Headquarters
Torrey, Utah 84775. Phone (801) 425-3791.

Seasons & Accessibility
Park open year-round. Most roads are unpaved and, except for the Scenic Drive, may close during rainy weather and in winter. Driving dirt roads, including Cathedral Valley Loop, may require high-clearance or four-wheel-drive vehicles. Call headquarters or ask at Visitor Center for latest weather and road conditions.

Visitor & Information Centers
Visitor Center on Utah 24 at north end of park open all year except Thanksgiving, Christmas, and New Year's Day. Call headquarters number for visitor information.

Entrance Fee
$3 per car per week allows multiple entries.

Pets
Permitted on leashes, except on trails and in backcountry.

Facilities for Disabled
Visitor Center, rest rooms, and part of the Fremont River Trail are accessible to wheelchairs.

Things to Do
Free naturalist-led activities: nature walks, evening programs. Also available, interpretive exhibits, auto tour, hiking, fruit picking, bird-watching. For guided daily or multi-day horseback trips and jeep tours, call Hondoo Rivers & Trails at (801) 425-3519.

Special Advisories
☐Always carry water, even on short hikes. Except for tap water, most water in park is not drinkable.
☐Watch out for flash floods between July and September.
☐Inform a ranger if you plan a cross-country hike.

Overnight Backpacking
Permits required. They are free and can be obtained at the Visitor Center or from any park ranger.

Campgrounds
Three campgrounds, all with 14-day limit. Open all year on a first-come, first-served basis. Fees: None to $6 per night. No showers. Tent sites at **Cathedral Valley** and **Cedar Mesa**. Tent and RV sites at **Fruita**; no hookups.

Hotels, Motels, & Inns
(unless otherwise noted, rates are for 2 persons in a double room, high season)
In Bicknell, Utah 84715:
Aquarius Inn 240 West Main St. (801) 425-3835. 27 units, 6 with kitchenettes. $37-$41. AC, RV park, restaurant.
Sunglow Motel (63 East Main St.) P.O. Box 158. (801) 425-3821. 18 units, half with AC. $30-$36. Restaurant.
In Torrey, Utah 84775:
Capitol Reef Inn (360 West Main St.) P.O. Box 100. (801) 425-3271. 10 units. $36. Restaurant. Open Easter to October 31.
Wonderland Inn Junction of Utah Hwys. 12 and 24. (801) 425-3775. 30 units. $44. AC, restaurant.

For a more complete list of accommodations near the park, write or call park headquarters.

Isis Temple from Hopi Point on the West Rim

Grand Canyon

Arizona

Established February 26, 1919

1,218,375 acres

The road to the Grand Canyon from the south crosses a gently rising plateau that gives no hint at what is about to unfold. You wonder if you have made a wrong turn. All at once an immense gorge a mile deep and 18 miles wide opens up. The scale is so vast that even from the best vantage point only a fraction of the Grand Canyon's 277 miles can be seen.

More than 4 million people travel here each year; 90 percent first see the canyon from the South Rim with its dramatic views into the deep inner gorge of the Colorado River. So many feet have stepped cautiously to the edge of major overlooks that in places the rock has been polished smooth. But most of the park's 1,904

square miles are maintained as wilderness. You can avoid crowds by hiking the park's many trails or driving to the cool evergreen forests of the North Rim where people are fewer and viewing more leisurely.

Canyon views are not always clear, though you can see 200 miles on a good day. Increasingly, air pollution blurs vistas that had once been sharp and rich hued. Hazy days have become more common, with visibility dropping as low as 20 miles. Haze from forest fires and pollen has always been present, but the recent increase is traced to sources outside the park, like copper smelters and urban areas in Arizona, southern California, and even Mexico.

It's hard to look at the canyon and not be curious about geology. Some of the oldest exposed rock in the world, dating back 1.7 billion years,

where temperatures reach 118°F, prefer spring and fall; the prime river season is April through October. During summer months on the South Rim, time your visit to midweek, arriving early to avoid the crowds.

How to Visit

On a 1-day visit to the South Rim take the **West Rim Drive** for classic views of the main canyon. In summer the drive is closed to automobiles, but buses take you to the overlooks. The best second-day activity is the **East Rim Drive** tour for great views of the **Colorado River** and eastern canyon. On a longer stay take the **North Rim**'s **Cape Royal Road** for broad panoramic vistas. You may also enjoy a hike on a backcountry trail; a mule ride down the **Bright Angel Trail;** a week-long raft trip through the canyon on the Colorado River; and a scenic flight for an above-the-rim bird's-eye view of the canyon. The mule and raft trips require reservations far in advance.

South Rim: West Rim Drive

8 miles; at least a half day

Begin at **Yavapai Point** about a mile from the visitor center for a classic panoramic view into the heart of the Grand Canyon. Great solitary buttes rise from narrow ridges reaching out from the distant **North Rim.** Far below, a green cluster of Fremont cottonwood trees marks **Phantom Ranch,** a lodge and campground reached only by mule or foot. The museum at Yavapai Point explores the canyon's geological history and identifies major landmarks. If bad weather threatens, duck into its glass-enclosed observation room and watch as storm clouds roll in.

Pick up the **West Rim Drive** in your car or, in summer, board a bus just west of **Bright Angel Lodge.** The free shuttle buses operate all summer. They can be crowded during peak times of day. The drive, which skirts the rim for 8 miles, ends at a limestone curio shop called **Hermits Rest.** Along the way are superb views of the **Colorado River** and the labyrinth of side canyons and broad platforms below the rim. The first stop is the **Trailview Overlook.**

lies at the bottom. Exactly how the river formed the canyon is still unclear, but geologists generally agree that most of the cutting occurred within the last five million years.

How to Get There

South Rim: From Flagstaff, Ariz. (about 90 miles away), take US 180 skirting the San Francisco Peaks to South Rim entrance, or take US 89 to Cameron, then Arizona Hwy. 64 with views of the Little Colorado Gorge to Desert View entrance.
North Rim: Take Arizona 67 from Jacob Lake through the Kaibab National Forest to North Rim entrance. The two rims are 10 air miles apart but 215 miles by car, a 5-hour drive. Airports: Grand Canyon near South Rim; Flagstaff; Las Vegas.

When to Go

South Rim is open all year; North Rim is closed from late October to mid-May due to deep snows. Hikers and mule riders to the inner canyon,

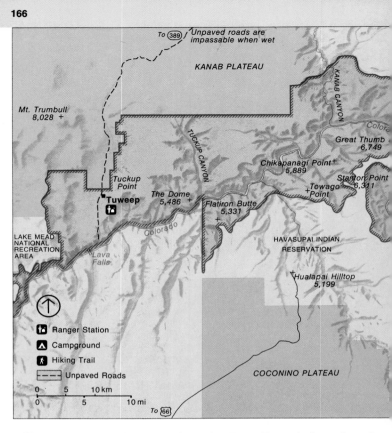

Unpaved roads are impassable when wet

To (389)

KANAB PLATEAU

KANAB CANYON

Mt. Trumbull
8,028 +

TUCKUP CANYON

Colora

Great Thumb
6,749

Chikapanagi Point +
5,889

Stanton Point
6,311

Tuckup
Point

The Dome
5,486 +

Flatiron Butte
5,331 +

Towago
Point

Tuweep

Colorado

LAKE MEAD
NATIONAL
RECREATION
AREA

Lava
Falls

HAVASUPAI INDIAN
RESERVATION

Hualapai Hilltop +
5,199

Ranger Station

Campground

Hiking Trail

Unpaved Roads

0   5   10 km
0   5   10 mi

To (66)

COCONINO PLATEAU

Here you get a hint of the canyon's size. To the southwest, the historic **El Tovar Hotel** and Bright Angel Lodge look small and insignificant perched on the brink of the great precipice. Mule strings and hikers file along the **Bright Angel Trail** as it zigzags 8 miles and 4,460 feet down to the river.

The **Rim Nature Trail**, generally level except for a steep stretch between the village and Trailview, hugs the canyon's edge for about 9 miles from **Mather Point** to Hermits Rest, roughly paralleling the West Rim Drive. The section between Yavapai Point and **Maricopa Point** is paved; the rest is a dirt path. Short hikes can be spliced together with rides by catching the shuttle bus at any of the main overlooks. Bypass Maricopa Point and the **Powell Memorial** for now.

Don't miss **Hopi Point**, a promontory jutting deep into the gorge. Magnificent views 45 miles eastward and 45 miles westward make this an ideal spot for watching sunset or sun-

rise. To avoid crowds, leave the main overlook and walk along the rim trail to find your own observation point. Across the river rise the intricately carved walls of **Isis Temple** and tree-topped **Shiva Temple,** described as "the grandest of all buttes."

Continue west passing **Mohave Point** and skirting breathtakingly close to **The Abyss,** where a sheer cliff plunges 3,000 feet to a plateau below. From here the road follows the sweep of the rim out to **Pima Point,** where you see the Colorado River threading through the deep gorge. On a still day you can hear the distant rumble of **Granite Rapids** almost a mile below. What looks like a stream from above is a river 300 feet wide that, with its tributaries, drains $1/12$ of the continental United States.

The road ends at Hermits Rest, a stone building that looks as if Hobbits built it on the canyon's rim. Those with time and stamina can hike partway down the steep **Hermit Trail** to **Dripping Springs,** 6 miles and

To Jacob Lake

KAIBAB   NATIONAL   FOREST

KAIBAB PLATEAU

Road closed in winter

67

Steamboat Mountain
+ 7,422

NAVAJO INDIAN RESERVATION

ELL PLATEAU

GRANITE GORGE

North Rim Entrance Station

Colorado

Point Imperial 8,803

+ Holy Grail Temple

Vista Encantadora

Cape Royal Road

Grand Canyon Lodge

+ Point Sublime 7,459

• Bright Angel Point

Cape Solitude 6,144

Havasupai Point 6,635

Shiva + Temple

Isis + Temple

Phantom Ranch

Zoroaster + Temple

Cape Royal

Vishnu Temple + 7,829

Watchtower 7,438

PAINTED DESERT

Hermits Rest

West Rim Drive

KAIBAB N.F.

Visitor Center
Grand Canyon Village

Yavapai Point

Yaki Point

GRANITE   GORGE

HORSESHOE MESA

Lipan Point

Desert View

East Rim Drive

Grandview Point

Tusayan

180

Grandview Point

Tusayan Ruins and Museum

Grand Canyon Airport

64

To Williams and Flagstaff

KAIBAB NATIONAL FOREST

64

To Cameron

White-water rafting down the Colorado River

Abert's squirrel

The trail eventually reaches the Colorado River at the bottom of the canyon, but a strenuous 3-mile, 2½-hour round-trip takes you only partway down to **Cedar Ridge**. Even though you drop 1,460 vertical feet, none of the major landforms of the canyon look any closer. Fossil ferns lie exposed in the bedrock on the left side of Cedar Ridge.

Return to your car and follow the main road as it climbs into a tall ponderosa forest. Take the turnoff to **Grandview Point**, one of the finest vistas on the **South Rim**. From the overlook, **Grandview Trail** drops a rugged 3 miles to **Horseshoe Mesa**, where miners once worked copper ore from the Last Chance Mine. John Hance, a prospector known for his tall tales and quick wit, led the first sightseeing parties into the canyon near here in the 1880s. On one trip a woman with a knowledge of botany described to him how trees breathe. "You know," Hance said, "that explains something that has puzzled me a long time; I used to make camp under a big mesquite tree, and night after night that thing would keep me awake with its snoring."

Drive farther east to **Moran Point** for the best view of one of the Colorado's major rapids. Here you look directly down on **Hance Rapids**; its rocky 30-foot drop is considered by river guides to be among the most difficult to run. Continue on down the road, and if you need a change of pace, stop at the small **Tusayan Museum**. It displays well-designed exhibits of American Indian cultures, and the nearby ruins offer a self-guided tour of an excavated Anasazi pueblo from AD 1185.

Take your time when you reach **Lipan Point**, the finest view of the eastern canyon. Here the Colorado River makes a great bend to the west, where it has carved through the **Kaibab Plateau** to form the deepest portion of the Grand Canyon. Below, the river makes an S-curve around **Unkar Delta**, which prehistoric people extensively farmed.

Bypass **Navajo Point** and continue on to Desert View, where you may be ready for a stop at the snack bar and curio shop. While here, climb the winding stairs to the top of the 70-foot **Watchtower**, built in 1932. On the tower's interior walls Indian artist

about 6 hours round-trip. Here the hermit Louis Boucher raised goldfish in a watering trough at the turn of the century. It's a good place to see some of the canyon's 302 species of birds. Permits are not needed for day hikes, but first ask a park ranger for conditions and advisories. Return to the parking lot and retrace your outward trip back to the village.

South Rim: East Rim Drive

23 miles; a half to full day

The **East Rim Drive** (Arizona Hwy. 64) begins just south of Mather Point. The drive skirts the rim for 23 miles to **Desert View**, providing numerous pull-offs for long views of the main canyon. In summer, parking at the major overlooks can be a problem. Along the roadside are shaggy-barked Utah juniper and low clumps of Gambel oak.

Turn off at **Yaki Point** for a fine view of the darkly shining **Granite Gorge**, the innermost canyon. The imposing pyramid-shaped profile of **Vishnu Temple**, 7,829 feet high, dominates the eastern skyline. The practice of naming major park landforms after world deities began with Clarence Dutton, who published a classic report on the geology of the Grand Canyon in 1882.

On the way back to the main road you can park your car and hike the **South Kaibab Trail**, which switchbacks down the west side of Yaki Point.

North Rim aspen in fall foliage

Fred Kabotie painted murals depicting Hopi legends.

North Rim: Cape Royal Road

23 miles; a half to full day

Averaging 1,000 feet higher than the South Rim, the North Rim's alpine vegetation and more varied vistas appeal to many travelers. Still, you won't find the South Rim crowds here. The focus is the historic **Grand Canyon Lodge** built in the 1920s on the lip of the canyon and rebuilt after a disastrous fire in 1932. From its Sun Room you'll get an excellent view of **Bright Angel Canyon** incised 11 miles into the plateau and overshadowed by **Deva, Brahma,** and **Zoroaster Temples.**

Pick up a self-guiding pamphlet from the box by the log shelter near the parking lot. Follow one of the paved trails to **Bright Angel Point,** which divides a side canyon called **The Transept** from **Roaring Springs Canyon.** Listen for the sound of the springs cascading from a cave 3,000 feet below the rim. This is a fine spot for watching sunrise or sunset. Those needing to stretch their legs can take the **Transept Trail,** 1½ miles along the nearly level canyon rim, or a short hike on the **North Kaibab Trail** (1 mile down takes you 650 feet beneath the rim—and that mile back up feels like 3).

From the lodge, drive north 3 miles to the **Cape Royal Road,** one of the most scenic drives in the park. It passes through forests of spruce, fir, locust, and ponderosa pine mixed with stands of quaking aspen, and through meadows of blue lupine and scarlet bugler. Often long-eared mule deer bound across the road, and you might glimpse the reclusive white-tailed Kaibab squirrel found only in North Rim forests on the Kaibab Plateau.

Those looking for a dramatic sunrise perch can turn off onto the 3-mile road to **Point Imperial,** at 8,803 feet the highest viewpoint on either rim. Here amid tall evergreens you look across the canyon to the high plateau of the Navajo Indian Reservation. Return to the main road and continue on, passing through the forested **Walhalla Plateau.** Stop at **Vista Encantadora** for superb views of the northeastern canyon and the carved pinnacles of **Brady** and **Tritle Peaks.**

The road ends at a parking lot on **Cape Royal.** A paved ½-mile nature trail leads along a narrow peninsula past **Angel's Window,** an opening eroded through the rock spur that frames the river below. *Watch your children.* From the overlook **Wotans Throne** and Vishnu Temple dominate the foreground. Across the canyon rise the **Palisades of the Desert.** The unusually broad vista here provides a fine vantage point to watch the sun set and to absorb what naturalist John Burroughs described as Grand Canyon's "strange new beauty."

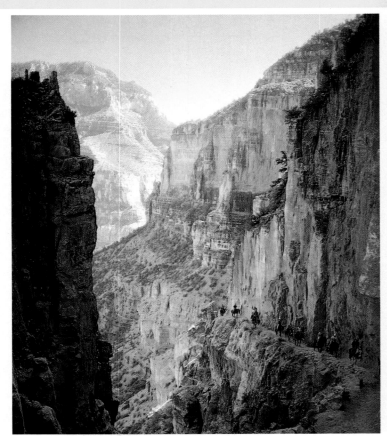

Mule trip on the North Kaibab Trail

Mule, River, & Air Trips

If the extremely challenging hike to the canyon floor (8 miles down the Bright Angel Trail and 6½ miles on the steeper South Kaibab Trail) is not for you, consider going by mule-back. (Though mule trips are not for everyone either—acrophobes especially!) Mules leave the South Rim for day trips and overnights at **Phantom Ranch,** which accommodates guests in rustic cabins and dormitories. The ranch lies in a deep gorge of the inner canyon near the confluence of **Bright Angel Creek** and the Colorado River. The creek's clear waters are known for their excellent trout fishing. The lodge is the only place within the canyon where you can spend the night without camping, and it serves as a good base for hikes up Bright Angel Canyon. Advance reservations—as much as 6 months ahead for mule trips—are necessary.

Many regard a raft trip through the Grand Canyon as the experience of a lifetime. Long, quiet stretches through the scenic heart of the canyon are broken by more than 150 major rapids, two of which are consistently rated 10 on a scale of 10. Most trips stop for day hikes at waterfalls, Indian ruins, and interesting side canyons. A number of river companies offer the raft trips, which generally take 1 to 2 weeks; some companies offer partial trips. Write the park for a list of the companies and reserve well in advance.

Companies giving helicopter and airplane tours are based at Grand Canyon Airport and Tusayan. Flights are no longer allowed below the rim, and because of safety and noise concerns, use of the canyon's airspace is being regulated.

Carving Grand Canyon

What looks timeless is constantly changing: The Grand Canyon's variegated layers encode two billion years of earth's history.

Some of the planet's oldest rock lies at the canyon's bottom. Thousands of feet thick, the rock formed from sediments. About 1.7 billion years ago, cataclysmic geological forces crumpled and uplifted this rock to create a range of mountains that towered probably 5 to 6 miles high. (1)

The tremendous heat and pressure recrystallized the rock to schist; molten material from deep inside the earth oozed up, forcing itself into the rock and hardening into veins of pink granite. Over eons, wind and water gnawed the mountain range into a plain, and a primordial sea submerged it. Again, sediments wafted to the sea bottom, solidifying into rock; magma continued to well up from inside the earth. (2)

About a billion years ago, the earth shuddered again, cracking its crust into giant fault blocks that tilted upward to form a second range of mountains. (3) The rains, frosts, and winds of millions of years wore away these mountains also.

Much of the Grand Canyon rock visible today (blue layers, 4) accumulated over the schist in the last 600 million years. During some ages the region sank beneath advancing seas; primitive shellfish fossilized in sea bottoms that hardened to shale. During other periods the restless region rose. Topping the Grand Canyon today—some 8,000 feet above sea level—is a 300-foot layer of cream-colored limestone, formed from the remains of countless corals, sponges, and other marine animals.

In recent geological time (about six million years ago) the young, southward-flowing Colorado River—perhaps later captured by the ancestral Hualapi River encroaching from the west—began to slice into the upper layers. Gouging inch by inch over the centuries, the river eventually reached the schist 4,000 feet below the rim and continued to cut. (5) Wind and water still wear away, ever widening, ever deepening the canyon's floor and walls.

Information & Activities

Headquarters
P.O. Box 129, Grand Canyon, Arizona 86023. Phone (602) 638-7888.

Seasons & Accessibility
South Rim open year-round. North Rim closed to vehicles mid-October to mid-May. For weather and road information, call (602) 638-7888.

Visitor & Information Centers
South Rim Visitor Center in Grand Canyon Village open all year. Call (602) 638-7888. North Rim information available in Grand Canyon Lodge's lobby. Call (602) 638-7864.

Entrance Fee
$10 per car per week.

Pets
Allowed, leashed, on rim trails, but not below the rim. Kennels available; phone (602) 638-2631.

Facilities for Disabled
Visitor center is wheelchair accessible. Free brochures available. West Rim Drive open to vehicles carrying disabled persons, with permit.

Things to Do
Free naturalist-led activities: day and evening nature walks, slide shows, talks, cultural demonstrations, and campfire programs. Also available, horse and mule trips into canyon, hiking, bicycling, fishing, river rafting, air tours, cross-country skiing. For recorded visitor activities call (602) 638-7888. Write headquarters for list of concessioners offering wide variety of tours.

Special Advisory
□Be very careful near the rim; protective barriers are intermittent.

Overnight Backpacking
Permits needed; issued free by mail or in person. Backcountry Reservations, P.O. Box 129, Grand Canyon, Ariz. 86023. Info.: (602) 638-7888.

Campgrounds
Four campgrounds, all with 7-day limit, all in South Rim except **North Rim. Mather** open all year; reservations recommended March to Dec.; available through MISTIX only (see page 11). Other times first come, first served. **Desert View** (first come, first served) and **North Rim** (reservations through MISTIX recommended) open mid-May to mid-Oct. **Trailer Village** open all year; reservations recommended. Contact Grand Canyon NP Lodges, see below. Fee $10 per night. Showers at **North Rim** and **Grand Canyon Village.** Tent and RV sites at all campgrounds; hookups only at **Trailer Village.** Two group campgrounds; must reserve. Food services in park.

Hotels, Motels, & Inns
(unless otherwise noted, rates are for 2 persons in a double room, high season)

INSIDE THE PARK (On South Rim):
The following 7 hotels and lodges are operated by Grand Canyon National Park Lodges, P.O. Box 699, Grand Canyon, Ariz. 86023. For reservations call (602) 638-2401 or (602) 638-2631. **Bright Angel Lodge & Cabins** 91 units, some share baths. Cabins $52-$200; rooms $31-$45. Rest. **El Tovar Hotel** 65 units. $100-$250. AC, rest. **Kachina Lodge** 47 units. $85-$95. AC. **Maswik Lodge** 280 units. Cabins $38-$44; rooms $55-$90. Rest. **Phantom Ranch** (reached by hiking, mule or raft trips) Dormitories $20 per person. Cabins $54 double. AC, restaurant, shared showers. Mule trip packages from $255 per night, per person, includes meals. Reserve early. **Thunderbird Lodge** 53 units. $85-$95. AC. **Yavapia Lodge** 348 rooms. $67-$77. Rest. Open mid-March to mid-November.

(On North Rim): **Grand Canyon Lodge** TW Services, Inc., P.O. Box 400, Cedar City, Utah 84720. (801) 586-7686. 201 units. $45-$67. Restaurant. Open mid-May through Oct.

OUTSIDE THE PARK:
In Grand Canyon, Ariz. 86023:
Moqui Lodge (in Kaibab NF) P.O. Box 699. (602) 638-2401 or (602) 638-2631. 127 units. $70. Rest. Open March through December. **Quality Inn** (on Ariz. 64) P.O. Box 520. (800) 228-5151 or (602) 638-2673. 196 units. $93-$108. AC, pool, rest. **Seven Mile Lodge** (on Ariz. 64) P.O. Box 56. (602) 638-2291. 20 units. $65-$72. AC. Closed January.

Excursions

Coconino National Forest
Flagstaff, Arizona

The ancient volcanic San Francisco Peaks, Arizona's highest, serve as backdrop to extensive stands of ponderosa pines, buttes, canyons, and plateaus. Here, ecosystems range from desert to tundra. Contains Oak Creek Canyon, spectacular Mogollon Rim, and all or portions of ten wilderness areas. 1,821,495 acres. Facilities include 544 campsites, hiking, boating, boat ramps, climbing, bicycling, fishing, horseback riding, hunting, picnic areas, winter sports, water sports, handicapped access. Open all year; most campsites open May-September. On I-17, I-40, and US 89 about 75 miles south of Grand Canyon NP. (602) 527-7400.

Apache-Sitgreaves National Forests
Springerville, Arizona

Twenty-four lakes and reservoirs and nearly 400 miles of rivers and streams provide more water-based recreation here than in any other southwest forest. Scenic drives along Mogollon Rim, the Coronado Trail, and through the White Mountains. 2,619,387 acres, part in N. Mex. Facilities include 860 campsites, hiking, boating, boat ramps, fishing, horseback riding, hunting, picnic areas, water sports. Open all year; most campsites open April-November. Headquarters at Springerville on US 60, 300 miles southeast of Grand Canyon NP. (602) 333-4301.

Kaibab National Forest
Williams, Arizona

This high country of pine, spruce, and aspen encompasses three sections of the Grand Canyon and boasts stunning fall color. Wildlife features rare Kaibab squirrel, North Kaibab mule deer, and bison. Contains four wilderness areas. 1,557,274 acres. Facilities include 374 campsites, 194 rooms, food services, hiking, boating, boat ramp, fishing, horseback riding, hunting, winter sports, handicapped access. Open all year; most campsites open May-October. Visitor center at Jacob Lake on Arizona 67, about 50 miles north of Grand Canyon NP. (602) 635-2681.

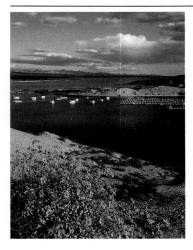

Lake Mead
National Recreation Area
Boulder City, Nevada

Lake Mead, water impounded from
the Colorado River by Hoover Dam,
forms the center of this NPS recreation area—the nation's first—established in 1936. More than 1,000 bighorn sheep roam the desert canyons
and plateaus surrounding the reservoir. 1,496,601 acres, part in Arizona. Facilities include 1,148 campsites, 214 rooms, food services,
boating, fishing, horseback riding,
hunting, picnic areas, naturalist programs, water sports, handicapped
access. Open all year. Adjoins Grand
Canyon NP on west. Visitor center at
junction US 93 and Nevada 166,
about 280 miles from the park's
South Rim entrance. (702) 293-8907.

Sunset Crater
National Monument
Flagstaff, Arizona

Sulphur and iron oxide deposits give
1,000-foot Sunset Crater its permanent fiery glow. Part of the 2,000-
square-mile San Francisco Peaks
lava field, this monument also features lava flows, a lava tube, spatter
cones, and "squeeze-ups," wedges of
rock formed when partially cooled
lava squeezed through cracks in the
surface. 3,040 acres. Facilities include 44 campsites, hiking, climbing,
picnic areas, scenic drives. Open
year-round; campsites open April 29-
October 15. Off US 89, about 75 miles
southeast of Grand Canyon NP.
(602) 527-7042.

Wupatki National Monument
Flagstaff, Arizona

Eight hundred years ago, people
moved to the Wupatki area to farm
the recently deposited volcanic soil.
They stayed a little more than a century and left behind extensive accomplishments, including a 100-room
pueblo, amphitheater, ball court, and
at least 30 types of pottery. 35,253
acres. Facilities include 44 campsites
(located near Sunset Crater NM),
hiking, picnic areas, scenic drives.
Open all year; campsites open April
29-October 15. Off US 89, about 85
miles southeast of Grand Canyon NP.
(602) 527-7040.

Navajo National Monument
Tonalea, Arizona

Around AD 1250, the Kayenta Anasazi farmed the canyon bottoms and built villages in the sandstone cliffs, which form part of today's Navajo Indian Reservation. Rangers guide visitors through the Betatakin and Keet Seel ruins, after a rigorous hike or horseback ride. Reservations required. 360 acres. Facilities include 30 campsites, hiking, horseback riding, picnic areas. Visitor center open year-round; tours available and campsites open mid-April to mid-October. Located off US 160, about 90 miles northeast of Grand Canyon NP. (602) 672-2366.

Montezuma Castle National Monument
Camp Verde, Arizona

Mistaken for an Aztec site by early settlers, this 5-story, 20-room "castle" remains one of the Southwest's best preserved cliff dwellings. Protected by a 150-foot cliff, it reflects the accomplishments of the Sinagua ("without water") people who farmed, hunted, and gathered here between AD 1150 and 1400. 850 acres. Picnic areas, handicapped access. Open year-round. Located on I-17, about 135 miles south of Grand Canyon NP. (602) 567-3322.

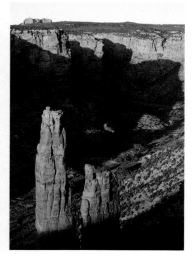

Canyon de Chelly National Monument
Chinle, Arizona

As a natural site alone, these spectacular red-rock canyons, spires, and mesas rival anything in the Southwest. The same is true of their cultural legacy: ancient Basketmaker pithouses, the remains of Anasazi dwellings on 1,000-foot cliffs, and the many reminders of the Navajo past and present. Park rangers and Navajo guides offer tours into the canyons; only the White House ruin may be visited without a guide. North and South Rim Drives have many scenic overlooks. 83,840 acres. Facilities include 75 campsites, 120 rooms, food services, hiking, horseback riding, jeep tour, scenic drives, handicapped access. Open all year. Off I-191, about 230 miles east of Grand Canyon NP. (602) 674-5436.

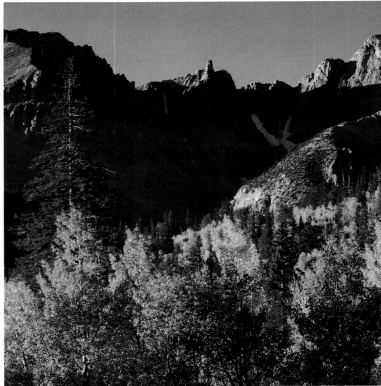

A fall morning on Wheeler Peak

Great Basin

Nevada

Established October 27, 1986

77,109 acres

An Ice Age landscape of glacier-carved peaks rises more than a mile from the desert floor. The park takes its name from the vast region encompassing most of Nevada and western Utah, where rivers all flow inland. Called Great Basin by explorer John C. Fremont in the mid-1800s, the region actually comprises not one but at least 90 basins, or valleys.

The park road winds up Wheeler Peak, the second highest in Nevada. When the road ends at 10,000 feet, trails lead to the 13,063-foot summit and to the region's only glacier, near a stand of bristlecone pine. Great Basin is a young park, yet it holds some of the world's oldest trees.

The bristlecones form the rear guard of a Pleistocene forest that once covered much of the region. Now surviving in scattered stands, some trees are 3,000 years old—alive when Tutankhamun ruled Egypt.

In the flank of the mountain, at 6,800 feet, lies Lehman Caves with $1\frac{1}{2}$ miles of underground passages. These formed when higher water tables during the Ice Age made pockets in the limestone. Here park rangers guide visitors past flowstone, stalactites, and delicate white crystals that grow in darkness.

The number of visitors has reached more than 65,000 since 1986, when the cave and neighboring mountains became a national park. But the park has 65 miles of trails, offering access to the hills and a chance to see glacial moraines, alpine lakes, and sweeping views of the surrounding basin and range country.

How to Visit
On a 1-day visit, take the **Wheeler Peak Scenic Drive** for dramatic views of high alpine landscapes. On your way back, stop at **Lehman Caves** for a chance to walk underground through intriguing passages.

Wheeler Peak Scenic Drive
12 miles; 1½ hours to most of a day

A paved road climbs steeply from the visitor center to the Wheeler Peak Campground at 10,000 feet. Those not used to mountain driving may find both the view and the drive breathtaking. The road passes from the tough, drought-resistant pinyon-juniper woodland into the high-elevation forest of Engelmann spruce, limber pine, and aspen.

Begin the scenic drive near the visitor center. A short trail at the first pull-off takes you to the historic **Osceola Ditch** built in the late 1880s to carry water for hydraulic gold mining. Save this for your next trip, if pressed for time.

Skip the **Serene Overlook**, but notice the old stand of mountain mahogany. These usually grow as a shrub but here reach tree height. Pull off at **Peak Overlook** for spectacular views of **Wheeler Peak** on the right and **Jeff Davis Peak** on the left. The north face of Wheeler drops 1,800 feet to a glacier below. Snow often dusts the jagged walls of gray quartzite.

How to Get There
From Las Vegas (about 300 miles away), take I-15 to US 93, then US 50 to Nevada Hwy. 487. At Baker, take Nevada Hwy. 488 to the park entrance. From Salt Lake City, Utah (about 250 miles away), take I-15 to US 50, then Nevada 487 to Baker and Nevada 488 to the park entrance. Airport: Ely (about 67 miles away).

When to Go
All-year park, but the Wheeler Peak Scenic Drive is closed from November to May, or as long as snow makes it impassable. In summer, the most popular season, temperatures are generally mild. September and October bring cool weather and fewer crowds. Hikers must beware of sudden storms that can catch them on exposed ridges anytime of year.

Spelunking in Little Muddy Cave and candlelight tours of Lehman Caves offered in summer only. Peak-viewing is best in early morning. Good cross-country skiing in winter.

Ancient bristlecone pine on Mt. Washington

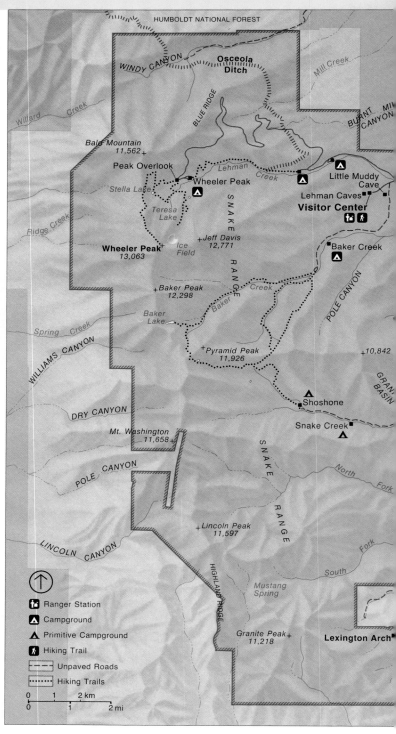

HUMBOLDT NATIONAL FOREST

WINDY CANYON

Osceola Ditch

Mill Creek

BLUE RIDGE

BURNT MILL CANYON

Willard Creek

Bald Mountain
11,562 +

Lehman Creek

Little Muddy Cave

Peak Overlook

Stella Lake

Wheeler Peak

Lehman Caves

Visitor Center

Teresa Lake

Ridge Creek

SNAKE RANGE

Wheeler Peak
13,063

Ice Field

+ *Jeff Davis*
12,771

Baker Creek

Baker Peak
12,298 +

Baker Creek

POLE CANYON

Spring Creek

Baker Lake

WILLIAMS CANYON

+ *Pyramid Peak*
11,926

+ *10,842*

GRANITE BASIN

DRY CANYON

Shoshone

Snake Creek

Mt. Washington
11,658 +

SNAKE RANGE

POLE CANYON

North Fork

Lincoln Peak
11,597 +

HIGHLAND RIDGE

Fork

South Fork

Mustang Spring

Granite Peak +
11,218

Lexington Arch

Ranger Station

Campground

Primitive Campground

Hiking Trail

Unpaved Roads

Hiking Trails

0   1   2 km
0   1   2 mi

Parry's primrose near alpine Stella Lake

Desert prickly pear cactus

Blue columbine on Baker Lake Trail

The road ends at Wheeler Peak Campground where you have your choice of several fine walks. One of the most popular follows the 3-mile **Alpine Lakes Loop Trail** past **Stella** and **Teresa Lakes.** This leads you to a dramatic alpine setting with a barren, sawtooth ridge rising above the smooth surface of the lake.

If time and stamina allow, follow the **Wheeler Summit Trail** to the ridge above the lakes for an overview of the park and sweeping views of

Bristlecone pines worn smooth by centuries of wind, sand, and ice

New-growth bristlecones and needles

Climbing the northwest face of Mt. Washington

Great Basin's seemingly endless succession of mountain ranges. The trail leaves the Alpine Lakes Loop Trail near Stella Lake and climbs another 3,000 feet to the summit. Once above tree line, watch for sturdy alpine flowers like primrose and phlox. And be prepared for harsh weather. A terse entry in the summit register reads, "Wind took no prisoners."

Just as spectacular is the 3-mile **Bristlecone/Ice Field Trail.** This leaves from Teresa Lake and takes you to **Wheeler Cirque,** a glacier-hollowed valley enclosed by sheer cliffs. At the far end lies the glacier, the Great Basin's only permanent one and one of the southernmost in the country.

Before reaching the glacier be sure to take the **Bristlecone Forest Loop.** This self-guided nature trail passes ancient trees with twisted trunks carved and polished by wind-driven snow and ice. Nearby a tree called Prometheus lived for almost 5,000 years until it was cut down in 1964.

Even after most of its trunk and branches die, a bristlecone pine can live on, sustained by very little moisture. The tree holds onto its needles for 20 to 30 years, assuring stable photosynthesis regardless of environmental stress.

Lehman Caves

⁶/₁₀ mile; 1¹/₂ hours

Rangers lead groups through underground chambers filled with intricate formations. Guided cave tours began

Stalactites and stalagmites in the Gothic Palace, Lehman Caves

in 1885 with Absalom Lehman, a miner turned rancher. Over the years dozens of legends have grown around his discovery of the cave.

One claims he was racing along on horseback when he suddenly dropped through the entrance. He lassoed a tree and managed to hold on until rescued 4 days later. The hard part was keeping his legs wrapped around the horse to prevent it from falling.

After purchasing tickets, meet your guide behind the visitor center near the cave entrance. The attraction of **Lehman Caves** does not lie in massive rooms and big drops, but in the beauty of its formations, well represented in the first room you visit, the **Gothic Palace.** The cave is so filled with columns, draperies, and stalactites that the first explorers used sledgehammers to break a trail through them. Because of the cave's manageable scale, you get closeup views of bizarre helictites and delicate aragonite crystals.

The walkway takes you past fine examples of rare cave shields. These large disks grow from cracks in the ceiling where seeping water deposits minerals in flat, circular forms. Continuing deeper, you reach two of the cave's most beautiful rooms. Rimstone pools and soda straws decorate the **Lake Room;** shields, massive columns, and bacon-rind draperies fill the **Grand Palace.**

A small variety of cave life makes its home here, including pack rats, cave crickets, and the rare pseudo-scorpion—an arachnid with scorpion-like pinchers. Bats, however, stay away, finding the cave's vertical entrance too hard to negotiate.

During summer, candlelight tours allow you to experience the cave much like early visitors did. For those who don't mind getting dirty or squeezing through tight passages, there's the **Little Muddy Cave** spelunking tour. Rangers guide you through this wild cave, but you carry your own light and do your own crawling.

Information & Activities

Headquarters
Baker, Nevada 89311. Phone (702) 234-7331.

Seasons & Accessibility
Park open year-round. Snow may close high-elevation trails until late June or July. Some park roads require four-wheel-drive vehicles. Call headquarters or ask a ranger about current trail and road conditions.

Visitor & Information Centers
Visitor Center and Lehman Caves, on Hwy. 488 at northeast end of park, open daily all year, except for Thanksgiving, Christmas, and New Year's Day. Phone park headquarters number for visitor information.

Entrance Fees
None for park. Fees for cave tours: adults, $3; children ages 6-15, $2; ages 5 and under, free. Spelunking tours $6.

Pets
Permitted on leashes except in Visitor Center, caves, backcountry, and on trails.

Facilities for Disabled
Visitor Center and first room in Lehman Caves are wheelchair accessible. Park is new; future facilities will be accessible.

Things to Do
Free naturalist-led activities: nature walks and talks, exhibits, movie, campfire programs. Also available, cave tours, candlelight cave tours and spelunking tours (summer only, reservations recommended), Wheeler Peak scenic drive, hiking, fishing (license required), climbing, cross-country skiing.

Special Advisories
☐Park's high elevation can cause altitude sickness. People who have heart or respiratory problems should take it slowly.
☐Don't expect to find water sources when hiking; always carry drinking water.
☐Watch out for rattlesnakes when walking.
☐Summer thunderstorms are common; check weather conditions with park before setting off on a hike.

Overnight Backpacking
No permits required, but registration at Visitor Center recommended.

Campgrounds
Four campgrounds, all with 14-day limit, all first come, first served. **Baker Creek** and **Upper Lehman Creek** open mid-May through October. **Wheeler Peak** open June 15 to October 1. **Lower Lehman Creek** open all year. Snowstorms may close campgrounds occasionally. Fees $5 per night. No showers. Tent and RV sites; no hookups. Food services in park.

Hotels, Motels & Inns
(unless otherwise noted, rates are for 2 persons in a double room, high season)
In Baker, Nevada 89311:
The Border Inn (on US 50) P.O. Box 548. (702) 234-7300. 14 units. $27-$37. AC, restaurant.
Silver Jack Motel (on Main Street) P.O. Box 166. (702) 234-7323. 7 units. $35. Open April through October.
In Ely, Nevada 89301:
Bristlecone Motel 700 Avenue I. (702) 289-8838. 31 units. $39-$41. AC.
Copper Queen Hotel and Casino 701 Avenue I. (702) 289-4884. 64 units. $48-$60. AC, pool, restaurant.
Hotel Nevada 501 Aultman Street. (702) 289-6665. 86 units. $29. AC, restaurant.
Jailhouse Motel and Casino 5th and High Streets. (702) 289-3033. 47 units. $45. AC, restaurant.
Petrelli's Fireside Inn (2 miles north of Ely) SR 1, Box 2. (702) 289-3765. 15 units. $41. AC, restaurant.

Excursions

Humboldt National Forest
Elko, Nevada

Although some of its major attractions were transferred to Great Basin National Park, this immense forest offers ample recreational opportunity. Contains glacier-carved Lamoille Canyon, historic mining towns, and Jarbridge Wilderness, one of the country's least used wilderness areas. 2,000,000 acres. Facilities include 300 campsites, hiking, boating, boat ramp, fishing, horseback riding, hunting, picnic areas, scenic drives, winter sports, water sports, handicapped access. Open year-round; most campsites open late May-October. The forest's Snake Division surrounds Great Basin NP. (702) 738-5171.

Desert National Wildlife Range
Las Vegas, Nevada

Wildlife, not nightlife, is the focus of this Mojave Desert refuge just a long roll of the dice from the gambling and entertainment mecca. Bighorn sheep, mule deer, coyotes, and more than 260 species of birds are found in the refuge, the largest in the lower 48 states. 1,600,000 acres. Facilities include primitive camping, hiking, hunting, picnic areas, scenic drives. Open year-round. Interpretive kiosk at Corn Creek Field Station entrance, off US 95, about 250 miles from Great Basin NP. (702) 646-3401.

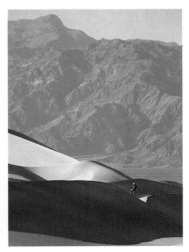

Death Valley National Monument
Death Valley, California

Named by forty-niners who found out the hard way, this 120-mile-long basin is the hottest spot on the continent. Features Devil's Golf Course, Scotty's Castle, borax works, and Badwater, at 282 feet below sea level the lowest point in the Western Hemisphere. 2,067,795 acres, part in Nevada. Facilities include 369 rooms, 1,600 campsites, food services, tour bus, hiking, bicycling, picnic areas, scenic drives, handicapped access. Open year-round. On Nevada Hwy. 267, about 240 miles from Great Basin NP. (619) 786-2331.

Winter at Cliff Palace, a 13th-century Anasazi ruin

Mesa Verde

Colorado

Established June 29, 1906

52,074 acres

At Mesa Verde, ancient multistoried dwellings fill the cliff-rock alcoves that rise 2,000 feet above Montezuma Valley. Unique for their number and remarkable preservation, the cliff dwellings cluster in sandstone canyons that slice the mesa into narrow tablelands fingering southward. Here, and on the mesa top, archaeologists have located more than 4,000 prehistoric sites dating from about AD 550 to 1270.

The sites, from mesa-top pithouses and multistoried dwellings to cliffside villages, document the dramatic changes in the lives of a prehistoric people that archaeologists call the Anasazi, a Navajo word that seems to mean "ancient ones." Some

40 pueblos and cliff dwellings are visible from park roads and overlooks; many of these are open to the public.

Beginning in about AD 750, the Anasazi grouped their dwellings in mesa-top pueblos, or villages. Around 1200 they moved down into recesses in the cliffs. Massive overhanging rock has so sheltered these later villages they seem to stand outside of time, aloof to the present.

In 1888 two cowboys tracking stray cattle through snow stopped on the edge of a steep-walled canyon. Through the drifting flakes they could make out traces of walls and towers of a great cliff dwelling across the canyon. Novelist Willa Cather, a later visitor, described the scene: "The falling snowflakes sprinkling the piñons, gave it a special kind of solemnity. It was more like sculpture than anything else . . . preserved

. . . like a fly in amber."

Climbing down a makeshift ladder to the deserted city, the excited cowboys explored the honeycombed network of rooms that they named Cliff Palace. Inside, they found stone tools and pottery. Later investigators learned that these rooms had been uninhabited for seven centuries.

Why the Anasazi eventually abandoned their homes may never be known. Early observers guessed warfare, but the evidence for this never turned up in later excavations. Archaeologists now think the Anasazi may have been victims of their own success. Their productive dry farming allowed their populations to grow perhaps as high as 5,000. Gradually woodlands were cut, wild game hunted out, and soils depleted. Years of drought and poor crops may have been aggravated by village squabbles. By the end of the 13th century the Anasazi had left the plateau, never to return.

How to Get There
From Cortez, take US Hwy. 160 east for 8 miles to the park entrance, then follow the winding park road 15 miles to Far View Visitor Center and 5½ miles farther to park headquarters area, which includes the museum and main cliff dwellings. Trailers are not allowed past Morefield Village. Airports: Cortez and Durango.

When to Go
All-year park. Wetherill Mesa, Far View Visitor Center, Cliff Palace Loop, Balcony House, and many services are closed in winter. Wildflowers bloom from April through September. In winter, cross-country skiing is allowed on parts of Ruins Road when conditions permit.

How to Visit
On a 1-day visit, begin early and stop first at the **Chapin Mesa Museum** for an overview; then visit nearby **Spruce Tree House.** From there take the **Cliff Palace Loop** of **Ruins Road.** In the afternoon, follow the **Mesa Top Loop.** Wear sturdy shoes and be prepared for some strenuous climbing if you plan to visit the cliff dwellings. Binoculars are useful for enhancing your views from across the canyon. With extra time, visit less crowded **Wetherill Mesa.**

Chapin Mesa Museum & Spruce Tree House
2 hours to a half day

Before descending to the ruins, go through the **Chapin Mesa Museum** located at the **Spruce Tree House Trailhead** and park headquarters area. Here you pick up self-guiding booklets to the major ruins and see excellent dioramas that bring to life the changing world of the Anasazi. Also displayed are some of the Southwest's finest artifacts and Indian arts and crafts.

View the collection of **Mesa Verde** pottery. Decorated with black geometric designs against a white background, the pots represent the highest artistic expression of the Anasazi people. Women were the community's potters.

The park naturally focuses on the dramatic cliff dwellings, but they represent only the final scene in a

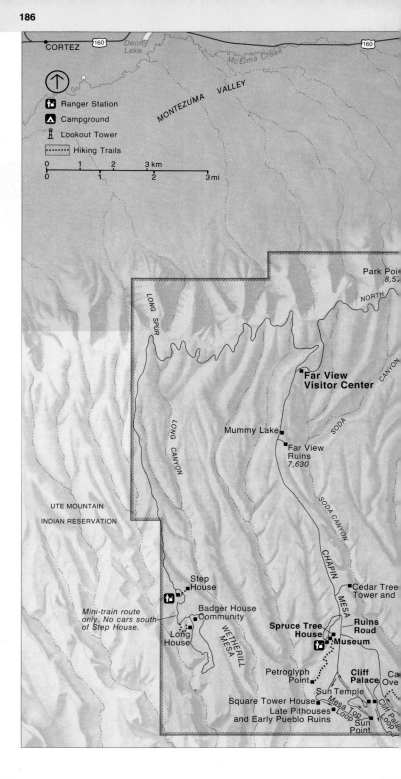

CORTEZ · 160 · Denny Lake

McElma Creek · 160

MONTEZUMA VALLEY

↑

Ranger Station
▲ Campground
Lookout Tower
······· Hiking Trails

0   1   2   3 km
0   1   2   3 mi

LONG SPUR

Park Poin
8,5

NORTH

LONG CANYON

Far View
Visitor Center

Mummy Lake

SODA CANYON

Far View
Ruins
7,630

UTE MOUNTAIN
INDIAN RESERVATION

SODA CANYON

Step
House

Mini-train route
only. No cars south
of Step House.

Badger House
Community

Long
House

WETHERILL MESA

Petroglyph
Point

Square Tower House
Late Pithouses
and Early Pueblo Ruins

CHAPIN MESA

Cedar Tree
Tower and

Ruins
Road

Spruce Tree
House

Museum

Cliff
Palace

Ca
Ove

Sun Temple
Mesa Top
Loop

Sun
Point

Cliff Pala

Cliff
Loo

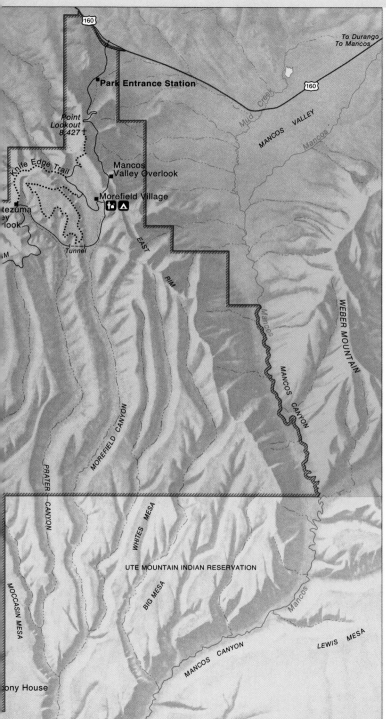

A narrow passageway in Balcony House

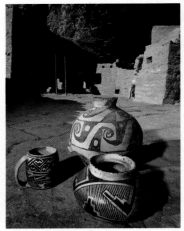

Anasazi pots in Spruce Tree House

long story. The genius of the earlier Anasazi was best expressed not in building but in weaving. Watch for outstanding examples in the museum, including a long sash of braided dog hair still as strong and pliable as it was when worn 1,500 years ago.

Look for an exhibit that hints at the human lives behind the artifacts. Leaning against a display case are a pair of carefully padded crutches, so small they must have been made for a crippled child.

During summer, pick up a self-guiding booklet to **Spruce Tree House** and walk the paved $\frac{1}{4}$-mile trail to the park's best preserved ruin. Here you will see the Anasazi's skillful building techniques and stone work; 90 percent of the stonework is original. Rangers will be on duty to answer questions. (From mid-October to late April, when the park is less crowded, the rangers lead guided tours.) The trail crosses the canyon bottom, thick with Gambel oak, whose acorns were eaten by the Indians. The ruin got its name from a tall Douglas-fir that, it is said, early explorers climbed down to reach the site—they thought it was a spruce.

The cliff dwelling, built in an alcove more than 200 feet wide, housed 100-125 people. Three of its eight kivas—underground ceremonial rooms—have reconstructed roofs. At one of them, you may climb down the ladder through the smoke hole into the dark chamber below.

Either now or later—if time and stamina allow—take the $2\frac{4}{5}$-mile **Pet-roglyph Point Trail,** a self-guided nature walk that branches off the Spruce Tree House Trail. Register and pick up a guidebook at the ranger's office next to the museum. The trail offers a good place to stretch your legs, familiarize yourself with plants and their prehistoric uses, and see one of the park's largest petroglyphs, a panel 12 feet across.

Ruins Road

12 miles; a half day

Two 6-mile one-way loops wind through **Chapin Mesa**'s thick pinyon-juniper woodland. Begin your tour by turning onto the **Cliff Palace Loop** and driving to the parking area at **Cliff Palace.** A short trail takes you to a striking view of the largest cliff dwelling in North America. The $\frac{1}{4}$-mile trail continues down to the 217-room ruin that once housed more than 200 Indians.

Pick up a self-guiding booklet and see the site at your own pace; rangers are posted to answer questions. Inside the square tower, be sure to look high at walls still decorated with painted designs.

The Anasazi built their dwellings in natural shelters formed by water percolating down through the sandstone. Where it reaches the denser shale layer, it seeps horizontally through the canyon wall, forming springs. These weaken the overlying rock, eroding the cliff face into eye-shaped alcoves.

Continue driving to the **Balcony House** parking area. This 40-room dwelling is one of the highlights of the park. The line to enter it can be long in summer. But it is not for everyone. *Acrophobes and claustrophobes beware!*

Rangers guide adventurous groups up a 32-foot ladder to an easily defended ledge ruin and a panoramic view of **Soda Canyon.** To leave Balcony House, you must crawl through a tunnel on your hands and knees. Balcony House is closed in winter; you can view it then from a promontory at the end of the ³/₄-mile **Soda Canyon Overlook Trail.**

Keep going along the road until the junction with the **Mesa Top Loop,** where you turn left. Stop at the first pull-off to pick up a guide booklet and continue on to the **Square Tower House** overlook. A 500-foot trail leads to a dramatic viewpoint above the park's tallest ruin, the four-story remnant of a more extensive, multi-tiered structure. The site itself is not open to the public.

Return to your car and continue a short distance to the **Late Pithouse** and **Early Pueblo Ruins** pull-off. The squarish, sunken pithouses, earliest of Mesa Verde's permanent dwellings, were forerunners of the kivas. Farther along the trail are the excavated remains of three villages built on the same site between AD 900 and 1075. They show the evolution in Anasazi style, from post-and-adobe construction to stone masonry.

Drive to **Sun Point Overlook,** saving **Sun Point Pueblo** for your next trip. Here at the junction of **Fewkes Canyon** and **Cliff Canyon** you see a dozen cliff dwellings—among them, distant views of Cliff Palace to the northeast; **Sunset House** perched on a high rock ledge to the east; and **Mummy House,** directly across the canyon. The house was named for the naturally desiccated mummy of a child discovered there.

Continue past **Oak Tree House** and **Fire Temple** pull-offs to **Sun Temple.** Built by skilled masons—the stones were molded and their surfaces "dimpled"—this D-shaped structure presents an enigma to archaeologists. Never inhabited, it may have been a ceremonial center. The canyon edge next to the parking area offers a superb view of Cliff Palace.

Sunset on Point Lookout, above Mancos Valley

Wetherill Mesa

13 miles; a half day or more

Accessible only in summer, the **Wetherill Mesa Road** starts on the west side of **Far View Visitor Center.** The steep road takes you to ruins opened to the public in 1972 after an extensive archaeological study. Under sponsorship of the National Geographic Society and National Park Service, several major cliff dwellings and mesa-top ruins were excavated.

Drive to the kiosk area and park. From here take the ¹/₂-mile, self-guided walk to **Step House,** named for its prehistoric stairway. The site is unusual, for pithouses have been uncovered next to a multistoried pueblo built in the same alcove.

Return to the kiosk area and take the mini-train to the head of **Long House Trail.** Rangers lead groups down the ¹/₄-mile trail to the park's second largest cliff dwelling—150 rooms with 21 kivas, an unusually high number. Gustaf Nordenskiöld, a Swedish scientist, excavated portions of **Long House** and other ruins in 1891, publishing the first scientific report on Mesa Verde.

You can extend your visit by taking the mini-train to the ¹/₂-mile, self-guided trail that threads through the ruins of **Badger House Community.** These excavated pithouses and pueblos show the contrast between life on the mesa top and that in the canyon alcoves below. The mini-train will return you to the kiosk area.

Information & Activities

Headquarters
Mesa Verde National Park, Colorado 81330. Phone (303) 529-4465.

Seasons & Accessibility
Park open year-round, but most visitor facilities and services available mid-May to mid-October only. Spruce Tree House open all year; Cliff Palace open mid-April to mid-October; Balcony House open late May to late September; Wetherill Mesa ruins open summer only. In winter, snow or ice may close Ruins Road. For weather and road conditions, call (303) 529-4461 or (303) 529-4475 or, if in vicinity of park, turn your radio dial to 1610 AM.

Visitor & Information Centers
Far View Visitor Center at northwest section of park open daily mid-May to Labor Day. Chapin Mesa Museum at southern end of park, 21 miles from entrance, open daily all year. Phone (303) 529-4475 for visitor information.

Entrance Fee
$5 per car per week, multiple entries allowed.

Pets
Permitted on leashes. Not allowed in public buildings, in ruins, or on trails.

Facilities for Disabled
Visitor center, museum, ½-mile trail at Wetherill Mesa, some campsites, and most rest rooms are wheelchair accessible. Ruin tours are not accessible, but most major cliff dwellings can be viewed from the mesa-top roads and overlooks. Free brochure.

Things to Do
Free naturalist-led activities: archaeological walks, tours of Balcony House (spring to fall), Spruce Tree House (fall to spring), and Long House (summer only); evening campfire programs. Also available, wayside exhibits, archaeological museum, self-guided tours; also, limited hiking (registration required for two trails), cross-country skiing, snowshoeing.

Special Advisories
☐Visits to the cliff dwellings are strenuous. Wear sturdy shoes and use caution, especially if you have heart or respiratory problems.
☐Hold onto your children on cliff trails and canyon rims.

Overnight Backpacking
Not permitted in park.

Campgrounds
One campground, **Morefield**, with a 14-day limit. Open mid-April to mid-October. First come, first served. Fees $7-$14.50 per night. Showers within 1 mile of campground. Tent and RV sites; 14 hookups. **Morefield Group Campgrounds** available first come, first served. Food services in park (mid-April to mid-October).

Hotels, Motels, & Inns
(unless otherwise noted, rates are for 2 persons in a double room, high season)
INSIDE THE PARK:
Far View Lodge Mesa Verde Co., P.O. Box 277, Mancos, Colo. 81328. (303) 529-4421. 150 units. $70-$80. Restaurant. Open late April through Oct.

OUTSIDE THE PARK:
In Cortez, Colorado 81321:
Anasazi Motor Inn 640 S. Broadway. (800) 972-6232 or (303) 565-3773. 87 units. $56-$63. AC, pool, rest. **Best Western Sands** 1120 E. Main St. (800) 528-1234 or (303) 565-3761. 81 units. $64. AC, pool, rest. **Best Western Turquoise Motor Inn** 535 E. Main St. (800) 528-1234 or (303) 565-3778. 46 units. $68. AC, pool, restaurant.
In Durango, Colorado 81301:
General Palmer Hotel 567 Main Ave. (800) 523-3358 or (303) 247-4747. 39 units. $135-$165. AC.
Strater Hotel (699 Main Ave.) P.O. Drawer E. (800) 247-4431; in Colo. (800) 227-4431. 93 units. $92-$135. AC, restaurant.
In Mancos, Colorado 81328:
Lake Mancos Ranch 42688 County Road N. (303) 533-7900. 12 cabins; 4 rooms. $680 per adult, per week, includes meals. Pool. Open June to October. **Mesa Verde Motel** (191 Railroad Ave.) P.O. Box 552. (800) 825-6372 or (303) 533-7741. 15 units, 1 kitchenette. $22-$52. AC.

Excursions

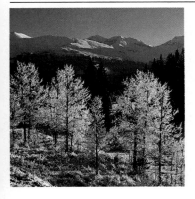

San Juan National Forest

Durango, Colorado

The vegetation ranges from high alpine forest to sage-and-pinyon desert in this rugged San Juan Mountains area. Contains lakes, rivers, wilderness areas, and an archaeological site. 1,870,561 acres. Facilities include 900 campsites, hiking, boating, boat ramps, climbing, bicycling, fishing, horseback riding, llama trekking, hunting, winter sports, water sports, handicapped access. Open all year; most campsites open May-November. Information at Durango on US 550, about 50 miles east of Mesa Verde NP. (303) 247-4874.

Aztec Ruins National Monument

Aztec, New Mexico

Misnamed by early Anglo settlers, this masonry-and-timber pueblo shows the influence of two distinct Anasazi groups—one with ties to Chaco Canyon in the south and the other to Mesa Verde. Features the Southwest's only restored great kiva. 319 acres. Facilities: exhibits, picnic areas. Open all year. Off US 550, about 60 miles southeast of Mesa Verde NP. (505) 334-6174.

Hovenweep National Monument

Cortez, Colorado

Hovenweep—a Ute term meaning "deserted valley"—consists of six Anasazi sites: two in Utah and four in Colorado. They feature stone pueblos and square, circular, and D-shaped towers. Square Tower Group—located in Utah midway between Cortez and Blanding, Utah—is best preserved and most accessible. 784 acres. Open all year. Facilities: 3l campsites, interpretive exhibits, hiking, picnic areas. Headquarters at Square Tower Group off Utah 262, about 55 miles from Mesa Verde NP. (303) 529-4461.

Fossilized logs, remnants of prehistoric conifers in Blue Mesa

Petrified Forest

Arizona

Established December 9, 1962

93,533 acres

A sun-swept corner of the Painted Desert draws up to 900,000 visitors each year. While most come to see one of the world's largest concentrations of brilliantly colored petrified wood, many leave having glimpsed something more. The 146 square miles of Petrified Forest open a window on an environment more than 200 million years old, one radically different from today's high desert.

Where you now see ravens soaring over a stark landscape, leathery-winged pterosaurs once glided over rivers teeming with armor-scaled fish and giant, spatula-headed amphibians. Nearby ran herds of some of the earliest dinosaurs. Scientists have identified more than a hundred species of fossil plants and animals in Petrified Forest.

The park consists of two main sections. In the south are the major concentrations of petrified wood; in the north are colorful badlands of the Painted Desert. Giant fossilized logs, many fractured into cordwood-size segments, lie scattered throughout.

Much of the quartz rock that replaced the wood tissue 200 million years ago is tinted in rainbow hues. Many visitors cannot resist taking rocks, despite strict regulations and stiff fines against removing any material. To see how fast the rock was disappearing, rangers placed a number of invisibly marked pieces next to a well-used trail. Within two weeks 20 percent of them were gone.

The problem is not new. Military survey parties passing through the region in 1851 filled their saddlebags

with its milder weather, also attracts many visitors. Winter in the high desert can be cold with brief snow-storms, but moderate afternoon temperatures are not uncommon. The desert blooms colorfully in spring; winds can be high.

How to Visit
Many of the features at Petrified Forest are on a scale best appreciat-ed by leaving the car. Plan enough time to walk among the fossil logs and **Painted Desert** badlands. For a $\frac{1}{2}$-day visit, follow the **park road** from the **Rainbow Forest Museum** to **Pintado Point.** If you can stay longer, include a walk to **Agate House**, take the trail into the **Blue Mesa** badlands, and con-sider a hike in the **Painted Desert Wilderness.**

The Park Road
27 miles; a half to full day

A scenic drive connecting the south and north entrances passes through high desert grasslands broken by un-expected escarpments and bare hills banded in pastels. Begin at the south entrance with a stop at the **Rainbow Forest Museum.** (Or, from the north, begin at the **Painted Desert Visitor Center** and reverse this tour.) Be sure to see the dioramas of ancient environments, the cast skeleton of a crocodile-like phytosaur, and the dis-play of pre-Columbian Indian arti-facts made from petrified wood.

The museum sits in the **Rainbow Forest,** one of four major concentra-tions of petrified logs called "for-ests." Behind it winds the $\frac{1}{2}$-mile **Gi-ant Logs Trail;** the largest fossil log is **Old Faithful** with a $9\frac{1}{2}$-foot diameter. If you are in a hurry, skip this trail and continue on to **Long Logs.** From the parking lot there, a $\frac{1}{2}$-mile loop trail, taking about 20 minutes, leads you to the largest concentration of petrified wood in the park. Here you see logs up to 170 feet long—many crisscrossed in logjams—and colorful cross sections of fossil trees.

Ninety-nine percent of the park's petrified wood comes from tall coni-fers called *Araucarioxylon,* which looked similar to modern Norfolk Island pines. The ancient trees grew 200 million years ago in distant high-lands, where great floods or perhaps

with petrified wood. As word of these remarkable deposits spread, fossil logs were hauled off by the wa-gonload for tabletops, lamps, and mantels. In the 1890s gem collectors began dynamiting logs searching for amethyst and quartz crystals. To prevent further destruction, the area was designated a national monument in 1906 and a national park over a half century later.

How to Get There
From the east on I-40, exit at Hol-brook, and drive about 20 miles on US 180 to the park's south entrance. Continue through the park, rejoining I-40 at the north entrance. From the west on I-40, exit at the north en-trance and drive through the park to US 180. Rejoin I-40 at Holbrook. Air-ports: Flagstaff and Winslow.

When to Go
All-year park. Summer's dramatic clouds and thunderstorms enhance the beauty of the landscape. Fall,

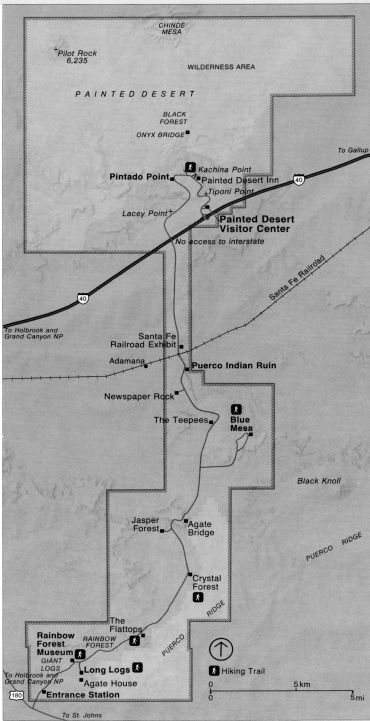

CHINDE MESA

+ *Pilot Rock*
6,235

WILDERNESS AREA

P A I N T E D   D E S E R T

BLACK FOREST

ONYX BRIDGE ■

To Gallup

Kachina Point

Pintado Point ■

■ Painted Desert Inn

+ *Tiponi Point*

40

Lacey Point +

Painted Desert Visitor Center

No access to interstate

Santa Fe Railroad

40

To Holbrook and Grand Canyon NP

Santa Fe Railroad Exhibit ■

Adamana ●

■ **Puerco Indian Ruin**

Newspaper Rock ■

The Teepees ■

■ **Blue Mesa**

Black Knoll

PUERCO   RIDGE

Jasper Forest ■

■ Agate Bridge

■ Crystal Forest

RIDGE

The Flattops

Rainbow Forest Museum

RAINBOW FOREST

PUERCO

GIANT LOGS

Long Logs

To Holbrook and Grand Canyon NP

■ Agate House

180 ■ **Entrance Station**

To St. Johns

Hiking Trail

0   5 km

0   5 mi

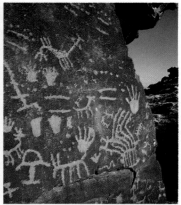
Anasazi petroglyphs on Newspaper Rock

mudflows triggered by explosive volcanic eruptions uprooted them. Tumbled and abraded, they washed into logjams and were quickly buried by silt and ash. Mineral-laden water percolated through the wood, replacing organic tissue with multicolored quartz.

Next, if you have time, strike out on the paved trail to **Agate House** (1 mile round-trip). During the 1930s crews restored two rooms of an eight-room Anasazi pueblo over 800 years old. What makes this site unusual are the masonry walls built entirely of vividly tinted petrified wood and adobe mortar.

Continue your drive north, bypassing three turnoffs—**Crystal Forest, Jasper Forest,** and **Agate Bridge**, unless you have plenty of time. Take the 3-mile spur road that climbs **Blue Mesa.** You loop through strange badlands layered in blue, purple, and cream colors that change with weather and time of day.

The **Blue Mesa Trail** winds along a 1-mile, 45-minute route through the badlands. The trail is paved and nearly level except for one very steep section. Even if you can't take the full hike, park your car and walk 100 feet to where the trail begins to descend. Here are good views of the intricately eroded mesa.

Return to the main road and drive north through **The Teepees,** bare, conical hills carved from blue and red mudstones. Near here paleontologists excavated a fossil graveyard filled with hundreds of metoposaurs, amphibians that resembled huge salamanders.

The trail to the **Newspaper Rock** petroglyphs has been closed, making them difficult to see from the overlook above. Skip this and continue driving a short distance to the **Puerco Indian Ruin,** one of the largest prehistoric sites in the park. Here you see the partially excavated remains of an Anasazi village abandoned in the early 1400s as well as many fine petroglyphs of animals and geometric designs pecked into the outcropping rock.

Scientists believe a chiseled spiral here was used by the Indians as a solar calendar. Early in the morning for several weeks around June 22, the summer solstice, rangers guide observers to the place where a shaft of sunlight pierces the very center of the ancient symbol.

The road crosses the intermittent **Puerco River** that divides the park in two. No permanent streams flow in Petrified Forest, and less than nine inches of precipitation fall each year, half in summer thunderstorms.

After crossing I-40, the drive reaches the edge of a volcanic escarpment overlooking a particularly colorful section of the **Painted Desert.**

Pull off at **Lacey Point,** the first of eight overlooks. Here the bare Chinle slopes are tinted in the shades of a Navajo rug. The colors are especially vivid when the sun shines on rock still wet from a thunderstorm.

Continue on to the sweeping panoramic vista at **Pintado Point**—the highest along the Painted Desert rim. Below lies **Lithodendron Wash,** braiding through the red badlands of the **Black Forest.** In the distance stands the dark profile of **Pilot Rock,** at 6,235 feet the park's highest point.

For a longer hike, walk through the rugged beauty of the **Painted Desert Wilderness.** The trail begins at **Kachina Point** behind the old **Painted Desert Inn,** originally built as a roadside inn, now open daily as a historical site. Once in the flats below the rim, the trail disappears, requiring you to do your own route-finding. Look for the Black Forest, an area of dark fossilized wood, standing tree stumps, and **Onyx Bridge.** Finding the bridge can be an adventure since there are no landmarks to guide you.

The scenic drive ends at the Painted Desert Visitor Center, the park headquarters at the north entrance.

Information & Activities

Headquarters
Petrified Forest National Park, Arizona 86028. Phone (602) 524-6228.

Seasons & Accessibility
Open year-round during daylight hours, except Christmas; extended hours May through September. Snow and ice may close park road temporarily in winter.

Visitor & Information Centers
Painted Desert Visitor Center at north entrance, just off I-40, and Rainbow Forest Museum near south entrance, just off US 180, both open daily all year except Christmas and New Year's Day.

Entrance Fee
$5 per car good for 7 days, multiple entries.

Pets & Horses
Pets permitted on leashes except in public buildings, wilderness areas, and on Giant Logs Trail. Horses permitted throughout park in groups of six or less when accompanied by riders, but grazing is prohibited.

Facilities for Disabled
Visitor centers, museum, and rest rooms are wheelchair accessible.

Things to Do
Free naturalist-led activities: nature talks, movie. Also available, a film, interpretive exhibits, self-guided auto tours, hiking, horseback riding (no rentals in area).

Special Advisories
☐Stay on trails to prevent damage to the fragile desert environment and personal injury from sharp edges of petrified logs.
☐Take nothing from the park but memories, not even a tiny piece of petrified wood; pieces quickly add up to tons.
☐Carry water whenever you hike; none is available outside developed areas.
☐Do not approach any wildlife; park animals may carry bubonic plague.

Overnight Backpacking
Allowed in most of the wilderness area. Permit required; available free at visitor centers or museum up to 1 hour before park closing.

Campgrounds
None inside park, but food service available.

Hotels, Motels, & Inns
(unless otherwise noted, rates are for 2 persons in a double room, high season)
In Chambers, Arizona 86502:
Best Western Chieftain Motel P.O.Box 39. (800) 528-1234 or (602) 688-2754. 52 units. $57-$61. AC, pool, restaurant.
In Holbrook, Arizona 86025:
Best Western Adobe Inn 615 W. Hopi Drive. (602) 524-3948. 54 units. $56. AC, pool.
Best Western Arizonian Inn 2508 E. Navajo Blvd. (800) 528-1234 or (602) 524-2611. 70 units. $49. AC, pool, restaurant.
Comfort Inn 2602 E. Navajo Blvd. (800) 228-5150 or (602) 524-6131. 84 units. $44-$58. AC, pool.
Rainbow 8 Motel 2211 E. Navajo Blvd. (602) 524-2654. 40 units. $35-$45. AC.

Contact the Holbrook Chamber of Commerce for additional accommodations: 100 E. Arizona Street, Holbrook, Arizona 86025. (602) 524-6558.

Excursions

Saguaro National Monument
Tucson, Arizona

The venerable saguaro, blossom-tipped arms reaching skyward, is the quintessential survivor: Perhaps only one seed in 40 million will make it to full maturity as an 8-ton, 50-foot, 150-year-old desert monarch. This monument's two districts protect the saguaro and the many other plants and animals of the Sonoran Desert. 83,576 acres. Facilities include hiking, horseback riding, scenic drives, handicapped access. Open year-round. Information for Saguaro West on Kinney Road, 16 miles west of downtown Tucson (some 325 miles from Petrified Forest NP). Saguaro East visitor center on Old Spanish Trail, about 17 miles east of downtown Tucson. (602) 296-8576.

El Morro National Monument
Ramah, New Mexico

Here in 1605 Spaniard Juan de Oñate scratched his name at the base of a sandstone cliff overlooking a rocky pool. Other desert travelers also added inscriptions to the carvings of pre-Columbian Indians. Two Anasazi ruins sit on the cliff-top mesa. 1,279 acres. Facilities include 9 campsites, hiking, picnic areas, handicapped access. Open year-round, but Mesa Top Trail closes when snow is heavy. On New Mexico Hwy. 53, off I-40, about 125 miles from Petrified Forest NP. (505) 783-4226.

El Malpais National Monument
Grants, New Mexico

El Malpais—"badlands" in Spanish—is a new national monument and conservation area located in the lava beds of western New Mexico. Featuring spatter cones, a 17-mile-long lava-tube system, and ice caves, the site also contains Anasazi ruins and the state's largest freestanding natural arch, as well as two wilderness areas. 376,000 acres. Facilities include primitive camping, hiking, bicycling, horseback riding, scenic drives. Open all year. Information at 620 E. Santa Fe Ave. in Grants, off I-40, about 140 miles east of Petrified Forest NP. (505) 285-5406.

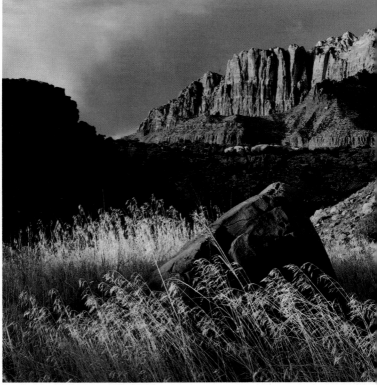

Sunset gilding Mt. Kinesava and The West Temple

Zion

Utah

Established November 19, 1919

146,551 acres

Rising in Utah's high plateau country, the Virgin River carves its way to the desert below through a gorge so deep and narrow that sunlight rarely penetrates to the bottom. As the canyon widens, the river runs a gauntlet of great palisade walls rimmed with slickrock peaks and hanging valleys.

The scale is immense—sheer cliffs dropping 3,000 feet, massive buttresses, deep alcoves. Nineteenth-century Mormon pioneers saw these sculptured rocks as the "natural temples of God." They called the canyon Little Zion after the celestial city.

A million years of flowing water has cut through the red and white beds of Navajo sandstone that form the sheer walls of Zion. The geologic heart of the canyon began as a vast desert millions of years ago; winds blew one dune on top of another until the sands reached a depth of 2,000 feet. You can see the track of these ancient winds in the graceful cross-bedded strata of Zion's cliffs.

Unlike the Grand Canyon where you stand on the rim and look out, Zion Canyon is usually viewed from the bottom looking up. Streamside on the canyon floor grow thick stands of Fremont cottonwood, boxelder, willow, and, a short distance away, cactus and thorny mesquite trees. Vegetation changes rapidly as the terrain rises almost a mile in elevation. The high plateaus support Douglas-fir and blue spruce.

The vertical topography confines most of Zion's 2.5 million yearly visitors between canyon walls. The park

and fall temperatures are ideal for hiking. Summer rains can bring spectacular clouds and numerous waterfalls. Rock colors are heightened by contrast with winter snows, green summer foliage, deep blue fall skies.

How to Visit
On a 1-day visit, take the **Zion-Mt. Carmel Highway** and the **Zion Canyon Scenic Drive** for the best overview of the park. For longer stays, begin with one of the classic walks in **Zion Canyon,** then take a road tour of the **Kolob Canyons** in late afternoon.

Zion-Mt. Carmel Highway & Zion Canyon Scenic Drive
18 miles; a half to full day

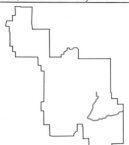

is considering a shuttle bus or tram system to reduce congestion in peak seasons. But solitude is never far.

Within the park's 229 square miles lies a landscape of remote terraces and narrow gorges. A number of these canyons are so well hidden that early surveyors overlooked some that are 20 miles long. More than 100 miles of wilderness trails crisscross the backcountry, while 23 miles of paved trails encourage casual visits.

How to Get There
From Cedar City to the Kolob Canyons Entrance, take I-15 about 18 miles to Exit 40. To Zion Canyon, take I-15 to Hwy. 17 then Hwy. 9 to the South Entrance (about 60 miles). From Kanab, take US 89 to Utah Hwy. 9 (at Mt. Carmel junction) to the East Entrance. Airports: Cedar City and St. George.

When to Go
Open all year, but main season is March through October. Mild spring

Zion-Mt. Carmel Highway (Utah 9) descends almost 2,000 feet from the high mesa country at the **East Entrance** to the **South Entrance** desert. Begin the drive on the east to see the park in the most dramatic possible

Pinyon pine near Checkerboard Mesa

200

way—from a tunnel on the wall of the canyon, 800 feet above the floor.

Shortly after passing through the East Entrance, stop at the **Checkerboard Mesa** pull-off. Here is a classic view of weathered sandstone beds crosshatched with vertical joints. Continue driving as the road winds along the normally dry creek bed. For the full impact of the approaching canyon, turn off at the **Canyon Overlook** parking area. If you are ready for a stop, this is a good place to stretch your legs along a 1-mile round-trip trail. You walk above the winding narrows of **Pine Creek** to an impressive view of **The West Temple** and the **Towers of the Virgin.**

The road disappears into the canyon wall at the narrow **Zion-Mt. Carmel Tunnel**, breaking into the blue sky again $1\frac{1}{10}$ miles farther. The tunnel was completed in 1930 at a cost of a half million dollars and the lives of two men. The road switchbacks down the side of **Pine Creek Canyon,** passing close to **The Great Arch,** which is 400 feet high. Geologists call it a blind arch because it is recessed into the cliff.

You next enter **Zion Canyon,** where Pine Creek meets the **North Fork** of the **Virgin River.** The canyon has an average width of $\frac{1}{2}$ mile, with walls 2,000 to 3,000 feet high. Turn north onto the $6\frac{3}{5}$-mile **Zion Canyon Scenic Drive** as it follows the winding course of the river. Pull off at the **Court of the Patriarchs.** A short trail leads up the slope to a view of the **Three Patriarchs,** sheer faces carved by wind

Isaac, one of the Three Patriarchs, in winter

Waterfall at Emerald Pools

Canyon treefrog

Indian paintbrush

and water from Navajo sandstone.

Back in the car, follow the drive past the **Emerald Pools** parking area. This is the trailhead for a popular stroll on a paved walkway to natural rock basins fed by small waterfalls. The lowest pool on the climbing path is a tiny oasis tucked into the side of the cliff and sheltered by bigtooth maple trees.

After a sojourn at the pools, drive past **Zion Lodge** to the Grotto picnic area, a good place to take a break. Here is the trailhead for **Angels Landing** and **West Rim Trail.**

Continue a short distance to the **Weeping Rock** parking area. Here is the trailhead of a self-guided nature trail (½ mile round-trip), which leads behind a curtain of water showering down from the ceiling of an alcove. Water percolates through the sandstone until it hits shale and then seeps through to the surface of Weeping Rock—2 years after falling as rain on the high plateau above. The strenuous **East Rim Trail** and a branch trail that climbs to **Hidden Canyon** start here.

Drive just past Weeping Rock to a pull-off that offers superb views of **The Great White Throne** rising some 2,500 feet above the river. The scenic drive ends where the canyon narrows at the **Temple of Sinawava,** named for the coyote-spirit of the Paiute Indians.

Here and elsewhere in the park, keep watch for the tiny creatures of Sinawava's realm—canyon treefrogs, pocket gophers, eastern fence lizards. There are also more than 270 species of birds, including roadrunners, Gambel's quail, and the water-skimming American dipper.

Kolob Canyons Road

5½ miles; 1 hour to a half day or more

One of the most spectacular and most accessible regions of the park is also one of the least visited. The **Hurricane Cliffs,** forming the western boundary of the park, screen the great towers of the Kolob from I-15. Follow the **Kolob Canyons Road** past the **Kolob Canyons Visitor Center** as it winds into **Taylor Creek Canyon.** Here you get a hint of what's to come when the jagged face of **Tucupit Point** appears.

Continue up the road, skirting the

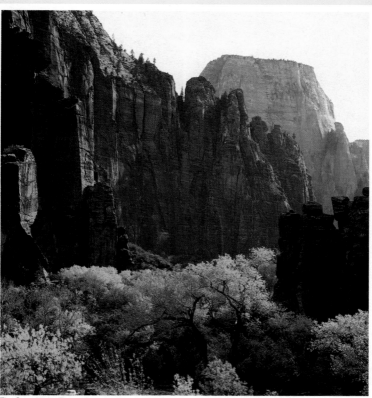

The Great White Throne from the Temple of Sinawava

The Narrows

beautiful **South Fork** of **Taylor Creek.** Each vista becomes more striking as you cross **Lee Pass,** the trailhead for routes into the hidden canyons of **La Verkin Creek.** If time and stamina allow, you can backpack (usually done as an overnight) the 14-mile round-trip to **Kolob Arch,** one of the world's largest freestanding natural arches, 310 feet long.

Drive to the parking area at the end of the road for a dramatic view of the **Finger Canyons.** Sheer cliffs of pale red sandstone lift more than 2,000 feet into the blue sky. Narrow canyons work deep into the sides of **Timber Top Mountain,** connecting **Shuntavi Butte** with **Nagunt Mesa.**

Other Hikes

The full impact of Zion's great carved landscape is best experienced from a high vantage point above the river. The park's extensive trail system gives you a wide range of choices, from walks of $\frac{1}{2}$ hour to backpacking trips lasting for days.

The park's most popular trail is the **Gateway to the Narrows,** an easy, 2-mile round-trip amble. This paved path can be negotiated by strollers

The Virgin River Valley from Observation Point

Mountain lion in western Zion

and assisted wheelchairs. Beginning where the Zion Canyon Scenic Drive ends at the Temple of Sinawava, the trail leads past hanging gardens of maidenhair fern and golden columbine and stands of shady cottonwood and ash. It ends where the North Fork rushes from a defile so narrow the only way to look is up.

Flash floods here are a real danger; deeper in **The Narrows** the walls are 2,000 feet high but in places only 18 feet apart. In the 1960s, a sudden flood caught 26 hikers, drowning 5. Rangers close The Narrows to hiking when flooding threatens.

Perched midway between the river and the rim of the canyon, Angels

Landing provides one of Zion's best overall views. The strenuous trail climbs $2\frac{1}{2}$ miles, at times cutting into a knife-edge ridge that joins the landing to the western wall. Sheer 1,500-foot drops surround the promontory on three sides and allow excellent cross-canyon views of The Great White Throne and down the deep cut of Zion Canyon. *Not recommended for those with a fear of heights.*

East Rim Trail, 8 miles round-trip, is not recommended for acrophobes either. One of the best routes to reach the very top of the canyon, the sometimes strenuous trail passes through a beautiful narrows and winds into the slickrock country. As it swings back to the main canyon, the trail cuts into the very edge of the cliff and opens to dramatic views. If you arrive after a thunderstorm, clouds steaming up from the white sandstone of the western wall look as if the rock itself is evaporating.

Once on top, the route crosses a sandy mesa through stands of pinyon pine and juniper to **Observation Point** with fine views down the length of the main canyon. You stand here and listen to what Frederick Dellenbaugh called "the whisper of the wind that comes and goes, breathing with the sound of centuries."

Information & Activities

Headquarters
Springdale, Utah 84767. Phone
(801) 772-3256.

Seasons & Accessibility
Park open year-round. Kolob Can-
yons Road and the main roads in
Zion Canyon are plowed in winter.
Dirt roads are impassable when wet.
Lava Point inaccessible in winter and
early spring due to snow. Call head-
quarters for weather conditions.

Shuttle bus service available on
the Zion Canyon Scenic Drive.
March to Oct. parking restriction in
canyon for vehicles over 21 feet.

Visitor & Information Centers
Zion Canyon Visitor Center, near
the South Entrance on Hwy. 9, and
Kolob Canyons Visitor Center, in the
northwest corner of the park off I-15,
are both open daily all year.

Entrance Fee
$5 per car per week, multiple en-
tries. Also, $10 charge for escorting
oversize vehicles through the mile-
long tunnel on East Entrance road.

Pets
Not permitted in backcountry, in
public buildings, or on trails; elsewhere allowed on leashes.

Facilities for Disabled
Visitor centers are wheelchair accessible, as are some rest rooms and
trails. Handicapped sites available in
campgrounds. Information sheet.

Things to Do
Free naturalist-led activities: nature
walks and talks, evening programs,
children's programs. Also, hiking,
horseback trail rides (inquire at Zion
Lodge or call 801-772-3967), tram
tours, climbing, bicycling (bicyclists
must transport their bikes through
the long tunnel—check at entrance
or visitor center), river tubing, limited cross-country skiing.

Special Advisories
☐Summer temperatures in park can
exceed 105°F. Always carry tap or
treated water when hiking—at least
a gallon a day per person in summer.
☐Rattlesnakes live here; watch out! `

Overnight Backpacking
Permits required; available free at
visitor centers.

Campgrounds
Three campgrounds, 14-day limit.
Watchman open all year; **South** open
May through Sept.; **Lava Point** open
May through Oct., depending on
weather. All first come, first served.
Fees $7 per night. Showers nearby
but outside park. Tent and RV sites;
no hookups. Must reserve for **Watchman Group Campsites**; contact headquarters. Food services in park.

Hotels, Motels, & Inns
*(unless otherwise noted, rates are for 2
persons in a double room, high season)*
INSIDE THE PARK:
Zion Lodge (off Utah Hwy. 9) TW
Recreational Services, Inc., Cedar
City, Utah 84720. (801) 586-7686 or
(801) 772-3213. 75 rooms, with AC; 40
cabins. Rooms $62; cabins $70.
Restaurant.

OUTSIDE THE PARK:
In Springdale, Utah 84767:
Best Western Driftwood Lodge (1515
Zion Park Blvd.) P.O. Box 98, Utah
Hwy. 9. (800) 528-1234 or (801) 772-
3262. 47 units. $58-$66. AC, pool,
rest. **Bumbleberry Inn** (897 Zion Park
Blvd.) P.O. Box 346. (801) 772-3224.
24 units. $44. AC, pool, rest. **Canyon
Ranch Motel** (668 Zion Park Blvd.)
P.O. Box 175. (801) 772-3357. 21
units, 5 kitchenettes. $44-$60. AC,
pool. **Cliffrose Lodge & Gardens** (281
Zion Park Blvd.) P.O. Box 510. (800)
243-8824. 36 units. $68-$100. AC,
pool. **Flanigan's Inn** (428 Zion Park
Blvd.) Zion Canyon, P.O. Box 100.
(801) 772-3244. 36 units. $36-$65. AC,
pool, rest. **Under the Eaves Guest
House** (980 Zion Park Blvd.) P.O. Box
29. (801) 772-3457. 5 rooms, 3 private
baths. $45-$75. Breakfast. AC.
In Kanab, Utah 84741:
Parry Lodge 89 E. Center St. (801)
644-2601. 88 units. $52-$57. AC, pool,
restaurant. **Shilo Inn** 296 West 100
North. (800) 222-2244 or (801) 644-
2562. 119 units. $64-$70. AC, pool.

*For additional accommodations near
Zion NP, call Kane County Travel at
(801) 644-5033.*

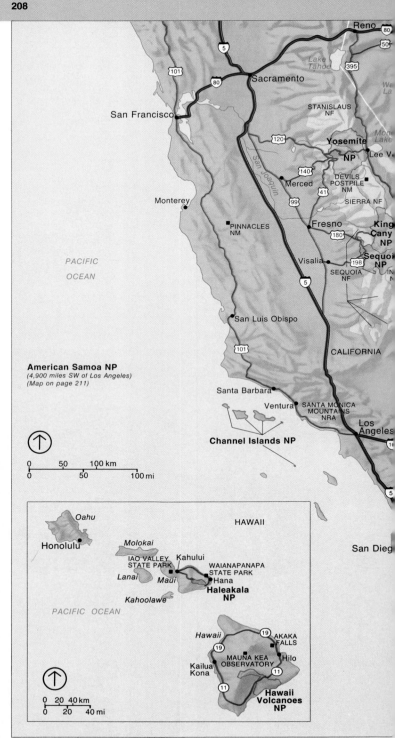

Reno

Lake Tahoe

Sacramento

San Francisco

STANISLAUS NF

Yosemite NP

Lee V

Monterey

DEVILS POSTPILE NM

Merced

SIERRA NF

PACIFIC OCEAN

PINNACLES NM

Fresno

King Cany NP

Visalia

Sequoi NP

SEQUOIA NF

San Luis Obispo

American Samoa NP
(4,900 miles SW of Los Angeles)
(Map on page 211)

CALIFORNIA

Santa Barbara

Ventura

SANTA MONICA MOUNTAINS NRA

Los Angeles

Channel Islands NP

0   50   100 km
0   50   100 mi

Oahu

HAWAII

San Dieg

Honolulu

Molokai

Kahului

IAO VALLEY STATE PARK

WAIANAPANAPA STATE PARK

Lanai   *Maui*   Hana

Haleakala NP

Kahoolawe

PACIFIC OCEAN

Hawaii

AKAKA FALLS

MAUNA KEA OBSERVATORY

Hilo

Kailua Kona

Hawaii Volcanoes NP

0   20   40 km
0   20   40 mi

Preceding pages: El Capitan, Yosemite

NEVADA

) NF

Las Vegas

Lake Mead

15

40

ernardino

JOSHUA TREE NM

Salton Sea

ARIZONA

Colorado

10

8

MEXICO

Golfo de California

50

The Pacific Southwest

Visitors to the national parks of the Pacific Southwest can bask on a tropical isle or climb a snow-clad peak. They can watch the vegetation change from tropical to subalpine in a single Hawaii drive, observe plants and animals that make their home in only one place in the world, and see the earth build itself.

The island parks, all of them on volcanoes except Channel Islands, are microcosms of evolution and laboratories of the effects of humans on the land. In Hawaii Volcanoes and Haleakala, preservation efforts seek to stem the damage done over centuries to the native plants, about 90 percent of which are endemic—found nowhere else. Some 2,300 miles south of Hawaii, American Samoa National Park shelters fragments of tropical rain forest and coral reef as well as an endangered 4,000-year-old human culture. Off the coast of California, the Channel Islands safeguard numerous threatened seals, sea lions, and seabirds. They also harbor some 70 endemic plants.

On the mainland, Sequoia & Kings Canyon and Yosemite National Parks provide haven for a multitude of plant and animal communities in what John Muir called "the range of light"—the Sierra Nevada. Chaparral and wild oats robe the foothills; cathedral-like groves of conifers embellish slopes; wildflowers overrun alpine meadows. Marmots and pikas scurry the granite, glacier-carved heights, some of which soar beyond 12,000 feet; mule deer graze deep, U-shaped valleys that resound with waterfalls. A century ago, Sequoia National Park was established to preserve the giant sequoia tree— most famous of the Sierra's vast numbers of flora and fauna species and the world's largest living thing.

Yosemite and Sequoia & Kings Canyon lie about 4 hours apart by car; another 5 road hours, plus a 90-minute boat ride, will bring you from Sequoia to Anacapa, nearest of the Channel Islands. To reach any of the Hawaiian islands, count on at least a $5\frac{1}{2}$-hour flight from California. An 11-hour plane trip from the west coast (plus layover in Honolulu) awaits visitors to American Samoa, the newest national park.

A fisherman casting his net off Tutuila's rocky coast

American Samoa

American Samoa

Authorized October 31, 1988

About 8,870 acres

For some 4,000 years, people of Polynesia's oldest culture have been keenly attuned to their island environment, holding it to be precious and managing it communally. The name they gave their land reflects their attitude: Samoa means "sacred earth."

Located about 2,300 miles southwest of Hawaii, American Samoa is a US territory comprising five volcanic islands and two coral atolls. In 1988 Samoan tribal chiefs agreed to lease a portion of their lands for a national park. Lease arrangements are still being negotiated, but planners expect the park to include parts of three islands and encompass rain forest, beach, and coral reef. Samoans will help manage the park, and their villages may offer guest facilities.

The park would protect hundreds of plant species in five distinct rain forest communities: lowland, montane, coast, ridge, and cloud. It is the only such rain forest on American soil, similar to forests in Africa and Asia. Among the fauna visitors can see are myriad tropical birds and the endangered flying fox—a fruit bat with the wingspan of an eagle.

On Tutuila, American Samoa's largest island, lofty volcanic ridges overlook the deep blue waters of Pago Pago Harbor. Except for a few settlements, and the scenic drive that skirts the harbor and the dramatic southern coastline, there is little level land. Atop this crumbled terrain and plunging steeply toward the sea on the island's northern side lies the park area—about 2,670 acres

or land, beach, water, and other park acreage on volcanic Ofu Island total about 260 acres, including what many call Samoa's loveliest beach and one of the best examples of healthy coral reef in the Pacific.

How to Get There
There are flights to Pago Pago from Honolulu five times a week that take $5\frac{1}{2}$ hours. Time from California is about 14 hours, including a 3- or 4-hour Honolulu layover. From the airport, taxi or rent a car to the Rainmaker Hotel. You can reach the park by bus or car, or by walking about 25 minutes. Accommodations are also available on Ta'u, Ofu, and Olosega. To get to Ta'u and Ofu requires about a $\frac{1}{2}$-hour flight each from Pago Pago. Ofu's park area begins at the edge of the airport; parkland on Ta'u is about a $\frac{1}{2}$-hour walk from the new airport, or hitch a ride.

When to Go
Any time. The islands are 14° south of the Equator, giving them a hot and rainy climate year-round. The heat abates slightly from June-Sept.

How to Visit
Until the leasing agreement is final, visitors will need to get permission to enter the park. For information, write or call the American Samoa Office of Tourism, P.O. Box 1147, Pago Pago, American Samoa, 96799. Phone (684) 699-9280. Or write National Park of American Samoa, Pago Pago, American Samoa, 96799.

of land and some 450 acres of ocean. Parkland on Ta'u, the easternmost island, would encompass about 5,190 acres of land—including Lata Mountain, American Samoa's highest peak—and 300 acres offshore. Interi-

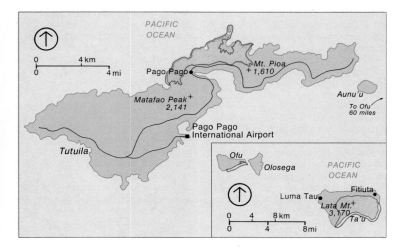

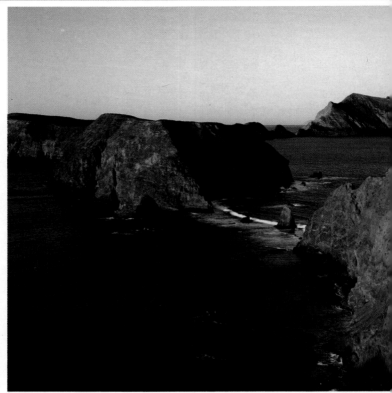

Sunrise over Anacapa Island

Channel Islands

California

Established March 5, 1980

248,515 acres

Strung along a stretch of California coast are five separate pieces of land surrounded by 1,252 square nautical miles of sea. Channel Islands National Park and Channel Islands National Marine Sanctuary protect these islands, the sea around them, and a dazzling array of wildlife.

Two of the islands in this unusual park, Anacapa and Santa Barbara, were earlier designated a national monument, a refuge for nesting seabirds, seals, sea lions, and other long-threatened marine animals. When those islands and three others were joined in a national park, the mission of refuge continued.

Today the park manages a long-term ecological research program that may be the best in the park system. The marine sanctuary, also established in 1980, extends for 6 nautical miles around each island. Among the resources it protects is a giant kelp forest with nearly a thousand kinds of fish and marine plants. The park and sanctuary also guard the area from encroachment by another kind of island—the seagoing oil rigs of the Santa Barbara Channel.

About 70 plants grow only on the Channel Islands, and some plants exist on but one of them. The islands shelter the only breeding colony of northern fur seals south of Alaska. To help native animals, park managers have gotten rid of such non-native species as burros, rabbits, and house cats gone feral. Efforts to eradicate black rats—descendants of ancestors that jumped ship—have been less successful.

When to Go
All-year park. Boat schedules peak in spring and summer, but you should be able to book a trip in any month. Best whale-watching time: end of December through March.

How to Visit
Your exploration of this unique park depends on your time and resources. Even a short stop at the mainland visitor center will give you an understanding and appreciation of the park. Displays include a tide pool alive with creatures. For a 1-day visit, see the closest island, **Anacapa**. Take all necessities, especially food and water, and dress warmly. Trips to the other islands require substantial advance planning. (See **Information & Activities**.) The park cautions people from doing more than treading lightly on the islands, which are maintained for the well-being of the residents, both flora and fauna.

Each island has a permanent ranger. Permits are needed for camping and, on some islands, even for landing a boat. Fishing and diving are strictly regulated and airplanes are asked to keep their distance.

Chumash Indians lived on the Channel Islands until the early 19th century. They traveled from island to island in plank canoes caulked with tar from oil seeps. The tar from such seeps still appears on mainland beaches, reminding strollers of the reason for the oil rigs on the horizon.

How to Get There
Take US 101 to Ventura. Northbound, exit at Victoria Avenue; southbound, at Seaward Avenue. Follow park signs to the harbor and then to the visitor center on Spinnaker Drive. Get oriented here and then go to the nearby Island Packers office and inquire about boat schedules to the islands. Airports: Oxnard, Santa Barbara, and Los Angeles International.

Anacapa Island
14 miles from Ventura; a full day

As the Island Packers boat plies through **Santa Barbara Channel,** flyingfish skip through the waves and pelicans skim over them. Oil rigs stand on dark stilts. Gray whales may glide by during winter trips. Seals appear and disappear in the channel waters year-round. Approaching the landing cove, the boat passes **Anacapa's Arch Rock** and sails close enough to the rocky coast for you to see resident California sea lions. At the end of the 90-minute voyage (which can be rough), a dinghy transports you to the landing platform. Then you climb 154 steps up a metal-and-concrete stairway to the top of the cliff-girt island.

There you can walk the 1½-mile nature trail on your own or fall in behind a ranger who dispenses island lore: That plain gray plant (giant coreopsis) is a tree sunflower; in late winter and spring it bursts into glorious gold. Those finely ground shells you are walking on are remnants of a Chumash midden. The Indians hunted on the island and used it as a stopover on trips to the mainland. The trail skirts the edge of a cliff 150 feet above the sea. Stand well back from the unstable cliff edges. You are

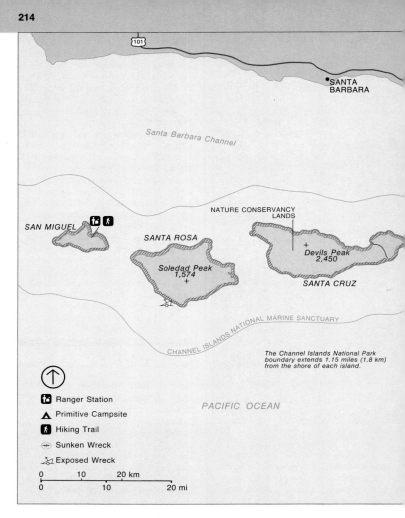

NATURE CONSERVANCY
LANDS

SAN MIGUEL

SANTA ROSA

Soledad Peak
1,574

Devils Peak
2,450

SANTA CRUZ

CHANNEL ISLANDS NATIONAL MARINE SANCTUARY

The Channel Islands National Park
boundary extends 1.15 miles (1.8 km)
from the shore of each island.

PACIFIC OCEAN

SANTA
BARBARA

Santa Barbara Channel

Ranger Station

Primitive Campsite

Hiking Trail

Sunken Wreck

Exposed Wreck

0   10   20 km
0   10   20 mi

warned: *Don't risk your life for a view.*

A building that looks like a Spanish mission church is not what it seems. The structure protects two large water tanks. Vandals who in years past took potshots at the wooden tanks refrain from sniping at a "church." The few buildings date to days when the island lighthouse, now automated, had a crew. Your day ends with a descent to the boat, which picks up the passengers about 3 or 4 hours after arrival; the time depends on tide and sea conditions.

Anacapa consists of three islets. You visit only **East Anacapa**. Scuba divers, subject to strict conservation laws, plunge off **Middle Anacapa** to see the kelp forests or the remains of the S.S. *Winfield Scott*, which sank

here in 1853 with no loss of life. Divers can take only photographs. **West Anacapa** is closed to the public to protect the largest nesting brown pelican population on the Pacific coast of the United States.

The Other Islands

If you decide to go to the other islands, your visits will be controlled by weather, regulations, and boat schedules. Island by island, here is what you can expect:

Santa Cruz (21 miles from Ventura; 60,000 acres) is the largest. The Nature Conservancy runs most of the island and strictly limits visitors. The park is negotiating to acquire

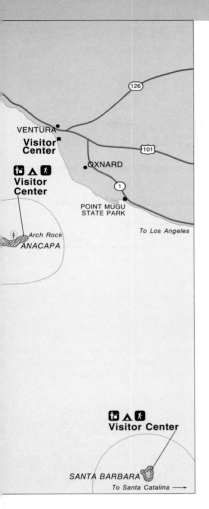

complete ownership of the east end, the end at which Island Packers stops. Among Santa Cruz's distinctive species are the island oak, the cat-size island fox, and the scrub jay.

Santa Rosa (45 miles from Ventura; 53,000 acres) has more than 160 archaeological sites; people may have lived there as long as 10,000 years ago. Ranchers have raised cattle on the island's grasslands since the mid-19th century and may continue to do so under an agreement with the NPS, which acquired the island in 1986. Someday the park hopes to create a "living history ranch" with 400 to 500 head of cattle. A freshwater marsh sustains waterfowl. There are more than 195 bird species on the island.

San Miguel (63 miles from Ventura; 9,325 acres), the westernmost island, is also rich in archaeological sites. Six seal species gather here; as many as 35,000 haul out at times. A bizarre caliche "forest" spikes a plateau. Caliche—a kind of limy sand—encrusted vegetation that died and decayed, leaving the hollow, calcified sand castings. Once used as a bombing range and missile test site, the island is owned by the US Navy and administered by the Park Service, which limits visitors to the beach unless accompanied by a ranger.

Santa Barbara (52 miles from Ventura; 640 acres), once a sheep pasturage, has 5½ miles of nature trails. In springtime, burrows on the island's steep hillsides house the world's largest known breeding population of the remarkable Xantus' murrelet.

Caliche "forest" on San Miguel Island

When a chick is two days old, it waits until night, then tumbles down to the sea where it joins its parents. Except for nesting season, it will spend the rest of its life on the ocean. In summer and spring, you can usually see pelicans and sea lions, but don't expect to see the rock-dwelling island night lizard. It is shy, secretive, and protected: You are forbidden to turn over any rock.

Protected elephant seal

Information & Activities

Headquarters
1901 Spinnaker Drive, Ventura, Calif. 93001. Phone (805) 658-5730.

Accessibility & Boat Information
Park open year-round. Access to islands is subject to weather conditions, which are unpredictable; the channel can be rough. Call headquarters for information.

Anacapa, Santa Rosa, San Miguel, and *Santa Barbara:* Boat trips offered by Island Packers, the park's authorized concessioner (see below). Visitors using private boats must obtain landing permits for Santa Rosa and San Miguel from park. Air service available to Santa Rosa via Channel Island Adventures (see below).

Santa Cruz: Island Packers offers day trips to east end and arranges overnight stays at historic Scorpion Ranch. For day trips to the west end and permits for private boats, contact well in advance the Nature Conservancy, Santa Cruz Island Project Office, 213 Stearns Wharf, Santa Barbara, Calif. 93101. Phone (805) 962-9111 (trips), 964-7839 (permits).

For boat schedules, check at headquarters, or contact Island Packers, 1867 Spinnaker Drive, Ventura, Calif. 93001. Phone (805) 642-7688 for information, and (805) 642-1393 for reservations. For weekend trips, reserve at least 2 weeks in advance.

For plane information, contact Channel Island Adventures, 233 Durley Avenue, Camarillo, Calif. 93010. Phone (805) 987-1301.

Visitor & Information Centers
Visitor Center on Spinnaker Drive in Ventura open daily year-round, except Thanksgiving and Christmas. Visitor Centers on East Anacapa and Santa Barbara also open year-round.

Ranger station on San Miguel.

Entrance Fee
None. But boat fares to islands; inquire at headquarters or Island Packers (see above).

Pets
Not permitted in park headquarters or on islands.

Facilities for Disabled
Visitor Center at Ventura, rest rooms, theater, exhibits, and observation tower are accessible to wheelchairs. Boats and islands are not.

Things to Do
Santa Barbara Channel: Whale-watching from late December through March. *Anacapa:* free ranger-led walks and evening programs; also, wildlife-watching, birdwatching, tide pool walks (access on special boat trips only), swimming and snorkeling, scuba and skin diving, fishing (license needed; certain areas closed). *Santa Barbara:* nature hikes, marine life observation, birdwatching, tide pool walks. *Santa Rosa:* free ranger-led nature hike. *San Miguel:* free ranger-led hike to caliche forest; also, seal- and sea lion-watching, tide pool walks. *Santa Cruz:* hikes, jeep tours, marine life observation, birdwatching.

Special Advisories
☐When hiking on the islands, stay on trails and away from cliffs.
☐All birds, animals, tide pools, shells, rocks, and plants are protected; do not take anything but photos.

Overnight Backpacking
Three backcountry boat-in campsites; 14-day limit. **Anacapa** and **Santa**

Barbara open all year; **San Miguel** open Memorial Day weekend to November 1. Reservations and permits required; contact park headquarters. No fees. No showers. Tent sites only. No water or supplies on islands. Group camping available.

Hotels, Motels, & Inns
(unless otherwise noted, rates are for 2 persons in a double room, high season)
In Ventura, Calif.:
Bella Maggiore Inn 67 S. California St. 93001. (805) 652-0277. 28 units. $70-$150, includes breakfast. **Best Western Inn of Ventura** 708 E. Thompson Blvd. 93001. (800) 528-1234 or (805) 648-3101. 75 units. $54-$70. AC, pool, restaurant. **Country Inn by the Sea** 298 S. Chestnut St. 93001. (800) 447-3529 or (805) 653-1434. 120 units. $79-$89, includes breakfast. AC, pool. **Harbortown Marina Resort** 1050 Schooner Dr. 93001. (805) 658-1212 or in Calif. (800) 622-1212. 150 units. $70. Pool, rest. **Inn on the Beach** 1175 S. Seaward Ave. 93001. (805) 652-2000. 24 units. $100-$130, includes breakfast. AC. **La Mer European Bed & Breakfast** (411 Poli St.) P.O. Box 23318. 93002. (805) 643-3600. 5 units. $105-$170, includes breakfast. **Seaview Inn** 1065 S. Seaward Ave. 93001. (805) 648-1084. 7 units with kitchenettes. $50.

For additional accommodations, write or call the Ventura Visitor and Convention Bureau, 89 S. California Street, Ventura, Calif. 93001. (805) 648-2075.

Excursions

Santa Monica Mountains National Recreation Area
Woodland Hills, California
Here southern California's rare Mediterranean climate offers habitats ranging from chaparral to oak woodlands to rocky canyons to marshes and sandy beaches. Government and private efforts preserve the area's natural and cultural resources including Paramount Ranch (a working Hollywood set), spectacular Mulholland Drive, Malibu Beach, Cold Creek Canyon Preserve, and the Will Rogers State Historic Park. 150,000 acre boundary. Facilities include 100 campsites, hiking, boating, fishing, horseback riding, water sports. Open all year, dawn to dusk (some areas 9 a.m.-5 p.m. or by reservation). Info. at NPS headquarters in Woodland Hills, about 30 miles from Ventura. (818) 888-3770.

Joshua Tree National Monument
Twentynine Palms, California
This monument preserves the unique high Mojave Desert habitat of the giant branching yucca, as well as the low, creosote- and cholla-bearing Colorado Desert to the east and five fanpalm oases. 559,960 acres. Facilities include 550 campsites, hiking, climbing, picnic areas, handicapped access. Open all year. Information at Oasis Visitor Center on Calif. 62, about 180 miles east of Channel Islands NP. (619) 367-7511.

Kalua o Ka Oo cinder cone in the volcanic desert near Sliding Sands Trail

Haleakala

Maui, Hawaii

Established August 1, 1916

28,655 acres

Haleakala, a giant dormant volcano, forms the eastern bulwark of the island of Maui. According to legend, it was here, in the awe-inspiring basin at the mountain's summit, that the demigod Maui snared the sun, releasing it only after it promised to move more slowly across the sky. Haleakala means "house of the sun"; the park encompasses the basin and portions of the volcano's flanks.

A United Nations International Biosphere Reserve, the park comprises starkly contrasting worlds of mountain and coast. The road to Haleakala's summit rises from near sea level to 10,000 feet in 38 miles—possibly the steepest such gradient for automobiles in the world. Visitors ascend through several climate and vegetation zones, from humid tropical lowlands to subalpine desert. Striking plants and animals such as the Haleakala silversword and the nene goose may be seen in this mountain section. The great summit-area depression, misnamed Haleakala Crater, formed as erosion ate away the mountain, joining two valleys. This 19-square-mile bowl, 2,720 feet deep, is the park's major draw.

From the crater's eastern rim, the great rain forest valley of Kipahulu drops thousands of feet down to the coast. The upper Kipahulu is a protected wilderness, home to a vast profusion of flora and fauna, including some of the world's rarest birds, plants, and invertebrates. Some insects evolved in the Kipahulu Valley and live nowhere else.

Visitors reach Kipahulu via a sliv-

mountain rangeland to the park entrance. Allow up to 2 hours.

For the 62-mile drive to Kipahulu, allow up to 3½ hours. Take Hwy. 36 from Kahului around the northeastern side of the island to the town of Hana. The road to Hana, which becomes Hwy. 360, is famous for its narrow, tortuous course along 1,000-foot sea cliffs, into deep gorges, and past many waterfalls. This drive includes many opportunities to pull over for a refreshing dip in cascade pools. Go past Hana on Hwy. 31 for about 7 miles. Just beyond 'Ohe'o Stream, signs or park rangers will point to off-road parking.

When to Go
All-year park. Most rain comes in winter, although the temperatures vary little month to month. To avoid the crowds, visit the crater after 3 p.m.; sunsets can be as spectacular as the famous sunrises. At Kipahulu, avoid crowds by arriving early or camping overnight. Weather varies most at higher elevations, and can change from very hot to rainy, cold, and windy in the same day. Temperatures can drop to freezing inside the crater, although snow is rare. Coastal Kipahulu stays warm but receives considerable rain all year.

er of parkland on Maui's southeastern coast. Dominated by intense hues—azure sea, black rock, silver waterfalls, green forest and meadow—the coastal area was farmed beginning in early Polynesian times, more than 1,200 years ago. Mark Twain, who traveled to Hawaii in 1866, may well have had this part of Kipahulu in mind when he wrote: "For me its balmy airs are always blowing, its summer seas flashing in the sun; the pulsing of its surfbeat is in my ear; I can see its garlanded crags, its leaping cascades, its plumy palms drowsing by the shore."

How to Get There
Fly directly from the mainland, or from another Hawaiian island, to Kahului in central Maui. To reach Haleakala Crater and summit, follow, sequentially, Hawaii Hwys. 36, 37, 377, and 378. The 37-mile route is well marked; last chance to buy food and gas is at Pukalani. Continue on the switchback road through miles of

How to Visit
With an early start, it's possible to tour both the **Haleakala** summit and **Kipahulu** coastal regions of the park in 1 day, but you will spend much time in your car. To absorb more of the ambience of this unique sea-girt volcano, try to spend a day on the mountain, with a hike through the crater's moonscape, and a second day on the coast. Van and bus tours—some starting in predawn hours to take in a magical summit sunrise—can be arranged from most island hotels. Some companies will drive a group to the summit, then provide bicycles to ride down the mountain.

Consider taking a guided walk from **Hosmer Grove** into the Nature Conservancy's **Waikamoi Preserve**, home of living treasures including various species of honeycreepers, Hawaii's premier family of native birds. Call ahead for the schedule.

Air tours of Maui and the park are available from Kahului, but regulations limit them to high altitude.

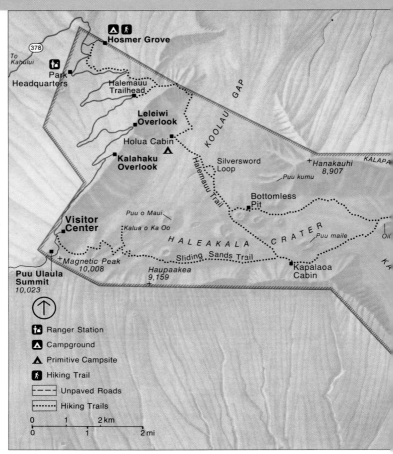

Map legend:

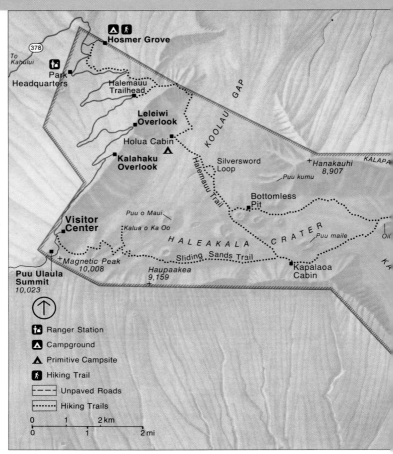

Ranger Station
Campground
Primitive Campsite
Hiking Trail
- - - - Unpaved Roads
.... Hiking Trails

0   1   2 km
0   1   2 mi

Hosmer Grove to Haleakala Summit & Crater

11 miles; at least a half day

A short distance above the park entrance lies **Hosmer Grove**, a cool, shady spot to picnic and camp. You may recognize some of the trees, which include Douglas-fir, California redwood, and eucalyptus. Around 1910, forester Ralph Hosmer planted trees from all over the world to test their potential for watershed protection and timber here. A ½-mile loop trail will refresh you after your drive. Guided nature walks are also available. Back on the road, you reach park headquarters 1³⁄₁₀ miles above the Hosmer turnoff. At this 7,000-foot elevation, you will see vegetation native to Hawaii. In front

of headquarters, plantings of Haleakala geranium and silversword offer photo opportunities and biology lessons in adaptation and evolution. These two plants are endemic—found only on Haleakala volcano.

Leaving headquarters, drive up the mountain through subalpine heath of soft earthy hues. In spring, mamane, a dominant shrub, brightens these slopes with sprays of yellow blossoms. The small birds here are mainly native. With luck you may see some of the famous honeycreepers—brightly feathered birds that may be descendants of the first land birds to reach Hawaii. From their original ancestors, the honeycreepers have evolved at least 47 species, some adapted to only one island, some spread more widely. More than half of these species have

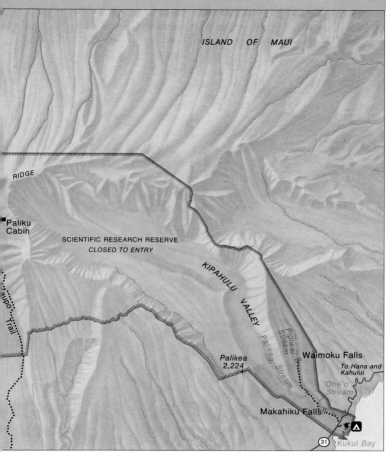

ISLAND OF MAUI

RIDGE

Paliku
Cabin

SCIENTIFIC RESEARCH RESERVE
CLOSED TO ENTRY

KIPAHULU VALLEY

Kaupō Trail

Palikea
2,224

Pipiwai Stream

Palikea Stream

Waimoku Falls

To Hana and
Kahului

'Ohe'o
Stream

Makahiku Falls

Kukui Bay

31

Nene geese, birds unique to Hawaii

Silky balls of Hawaiian silversword

A tiny, rare honeycreeper

become extinct. Driven from the lowlands by habitat change and disease, others are making their last stand high on the mountain.

Crater hikers often start at the **Halemauu Trailhead,** 3 miles above headquarters. This trail takes you through rolling country to the crater rim, then switchbacks as it steeply drops 1,000 feet down the spectacular northwest wall of the crater to **Holua Cabin** and campground (4 miles from the trailhead). The crater wall is broken here by **Koolau Gap,** a wide, wet canyon that descends to the sea. In this corner of the crater, vegetation thrives on moisture carried by waves of clouds that slowly ebb and flow in the gap, and you will find leathery ferns ('ama'u) and other

unusual plants.

Motorists can get first views of the crater at **Leleiwi** and **Kalahaku Overlooks.** At Kalahaku, look for silverswords in a protected area below the parking lot. Do not walk near the plants; soil compaction damages their roots. Drive 2 more miles to the visitor center, where rangers lead hikes part-way into the crater (call ahead for schedules).

An exhibit shelter crowns the highest point—**Puu Ulaula,** or "red hill"—where park naturalists give several informal lectures daily. At 10,023 feet, Puu Ulaula offers the ultimate view: Often you can see the giant volcanoes of the Big Island, as well as Maui's neighboring islands of **Lanai** and **Kahoolawe** and sometimes, far to the northwest, **Oahu.** Nearby is Science City, a cluster of observatories and laboratories outside the park and closed to the public.

The best way to experience the crater is on a 2-day hike, spending the night at one of the three cabins or two campgrounds inside the crater. (Reserve well ahead for cabins—see **Information & Activities.**) One popular trip involves hiking the **Sliding Sands Trail** to **Kapalaoa Cabin** (5$\frac{4}{5}$ miles from the visitor center). Because of the difficulty in climbing back up the trail's loose cinder, many choose to exit the crater via Halemauu Trail, an 8-mile hike from the cabin back to the road. You'll need to arrange a ride between the two trailheads, possibly leaving your car near Halemauu Trailhead and hitchhiking

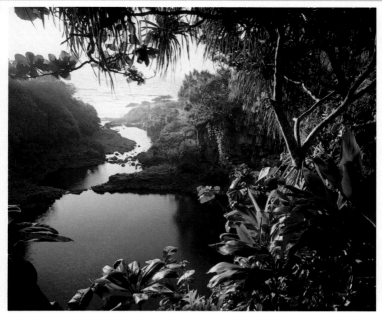
'Ohe'o Stream on its way to the ocean

to the Sliding Sands Trailhead. For a challenging day hike from the visitor center, take the Sliding Sands Trail down to **Kalua o Ka Oo**, the first big cinder cone, 5 miles round-trip.

Kipahulu: 'Ohe'o Stream
at least a half day

Swimming and hiking are primary pastimes in this strip of parkland along the gorge of **'Ohe'o Stream.** Most swimmers congregate around the big pools and waterfalls below the highway bridge, but less crowded spots await upstream. Some pools are deep, but beware of slippery or hidden rocks. Also, flash floods can follow heavy rains in the watershed above. Ocean swimming is generally ruled out by big breakers and a rugged shoreline. Camping is permitted on the oceanfront meadows south of the stream. Bring your own drinking water, or boil stream water or treat it with halozone.

If you have 2 or 3 hours, take **Pipiwai Trail**, one of the most memorable short hikes in the islands. This walk is easy for anyone in good health, but is usually slippery with mud in spots; wear sturdy footgear. Begin about 200 yards south of the 'Ohe'o bridge. Walk up through gently sloping pasture about ½ mile to overlook **Makahiku Falls**, 184 feet high. After another ½ mile, the trail enters the woods and crosses the stream at a shallow ford near a lovely double falls. Continue about a mile more through lush forest, including a stand of dense, 50-foot-high bamboo, which on a breezy day clacks and creaks with a mysterious percussive music. Your destination looms above the forest as you get close: **Waimoku Falls**, more than 300 feet high, fills its jungle clearing with cool mists. On your way back down through the pastures, the view of the Big Island across 30-mile-wide **Alenuihaha Channel** is majestic. Much of the year, mango, guava, and mountain apple provide refreshment au naturel.

Archaeological evidence shows that large numbers of Hawaiians once lived in the lower Kipahulu Valley. Look carefully for traces of stone-walled gardens, taro patches that continue to grow, and temple and shelter sites. From about 1888 to 1923, sugarcane plants lined both sides of 'Ohe'o Stream; wild cane still grows in patches. More recently, the economy of Kipahulu relied on cattle ranching; alien shrubs and trees are taking over the deserted ranchlands.

Information & Activities

Headquarters
P.O. Box 369, Makawao, Maui, Hawaii 96768. Phone (808) 572-9306.

Seasons & Accessibility
Park open year-round. Call (808) 572-7749 for recorded information on weather and roads.

Visitor & Information Centers
Main Visitor Center near the summit, 11 miles from the park entrance, open daily all year. Information also available at headquarters, 1 mile from the park entrance, or by phoning. Rangers provide information year-round in the Kipahulu-'Ohe'o Stream area. Call (808) 248-8260.

Entrance Fees
$3 per car per day, $10 for an annual pass; members of tour groups, $1.

Pets
Permitted on leashes except in backcountry.

Facilities for Disabled
Visitor Center and park headquarters are wheelchair accessible. A free brochure about visiting Maui is available from: Commission on the Handicapped, Old Federal Building, 335 Merchant St., No. 215, Honolulu, Hawaii 96813.

Things to Do
Free naturalist-led activities: nature walks and hikes, interpretive talks. Also available, hiking, horseback riding in crater, swimming in 'Ohe'o Stream.

Special Advisory
☐Crater hikes are at high altitude, where air is thin; take it easy. Be prepared for unpredictable weather that can change quickly from heat to cold and rain.

Overnighting in the Crater
Tent camping allowed only at Holua and Paliku campsites; free permit required; issued first come, first served at park headquarters on the day of the hike; 2-night limit at each campground; limit of 3 nights total per month.

Cabins: 3 small, primitive ones at Holua, Kapalaoa, and Paliku contain 12 bunks, minimum equipment; can be reached by trail only. Reservation requests must be received by mail before the first of the month, 3 months prior to desired stay; give alternate dates; assignments made by lottery; limited to 3 nights per month (2 consecutive nights in one cabin); $5 adults per night, $2.50 children; $15 deposit after confirmation. Send request to headquarters. Call (808) 572-9177 for recorded information on cabins and campgrounds.

Campgrounds
Two drive-in campgrounds, both with 3-day limit. **Hosmer Grove** and 'Ohe'o open all year first come, first served. No fees. No showers. Tent and RV sites; no hookups.

Hotels, Motels, & Inns
(unless otherwise noted, rates are for 2 persons in a double room, high season)
In Hana, Hawaii 96713:
Aloha Cottages P.O. Box 205. (808) 248-8420. 5 small cottages, all with full kitchens, in residential areas of Hana. $55-$75. **Hana Bay Vacation Rentals** P.O. Box 318. (808) 248-7727. 8 cottages, all with full kitchens, in various areas of Hana. $85-$220.
Hana Kai Maui Resort Condominiums P.O. Box 38. (800) 346-2772. 11 units, kitchenettes. $120. **Heavenly Hana Inn** P.O. Box 146. (808) 248-8442. 6 units; cottages and 2-bedroom suites, kitchens. $75-$85. **Hotel Hana Maui** P.O. Box 8. (800) 321-4262. 96 units. $305-$795. Restaurant.
In Kahului, Hawaii 96732:
Maui Beach Hotel (170 Kaahumanu Ave.) Hawaiian Pacific Resorts, 1150 S. King St., Honolulu, Hawaii 96814. (800) 367-5004. 154 units. $60-$85. AC, pool, rest. **Maui Palms Hotel** (170 Kaahumanu Ave.) Hawaiian Pacific Resorts, see above. 103 units. $50-$56. AC, pool, rest. **Maui Seaside Hotel** 100 W. Kaahumanu Ave. (800) 367-7000 or (808) 877-3311. 192 units. $69-$78. AC, pool, restaurant.
In Kula, Hawaii 96790:
Kula Lodge (on Hawaii Hwy. 377) RR 1, Box 475. (808) 878-1535. 5 units. $120-$140. Restaurant.

Excursions

Waianapanapa State Park
Hana, Maui, Hawaii

Low volcanic cliffs and native hala
(pandanus) forest line the coast in
this remote, rugged park. Here, visitors can fish in the surf, explore a
cave, observe an immense seabird
colony, and hike the ancient coastal
trail leading to Hana. 120 acres. Facilities include 1 campground (permits required), 12 cabins, hiking,
fishing, picnic areas, swimming.
Open year-round. Off Hawaii Hwy.
360 (Hana Highway) about 35 miles
from Haleakala NP. (808) 244-4354.

Iao Valley State Park
Wailuku, Maui, Hawaii

Velvety moss-covered cliffs surround
the verdant Iao Valley and its centerpiece, the Iao Needle, a 2,250-foot
basalt spire sacred to the people of
Maui. Swirling waters fashioned the
Needle from a natural altar in an ancient volcanic caldera; today they
provide many refreshing pools. 6
acres. Facilities: hiking, observation
pavilion, swimming. Open year-
round from 7 a.m. to 7 p.m. On Iao
Valley Road, off Hawaii Hwy. 30,
about 40 miles from Haleakala NP.
(808) 244-4354.

Hawaiian ferns and ohia blossoms near Halemaumau crater, atop Kilauea

Hawaii Volcanoes

Hawaii

Established August 1, 1916

229,177 acres

Hawaii Volcanoes National Park, on the Big Island of Hawaii, offers the visitor a look at two of the world's most active volcanoes: Kilauea and Mauna Loa.

More than 4,000 feet high and still growing, Kilauea abuts the southeastern slope of the older and much larger Mauna Loa, or "long mountain." Mauna Loa towers some 13,680 feet above the sea: Measured from its base 18,000 feet below sea level, it exceeds Mt. Everest in height. Mauna Loa's gently sloping bulk—some 10,000 cubic miles in volume—makes it earth's most massive single mountain.

The park stretches from sea level to Mauna Loa's summit. Beyond the end of the road lies Mauna Loa's wilderness area, where the rugged backpacker encounters freezing nights and rough lava trails amid volcanic wonders: barren lava twisted into nightmarish shapes, cinder cones, gaping pits. Kilauea, however, provides easy access to a greater variety of scenery and cultural sites.

On the slopes of Kilauea, whose name means "spreading, much spewing," patches of vegetation border stark, recent lava flows. This natural laboratory of ecological change displays all stages of forest regeneration—from early regrowth of lichens and ferns to dense forest. The patchwork of lava and greenery gives way to the black Mars-scape of the Kau Desert on the hot, dry southwestern slope. At the shore, waves create lines of jagged cliffs; periodic eruptions send fresh lava flows to meet

island on Hwy. 11 past Kealakekua Bay, where Captain Cook met his death, and Ka Lae, or South Point, southernmost land in the 50 states. You'll reach the Kilauea summit after a 95-mile drive on a good road.

From Hilo, Hwy. 11 rises for 30 miles past small settlements, macadamia orchards, abandoned sugarcane fields, and rain forest, to reach the park at Kilauea's summit.

When to Go
All-year park. The weather is often driest in September and October. The climate ranges from warm and breezy on the coast, to cool and frequently wet at Kilauea, to nightly freezing with occasional snowstorms above about 10,000 feet on Mauna Loa. To avoid most tour bus crowds, plan to visit the major sights before 11 a.m. or after 3 p.m.

How to Visit
An intensive 1-day visit can encompass highlights of the **Kilauea** summit via **Crater Rim Drive** and the coastal region via **Chain of Craters Road.** Regular tours by bus and small van operate daily from many Hilo and Kona hotels. Those with botanical or ornithological interests may wish to explore the **Mauna Loa Strip Road** (accessible from Hwy. 11) which takes you through upland forest to the **Mauna Loa Trailhead** at 6,660 feet: At **Bird Park**, be sure to take the 1$\frac{1}{5}$-mile self-guided trail wending through one of Hawaii's richest concentrations of native plants and birdlife.

the sea amid colossal clouds of steam.

Geological dynamism forms the park's primary natural theme, followed closely by evolutionary biology. Thousands of unique species have evolved on the isolated Hawaiian islands. Cultural sites abound as well, reminders of the Polynesian pioneers who steered their great double-hulled canoes to Hawaii beginning some 1,500 years ago.

The United Nations has named the park both an International Biosphere Reserve and a World Heritage site. Many of the park's intriguing native plants and animals, however, are in peril, defenseless against alien species including weedy plants and feral goats and pigs.

How to Get There
Fly to the island of Hawaii, also called the Big Island. Airlines serve the Kona airport from the mainland and from other Hawaiian islands; only interisland flights land in Hilo. From Kona, head south around the

Puu Oo spewing molten lava

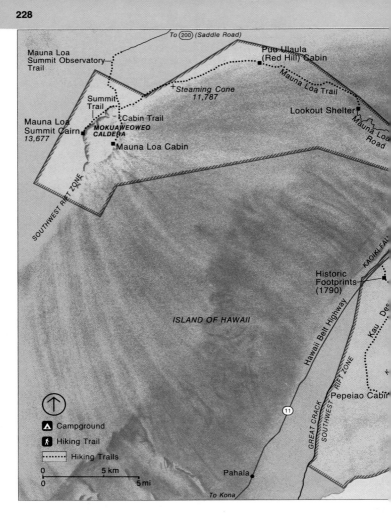

To (200) (Saddle Road)

Mauna Loa
Summit Observatory
Trail

Puu Ulaula
(Red Hill) Cabin

Mauna Loa Trail

Steaming Cone
11,787

Lookout Shelter

Summit
Trail

Cabin Trail

Mauna Loa
Summit Cairn
13,677

MOKUAWEOWEO
CALDERA

Mauna Loa Cabin

SOUTHWEST RIFT ZONE

Mauna Loa Road

KAOIKI FAL

Historic
Footprints
(1790)

Kau Des

ISLAND OF HAWAII

Hawaii Belt Highway

SOUTHWEST RIFT ZONE

GREAT CRACK

Pepeiao Cabin

11

↑

▲ Campground

🚶 Hiking Trail

········ Hiking Trails

| | |
0   5 km
0   5 mi

Pahala

To Kona

Kilauea Summit:
Crater Rim Drive

11-mile loop; about a half day

Begin at the **Kilauea Visitor Center.**
Don't miss the short, stunning film of
recent volcanic eruptions. The rustic
Volcano House and the **Volcano Art
Center** are just a short stroll. Walk
through the Volcano House lobby to
the rear of the hotel for a first dramatic view across **Kilauea Caldera,** the
great depression that marks the volcanic summit.

After leaving the visitor center,
continue clockwise on **Crater Rim
Drive.** For a time, the road traverses
rain forest featuring Hawaiian tree
ferns that lend the roadsides a pre-

historic look. Scenic turnouts begin
with a huge crater, **Kilauea Iki** ("little
Kilauea") just east of the main caldera. In 1959 Kilauea Iki erupted in a
lava fountain 1,900 feet high, a
record for Hawaiian volcanism.

Visit the **Thurston Lava Tube** by
taking an easy 15-minute loop trail
that starts in lush jungle. The lava
tube formed when the exterior of a
lava flow cooled to a crust while the
still molten interior lava flowed out.

From the Thurston parking area,
trails lead down to the floor of Kilauea Iki and along its rim. You can take
a loop hike or walk back to Volcano
House in 2 to 3 miles. Either way,
you'll pass dramatic vistas of the Kilauea Caldera, vertical lava cliffs,
and verdant rain forest.

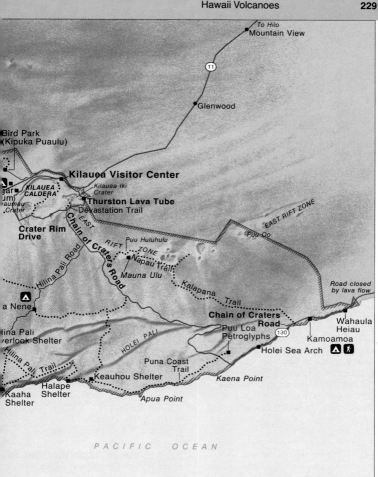

Thurston Lava Tube, a natural tunnel

New growth among cinders at Devastation Trail

Continuing along Crater Rim Drive, look for white-tailed tropic-birds, graceful seabirds with long tail streamers. These ethereal-looking creatures nest on cliffside ledges, often soaring above Kilauea Caldera. With luck, you may spot a nene goose, an endemic Hawaiian bird probably descended from lost Canada geese that landed here. **Devastation Trail** is a short (½ mile) but unforgettable walk through remains of a forest killed by falling cinder during the 1959 eruption. The forest is now beginning to recover.

As the road descends along the southwestern side of Kilauea Caldera, you will notice the landscape becoming more arid. In the rain shadow of the summit, the **Kau Desert** receives about half as much rain as Kilauea Visitor Center. It also bears the brunt of hot winds blowing volcanic fumes and natural acid rain—which stunt plants—down from above. Legend tells that in 1790, Hawaiian soldiers returning from battle through the Kau Desert were overcome by volcanic gases and debris when they failed to pacify Pele, the volcano goddess. (To see solidified footprints said to be those of the stricken soldiers, take Hwy. 11 toward Kona after the tour and stop at the marked display.)

Ascending again, you reach the **Halemaumau Crater** overlook. Walk the short path to look into the fire pit, a favorite abode of Pele. Many native Hawaiians still revere her, and you may see offerings of flowers, fruit, and even liquor. The Park Service honors the practice.

The **Hawaiian Volcano Observatory** of the US Geological Survey, and the small, excellent **Jaggar Museum** of volcano lore and research are next on your route. Nearing the visitor center once more, you'll pass fumaroles, or steam vents. These have produced the **Sulphur Banks** with crystalline deposits of pure sulphur. From here you can opt for a short hike back toward the visitor center. Alternatively, a 1-to-2-mile walk along the caldera rim provides fine views.

Chain of Craters Road: Kilauea to Wahaula

28 miles one way; about a half day

From the summit visitor center follow Crater Rim Drive clockwise to the well-marked turnoff for **Chain of Craters Road.** For about 4 miles as you head toward the coast, your route closely approximates the active **East Rift Zone** of Kilauea volcano. Scenic turnouts and short walks bring you to the rims of several impressive craters. If you have time, hike the **Napau Trail** up **Puu Huluhulu** ("shaggy hill") to the overlook at the top, just over 1 mile. The overlook provides splendid views of the East Rift Zone and **Mauna Ulu**, the large, steaming domelike hill directly to the south. Look for steam from **Puu Oo**, a major vent of Kilauea's ongoing eruption, far to the east.

Walk back to your car; the road

Lava sizzling into ocean near the park

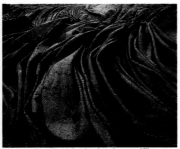

Ripples of hardened pahoehoe lava on Kilauea

farther on was covered during the 1970s by a series of huge lava flows from Mauna Ulu. At the turnouts, you stand on some of the newest ground on earth. Most of this lava is pahoehoe (pa-hoy-hoy): Fluid when fresh, it freezes in fairly smooth mounds with swirls and ropy strands. This rock contrasts with aa (ah-ah)—thicker, slow-moving lava that has hardened into a chaotic jumble of rough chunks and boulders.

The climate becomes drier, and patches of forest in various stages of recovery appear, as you descend toward the sea. Sulphur fumes sweep down from active volcanic vents on the rift to the east. Turnouts offer sweeping views of the Kau Desert and white-capped waves pounding the black shoreline. About 21 miles off this coast, a huge undersea volcano is building a future Hawaiian island. Called Loihi, the volcano could breach the ocean's surface in some 10,000 years.

A steep descent of about 800 feet marks **Holei Pali**, a cliff formed by vertical faulting; the huge coastal shelf is breaking away from the uplands and sinking into the sea, albeit slowly on a human time scale. Reaching the lowlands, look for the **Puu Loa Petroglyphs** turnout; a modest hike will bring you to some fine examples of ancient Hawaiian rock carvings.

Hawaiians lived on this dry, rocky land for centuries. Your route along the coast takes you past several of their ancient settlements, often marked by groves of coconut trees; short, rough walks take you to these sites as well as to scenic, wave-carved sea arches. Hawaiian heritage becomes conspicuous at **Kamoa-moa**—once a large fishing village, now a beautiful picnic site and campground. The black-sand beach cloaked a former rocky shoreline here in 1988, when a lava flow reached the sea about 3 miles to the east and exploded into tiny black particles. Swimming is unsafe due to powerful breakers and undertow.

The road ends near the site of the former **Wahaula Visitor Center**, destroyed in a 1989 lava flow. If it has not met the same fate, visit **Wahaula Heiau**, an open-air temple dating from the 13th century. When active lava is accessible, rangers lead walks to the best and safest vantage points.

Information & Activities

Headquarters
Hawaii Volcanoes National Park, Hawaii 96718. Phone (808) 967-7311.

Seasons & Accessibility
Park open year-round. Chain of Craters Road is closed by lava flow at its eastern end, beyond Kamoamoa Campground. For eruption bulletins call (808) 967-7977.

Visitor & Information Centers
Kilauea Visitor Center, just off Hwy. 11 on Crater Rim Drive $\frac{1}{4}$ mile from park entrance, and the new Thomas A. Jaggar Museum on Crater Rim Drive, 3 miles from park entrance, are both open all year. For information write or call the park.

Entrance Fee
$5 per car per week, multiple entries.

Pets
Not allowed on trails or in backcountry; elsewhere must be leashed.

Facilities for Disabled
Visitor center and museum are accessible to wheelchairs, with assistance. One trail and many scenic overlooks along Crater Rim Drive also accessible. Free brochure about visiting the Big Island from: Comm. on the Handicapped, Old Federal Bldg., 335 Merchant Street, No. 215, Honolulu, Hawaii 96813.

Things to Do
Free naturalist-led activities: nature walks and talks, slide shows, films, museum exhibits on volcanism. Also, hiking, backcountry fishing (check headquarters for regulations), art center, workshops, seminars.

Special Advisories
☐Be prepared for intensive sunlight.
☐Persons with heart or respiratory problems must beware of noxious sulphur fumes.
☐Stay on marked trails; vegetation may conceal deep cracks.
☐Coastline collapse can occur fast; do not go beyond barriers.
☐Strong winds and unpredictable surf along the coast make swimming dangerous; it is prohibited in places.

Overnight Backpacking
Registration at the visitor center is required. No fee.

Campgrounds
Three campgrounds, **Kamoamoa, Kipuka Nene,** and **Namakani Paio,** all with a 7-day limit. Open all year first come, first served. No fees. No showers. Tent sites only. Two patrol cabins on **Mauna Loa Trail** and one at **Kipuka Pepeiao** may be used free first come, first served. Must register at headquarters. Food services in park.

Hotels, Motels, & Inns
(unless otherwise noted, rates are for 2 persons in a double room, high season)
INSIDE THE PARK:
Volcano House (Crater Rim Dr.) P.O. Box 53, Hawaii Volcanoes NP, Hawaii 96718. (808) 967-7321. 42 rooms. $79-$131. Restaurant. **Namakani Paio Cabins** (off Hawaii Hwy. 11) P.O. Box 53, Hawaii Volcanoes NP, Hawaii 96718. (808) 967-7321. 10 cabins with central bath. $31.

OUTSIDE THE PARK:
In Hilo, Hawaii 96720:
Country Club Apartment Hotel 121 Banyan Dr. (808) 935-7171. 155 units, 24 with kitchenettes. $55-$80. AC, pool, restaurant. **Dolphin Bay Hotel** 333 Iliahi St. (808) 935-1466. 18 units with kitchenettes. $36-$77. **Hawaii Naniloa Hotel** 93 Banyan Dr. (800) 367-5360 or (808) 969-3333. 325 units. $96-$574. AC, pool, restaurant.
In Kailua-Kona, Hawaii 96740:
Hotel King Kamehameha 75-5660 Palani Rd. (800) 367-2111. 452 units. $105-$180. AC, pool, restaurant.
In Pahala, Hawaii 96777:
SeaMountain at Punaluu (on Hawaii Hwy. 11) P.O. Box 70. (800) 367-8047, ext. 145 or (808) 928-8301. 27 condominiums, kitchens or kitchenettes. $73-$135. Pool, restaurant.

Contact the Chamber of Commerce of Hilo, 180 Kinoole St., Suite 118, Hilo, Hawaii 96720 (808) 935-7178, and Kailua-Kona (808) 329-1758 for additional accommodations.

Excursions

Mauna Kea Observatory
Hilo, Hawaii

Mauna Kea, the world's highest island mountain, is the world's premier astronomical site. Clear, dry skies and a 13,796-foot elevation provide ideal viewing conditions; six countries have built state-of-the-art telescopes on the dormant volcano's summit. Mauna Kea Support Services operates a visitor center at 9,200 feet with astronomical displays and, on Friday nights, stargazing from an 11-inch telescope. Saturday and Sunday tours to the summit available for persons 16 and older with no heart or respiratory problems. Summit goers must provide their own four-wheel-drive vehicle. Hiking to the summit discouraged. Open year-round. Located off Hawaii Hwy. 200 (Saddle Road), about 55 miles from Hilo. (808) 961-2180.

Akaka Falls State Park
Honomu, Hawaii

This park's ancient legend bears a decidedly modern ring: It says that the god Akaka, fleeing across the canyon after his wife returned home unexpectedly and discovered his infidelity, slipped and fell off 442-foot Akaka Falls. A self-guided paved path leads visitors through a lush jungle ablaze with colorful and fragrant blossoms to viewpoints over these falls and the 100-foot cascading Kahuna Falls. 65 acres. No facilities other than the hiking trails. Located on Hawaii Hwy. 220, about 15 miles north of Hilo. (808) 961-7200.

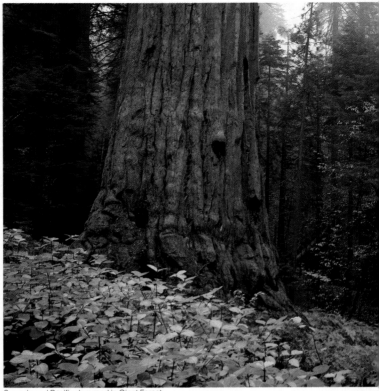

Sequoia and Pacific dogwood in Giant Forest

Sequoia & Kings Canyon

California

Established September 25, 1890; March 4, 1940

863,159 acres

Bigness—big trees and big canyons—inspired the separate founding of each of these parks. In 1943 Sequoia and Kings Canyon National Parks began to be jointly administered. The result was a dual-named superpark 66 miles long and 36 miles across at its widest point.

Nearly every square mile of this vast park is wilderness. A backpacker here can hike to a spot that is farther from a road than any other place in the 48 contiguous states. But the park's famed attraction, the Giant Forest of sequoias, is easily reached.

Relatively few visitors hike any of the park's hundreds of miles of trails. Still, there are enough backpackers to worry officials, who protect the backcountry by regulating the number of people entering it.

Mt. Whitney, at 14,495 feet the highest peak in the United States south of Alaska, rises at the border. Backpackers coming in from the east can get to Whitney in 1 or 2 days. From the park's western trailheads, backpackers reach it by a 70-mile, 8-day trek across the park's snow-swept, glacier-dotted heights.

Visitors are startled to learn that the smoke they sometimes see rises from "prescribed burning"—controlled fires deliberately set by park employees to help the sequoias by removing undergrowth. In the past, when the park fought all fires, brush and deadwood built up. This fueled fires that imperiled the sequoias, which resist flames at their bases but can die if fire attacks their crowns.

How to Get There

From Visalia (about 35 miles west), take Calif. Hwy. 198 to Sequoia's Ash Mountain Entrance. From Fresno, take Calif. Hwy. 180 to Kings Canyon's Big Stump Entrance. The only road entrance into the main part of Kings Canyon is a dead-end, summer-only extension of Calif. 180 into Cedar Grove. Airport: Fresno.

When to Go

Spring through fall is the best time for sequoia gazing. Generals Highway, which connects Sequoia and Kings Canyon, is open all year except when snow is heavy. From December to April, there are cross-country skiing and snowshoeing in the Giant Forest area and at Grant Grove.

How to Visit

This immense double park challenges anyone planning a 1-day visit. To appreciate the rugged splendor, you must hike a trail. No east-west road

crosses either park. But a drive-in visitor, in a day, can see sequoias in **Giant Forest,** along the **Generals Highway,** and in **Grant Grove.** A quiet walk in a grove of sequoias will give you more than a drive to named trees, which are constantly surrounded by shutterbugs.

Stay long enough to explore both vast parks. Drive to Kings Canyon's beautiful valley, **Cedar Grove.** On another day visit **Crystal Cave** and climb **Moro Rock.** Hike in Sequoia's spectacular **Mineral King** area.

Giant Forest & Grant Grove

48 miles; a full day

From the **Ash Mountain Entrance,** on **Generals Highway,** drive 17 miles to **Giant Forest,** home of the **General Sherman Tree,** the world's largest tree and the largest living thing on earth. About 6 miles along the road from the Ash Mountain Entrance, stop to see the Indian exhibit at **Hospital Rock.** Indians lived here from prehistoric times until the 1870s, when the white man's diseases killed off the last of them. The Western Mono made flour from acorns—the most important staple food of California Indians. They crushed the acorns in small hollows gouged into streamside bedrock; you can see several such rock mortars at the exhibit.

The **Four Guardsmen,** a quartet of sequoias, stand as sentinels near the **Giant Forest Village.** Trails radiate

A towering sequoia

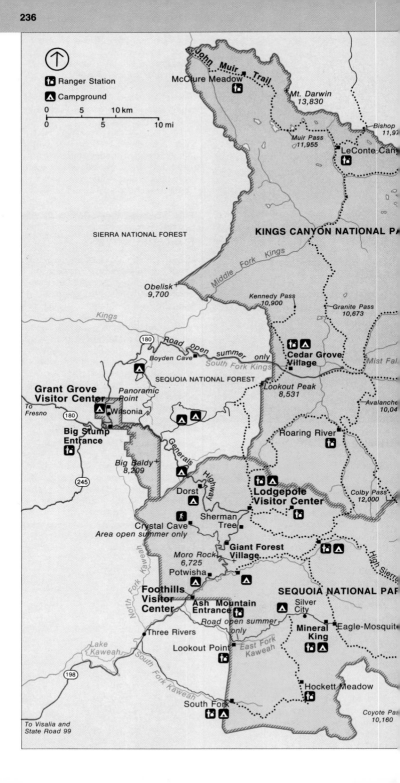

Ranger Station

Campground

0   5   10 km

0   5   10 mi

John Muir Trail

McClure Meadow

Mt. Darwin
13,830

Bishop
11,97

Muir Pass
11,955

LeConte Can

SIERRA NATIONAL FOREST

KINGS CANYON NATIONAL PA

Middle Fork Kings

Obelisk
9,700

Kennedy Pass
10,900

Granite Pass
10,673

Kings

Road open summer only

Boyden Cave

South Fork Kings

Cedar Grove
Village

Mist Fal

SEQUOIA NATIONAL FOREST

Lookout Peak
8,531

Avalanche
10,04

Grant Grove
Visitor Center

Panoramic
Point

Wilsonia

To
Fresno

Roaring River

Big Stump
Entrance

Big Baldy
8,209

Generals

Dorst

Highway

Big Baldy
8,209

Lodgepole
Visitor Center

Colby Pass
12,000

Crystal Cave
Area open summer only

Sherman
Tree

Moro Rock
6,725

Giant Forest
Village

High Sierra

Potwisha

Foothills
Visitor
Center

Ash Mountain
Entrance

SEQUOIA NATIONAL PA

North Fork Kaweah

Road open summer only

Silver
City

Three Rivers

East Fork
Kaweah

Mineral
King

Eagle-Mosquit

Lake
Kaweah

South Fork Kaweah

Lookout Point

Hockett Meadow

Coyote Pas
10,160

South Fork

To Visalia and
State Road 99

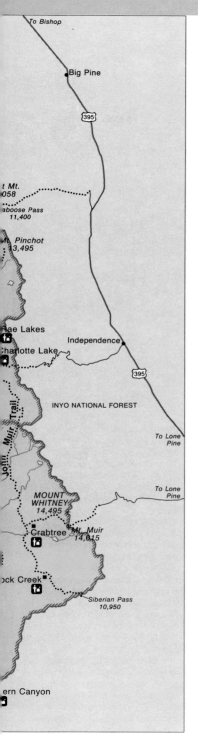

from the star attraction, the General Sherman Tree, between 2,300 and 2,700 years old, 274$\frac{9}{10}$ feet tall and 102$\frac{3}{5}$ feet in circumference, with a volume of 52,500 cubic feet. (In board feet, this is the equivalent of 119$\frac{1}{3}$ miles of 1-by-12-inch planks.) A 13-story building would fit beneath its first large branch. The tree was named by a pioneer cattleman who had served in the Civil War under Gen. William Tecumseh Sherman.

The easy 2-mile **Congress Trail** (the name honors the institution that gave legal protection to the sequoias) takes 2 to 3 hours and begins at the base of the champion tree, where you can buy a self-guiding pamphlet. At stops along the way, you will see young sequoias (a mere 140 or so years old); sequoias scarred by fire but standing tall because their bark, thick and lacking resin, protects them; and fallen sequoias, not rotting because they contain tannin, which helps them resist decay.

From the village, return to Generals Highway and begin the 30-mile drive to **Grant Grove** in Kings Canyon by heading northwest through Sequoia National Forest to Calif. Hwy. 180. Turn north on Calif. 180. On your right a road loops in and out of Wilsonia, a private community.

Just beyond the **Grant Grove Visitor Center,** take the road on your left to **General Grant Tree Trail,** a $\frac{1}{2}$-mile loop leading to the **General Grant Tree** (267$\frac{2}{5}$ feet tall, 107$\frac{3}{5}$ feet in circumference at ground). The name of the tree recalls the original 1890 name of the park, created to preserve Grant Grove. To counteract lumbering, champions of the sequoias bought more and more land to expand the 4-square-mile grove. When **Kings Canyon** and its trees were added to the park system in 1940, sequoias within the boundaries were forever protected from logging.

On the trail are many giants saved by the park, along with a reminder of the years of casual havoc: **Centennial Stump,** a sequoia cut down for exhibition at the 1875 Centennial in Philadelphia. In the southern part of Grant Grove is **Big Stump Trail** (1-mile loop), where stumps, logs, downed trees, and a pile of sawdust help you imagine the sequoia logging of the past and where regenerating trees grow into the giants of the future.

Woods Creek near Rae Lakes

Drive back to the visitor center and head east on the steep, narrow, 2½-mile road to **Panoramic Point** (no trailers or large vehicles allowed). From the parking lot, take the ¼-mile trail to the 7,520-foot ridge. Before you stretches the Sierra Nevada. A trailside diagram of the landscape names the mountains. You won't see Mt. Whitney; the Great Western Divide blocks the view.

Cedar Grove

36 miles; a full day

Drive north and east on Generals Highway; from Grant Grove follow Hwy. 180 for 30 miles through Sequoia NF. The road winds into the canyon of the **South Fork** of the **Kings River.** Stop at **Junction View** to gaze down on a wild river flanked by sheer canyon walls glistening in the sun. The road dead-ends at **Cedar Grove,** a mile-deep valley. Scouring streams began the carving of the val-

ley, which got its U-shape from subsequent glaciers that pushed into the canyon and widened the floor.

Incense-cedar, ponderosa pine, black oak, live oak, white fir, and sugar pine grow in the valley's flats. In the 1870s the area attracted stockmen as well as gold and silver prospectors. Even so, John Muir, who explored here in 1873, would still recognize this well-preserved high-country valley.

The **Cedar Grove Motor Nature Trail,** just beyond **Cedar Grove Village,** gives the drive-in visitor a tame tour on what had been a livestock trail. Better to park, get out, and walk, even for a short distance, to savor this beautiful hidden valley. The easy ½-mile **River Trail** takes you from the South Fork of the Kings River to **Roaring River Falls.** Back at the parking lot you can return to your car or continue on for a hike along the curves of the river. Cross a suspension bridge and climb a slight rise for a view of the valley. Retrace your steps to the bridge and take the **Zumwalt Meadow Trail,** a 1-mile loop.

Crystal Cave

18 miles; a half day

The cave temperature is a constant 55°F, so bring a jacket. Take the Generals Highway south from Giant Forest Village. Turn right down the rough, summer-only road (no trailers or large vehicles) to **Crystal Cave.** The twisting 9-mile trip consumes about 45 dusty minutes. From the parking lot you walk a paved, narrow path along a canyon wall, down to the entrance. To enter you need to buy a ticket and follow a guide. Don't expect multicolored lights or tales of goblins; the 1-hour tours, conducted from 10 a.m. to 3 p.m., introduce you to a cave that got its name from an unusual geological phenomenon. The cave is formed of marble—instead of limestone—that underground water slowly dissolved and then redeposited as dazzling stalactites, stalagmites, and columns.

Moro Rock

4³/₅ miles round-trip; a half day

Although you can drive to **Moro Rock,** a huge granite monolith, via the 2-mile **Moro Rock-Crescent Meadow Road** from Giant Forest Village, you get a better perception of its setting by hiking to it. Either way, try to be there at sunset when the view is spectacular. The 2-mile **Moro Rock Trail** begins near the cafeteria in the village and quickly leads you away from the throngs. About 1⅓ miles along the trail, a short path veers off to **Hanging Rock,** a high granite stage for viewing Sierra Nevada scenery.

Return to the trail and continue to the base of Moro Rock. Here you start climbing a stone stairway of nearly 400 steps (and several welcome spots for resting). Your 300-foot ascent takes you to an elevation of 6,725 feet, about 4,000 feet above the canyon floor. From here you can look down on the *tops* of the sequoias you craned at from the ground. On clear days you can see the Coast Ranges, more than 100 miles west.

When you return from the summit, you can retrace your steps on the Moro Rock Trail or return to the village via the 2¹/₃-mile **Soldiers Trail,** named for the US Cavalry troopers who patrolled the sequoias before the Park Service's rangers took over the task.

Mineral King

50 miles round-trip; at least a full day

Three miles north of the town of Three Rivers, near the Ash Mountain Entrance, is the sign for **Mineral King,** in 1978 the park's last major addition. It was named in the 1870s by prospectors who got little more than unfulfilled dreams from it. In the 1960s dreams of a ski resort also failed to come true because of public opposition.

Turn off Calif. 198 onto a narrow, twisting, 25-mile road. (One driver counted 29 turns in a single mile.) To avoid driving it twice in one grueling day, plan to stay at least a night. But, if you must do it in a single day, start early. Mineral King is a hiker's paradise. And the road is the secret to the paradise's solitude. "The road is terrible," one grinning hiker said. "And we hope it stays that way."

During the summer, stop at the **Mineral King Ranger Station** and check to see whether a ranger-guided walk is scheduled that day. Or take a hike on your own. Get a map at the station, find a legal parking place, and select a trail. Remember that all trails here begin at altitudes of at least 7,500 feet and climb steeply. If you are not acclimated to the high elevations here, you may suffer altitude sickness.

A good hike for beginners: **Eagle Lake Trail,** which starts at the Eagle-Mosquito Parking Area. This trail starts gently, then begins to get steep near **Spring Creek,** which sprouts from the rocky mountainside. Every switchback is an overlook for a stunning view. Watch for marmots, which sometimes stand up and watch back, and tiny pikas, which whistle and scurry around. After a 2-mile climb, you come to the **Eagle Sink Holes,** where water disappears just as suddenly as the creek appeared. Here you can choose to turn around and start down or continue up another 1½ miles to **Eagle Lake,** a tarn.

Information & Activities

Headquarters
Ash Mountain, Three Rivers, California 93271. Phone (209) 565-3134.

Seasons & Accessibility
Park open year-round. Roads to Mineral King (Sequoia) and to Cedar Grove (Kings Canyon) closed in winter; Generals Highway from Lodgepole to Grant Grove may close after heavy snowstorms; also at night in winter. Call (209) 565-3351 for current weather and road information.

Visitor & Information Centers
Sequoia: Lodgepole Visitor Center and Giant Forest Village Information Booth, both in Giant Forest; Foothills Visitor Center in Ash Mountain, where Hwy. 198 enters park; Mineral King Ranger Station in south of park. Lodgepole and Foothills open daily all year; others open summer only. *Kings Canyon:* Grant Grove Visitor Center open daily all year; Cedar Grove Ranger Station open daily in summer; both on Hwy. 180. For visitor information call (209) 565-3134 or 3341.

Entrance Fees
$5 per vehicle per week, good for multiple entries. $2 per person on bus, foot, bicycle, motorcycle.

Facilities for Disabled
Visitor centers and Cedar Grove Ranger Station are wheelchair accessible, as are some trails in Grant Grove and Giant Forest. Info. sheet.

Things to Do
Free naturalist-led activities (many offered in summer only): nature walks and talks, camera walks, night sky watches, children's programs, firefighting demonstrations, evening programs, snowshoe walks. Also, bus tours, Crystal Cave tours, nature center, fishing (license needed), horseback trail rides, pack trips, cross-country skiing.

Overnight Backpacking
Free permits required. Reservations for specific trails and dates must be made by mail. A few permits issued on departure day, first come, first served. Information: (209) 565-3306.

Campgrounds
Sequoia: seven campgrounds, 14-day limit mid-June to mid-Sept. **Lodgepole, Potwisha** open all year. Others open spring to fall, depending on weather. First come, first served, except **Lodgepole,** which requires reservations through MISTIX (see page 11) from mid-May to mid-Sept. Fees $5-$10 per night. Showers near **Lodgepole,** closed in winter. RV sites at **Dorst, Lodgepole,** and **Potwisha;** no hookups. Food services in park. *Kings Canyon:* seven campgrounds, 14-day summer limit. **Azalea** open all year, others late April to mid-Sept. First come, first served. Fees $8 per night. Showers nearby. Tent and RV sites; no hookups. Reservations required for **Canyon View Group Campground;** write Canyon View Group Sites, Box 948, Kings Canyon NP, Calif. 93633. Food services in park.

Hotels, Motels, & Inns
(unless otherwise noted, rates are for 2 persons in a double room, high season)
INSIDE THE PARKS:
The following camps and lodges are operated by Guest Services, P.O. Box 789, Three Rivers, Calif. 93271. To reserve call (209) 561-3314. **Bearpaw Meadow Camp** *(Sequoia)* 6 tent cabins, central showers. $85, includes meals. Open mid-June to mid-Sept. **Giant Forest Lodge** *(Sequoia)* 243 units. Rooms $66-$85; cabins $53-$100; rustic cabins, central showers $30-$36. Restaurant open May through October. **Cedar Grove Lodge** *(Kings Canyon)* 18 units. $75. AC, rest. Open May through Oct. **Grant Grove Lodge** *(Kings Canyon)* 52 cabins, 9 with private baths. $30-$53. Restaurant.

Also, in *Sequoia National Forest:*
Stony Creek Lodge 11 rooms. $75. Rest. Open late May to Labor Day.
OUTSIDE THE PARKS:
In Three Rivers, Calif. 93271:
Best Western Holiday Lodge (on Calif. Hwy. 198) P.O. Box 129. (209) 561-4119. 45 units. $51-$80. AC, pool.
Lazy J Ranch Motel 39625 Sierra Dr. (800) 341-8000 or (209) 561-4449. 19 units, 6 kitchenettes. $50. AC, pool.
The River Inn 45175 Sierra Dr. (209) 561-4367. 12 units. $51-$55. AC.

Excursions

Sequoia National Forest
Porterville, California

Thirty-eight groves of giant sequoias, including the largest tree in any national forest, are only part of the attractions here. Four stretches of Wild and Scenic Rivers and five wilderness areas provide recreational challenges. 1,123,100 acres. Facilities include 1,100 campsites, hiking, boating, white-water rafting, climbing, bicycling, fishing, horseback riding, hunting, picnic areas, scenic drives, winter sports, handicapped access. Open year-round. Adjoins Sequoia & Kings Canyon National Parks on south, west, and north. (209) 784-1500.

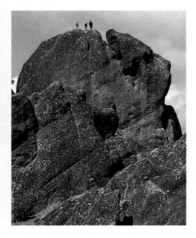

Pinnacles National Monument
Paicines, California

Rising abruptly from gentle hill country, the spires and crags of the Pinnacles formation are remains of a volcanic mountain formed some 200 miles to the south. Pulled north and west by the San Andreas Rift, the Pinnacles are still in migration. Hiking trails, ranging from easy to extremely strenuous, take visitors from chaparral-covered slopes, through caves, to the high peaks. 16,265 acres. Facilities include 24 campsites, climbing, picnic areas, handicapped access. Visitor center near east entrance off Calif. Hwy. 25, about 130 miles west of Sequoia & Kings Canyon NPs. (408) 389-4485.

Inyo National Forest
Bishop, California

Inyo boasts Mt. Whitney, at 14,495 feet the highest peak in the lower 48 states; the spectacular saline Mono Lake; and bristlecone pines, earth's oldest living things. Also contains parts of five wilderness areas, notably the John Muir and Ansel Adams areas. 2,046,346 acres. Facilities: 2,600 campsites, hiking, boating, boat ramp, climbing, bicycling, fishing, horseback riding, hunting, picnic areas, scenic drives, winter sports, water sports, handicapped access. Open year-round; most campsites open May-October. Visitor center at Mammoth Lakes on Calif. Hwy. 203. (619) 873-5841.

Wintry Yosemite Valley; at left, El Capitan

Yosemite

California

Established October 1, 1890

748,542 acres

In a high-country meadow two hikers crouch near the edge of a mirroring lake and watch a pika as it harvests blades of grass for a nest deep within a huge rock pile. When they resume walking, there is no other person in sight for as far as they can see. And on this sparkling summer's day, the view seems endless.

In the valley's crowded mall, families stroll by, eating ice cream, dodging bicycles. People pile in and out of buses. Shoppers hunt for souvenirs. Kids hang around a pizza place. Rock-climbers, coils of rope slung over their shoulders, swap stories over beers at an outdoor bar. On this summer's day about 14,000 people are in the valley village.

Both the solitude of the alpine ridge and the throngs of the valley are part of the experience when you visit Yosemite National Park. "No temple made with hands can compare with Yosemite," wrote naturalist John Muir, whose crusading led to the creation of the park. To this temple come more than three million visitors a year. And about 90 percent of them go to the valley, a mile-wide, 7-mile-long canyon cut by a river, then widened and deepened by glacial action. Walled by massive domes and soaring pinnacles, it covers about one percent of the park. In summer, the concentration of automobiles brings traffic jams and air pollution.

Beyond the valley some 800 miles of marked trails offer hikers easy jaunts or grueling tests of endurance in the High Sierra wilderness. Even the casual visitor can explore this

check with Amtrak about connecting buses to Yosemite. Airports: Fresno and Merced.

When to Go
All-year park. Avoid holiday weekends. Expect filled campgrounds from June through August and some crowding in late spring and early fall. Be sure you have reserved accommodations before attempting an overnight visit. You will find skiing and other winter activities in the Badger Pass Ski Area from about Thanksgiving to mid-April.

How to Visit
When a visitor asked a Yosemite ranger what he would do if he had only a day to visit the park, the ranger answered, "I'd weep." If you must zip through this huge park in a day, begin with **Yosemite Valley.** But even a dawn-to-dusk, 1-day visit hardly allows enough time for more than a tour of the valley plus a look at one or two of the park's other major areas, such as the vistas from **Glacier Point** (in winter, road closed beyond the ski area) and the sequoias of the **Mariposa Grove.** As an alternative or on another day between late May and early November, take the High Sierra **Tioga Road** to explore the park's alpine country. Better still, stay long enough to get beyond the crowds and discover the sense of seclusion this great park can give you.

solitude without getting outfitted for a backpack expedition.

The park, roughly the size of Rhode Island, is a United Nations World Heritage site. Here, in five of the seven continental life zones, live the mule deer and chipmunks of the valley and the marmots and pikas of the heights; the brush rabbit and chaparral of the near desert; the dogwood and warblers of mid-elevation forests; the red fir and Jeffrey pine of mile-high forests; the dwarf willow and matted flowers of Yosemite's majestic mountains.

How to Get There
From Merced (about 70 miles away): Calif. Hwy. 140 to the Arch Rock Entrance. Also from the west: Calif. Hwy. 120 to the Big Oak Flat Entrance. From the south, via Fresno: Calif. Hwy. 41 to the South Entrance. From the northeast, via Lee Vining: Calif. 120 to the Tioga Pass Entrance (closed mid-November to late May). Trains stop at Merced;

Yosemite Valley

12 miles; at least a half to full day

Don't add to the traffic congestion by driving the heavily used one-way valley roads. Park at one of the lots along the shuttle bus route and take the free bus, which loops through the east end of the valley. (See **inset map** on pages 246-247.) You can also explore the valley on a rented bike or on foot. Or, buy a ticket for a 2-hour guided tram tour. (The roofless trams also venture out on moonlit nights and glide through the ghostly light that bathes the valley.)

If you're traveling by shuttle bus, get off at the **Valley Visitor Center** in **Yosemite Village,** where a short slide presentation introduces Yosemite's history, grandeur, and geology. For an easy stroll in an oasis of quiet,

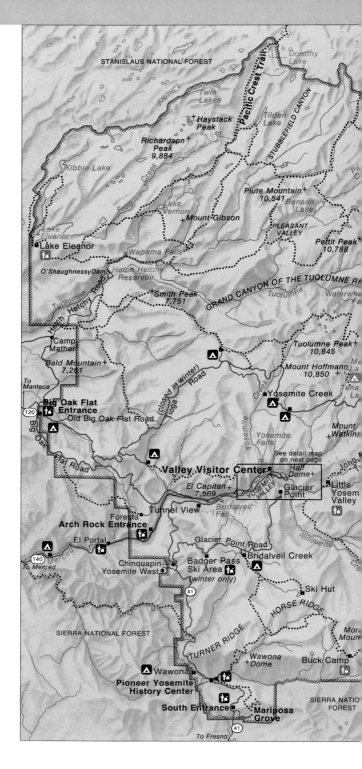

STANISLAUS NATIONAL FOREST

Dorothy Lake

Pacific Crest Trail

Twin Lakes

Haystack Peak

Tilden Lake

STUBBLEFIELD CANYON

Richardson Peak
9,884

Kibbie Lake

Creek

Piute Mountain
10,541

Benson Lake

Lake Vernon

Mount Gibson

PLEASANT VALLEY

Frog

Pettit Peak
10,788

Lake Eleanor

Lake Eleanor

Wapama Falls

GRAND CANYON OF THE TUOLUMNE RI

O'Shaughnessy Dam

Hetch Hetchy Reservoir

Tuolumne

Waterwh Fa

Smith Peak
7,751

Hetch Hetchy Road

Camp Mather

Tuolumne Peak
10,845

Tioga Road (closed in winter)

Bald Mountain
7,261

M La

Mount Hoffmann
10,850

Tena La

To Manteca

120

Big Oak Flat Entrance

Creek

Yosemite Creek

Old Big Oak Flat Road

Big Oak Flat Road

Yosemite Falls

Mount Watkins

Yosemite

See detail map on next page

Valley Visitor Center

Half Dome

John

El Capitan
7,569

YOSEMITE VALLEY

Glacier Point

Little Yosemite Valley

Foresta

Tunnel View

Bridalveil Fall

Illouette Cr

Arch Rock Entrance

140

El Portal

Glacier Point Road

Bridalveil Creek

To Merced

Merced

Chinquapin
Yosemite West

Badger Pass Ski Area
(winter only)

Ski Hut

41

HORSE RIDGE

SIERRA NATIONAL FOREST

TURNER RIDGE

Wawona Dome

Mor Moun

Buck Camp

Wawona

Pioneer Yosemite History Center

South Entrance

Mariposa Grove

SIERRA NATIO FOREST

41

To Fresno

Yosemite Falls above meadows of cow parsnip

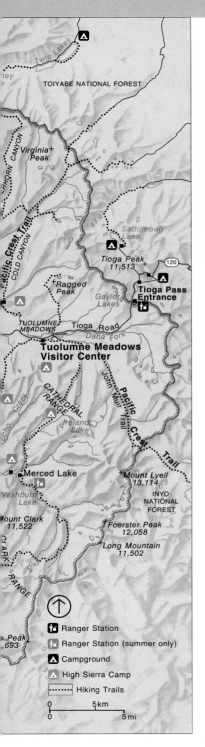

look for **Cook's Meadow** just south of
the visitor center. The trail begins at
the west end of the mall; pick up a
self-guiding brochure. Deer and human sometimes encounter each other
here. Keep your distance.

Walk around the nearby **Indian Village,** where exhibits and bark houses
evoke the life of the valley's earlier
dwellers. Visit the **Indian Cultural Exhibit** to see the baskets and other
works of art produced by Yosemite
area tribes. At the bustling village
shops you can find just about what
you would find in any resort-town
mall. But if you want to see the *park*,
don't tarry here.

Get back on the bus and travel to
the **Yosemite Falls** shuttle bus stop.
The upper and lower falls together
form the highest waterfall in North
America (2,425 feet) and the second
highest in the world. A ¼-mile walk
takes you to the base of **Lower Yosemite Fall.** (If you have the stamina
and another full day, take the strenuous 3⅖-mile hike to **Upper Yosemite
Fall,** where you will be rewarded with
spectacular valley views away from
the crowds. Look for the trailhead
behind the gas station and the Sun-
nyside Campground parking lot.)

Back on the bus, crane your neck
for other scenic wonders. And get off
when you want to absorb them; there
will be another bus soon. On the
3,000-foot vertical wall of **El Capitan**
you may spot the tiny figures of
climbers. During their ascent, which

Ranger Station
Ranger Station (summer only)
Campground
High Sierra Camp
Hiking Trails

0   5km
0   5mi

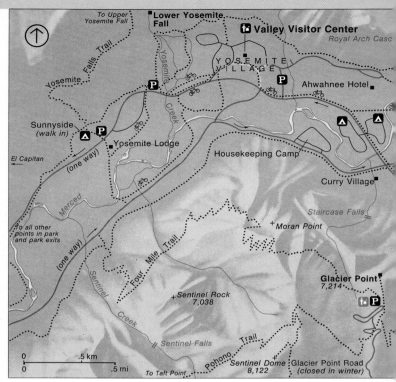

Cathedral Peak, near Tuolumne Meadows

Steller's jay

may take days, they sleep in slings hanging from the cliff. After looping east you'll pass **Sentinel Rock** and then **Glacier Point,** both giant granite blocks shaped by glaciers. (An arduous hike up **Four Mile Trail** takes you in 3 or 4 hours to Glacier Point's breathtaking vistas; for the trailhead, get off the bus at Yosemite Lodge and walk behind it to Southside Drive, then west $\frac{1}{4}$ mile to road marker V18.)

If you're still on the shuttle bus, alight at the stop near the **Happy Isles Nature Center.** After a walk around these two bridge-linked river islands, consider hiking the moderately strenuous $1\frac{1}{2}$-mile trail to the top of 317-foot **Vernal Fall.** From this trail you can also see 594-foot **Nevada Fall.** Massive **Half Dome,** a cracked block of granite gnawed by a glacier, soars 4,733 feet, dominating this part of the valley.

A gentle hike from the next shuttle bus stop takes you to lovely **Mirror Lake** a mile away; a 3-mile trail loops around it and above it. In spring and early summer, the lake reflects stun-

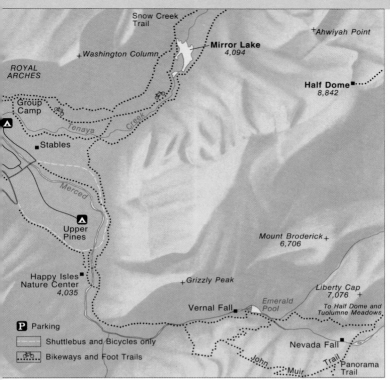

Eroded granite atop Sentinel Dome

ning mountain scenery; during the summer, it mostly dries up.

On the way back to Yosemite Village, you'll pass the **Royal Arches,** glacier-carved granite shells. You will see the full spectrum of Yosemite accommodations along the bus route: from tents, trailers, and clusters of concrete shelters to lodges, cabins, and a luxury hotel.

Glacier Point & Mariposa Grove

52 miles one way; a half to full day

Leave the valley by taking Calif. 41 (the Wawona Road) to the **Wawona Tunnel.** Park at the turnout at the tunnel's eastern end and walk over to the **Tunnel View Overlook** to see what

Staghorn lichens on conifer

Wildflowers at Tuolumne Meadows

has been called the most photographed vista on earth. Spread before you is a granite panorama encompassing El Capitan, Half Dome, Sentinel Rock, **Cathedral Rocks**, and 620-foot **Bridalveil Fall**, in the late afternoon a scrim of shimmering rainbows. About 7 miles beyond the tunnel, turn left on the **Glacier Point Road** (in winter, closed beyond the ski area). The 16-mile road, flanked by fir-and-pine forests, ends in a parking lot. Walk about 300 yards to the first of several overlooks on Glacier Point, which thrusts 3,214 feet above the valley, providing an enormous stage for a scenic spectacular of lights and shadows. Mirror Lake lies below; Half Dome looms across; Vernal Fall and Nevada Fall hang like white tassels in the distance.

Return to the intersection of Calif. 41 and drive south 13 miles to **Wawona**, site of a hotel, golf course, and other facilities. Stop at the **Pioneer Yosemite History Center**, where, in summer, visitors enter restored buildings and chat about the past with costumed interpreters who portray such real people as a cavalry trooper, a 19th-century homesteader, and a mountaineer. From conversations with these players in the bygone you learn Yosemite Valley's modern history, which began in 1851, when members of the Mariposa Battalion were tracking down Indians accused of raiding nearby trading posts. The story goes that some of the Indians yelled *"Yohamite,"* which meant "there are killers

among them." Thinking that this was the Indians' name, the whites gave an approximation of it to the valley.

Word of the radiantly beautiful valley spread quickly, and the first tourists arrived in 1855. They were soon followed by homesteaders and hotelkeepers. Next came the nation's early conservationists, who campaigned to protect not only the valley but also a grove of giant sequoias.

Return to Calif. Hwy. 41 and continue south. At the **South Entrance** continue straight to Yosemite's other long-cherished feature, the **Mariposa Grove**. From early May to late October you can take a guided tram tour of the grove's giant sequoias ($7 adult, $5 child). Or, you can walk among them at any time of year.

On June 30, 1864, President Lincoln took time out from the Civil War to sign a bill granting both the valley and this grove to the State of California. Never before had a nation set aside land as a wilderness preserve. Yosemite became a national park in 1890, although not until 1906 did California formally give the original grants back to the federal government. More land was added in 1913, the year automobiles were again allowed in the park after a ban.

The best known of the grove's more than 200 giant sequoias is the **Grizzly Giant**, whose estimated age, 2,700 years, makes it one of the oldest living sequoias. A trail takes you past the **Fallen Monarch;** its shallow roots help explain why winds sometimes topple these giants. Another

Mule deer in Yosemite Valley

fallen star, the **Wawona Tunnel Tree**, recalls another era. The living sequoia, gutted in 1881 to make a drive-through tree for horse-drawn wagons, became a photogenic attraction for generations of automobile travelers. The tree toppled in 1969. The decision not to cut a hole in another tree symbolized the dawning of an ecologically enlightened age.

Tioga Road & Tuolumne Meadows

124 miles round-trip; at least a full day

Take the **Big Oak Flat Road**, a modern version of an old mining town road, west out of the valley for 9 miles to 6,200-foot **Crane Flat** (a local term for "meadow") and turn right onto **Tioga Road**, which climbs into an alpine world of snowy peaks, crystal lakes, wind-tousled meadows, and relatively few people. The road (closed in winter) crosses the park. Even in July you may see snow alongside the road. Stop at the frequent turnouts for magnificent views and interpretive signs that explain the geology behind the splendor. Gauge your time and gasoline. The nearest gas station on this winding, climbing mountain road is 1 mile east of the **Tuolumne Meadows Visitor Center**, 40 miles from **Yosemite Valley.**

At the visitor center are **Tuolumne Meadows**, which, millions of years ago, were under a sea of ice more than 2,000 feet deep. Wildflowers—among them Jeffrey shooting stars, Lewis paintbrushes, monkeyflowers, and marsh marigolds—carpet this High Sierra realm in spring and summer. Trails of varying difficulty branch out here and elsewhere along the road. Some trails link five commercially run High Sierra camps with showers and dining halls (reservations required). The camps are spaced 8 to 10 miles apart.

The road climbs to 9,945-foot **Tioga Pass**, highest automobile pass in California, at the park's eastern boundary. At a trailhead here you can take a $\frac{1}{2}$-day alpine hike that rewards you with glimpses of both beauty and history. The $2\frac{1}{2}$-mile trail climbs sharply from 9,945 feet to about 10,500, then descends to **Middle Gaylor Lake**, a gem set in a broad meadow prowled by marmots and ground squirrels. The trail again winds upward, first to **Upper Gaylor Lake**, then to a surprise: the ruins of a stone cabin, rusting bits of machinery, and half-filled shafts—relics of a failed 19th-century silver mine.

Information & Activities

Headquarters
P.O. Box 577, Yosemite National Park, Calif. 95389. Phone (209) 372-0200.

Seasons & Accessibility
Park open year-round. Tioga (Hwy. 120 east) and Glacier Point Roads closed by snow from about mid-November to late May. Call (209) 372-0209 for recorded conditions. In winter, call (209) 372-1338 for Badger Pass ski information.

Free shuttle buses operate in the valley year-round and at Wawona and Tuolumne Meadows in summer.

Visitor & Information Centers
Valley Visitor Center open all year. Tuolumne Meadows Visitor Center near Tioga Pass Entrance open summer only. Information also available at Happy Isles Nature Center, in valley, and at Big Oak Flat Entrance on Hwy. 120 at western edge of park, both open spring through fall. For information call (209) 372-0264.

Entrance Fee
$5 per car per week, multiple entries.

Pets
Not permitted in buildings, backcountry, on beaches, or trails. Kennel at Yosemite stables in summer.

Facilities for Disabled
Visitor centers, the nature and art centers, and some trails are wheelchair accessible. Free brochure.

Things to Do
Free naturalist-led activities: day and evening walks and talks, hikes, camera walks, children's and evening programs, living history; Indian cultural interpretation. Also, auto tape tours, bus and tram tours, stagecoach rides, films, plays, concerts, art and photography classes, museums, horseback riding (call 209-372-1248), climbing, fishing, bicycling, swimming, boating, ice-skating, downhill and cross-country skiing.

Overnight Backpacking
Free permit required; issued first come, first served; apply up to 24 hours in advance of trip to a park wilderness permit station. Advance summer reservations available by mail Feb. 1 to May 31; write wilderness office at park address.

Campgrounds
Eighteen campgrounds; in summer, 7-day to 14-day limits; other times some have 30-day limit. Four open all year; others open mid-spring to mid-fall or summer only. Reservations through MISTIX (see page 11) required year-round for all in the valley, for **Hodgdon Meadow** spring through fall, and for **Crane Flat** and half of **Tuolumne Meadows** in summer. Fees $2-$12 per night. Most have RV sites. Five group campgrounds; reserve through MISTIX, except for **Bridalveil** and **Wawona**—write Wawona Ranger Office, P.O. Box 2027, Yosemite, Calif. 95389.

Hotels, Motels, & Inns
(unless otherwise noted, rates are for 2 persons in a double room, high season)

INSIDE THE PARK:
The Yosemite Park and Curry Co., 5410 East Home Ave., Fresno, Calif. 93727, operates the following. Reservations: (209) 252-4848. **The Ahwahnee** (Yosemite Valley) (209) 372-1407. 123 units. $175-$200. AC, pool, rest. **Curry Village** (Yosemite Valley) (209) 372-1233. 18 rooms; 183 cabins, 103 private baths; 427 tent-cabins, central showers. $25-$69. Pool, rest. **High Sierra Camps** (209) 454-2002. 5 camps with tent-cabins, central showers. $72 per person, 2 meals. Open summer. Reserve by mail from early Dec. **Tuolumne Meadows Lodge** (8,600 ft., at Tuolumne Meadows) (209) 372-1313. 69 tent-cabins, central showers. $36. Rest. Open summer. **Wawona Hotel** (Hwy. 41, 27 miles south of valley) (209) 375-6556. 105 rooms, 50 private baths. $60-$80. Pool, rest. Open all year. **White Wolf Lodge** (Tioga Road) (209) 372-1316. 4 cabins, private baths; 24 tent-cabins, central bath. $32-$55. Restaurant. Open summer. **Yosemite Lodge** (Yosemite Valley) (209) 372-1274. 495 rooms/cabins, some private baths. $44-$85. Pool, rest. Open all year.

Also, **The Redwoods** (Chilnualna Falls Rd.) P.O. Box 2085, Wawona Station, Calif. 95389. (209) 375-6666. 81 cottages with kitchens. $68-$393.

Excursions

Stanislaus National Forest
Sonora, California

This High Sierra forest offers a vast array of recreational activities ranging from white-water rafting on the Wild and Scenic Tuolumne River to pack riding to trout fishing on timbered Alpine Lake. Contains parts of three wilderness areas. 898,322 acres. Facilities include 1,143 campsites, hiking, boating, boat ramp, fishing, horseback riding, hunting, off-road vehicle routes, scenic drives, winter sports, water sports. Open all year; backcountry open June-October. Most campsites open May-October. Adjoins Yosemite NP on north and east. Information at Buck Meadows Ranger Station on Calif. Hwy. 120. (209) 962-7825.

Devils Postpile National Monument
Mammoth Lakes, California

Surrounded by the Inyo National Forest, this monument boasts a spectacular formation of basalt columns 60 feet high, which were born of the fire of volcanic eruptions and carved by the ice of overriding glaciers. At Rainbow Falls, water plunges 101 feet over a rhyodacite cliff. 798 acres. Facilities include 23 campsites (open July-Oct.), hiking, fishing, shuttle bus. Open July-Oct. Off Calif. Hwy. 203 about 40 miles from Yosemite NP. (619) 934-2289.

Sierra National Forest
Mariposa, California

Like the Stanislaus NF to the north, Sierra offers both rugged backcountry and developed recreational facilities. Contains parts of five wilderness areas, a stretch of white water on the Kings River, groves of giant sequoias, and the mountain-ringed Mammoth Pool Reservoir. 1,303,037 acres. Facilities include 1,500 campsites, food services, hiking, boating, boat ramp, bicycling, fishing, horseback riding, hunting, picnic areas, water sports, winter sports, handicapped access. Open all year; some backcountry areas closed in winter. Most campsites open May-Oct. Adjoins Yosemite NP. Info. at Mariposa on Calif. Hwy. 49. (209) 966-3638.

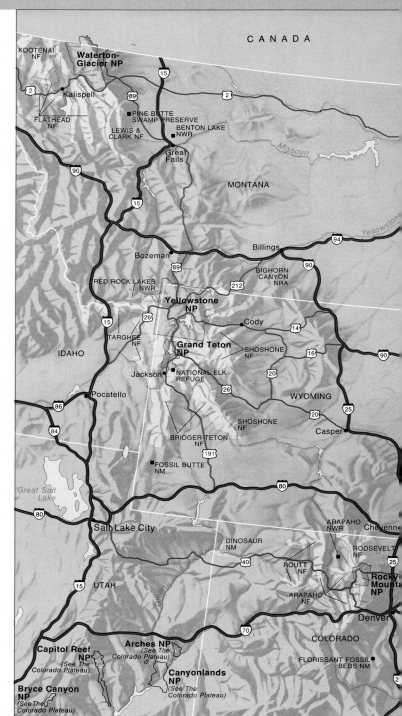

CANADA

KOOTENAI NF

Waterton-Glacier NP

Kalispell

FLATHEAD NF

PINE BUTTE SWAMP PRESERVE

LEWIS & CLARK NF

BENTON LAKE NWR

Great Falls

MONTANA

Missouri

Billings

Yellowstone

Bozeman

RED ROCK LAKES NWR

BIGHORN CANYON NRA

Yellowstone NP

Cody

TARGHEE NF

Grand Teton NP

SHOSHONE NF

IDAHO

Jackson

NATIONAL ELK REFUGE

Pocatello

BRIDGER-TETON NF

SHOSHONE NF

WYOMING

Casper

FOSSIL BUTTE NM

Great Salt Lake

Salt Lake City

DINOSAUR NM

ARAPAHO NWR

Cheyenn

ROOSEVELT NF

ROUTT NF

UTAH

Green

ARAPAHO NF

Rocky Mountain NP

Denver

COLORADO

Capitol Reef NP
(See The Colorado Plateau)

Arches NP
(See The Colorado Plateau)

Canyonlands NP
(See The Colorado Plateau)

FLORISSANT FOSSIL BEDS NM

Bryce Canyon NP
(See The Colorado Plateau)

Preceding pages: Aspens, Rocky Mountains

The Rocky Mountains

Craggy peaks capped by glimmering glaciers, fields run riot with wildflowers, lakes as smooth and blue as a summer sky—these images from the Rocky Mountains epitomize for many just what a national park should look like. Not surprisingly, four of the Rockies' parks rank among the country's most visited.

Yet this region offers more than mountains, since the forces that created the peaks contoured neighboring landscapes as well. The Black Hills of South Dakota uplifted along with the Rocky Mountains some 70 million years ago, cracking as they buckled upward. Enlarged by acidic groundwater, the cracks eventually produced the numerous underground passageways of Wind Cave. Streams flowing from the young Rockies also laid down the colorful mud that rivers would later carve into the buttes and gorges of the Dakota badlands, showcased in Badlands and Theodore Roosevelt National Parks.

The Rockies' parks and forests preserve the spirit of America's western frontier not only in their rugged scenery, but also in historic ranches, ghost towns, and in their abundance of wildlife. Yellowstone and Waterton-Glacier—together with their surrounding public lands—remain two of the last strongholds of the grizzly bear. In some of the parks visitors can watch elk, bighorn sheep, mule deer, and remnants of the great bison herds that once thundered across the Great Plains.

Rockies parks provide case studies in how wilderness manages itself. In Yellowstone, for instance, the visitor can get excellent glimpses of natural recovery in the wake of the 1988 fires. Less encouraging are the real estate development and plans for oil and gas drilling on the fringes of some parks. Such activities can shrink the habitats of wide-roaming animals, endangering their future.

The Rocky Mountain region invites the visitor to experience peaks along the Continental Divide, plus geysers, prairies, caverns, badlands—and lots of driving. Count on a drive of 520 miles from Rocky Mountain National Park to Grand Teton and nearly 400 miles from Yellowstone to Waterton-Glacier.

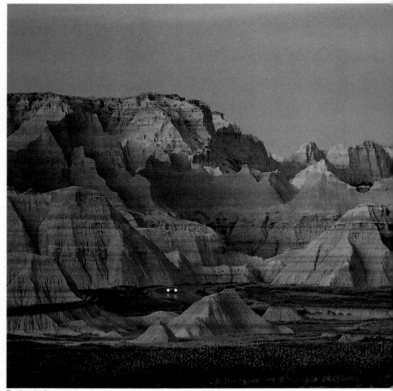

Badlands, feared by early pioneers, dwarfing a car headed west through the North Unit

Badlands

South Dakota

Established November 10, 1978

244,300 acres

They call it The Wall. It extends for a hundred miles through the dry plains of South Dakota—a huge natural barrier ridging the landscape, sculptured into fantastic pinnacles and tortuous gullies by the forces of water. Those who pass through the upper prairie a few miles north might not even know it exists. Those who traverse the lower prairie to the south, however, can't miss it; it rises above them like a city skyline in ruins, petrified.

The Badlands Wall, much of which is preserved within the boundaries of Badlands National Park, may not conform to everyone's idea of beauty, but nobody can deny its theatricality. It's been compared to an enormous stage set—colorful, dramatic, and not quite real. Water, the main player on this stage, has been carving away at the cliffs for the past half million years or so, and it carves away an entire inch or more in some places each year. But there have been other players, too. Beasts with names like titanothere and archaeotherium once roamed here; their fossilized bones can be found by the hundreds. And today the Badlands Wall serves as a backdrop for bison, pronghorn, and bighorn sheep, as well as the 1.2 million human visitors who pass through the park every year.

A national monument since 1939, Badlands acquired the South Unit in 1976, adding yet another dimension to the drama. This large stretch of land belongs to the Oglala Sioux, and one of their most sacred places is

now preserved within it. It was here, on Stronghold Table, that the final Ghost Dance took place in 1890, just a few days before more than 150 Sioux were massacred at Wounded Knee, 25 miles south.

How to Get There
The park is about 3 miles south of I-90 at Exit 131, 75 miles east of Rapid City and 27 miles west of Kadoka. Airport: Rapid City Regional.

When to Go
All-year park. As with most parks this far north, summer is the most popular season, though daytime temperatures may top 100°F. Spring and fall are usually pleasant, with moderate temperatures and fewer crowds. Winters can be bitter cold, but snow accumulations are rarely a problem in this arid climate.

How to Visit
The 89-mile **Badlands Loop** provides a rich eyeful of classic badlands for a 1-day **North Unit** visit (a shorter loop can be devised as described below). Make sure to take advantage of the informative nature trails. For those with a second day and a pioneering spirit, a trip to the park's undeveloped **South Unit** can be rewarding; don't fail to check with rangers about road conditions before going.

North Unit: Badlands Loop
32 or 89 miles; a half day or full day

Enter the park at the **Northeast Entrance** on Hwy. 240 and then stop at the **Big Badlands Overlook** for your first, but by no means best, view of **The Wall** from above. Before you are the characteristic tiered cliffs of the badlands, dropping precipitously to the lower prairie, where the **White River** meanders between a fringe of cottonwood trees.

Stop next at the **Windows Overlook**, which serves as the trailhead for three short nature trails—the **Door**, **Window**, and **Notch Trails.** Guide leaflets are available for the Door Trail. While these trails may sound like the components of an architectural tour, they are actually brief forays into the Badlands Wall. The Door Trail ($^3/_4$-mile round-trip, partly paved) passes through a narrow opening in The Wall into a jumble of barren, eroded hills reminiscent of the lunar surface. The Window Trail ($^1/_4$-mile round-trip, paved) leads to a natural window overlooking a deeply cut canyon. And the Notch Trail ($1^1/_2$ miles round-trip, very rough) leads up a shaky ladder and along the side of a gully to a break in The Wall, where you can look out over prairie and badlands, the White River, and the Pine Ridge Indian Reservation on the plain below.

Back in the car, a short drive brings you to the head of the **Cliff Shelf Nature Trail.** This $^1/_2$-mile very steep, but paved loop takes you through a fascinating microenvironment in the badlands. Many years ago, a giant block of stone fell from the surrounding cliffs, creating this relatively flat shelf. The impact of the fall compacted the stone, making it less porous and allowing water to collect here. The resulting vegetation makes this place a delightful oa-

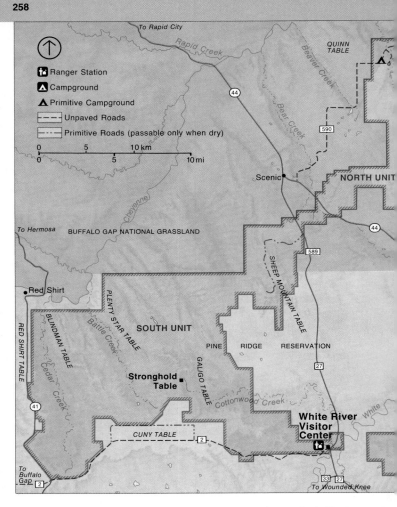

Ranger Station
Campground
Primitive Campground
----- Unpaved Roads
-·-·- Primitive Roads (passable only when dry)

0   5   10 km
0   5   10 mi

To Rapid City

Rapid Creek

QUINN TABLE

Beaver Creek

Bear Creek

44

590

Scenic

NORTH UNIT

44

Cheyenne

To Hermosa   BUFFALO GAP NATIONAL GRASSLAND

589

SHEEP MOUNTAIN TABLE

Red Shirt

PLENTY STAR TABLE

BLINDMAN TABLE

Battle Creek

SOUTH UNIT

PINE   RIDGE   RESERVATION

RED SHIRT TABLE

Cedar Creek

Stronghold Table

GALIGO TABLE

27

41

Cottonwood Creek

White River Visitor Center

CUNY TABLE

2

White

To Buffalo Gap
2

33   27
To Wounded Knee

sis in the otherwise barren wall. You can see mule deer browsing at dawn or dusk, and flamboyant magpies careening across the sky anytime.

Stop next at the **Ben Reifel Visitor Center**, where a video and various other exhibits provide a good introduction to the park's history and geology. From this point, the road descends to the lower prairie for a brief stretch and then begins a gradual, stunning climb back up the Badlands Wall. The **Fossil Exhibit Trail** takes you on a $1/4$-mile paved walk through an area dense with fossils. Replicas of some are displayed at trailside under clear plastic domes.

The road then continues level for 15 miles, punctuated by a dozen or so pullouts; each offers a slightly differ-

ent perspective on the knife-sharp ridges, twisted canyons, and multi-colored hills that characterize this broken terrain. Particularly spectacular among these are the **Yellow Mounds** and **Pinnacles Overlooks.**

If you're short of time, exit the park at this point and rejoin the interstate at the town of Wall. Otherwise make a left turn onto Sage Creek Rim Road and continue along the **Sage Creek Wilderness Area.** This is excellent wildlife country; bison and pronghorn are numerous, and the road passes a town of those always entertaining prairie dogs. Longer hikes into the wilderness area start at the primitive campground about a mile off the road near the park's western boundary.

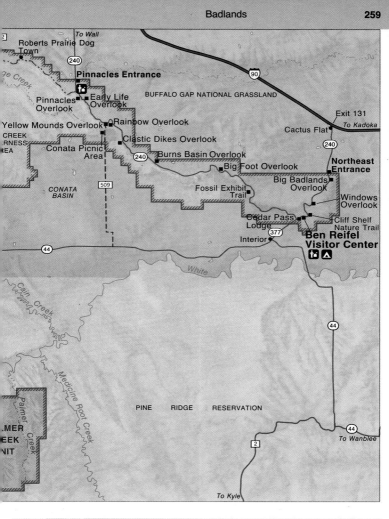

Roberts Prairie Dog Town
To Wall
240
Pinnacles Entrance
Early Life Overlook
Pinnacles Overlook
BUFFALO GAP NATIONAL GRASSLAND
Yellow Mounds Overlook
Rainbow Overlook
CREEK
RNESS
AEA
Clastic Dikes Overlook
Conata Picnic Area
240
Burns Basin Overlook
Exit 131
To Kadoka
Cactus Flat
240
Northeast Entrance
Big Foot Overlook
CONATA BASIN
509
Big Badlands Overlook
Fossil Exhibit Trail
Windows Overlook
Cedar Pass Lodge
Cliff Shelf Nature Trail
Ben Reifel Visitor Center
377
Interior
44
White
44
Cain Creek
Medicine Root Creek
Palmer Creek
MER
EEK
NIT
PINE   RIDGE   RESERVATION
2
44
To Wanblee
To Kyle

The prairie beyond Big Foot Overlook, North Unit

Frosty sunrise on the Badlands

A pronghorn, Badlands denizen

Beyond the campground turnoff, the road leaves the park. To complete the loop, continue along unpaved County Road 590 and make a left onto Hwy. 44. If you're heading toward Rapid City, turn right; this stretch takes you through beautiful **Cheyenne River Valley** prairie and gives you views of the Black Hills. The highway goes through Scenic, the turnoff for the **South Unit**, if you want to continue directly there.

South Unit Drive

about 54 miles; at least a half day

The South Unit is almost entirely undeveloped, so exploring it by car will involve backtracking, driving on rough dirt roads, and generally putting a lot of wear and tear on your vehicle. Don't fail to check with a ranger before setting out.

Begin at the town of Scenic, with its automobile graveyard and shantylike saloon, and head south on County Road 589 for 4 miles. The turnoff for **Sheep Mountain Table** is marked. Follow the road across the flats and up a seemingly impregnable cliff to a grass-topped table dotted with yuccas. If you go on to the juniper grove at the road's end, you can stand on a finger of high land and be almost surrounded by a stunning assortment of rock spires and pinnacles—perhaps the park's best view.

Return to the paved road and continue south for 16 miles to the **White River Visitor Center.** The center, which is open only in summer, features exhibits of Indian culture and a videotape about the Oglala Sioux. Here you can also get detailed directions to other sites in the South Unit.

A visit to the **Stronghold Table** will either be a letdown or the emotional culmination of your visit, depending on your own attitudes. Getting there involves driving some extremely rutted tracks through lonely grasslands, where you will probably get lost (bring a topographical map). It also involves opening and closing many gates. The reward for this effort? An unspectacular view, but the chance to stand in the place where, in December 1890, a group of Sioux danced the Ghost Dance for the last time. In this impassioned ritual, converts fell into hypnotic trances, "died," and envisioned the paradise soon to come, sweeping the white man from the land and repopulating it with buffalo, elk, and antelope. If you go there, keep in mind that for Indians this is a sacred place.

Information & Activities

Headquarters
Interior, South Dakota 57750. Phone (605) 433-5361.

Seasons & Accessibility
Park open year-round. Snowstorms may block roads temporarily in winter. Call park headquarters to check on current road and weather conditions and accessibility to the undeveloped South Unit.

Visitor & Information Centers
Ben Reifel Visitor Center, in the North Unit, open daily all year except Thanksgiving, Christmas, and New Year's Day. White River Visitor Center, in the South Unit, open only in summer.

Entrance Fee
$5 per car per week, collected May through September only.

Pets
Permitted on leashes except in the Sage Creek Wilderness Area.

Facilities for Disabled
Visitor centers and some trails are wheelchair accessible. Free brochure available.

Things to Do
Free naturalist-led activities: nature walks and hikes, evening programs, night walks, fossil demonstrations. Also available, interpretive exhibits and audiovisual programs, hiking, wildlife-watching.

Special Advisories
☐Prairie rattlesnakes and cactuses live here: Watch your step when walking.
☐Bison are unpredictable and can be dangerous: Keep your distance.
☐Be prepared for sudden changes in weather and severe thunderstorms in summer. Check weather conditions by contacting headquarters or a visitor center before you hike.

Overnight Backpacking
No permit required; ask a ranger for advisories.

Campgrounds
Two campgrounds, both with a 14-day limit. **Cedar Pass** and **Sage Creek** rarely fill up and are open all year, first come, first served. (Heavy snows may close them in winter.) Fees $8 per night, May to October only; no water rest of year. No showers. Tent and RV sites; no hookups.
Cedar Pass Group Campground; reservations accepted Memorial Day to Labor Day; campsites $2 per person, $20 minimum; contact park headquarters. Food service in park.

Hotels, Motels, & Inns
(unless otherwise noted, rates are for 2 persons in a double room, high season)
INSIDE THE PARK:
Cedar Pass Lodge (on Hwy. 240 near visitor center) P.O. Box 5, Interior, S. Dak. 57750. (605) 433-5460. 24 cabins. $39. AC, restaurant. Open mid-April through October.
OUTSIDE THE PARK:
In Interior, South Dakota 57750:
Badlands Inn ($\frac{1}{2}$ mile from park entrance) P.O. Box 103. (605) 433-5401. 24 units. $38. AC, pool. Open April through October.
In Wall, South Dakota 57790:
Best Western Plains Motel (1 block off I-90) P.O. Box 393. (800) 528-1234 or (605) 279-2145. 74 units. $45-$68. AC, pool. Open March through November.
Elk Motel (South Blvd.) P.O. Box 424. (605) 279-2127. 47 units. $39-$49. AC, pool.
Hitching Post Motel (Tenth Ave.) P.O. Box 171. (800) 456-2018 or (605) 279-2133. 30 units. $50-$58. AC, pool. Open May through October.
Kings Inn Motel 608 Main St. (605) 279-2178. 26 units. $48-$52. AC.
Sands Motor Inn (804 Glenn St.) P.O. Box 426. (800) 341-8000 or (605) 279-2121. 49 units, 2 with kitchenettes. $50-$60. AC, pool.

For additional accommodations contact the Wall Chamber of Commerce, P.O. Box 527, Wall, S. Dak. 57790. (605) 279-2665.

The Snake River meandering through Jackson Hole toward the Tetons

Grand Teton

Wyoming

Established February 26, 1929

310,516 acres

The peaks of the Teton Range, standing a sheer 7,000 feet above the valley floor, make one of the boldest geologic statements in the Rockies. Unencumbered by foothills, they rise through steep coniferous forest into alpine meadows strewn with wildflowers, past blue and white glaciers to naked granite pinnacles. The Grand, Middle, and South Tetons form the heart of the range. But their neighbors, especially Mt. Owen, Teewinot Mountain, and Mt. Moran, are no less spectacular.

A string of jewel-like lakes, fed by mountain streams, are set tightly against the steep foot of the mountains. Beyond them extends the broad valley called Jackson Hole, covered with sagebrush and punctuated by occasional forested hills and groves of aspen trees—excellent habitats for pronghorn, deer, elk, and other animals. The Snake River, having begun its journey in the Teton Wilderness, winds leisurely past the Tetons on its way to Idaho. The braided sections of the river create wetlands that support moose, elk, deer, beavers, trumpeter swans, sandhill cranes, Canada geese, and all sorts of ducks.

The Tetons are fault-block mountains. About nine million years ago, two blocks of the earth's crust began to shift along a fault line, one tilting down while the other went up. So far, movement has measured some 30,000 vertical feet, most of it from the subsidence of Jackson Hole.

Before Europeans arrived, the Teton area was an important plant-

where visitors see moose, elk, deer, and all kinds of birds.

How to Get There

From Jackson, take US 26/89 north past the National Elk Refuge; Moose Visitor Center and Entrance Station are at Moose. From Dubois, follow US 26 to Moran Junction and turn west to the Buffalo Entrance Station. From Yellowstone NP, the South Entrance road leads directly into the park. The Jackson Hole Airport is inside the park—to the continuing dismay of environmentalists.

When to Go

Something happens all year in the Tetons. Most people visit during July and August, when it's sunny and warm, after the snow has melted in the high country. In September and October, the days are pleasant, nights are brisk, the park is uncrowded, and the animals are still active. You have a better chance of seeing elk than in summer.

Winter, although spectacular, can be very demanding; snowshoeing and cross-country skiing are popular. The main park road, US 26/89, remains open all year, but snow closes Teton Park Road (the "inner road") north of Cottonwood Creek from about the end of October until early May. The Moose-Wilson Road inside the park is also closed. Moose Visitor Center stays open all year. At Teton Village, just south of the park, you'll find excellent downhill skiing.

gathering and hunting ground for Indians of various tribes. In the early 1800s, mountain men spent time here; it was they who called this flat valley ringed by mountains Jackson's Hole after the trapper Davey Jackson. (In recent times the name has lost its apostrophe *s*.) The first settlers were ranchers and farmers. Some of their buildings are historic sites today, although ranching is still done in the vicinity. When the park was established, it included only the mountains. Portions of the valley were added in 1950.

Today the park's 485 square miles encompass both the Teton Range and much of Jackson Hole. Park roads, all of which are in the valley, offer an ever changing panorama of the Tetons. For this reason, most visitors never go far from the road. But the Tetons are also popular with hikers; backcountry trails climb high into the mountains—and behind them. Easy trails in the valley lead around lakes and beside wetlands

Arrowleaf balsam root, common in park

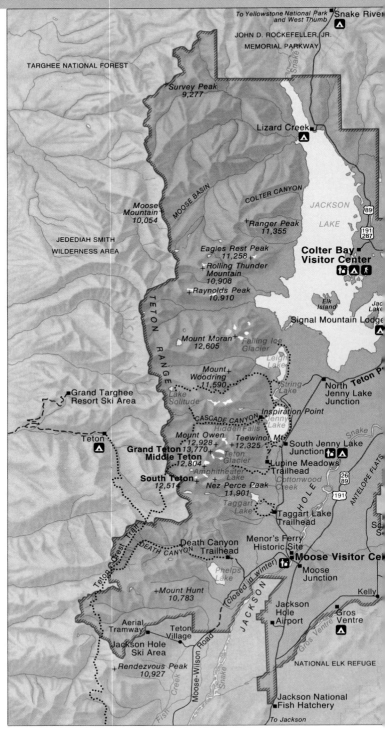

To Yellowstone National Park
and West Thumb

Snake River

JOHN D. ROCKEFELLER, JR.
MEMORIAL PARKWAY

TARGHEE NATIONAL FOREST

*Survey Peak
9,277*

Lizard Creek

COLTER CANYON

*Moose
Mountain
10,054*

MOOSE BASIN

JACKSON

LAKE

89

*Ranger Peak
11,355*

191
287

JEDEDIAH SMITH

WILDERNESS AREA

*Eagles Rest Peak
11,258*

**Colter Bay
Visitor Center**

*Rolling Thunder
Mountain
10,908*

*Raynolds Peak
10,910*

Elk
Island

Jac
Lake

Signal Mountain Lodge

*Mount Moran
12,605*

*Falling Ice
Glacier*

TETON RANGE

*Leigh
Lake*

*Mount
Woodring
11,590*

*String
Lake*

North
Jenny Lake
Junction

Teton P

**Grand Targhee
Resort Ski Area**

*Lake
Solitude*

CASCADE CANYON

Hidden Falls

Inspiration Point

*Jenny
Lake*

Snake

Teton

*Mount Owen
12,928*

*Teewinot Mtn.
12,325*

**South Jenny Lake
Junction**

Grand Teton 13,770

Middle Teton
12,804

*Teton
Glacier*

**Lupine Meadows
Trailhead**

26
89

*Amphitheater
Lake*

*Cottonwood
Creek*

ANTELOPE FLATS

South Teton
12,514

*Nez Perce Peak
11,901*

191

*Taggart
Lake*

HOLE

**Taggart Lake
Trailhead**

**Menor's Ferry
Historic Site**

Moose Visitor Cer

So
S

Teton Crest Trail

**Death Canyon
Trailhead**

DEATH CANYON

*Phelps
Lake*

(closed in winter)

**Moose
Junction**

JACKSON

Kelly

*Mount Hunt
10,783*

**Jackson
Hole
Airport**

**Gros
Ventre**

Fish Creek

Moose-Wilson Road

Snake

**Aerial
Tramway**

**Teton
Village**

**Jackson Hole
Ski Area**

NATIONAL ELK REFUGE

Gros Ventre

*Rendezvous Peak
10,927*

**Jackson National
Fish Hatchery**

To Jackson

Ranger Station

Campground

Hiking Trail

- - - - **Unpaved Roads**

········ **Hiking Trails**

0   5 km

0   5 mi

TETON NATIONAL FOREST

Two Ocean Lake

Emma Matilda Lake

ckson Lake
ction

Buffalo
Entrance Station

Moran
Junction

26
287   To Dubois

Hatchet

26
89

191

TETON NATIONAL FOREST

Atherton
Creek

Lower Slide
Lake

Red Hills   Crystal Creek

Gros Ventre

How to Visit

On a 1-day visit take the **Teton Park Road** from **Moose Junction** to **Jenny Lake** for excellent views of the **Tetons** and short walks or longer hikes. On the second day, go farther north to **Signal Mountain** and **Jackson Lake.** For a longer stay, consider floating the **Snake River,** taking some superb day hikes, canoeing, climbing, or enrolling in a nature seminar.

Teton Park Road & Jenny Lake Loop

17 miles; at least a half day

From **Moose Junction,** cross the **Snake River** to the **Moose Visitor Center,** which includes a small exhibit area. The first right turn after the entrance station leads to **Menor's Ferry Historic Site,** a pioneer homestead. Save that for another day; there are mountains ahead. The **Teton Park Road** climbs up from the river onto a sage-covered flat with the whole Teton panorama in view. You will see the mountains clearly throughout this drive from various changing angles; each viewpoint reveals striking perspectives different from the last.

If you look toward the mountains at **Taggart Lake Trailhead,** you can see the results of a 1985 forest fire. An easy trail offers a closeup view of forest regeneration—an especially interesting and encouraging sight if you plan to visit Yellowstone, where fires burned extensively in the summer of 1988.

Stop at **Glacier Gulch Turnout** for a close-in view of the three **Tetons.** The **Grand Teton,** at 13,770 feet, is the highest point in the range. A major route used by climbers follows the left-hand, southern skyline; just as it appears, there is no easy way to the

Near the base of South Teton

Looking over a field of wildflowers into Targhee National Forest

top. Looking to the left of the Grand, you see the **Middle** and **South Tetons.** The sharp pinnacle jutting up over the shoulder of the South Teton (actually in front of it), is the peak called **Nez Perce.** To the right of the Grand are the sharp peak of **Mt. Owen** and, in the foreground, the craggy battlements of **Teewinot Mountain.**

Notice the steep, glacier-carved gulch coming straight down from the Grand Teton. At the head of the gulch, beneath the mountain's near-vertical north face, lies **Teton Glacier.** During an ancient ice age, glaciers covered **Jackson Hole** to a depth of 3,000 feet and carved the canyons in the **Teton Range.** The glaciers that exist now only at high elevations established themselves more recently.

If you can take your eyes off the mountains, scan the sage flats on both sides of the road for pronghorn, elk, deer, and coyotes, especially in the fall. Across Jackson Hole to the southeast is the **Gros Ventre Range,** where herds of elk and mule deer roam the deeply forested gorges and bighorn sheep the highest peaks.

Heading north, the **Lupine Meadows** spur road leads to a major trailhead. From here you can take a very rewarding but strenuous hike, which climbs 3,000 feet to **Amphitheater Lake** near timberline. Lupine Meadows itself is a good place to look for wildlife in the evening.

Back on the main road, **South Jenny Lake Junction** is next, but unless you're planning to hike around the lake, or to take the boat across to **Cascade Canyon** at this point in your tour, you should drive past it for now. Four miles ahead is **North Jenny Lake Junction,** where a narrow one-way road provides the best approach to the area, which many consider to be the scenic heart of the Tetons. The one-way road angles back to the southwest, offering stunning views of the central peaks. Stop at **Cathedral Group Turnout** to take it all in.

The north face of the Grand is visible from here, flanked by Teewinot on the left, and Owen on the right. North of them, in order, are precipitous Cascade Canyon (one of the park's best hikes), **Mt. Saint John, Mt. Woodring,** and then the massive, flat-topped **Mt. Moran.** Moran's **Falling Ice Glacier** is prominent. Notice also the obvious line of black rock rising above the glacier. Called the **Black Dike,** it was caused when molten rock intruded into a crack in the older granitelike rock called gneiss, before the Tetons rose. The dike, now exposed by erosion of the gneiss, actu-

The Grand, highest peak in the Tetons, towering over skiers on Blacktail Butte

ally stands out from the mountain face near the summit. There is a similar dike on the Middle Teton (not visible from here).

Just ahead, a short road forks off the one-way road and leads to tiny **String Lake.** An easy trail leaves from the end of the road to follow the shoreline through open forest to sparkling **Leigh Lake,** named after a 19th-century mountain man named Richard "Beaver Dick" Leigh, who, it was said, could "trap beaver where there warn't any." The lake has sand beaches, superb views of soaring Mt. Moran, and, in summer, water sometimes warm enough for swimming.

Continuing on, the one-way road reaches **Jenny Lake.** For understandable reasons, this place is highly popular; the road in summer is crowded with vehicles. Even so, if you desire solitude amid the grandeur, you can usually find it. Park in a safe pullout and walk down to the shore. Instantly you are isolated from the world of automobiles. If you have more time, catch the boat that usually leaves twice an hour from the south end of the lake. Near the parking area you will find the **South Jenny Lake Junction Ranger Station** and a campground for tents only.

The passenger boat crosses Jenny

Hidden Falls

Lake to join **Cascade Canyon Trail.** It is a $\frac{1}{2}$-mile walk to **Hidden Falls,** one of the park's beauties. Ten minutes farther, aptly named **Inspiration Point** overlooks the lake. If you still have the energy, go up the canyon as far as you'd like before turning around. The trail is not steep after Inspiration Point, and the views keep getting better. You might consider walking back to the ranger station along the south shore; the easy trail is nearly 3 miles long.

Jackson Lake

about 30 miles; at least a half day

Start at North Jenny Lake Junction on the Teton Park Road. Drive north $2\frac{1}{2}$ miles through sage land and lodgepole pine to the **Mt. Moran Turnout.** Moran, at 12,605 feet, is more than a thousand feet lower than the Grand, but you wouldn't know that looking up. On its summit there is a patch of sandstone which corresponds to a sandstone layer an estimated 24,000 feet below where you stand; nine million years of movement on the Teton fault has separated the layers by some 30,000 feet.

North of Mt. Moran, **Raynolds Peak, Rolling Thunder Mountain,** and **Eagles Rest Peak** dominate the most remote section of the park, cut off from roads and easy trail access by **Jackson Lake,** just ahead. The natural lake was enlarged by a dam built before the park was established.

Before you get to the lake, take the right-hand turn to **Signal Mountain.** The road, on which trailers and RVs are not allowed, winds to the summit of a low mountain which, because it stands alone in Jackson Hole, provides a panoramic view of the region. There's no better place than here to appreciate the unusual geology of the Teton area: the abrupt meeting of valley floor and the Teton Range; the meandering course of the Snake River through deposits of gravel and clay brought down by ice age glaciers; and the ranges to the east. From Signal Mountain, it is easy to see why the early trappers thought of mountain-ringed valleys like this one as holes.

Back on the Teton Park Road, you pass Signal Mountain Campground and cross the Snake River over the newly rebuilt dam. A mile farther, the road joins US 89/191/287. If you're headed north toward Yellowstone, it's worthwhile to turn right and take a short side trip (about a mile) to **Oxbow Bend,** for a classic view of the Tetons dominated by Mt. Moran. Wildlife frequent this area.

Going north once again, stop at **Willow Flats Overlook.** The willows are a likely place to see moose. Failing that, watch the meadows below the bridge just to the north as you cross **Christian Creek.**

Day breaking over Mt. Moran and Oxbow Bend

A bull moose in rut

Climbing Blacktail Butte, just east of Moose

A few minutes north, **Colter Bay Visitor Center** has an excellent **Indian Arts Museum.** Consider stretching your legs on the easy 2-mile **Colter Bay Nature Trail;** self-guiding booklets can be had at the trailhead or at the visitor center.

North of **Colter Bay,** the main road stays close to the lake. Just before Lizard Creek Campground, you catch one last glimpse of the Tetons and Jackson Lake, before entering dense lodgepole forest. Ten miles farther, through the John D. Rockefeller, Jr., Memorial Parkway, is the South Entrance to Yellowstone.

Other Hikes & Activities

The park has more than 200 miles of maintained trails; many lead up canyons separating the major peaks. All the trails have something to offer, but they vary in difficulty, and some are more scenic than others. Keep in mind that most trails begin at about 6,800 feet, so shortness of breath can come quickly.

Cascade Canyon is most popular. Begin at Jenny Lake, and either walk along the lakeshore or take the boat across to Hidden Falls and Inspiration Point. It is a long hike to Lake Solitude—$7\frac{1}{5}$ miles if you take the boat, $9\frac{1}{5}$ miles if you walk the lakeshore—but it's worthwhile to go at least partway up the canyon.

From Lupine Meadows parking area, the **Amphitheater Lake Trail** climbs to 9,700 feet and rewards those who make the strenuous 9-mile round-trip with a breathtaking view of Jackson Hole. The lake nestles beneath craggy peaks; allow 6 hours minimum.

Death Canyon Trailhead, off the **Moose-Wilson Road,** leads up to a nice view of **Phelps Lake;** from there, it climbs to join the **Teton Crest Trail,** a magnificent backcountry route that traverses the range and ends at **Paintbrush Canyon** near String Lake, a trip of about 40 miles and 3 days.

Consider taking a raft trip on the Snake River for fine Teton views and a chance to see beavers, otters, moose, eagles, ospreys, and waterfowl. Ask about outfitters at a visitor center or check the park newspaper.

You can also sign up for a mountain climbing lesson; rent a canoe and paddle on a lake; or join one of the summer seminars (1 to 5 days) taught by the **Teton Science School.** The school offers courses on ecology and the region's natural history for ages 8 and up.

Information & Activities

Headquarters
Post Office Drawer 170, Moose, Wyoming 83012. Phone (307) 733-2880.

Seasons & Accessibility
Main road into park (US 26/89) open year-round. Side roads closed from about November 15 to May 15 due to snow. Call headquarters number for winter road conditions.

Visitor & Information Centers
Moose Visitor Center at park's south end, open daily all year except Christmas. Colter Bay Visitor Center on Jackson Lake, open mid-May through Sept. Call (307) 733-2880.

Entrance Fee
$10 per car, good for 1 week at both Grand Teton and Yellowstone.

Pets
Permitted on leashes except on trails, ranger-led activities, in backcountry and visitor centers; not permitted on boats on the Snake River or on lakes other than Jackson Lake.

Facilities for Disabled
Visitor centers, Indian Arts Museum, some rest rooms, and some ranger-led activities are wheelchair accessible. Free brochure available.

Things to Do
Free naturalist-led activities: wildlife walks and talks, day and twilight hikes, bicycle tours, slide talks, illustrated campfire programs, children's programs, skill development programs, tepee demonstration, wildlife watches, snowshoe walks. Also, boat cruise, Indian arts workshop, natural history seminars, wayside exhibits, boating (permit required), river rafting, climbing, bicycling, horseback riding (stables in park), fishing and ice fishing (license required), snowshoeing, cross-country skiing, dogsledding, snowmobiling. Ask park for list of concessioners offering variety of rental and guide services.

Overnight Backpacking
Permits required. They are free and can be obtained at the visitor centers and South Jenny Lake Ranger Station. One-third of the permits can be reserved; the rest are issued first come, first served. Mail requests to Permits Office c/o park.

Campgrounds
Six campgrounds, **Jenny Lake** has 7-day limit, all others 14-day limit. Open generally late May to October, except **Lizard Creek**, which is open mid-June to early September. Reservations required for **Colter Bay Trailer Village**; contact Grand Teton Lodge Co., P.O. Box 240, Moran, Wyo. 83013. (307) 543-2855. All other campgrounds first come, first served. Fees $8 per night; **Trailer Village** $17 per night. Showers at **Colter Bay**. Tent sites only at **Jenny Lake**; RV sites only at **Colter Bay Trailer Village**, with hookups; all others have tent and trailer sites, no hookups. Two group campgrounds; reservations suggested; contact park headquarters. Food services in park.

Hotels, Motels, & Inns
(unless otherwise noted, rates are for 2 persons in a double room, high season)
INSIDE THE PARK:
The following 3 lodges and cabins are operated by Grand Teton Lodge Co., P.O. Box 240, Moran, Wyo. 83013. (307) 543-2855. **Colter Bay Village** 209 cabins. $25-$92. Rest. Open mid-May to Oct. **Jackson Lake Lodge** (1 mi. N. of Jackson Lake Junct.) 385 units. $79-$135. Rest. Open late May to Sept. **Jenny Lake Lodge** 30 luxury cabins. $280-$400, includes 2 meals. Rest. Open May 31 to mid-Sept.

Also, **Lost Creek Ranch** P.O. Box 95, Moose, Wyo. 83012. (307) 733-3435 or (307) 856-6789. 10 cabins. $2,975-$6,808 per week, includes meals and activities. Open late May to Oct. **Signal Mountain Lodge** P.O. Box 50, Moran, Wyo. 83013. (307) 543-2831 or (307) 733-5470. 80 cabins, some kitchenettes. $60-$125. Rest. Open mid-May to mid-Oct. **Triangle X Ranch** Moose, Wyo. 83012. (307) 733-2183. 20 cabins. $660-$940 per person, per week, all inclusive. Open May through Oct., and Jan. through March for cross-country skiing.

Contact the Jackson, Wyo., Chamber of Commerce for a full list of accommodations open year-round. (307) 733-3316.

Excursions

National Elk Refuge
Jackson, Wyoming
In winter, visitors here can ride a horse-drawn sleigh into the protected winter range of a 7,500-head herd of elk. The refuge offers supplemental feeding to the animals, many of which migrate south from Yellowstone. 24,700 acres. Facilities include hiking, fishing, scenic drives, winter visitor center. Open year-round, dawn to dusk. Adjoins Grand Teton NP on south. (307) 733-9212.

Bridger-Teton National Forest
Jackson, Wyoming
This immense forest encompasses many types of terrain and recreational opportunities: wildlife-rich Jackson Hole; the glaciers and lakes of the Wind River Range; Two Ocean Creek along the Continental Divide. Contains three wilderness areas. 3,400,258 acres. Facilities: 40 campgrounds, hiking, boating, boat ramp, fishing, horseback riding, hunting, water sports, winter sports. Open all year; campgrounds open spring to fall. Adjoins Grand Teton NP on east. (307) 733-2752.

Targhee National Forest
St. Anthony, Idaho
Here, on the Tetons' western flank, lies a forest of lodgepole pine and fir with many rivers, streams, and lakes. Contains two wilderness areas. 1,642,493 acres, part in Wyo. Facilities include 899 campsites, food services, hiking, boating, boat ramp, fishing, horseback riding, hunting, picnic areas, winter sports, water sports. Open all year; campsites open late May-Sept. Adjoins Grand Teton & Yellowstone NPs. (208) 624-3151.

Fossil Butte National Monument
Kemmerer, Wyoming
Fifty million years ago, this semi-arid sagebrush country was the site of Fossil Lake, a rich depository of the Eocene. Features exquisitely preserved freshwater fishes. 8,180 acres. Facilities: hiking, picnic areas, scenic drives. Visitor center open May-September; site usually closed by snow November-early May. Off US 30, about 180 miles south of Grand Teton NP. (307) 877-3450.

Tundra along Trail Ridge Road; Longs Peak in the distance

Rocky Mountain

Colorado

Established January 26, 1915

265,668 acres

Nowhere else in the United States can a visitor see so much alpine country with such ease. Only 2 hours' drive from Denver, Trail Ridge Road takes visitors into the heart of Rocky Mountain National Park, traversing a ridge above 11,000 feet for 10 miles. Along the way, tiny tundra flowers contrast with sweeping vistas of towering summits; 78 of them exceed 12,000 feet. Alpine lakes reflect the grandeur.

The summits form at least the third generation of mountains to rise in this region. The first probably protruded as islands above a shallow sea more than 135 million years ago, when dinosaurs reigned. Another range grew out of a later sea some 75 million years ago. Over the eons these summits eroded to rolling hills, which rose once again, although unevenly: Some portions sank along fault lines, helping create the striking texture of the current scenery.

Rock as old as that at the bottom of the Grand Canyon—nearly two billion years—caps the Rockies' summits. Within the last million years, glaciers, grinding boulders beneath them, carved deep canyons. Erosion later scoured the more jagged summits into their present profiles.

Rocky Mountain, though only about $\frac{1}{8}$ the size of Yellowstone, accommodates nearly as many visitors—2.7 million or more a year. In 1917 a superintendent promoted the park by hiring a young woman to live off the land, clad in a leopard-skin; visitation soared. But today overcrowding worries park officials and

elevations, and you can hear their mating bugles. The tundra turns crimson early in the month; aspens turn golden later. In the winter there is skiing and snowshoeing.

How to Visit

On a 1-day blitz, drive **Trail Ridge Road** as far as **Farview Curve** for the classic overview of the park's mountains, valleys, and tundra, then double back and take **Bear Lake Road** to see a collection of scenic lakes (which can get very congested in summer). If you wish, make a loop of the first leg by driving one-way, unpaved **Old Fall River Road** west, then Trail Ridge Road east. Old Fall River Road gives you an intimate look at a wooded mountainside, but it's usually closed by snow until early July.

With more time, drive all the way to **Grand Lake** on the west side the first day, then take your trip to **Bear Lake** the second day. Spend extra time on the excellent nature trails and day hikes.

If you go in summer and plan to backpack and hike, *be sure not to be caught above timberline between about 1:30 and 3 p.m.,* when lightning storms are frequent.

Trail Ridge Road to Grand Lake, via Farview Curve

50 miles; at least a full day

Trail Ridge Road roughly follows a 10,000-year-old trail; prehistoric people once hunted where you'll drive. The road climbs to a land like the vast arctic expanses of Siberia, Alaska, and northern Canada. Take warm clothing and sunscreen. From Estes Park, enter the park on US 36 and stop by the visitor center to pick up information—including a useful flyer about Trail Ridge Road—and a weather report. (If coming from the west on US 34, stop at the visitor center near **Grand Lake** and reverse this tour.) Continue straight on US 36 after the entrance station. The road ascends **Deer Mountain** through open ponderosa woodland.

At **Deer Ridge Junction,** either bear left onto Trail Ridge Road, or, if it's summer, detour to the right, circling through **Horseshoe Park** and past

conservationists, who cite distressed animals, trodden plants, and eroded trails. Condominium development is crowding the park's borders also, shrinking the habitats of elk and other wildlife and threatening to turn the park into an island of nature.

How to Get There

Take I-25 north from Denver (about 65 miles away) or south from Cheyenne, Wyo., (about 90 miles away), then US 34 west at Loveland. From the west, pick up US 34 at Granby. Airports: Denver and Cheyenne.

When to Go

If possible, avoid mid-June to mid-August, when the park receives about half its yearly visitors. Trail Ridge Road stays open from roughly late May to mid-October; trails thaw out by around July 4. In May, subalpine wildflowers bloom; in late June, the tundra flowers. September, the sunniest month, is a prime time to visit: Elk move to lower

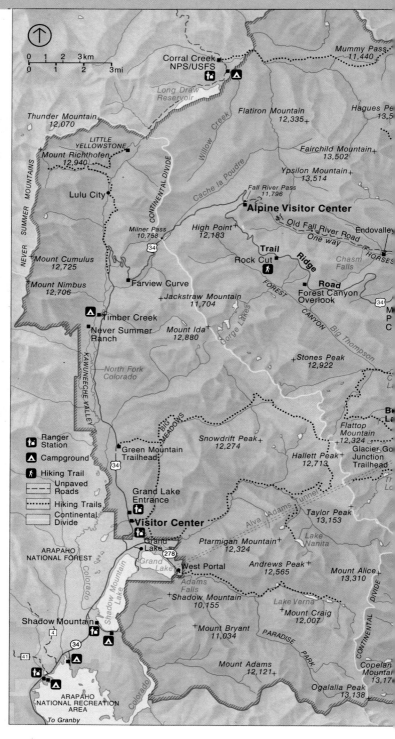

N

0 1 2 3km
0 1 2 3mi

Corral Creek
NPS/USFS

Long Draw
Reservoir

Mummy Pass
11,440

Thunder Mountain
12,070

Flatiron Mountain
12,335

Hagues Pe
13,5

LITTLE
YELLOWSTONE

Mount Richthofen
12,940

Fairchild Mountain
13,502

Ypsilon Mountain
13,514

Lulu City

Fall River Pass
11,796

Alpine Visitor Center

Milner Pass
10,758

High Point
12,183

Old Fall River Road
One way

Endovalle

34

Mount Cumulus
12,725

Trail

Rock Cut

Ridge

Chasm
Falls

HORSES

Road

34

Mount Nimbus
12,706

Farview Curve

Jackstraw Mountain
11,704

Forest Canyon
Overlook

M
P
C

Timber Creek

Never Summer
Ranch

Mount Ida
12,880

Stones Peak
12,922

North Fork
Colorado

Snowdrift Peak
12,274

Flattop
Mountain
12,324

Be
La

Green Mountain
Trailhead

Hallett Peak
12,713

Glacier Go
Junction
Trailhead

Grand Lake
Entrance

34

Taylor Peak
13,153

Visitor Center

Grand
Lake

278

Ptarmigan Mountain
12,324

Andrews Peak
12,565

Lake
Nanita

West Portal

Mount Alice
13,310

ARAPAHO
NATIONAL FOREST

Grand
Lake

Adams
Falls

Shadow Mountain
10,155

Lake Verna

Mount Craig
12,007

Shadow Mountain

4

41

34

Mount Bryant
11,034

PARADISE PARK

CONTINENTAL DIVIDE

Mount Adams
12,121

Copelan
Mountai
13,17

ARAPAHO
NATIONAL RECREATION
AREA

To Granby

Ogalalla Peak
13,138

Ranger
Station

Campground

Hiking Trail

Unpaved
Roads

Hiking Trails

Continental
Divide

CONTINENTAL DIVIDE

NEVER SUMMER MOUNTAINS

KAWUNEECHE VALLEY

Cache la Poudre

Willow Creek

FOREST CANYON

Big Thompson

Gorge Lakes

BIG MEADOWS

Alva Adams Tunnel

Colorado

Shadow Mountain Lake

Indian paintbrush and death camas

Sheep Lakes to look for bighorn sheep, which sometimes visit the natural mineral lick there. (In fall, take time to see Horseshoe Park at dawn or dusk to view elk; bugling-mating calls start soon after sunset.) If you made the detour, either continue on **Old Fall River Road** to **Fall River Pass** (see next tour), or return to Deer Ridge Junction and turn west onto US 34, Trail Ridge Road.

Stop at an unmarked pullover on the right in just under 2 miles. Here, among the willows and alders, beavers have dammed **Hidden Valley Creek**, creating a series of ponds. Take a few minutes to stroll the boardwalk. Watch, too, for greenback cutthroat trout, a native fish being restored to park waters.

Continue along Trail Ridge Road, which soon enters the subalpine zone, dominated by forests of Engelmann spruce and subalpine fir. Stop again on the right just past **Many Parks Curve**, and walk back to the overlook. The "parks" in the Rockies are mountain meadows: When the glaciers of the last ice age melted, they often left lakes, dammed in by debris the glaciers had pushed along their edges. The lakes eventually silted up and drained, becoming flat meadows. In another $5\frac{4}{5}$ miles, the road crosses timberline, where sub-zero winter temperatures and 100-mph winds blast trees into twisted shrubs. Higher still, the road enters tundra. Don't miss the 5-minute stroll to the overlooks of **Forest Canyon**, a glacier-carved, U-shaped valley 2,500 feet below. *Do stay on the trail*—damaged tundra plants take decades to recover.

Back in your car, drive on 2 miles, crossing smooth mountaintops that are part of a plain formed when an ancestral mountain range eroded.

Bighorn sheep on a winter slope near Fall River

The plain was uplifted largely intact and remained above the ice age glaciers. Stop at **Rock Cut** (12,110 feet) and hike the relatively easy 1-mile round-trip nature trail. High altitude can cause dizziness and nausea, *so walk slowly and don't overdo.* (If you feel ill, you'll most likely recover as soon as the road descends.) The trail leads from a parking lot to the **Toll Memorial Mountain Index**, a peak-finder atop a rock pile. The 360-degree views of mountain, tundra, and weird rocks are splendid. Plaques introduce the geology, animals, and plants of this environment. About 4 miles farther along the road, exhibits on alpine life—and a chance to quench your thirst—await you at the **Alpine Visitor Center** and snack shop at Fall River Pass.

To continue the tour, exit the visitor center parking lot and turn right. Trail Ridge Road crosses the Continental Divide after about 4 miles, at **Milner Pass,** named for the surveyor of a never built railway route through the Rockies. Water flowing east of the Divide will eventually find its way to the Atlantic, and water wending west will flow to the Pacific. The overlook at **Farview Curve,** about 2 miles farther, provides a riveting view of the **Never Summer Mountains** and glacier-carved **Kawuneeche Valley.** Through this valley winds the infant **Colorado River,** whose headwaters lie just 5 miles north. About halfway up on the western part of the Never Summer range, you can see a horizontal scar. It is the 14-mile-long **Grand Ditch,** built between 1890 and 1932 to divert water from the wetter western side of the Continental Divide to the drier Great Plains to the east.

If short of time, turn back now. Otherwise continue the 14 miles remaining on Trail Ridge Road, descending to the beaver ponds, willows, and conifer forests of the valley floor. You might spot moose, reintroduced in 1978 after settlers eliminated them in this area. Hunters also killed off wolves, grizzly bears, and bison in the region.

In the late 19th century, smatterings of silver and gold lured miners by the hundreds to the valley. Resulting boomtowns vanished as quickly as they arose when mining claims proved worthless. From the **Colorado River Trailhead,** about 4 miles past Farview Curve, an easy 1⁴⁄₅-mile hike brings you to the decaying 1870s cabins of miner Joe Shipler. About 2½ miles farther up the trail lies the site of **Lulu City,** once a bustling mining camp. Whether or not you hike, pick up an engaging leaflet on the human and natural history of this area at the trailhead or a visitor center.

Stop again 2 miles down the road to stroll the easy ½ mile through the rippling grasses, and over the Colorado River, to **Never Summer Ranch,** a dude ranch dating from the 1920s. By that time it had become clear that the real gold was in tourists' pockets. Return to your car; the road exits the park near Grand Lake.

Sunrise over Sprague Lake

Old Fall River Road to Fall River Pass

9²/₅ miles; a scant half day

Old Fall River Road provides an unpaved, leisurely (15 mph) drive through conifer forest and tundra. It is also a self-guided auto tour (no RVs), with leaflets for sale at the start, about 4 miles from the **Fall River Entrance Station.** En route you'll see traces of ancient glaciers and of recent rockslides and avalanches.

You can enter the park at the entrance station on US 34 or begin the tour off 34 shortly before Sheep Lakes. (See **Trail Ridge Road** tour for information on Sheep Lakes and Horseshoe Park.) Turn onto the **Endovalley** road. The huge assembly of boulders the road crosses is a reminder of the 1982 Lawn Lake flood. A dam, built prior to the creation of the park, burst one July morning, releasing a flood that turned the **Roaring River** into a tree-ripping torrent and deposited boulders, mud, and debris as far as the main street of Estes Park.

Pull over at the alluvial fan trailhead and take a few minutes to stroll the short paved pathway over the debris—up to 44 feet thick—and observe how nature recovers: Young aspens and dozens of species of willows and grasses are claiming the area, as are a wide variety of birds and other animals. Walk back to your car along the trail, not the road.

As you drive on, note the scars on the aspens: Elk and other animals gnaw the bark, which then becomes infected with the black fungus you see; given enough damage, the aspens eventually die. Some observers cite the extent of aspen damage within the park as evidence that elk have reached or exceeded their population limit here. At Endovalley, continue on to the one-way Old Fall River Road with your self-guiding leaflet. Join Trail Ridge Road at Fall River Pass.

Bear Lake Road

10 miles; at least a half day

Popular especially for its trails, wildflowers, and fall foliage, **Bear Lake Road** starts off US 36 just past **Beaver Meadows Entrance Station.** Make your first stop the **Moraine Park Visitor Center,** near the homestead of pioneer and resort owner Abner Sprague. Buy a pamphlet for the nature trail, an easy stroll that starts in front of

A beaver damming a river to make a pond and home

the building. Along the trail, be sure to smell the ponderosa pine bark; its vanilla scent is luscious.

Except in summer, drive on to the Bear Lake Road terminus. If the park is crowded, avoid the frustration of finding the parking lot full; park instead at the shuttle bus lot at **Glacier Basin.** The bus comes frequently; its schedule is in the park newspaper. Ride on through stands of lodgepole pine and aspen—dazzling in fall—to **Bear Lake.** Buy a pamphlet and stroll the $\frac{1}{2}$-mile **Bear Lake Nature Walk,** enjoying this dramatic, oft-photographed scenery while you learn about forest ecology. The park's most popular hike climbs a mile from Bear to **Dream Lake,** over which tower the distinctive profiles of **Hallett Peak** and **Flattop Mountain.**

For a somewhat less crowded walk to another spectacular lake, start from **Glacier Gorge Junction Trailhead,** about $\frac{3}{4}$ mile back down the road. The **Loch Vale Trail** passes **Alberta Falls** in $\frac{1}{2}$ mile, and reaches the rocky shoreline of **The Loch** in a moderately steep $2\frac{7}{10}$ miles.

Other Hikes

The park's excellent 355-mile trail system presents you with endless possibilities, just a few of which are listed below. See a ranger for details and ideas on less crowded walks.

Sprague Lake: Located off Bear Lake Road, Sprague Lake is a fishing pond created by Abner Sprague.

Here's an easy, $\frac{1}{2}$-mile self-guided nature walk, a loop dominated by views of Continental Divide peaks.

Wild Basin: This less congested corner of the park—14 miles south of Estes Park off Colo. Hwy. 7—offers fine day hikes, including those to **Calypso Cascades** ($1\frac{4}{5}$ miles) and **Ouzel Falls** ($2\frac{7}{10}$ miles) through spruce-fir and mixed conifer forests along **North Saint Vrain Creek** and its tributaries. Pick up a nature booklet to learn how the forest has been making a comeback since a major fire in 1978.

Longs Peak, Chasm Lake: Eight hundred people were counted climbing Longs on a summer's day. The predawn climb (8 miles one way) to the park's tallest peak requires planning—check with a ranger, *especially about lightning.* Some consider the challenging trail to Chasm Lake ($4\frac{1}{5}$ miles one way) the park's most beautiful hike. Both hikes begin at **Longs Peak Ranger Station,** 1 mile off Hwy. 7, 10 miles south of Estes Park.

Cub Lake: The less traveled **Cub Lake Trail** (an easy $4\frac{3}{5}$-mile round-trip) is known for birding and wildflowers, including the yellow water lilies afloat on Cub Lake in summer. The trail begins from a spur road off Bear Lake Road at **Moraine Park.**

Green Mountain Trail to **Big Meadows:** This easy, lightly used trail ($3\frac{3}{5}$ miles round-trip) passes diverse terrain: spruce-aspen woods, lodgepole forest, marshland, beaver ponds, meadow. It starts from Trail Ridge Road, about 3 miles north of the **Grand Lake Entrance.**

Information & Activities

Headquarters
Estes Park, Colorado 80517. Phone (303) 586-2371.

Seasons & Accessibility
Park open year-round. Trail Ridge Road closes mid-October to late May, depending on snow. Old Fall River Road closes Oct. to early July. In summer, free shuttle bus service on Bear Lake Road.

Visitor & Information Centers
Headquarters Visitor Center, on Hwy. 36 at east entrance to park, and Kawuneeche Visitor Center, on Hwy. 34 at Grand Lake on west side of park, open all year. Alpine Visitor Center, on Trail Ridge Road at Fall River Pass, open June through September. Moraine Park Museum and Visitor Center on Bear Lake Road, open May to October. Call (303) 627-3471 for visitor information.

Entrance Fee
$5 per car per week, multiple entries.

Pets
Permitted on leashes except in backcountry and on trails.

Facilities for Disabled
Visitor centers and museum are wheelchair accessible, as are amphitheaters in campgrounds, but not all rest rooms. Also accessible, the Bear Lake and Sprague Lake nature walks and the boardwalk at Hidden Valley Creek beaver ponds. Handicamp, at Sprague Lake, accommodates wheelchair backcountry campers—call (303) 586-4459.

Things to Do
Free naturalist-led activities: nature and history walks, hikes, campfire talks, slide shows, arts programs, snowshoe walks. Also, hiking, horseback trail rides (stables in Grand Lake; phone 303/627-3514), bicycling, fishing and ice fishing, rock- and mountain climbing, cross-country skiing, snowshoeing, snowmobiling.

Overnight Backpacking
Permits required, obtainable free by mail or in person from headquarters or the Kawuneeche Visitor Center. Call Backcountry Office at (303) 586-4459 for information.

Campgrounds
Five campgrounds. **Longs Peak** has 3-day limit, others 7-day limit June through Sept. Additional days permitted other times of year. **Glacier Basin** and **Moraine Park** open June through September; reservations required late May through Labor Day. Reserve through MISTIX (see page 11). Other campgrounds open all year—first come, first served. Fees $7-$9 per night. No showers. RV sites except at **Longs Peak**; no hookups. Reservations required at **Glacier Basin Group Campground**; contact MISTIX. Cafeteria in park.

Hotels, Motels, & Inns
(unless otherwise noted, rates are for 2 persons in a double room, high season)
In Estes Park, Colorado 80517:
Aspen Lodge Ranch Resort 6120 Hwy. 7, Longs Peak Route. (800) 332-6867 or (303) 586-8133. 57 units. $125 per person, includes all meals and activities. Pool. **RiverSong Bed & Breakfast Inn** P.O. Box 1910. (303) 586-4666. 9 units. $85-$150, includes breakfast. **The Stanley Hotel** P.O. Box 1767. (800) 762-5437 or (303) 586-3371. 95 units, 2 with kitchenettes. $80-$150. Pool, restaurant. **Wind River Ranch** P.O. Box 3410 NG. (303) 586-4212. 16 units. $115-$135 per person per day; $700-$800 per person per week, includes all meals. Pool. Open June to early September.
In Grand Lake, Colorado 80447:
Bighorn Lodge P.O. Box 1260. (800) 341-8000 or (303) 627-8101. 20 units. $55-$60. **Driftwood Lodge** P.O. Box 609. (303) 627-3654. 17 units, 10 with kitchenettes. $50-$80. Pool. **Western Riviera Motel** P.O. Box 1286. (303) 627-3580. 25 cabins with kitchenettes. $40-$70. Open mid-Dec. through February and mid-May through Oct.

Contact the Chambers of Commerce of Estes Park (800-443-7837) and Grand Lake (303-627-3402) for additional accommodations.

Excursions

Roosevelt National Forest
Fort Collins, Colorado
This high mountain forest in the Front Range offers craggy peaks with canyons and passes and clear alpine lakes. Contains five wilderness areas. 788,333 acres. Facilities include 662 campsites, hiking, boating, boat ramp, fishing, horseback riding, hunting, picnic areas, scenic drives, water sports, winter sports. One campground open all year; others open May-September. Backcountry open July-October. Adjoins Rocky Mountain NP on east. Information at Fort Collins off I-25, about 45 miles from the park. (303) 498-1100.

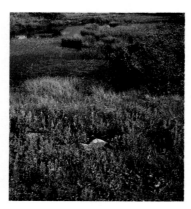

Routt National Forest
Steamboat Springs, Colorado
Routt's three sections encompass high grasslands, forests, and jagged peaks along the Continental Divide. Alpine lakes brim with trout. Also contains waterfalls and parts of three wilderness areas. 1,127,164 acres. Facilities include 372 campsites, hiking, boating, boat ramp, fishing, horseback riding, hunting, picnic areas, winter sports, water sports, handicapped access. Open all year; most campsites open May-October. Information at Steamboat Springs, off US 40, about 75 miles from Rocky Mountain NP. (303) 879-1722.

Arapaho
National Wildlife Refuge
Walden, Colorado
Set in a glacial basin ringed by mountains, Arapaho offers carefully maintained irrigated meadows that provide essential nesting habitat for waterfowl such as mallard, pintail, scaup, and redhead. Black-crowned night-herons breed along the Illinois River and sage grouse winter in upland hills. Features 6-mile-long self-guided auto tour. 18,253 acres. Facilities include fishing, hunting, scenic drives. Open all year, dawn to dusk. Headquarters on Colo. Hwy. 125 south of Walden, about 50 miles from Rocky Mountain NP. (303) 723-8202.

Arapaho National Forest
Fort Collins, Colorado

The nation's highest paved highway traverses the steep mountains of this ski-country forest. Four wilderness areas feature stands of virgin timber, alpine lakes and streams. 1,025,077 acres. Facilities include 931 campsites, hiking, boating, boat ramp, climbing, bicycling, fishing, horseback riding, hunting, picnic areas, scenic drives, winter sports, water sports. Open year-round, most campsites open June-September. Visitor center at Idaho Springs on I-70, about 50 miles from Rocky Mountain NP. (303) 498-1100.

Florissant Fossil Beds National Monument
Florissant, Colorado

Some 35 million years ago a nearby volcanic field erupted, trapping all manner of wildlife within the ash that fell on ancient Lake Florissant. More than 1,000 species of fossil insects, 140 plants, and numerous fish, bird, and small mammal species have been excavated from the Florissant shales—making this one of the world's most comprehensive fossil sites. 5,992 acres. Facilities include hiking, horseback riding, picnic areas, cross-country skiing, handicapped access. Open all year, dawn to dusk. Visitor center on Route 1, off US 24, about 150 miles from Rocky Mountain NP. (719) 748-3253.

Dinosaur National Monument
Dinosaur, Colorado

Apatosaurus, Diplodocus, Stegosaurus, Allosaurus—these Jurassic period giants once roamed here. Now their bones lie exposed in a fossil-filled cliff in the Dinosaur Quarry building. Each summer excavators add to the specimens. White-water rafting on Green and Yampa Rivers and Fremont pictographs and petroglyphs also featured. 211,141 acres, part in Utah. Facilities include 134 campsites, boating, fishing, picnic areas, handicapped access. Open all year; most campsites open May-Oct. Dinosaur Quarry on Utah 149, off US 40, about 220 miles from Rocky Mountain NP. (303) 374-2216.

Trail riders from the Peaceful Valley Ranch crossing the Little Missouri River

Theodore Roosevelt

North Dakota

Established November 10, 1978

70,416 acres

Theodore Roosevelt is unique among the scenic parks in that it preserves not only an extraordinary landscape but also the memory of an extraordinary man. It honors the president who probably did more for the National Park System than anyone before or since.

Theodore Roosevelt, who would later establish five national parks and help found the US Forest Service, first came to the North Dakota badlands as a young man in 1883 to bag a buffalo. He tried cattle ranching with no luck, but returned many times over the next 13 years, developing into a confirmed conservationist. It was the rugged badlands that taught him a healthy respect for

nature while toughening him physically and mentally. "I would not have been President," he would later say, "had it not been for my experience in North Dakota."

The history of the North Dakota badlands, however, goes back long before Roosevelt—65 million years, to be exact. It was then that streams flowing from the newly arisen Rockies began depositing sediments here that would later be carved by the Little Missouri River and its tributaries. The results of this ongoing process of deposition and erosion are spectacular: wildly corrugated cliffs; steep, convoluted gullies; and dome-shaped hills, their layers of rock and sediment forming multicolored horizontal stripes that run for miles.

This austere landscape is home to a surprisingly dense population of wildlife. Bison, pronghorn, elk,

white-tailed and mule deer, wild horses, and very occasionally mountain lions inhabit the three units of the park, as do numerous smaller mammals, amphibians, and reptiles. After a rainy spring, a wealth of wildflowers colors the river bottomlands and prairie flats. And perhaps best of all is the shortage of one particular mammal—human beings. This relatively isolated park is hardly ever crowded, so you can experience the gorgeous loneliness of the badlands much the way Roosevelt did more than a hundred years ago.

How to Get There
South Unit: From Bismarck, 130 miles east, take I-94 west across the prairie to the entrance near Medora. From points south, take US 85 north to Belfield, then I-94 west 17 miles to Medora. **North Unit:** US 85 north from Belfield will bring you to the North Unit entrance.

Airports: Bismarck and, from the west, Billings, Mont. (280 miles).

When to Go
Although this is an all-year park, portions of the park road may close in winter, and services are quite limited from October to May. Summer is the most popular time to visit; the days are very long.

Late spring and early autumn are best for wildflower enthusiasts.

How to Visit
If you have only 1 day, take the **Scenic Loop Drive** in the **South Unit,** allowing yourself time for nature trails and longer hikes. A second day can be devoted to the **Scenic Drive** in the **North Unit,** 70 miles away. A visit to the undeveloped site of Roosevelt's **Elkhorn Ranch** or an overnight horsepacking trip from the **Peaceful Valley Ranch** in the South Unit can fill out a longer stay.

South Unit: Scenic Loop Drive
36 miles; a half to full day

Start at the visitor center near **Medora,** where you can visit the relocated **Maltese Cross Cabin,** the rustic headquarters of Roosevelt's first ranch, which has been fitted with period furnishings and ranching equipment. Then follow the road up the side of the eroded cliff to the **Medora Overlook.** Here you get a good view of the rough little town that epitomized the Wild West back in Roosevelt's day.

Continue on, making sure to stop

Cabin from Roosevelt's Maltese Cross Ranch

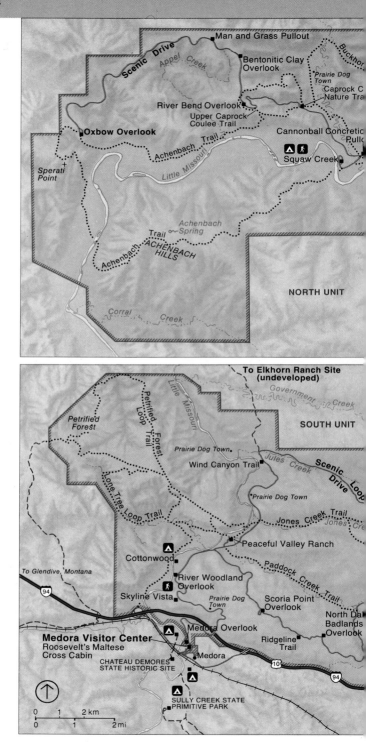

North Unit

Scenic Drive

Appel Creek

Man and Grass Pullout

Bentonitic Clay Overlook

Buckhorn

Prairie Dog Town

River Bend Overlook

Caprock C
Nature Tra

Upper Caprock
Coulee Trail

Oxbow Overlook

Achenbach Trail

Cannonball Concretic
Pullo

Little Missouri

Squaw Creek

Sperati Point

Achenbach Spring

Achenbach Trail

ACHENBACH HILLS

NORTH UNIT

Corral Creek

South Unit

To Elkhorn Ranch Site
(undeveloped)

Government Creek

Little Missouri

Petrified Forest

Petrified Forest Loop Trail

SOUTH UNIT

Prairie Dog Town

Wind Canyon Trail

Jules Creek

Scenic Loop

Prairie Dog Town

Lone Tree Loop Trail

Jones Creek Trail

Jones Cre

Peaceful Valley Ranch

Cottonwood

Paddock Creek Trail

River Woodland Overlook

To Glendive, Montana

94

Skyline Vista

Prairie Dog Town

Scoria Point Overlook

North Da
Badlands
Overlook

Medora Overlook

Medora Visitor Center
Roosevelt's Maltese
Cross Cabin

Ridgeline Trail

Medora

CHATEAU DEMORES
STATE HISTORIC SITE

10

94

SULLY CREEK STATE
PRIMITIVE PARK

0   1   2 km
0   1   2 mi

at the roadside prairie dog town (they bark warnings to each other as you approach). A little farther along is the **Skyline Vista.** Here you are on a high plateau, looking over the broken badlands. Actually, you are not so much "up" as the badlands are "down." The plateau is just a remnant of the original prairie before erosion took its toll, scooping out the bewildering landscape below.

The road descends again to the **River Woodland Overlook.** Beyond the row of cottonwood trees on the left lies an agent of the visual feast around you—the **Little Missouri River.** Notice how, in this arid environment, the vegetation is rigidly stratified according to the availability of water. There are tall cottonwoods near the river, and dark green junipers on the relatively moist northern hillsides and in places where water-bearing layers are exposed. On the dry southern slopes, where the sun quickly evaporates rainwater, little grows except grasses.

Turn right at the T to begin the **Scenic Loop Drive.** When you reach **Scoria Point,** you are deep into classic badlands territory. The bricklike material around you, which provides the brightest color in the badlands pallette, was formed when a layer of black lignite ignited. It baked the gray clay above, turning it into the reddish material known locally (but inaccurately) as scoria.

Along the next 6 miles of road, you will encounter two self-guided nature trails that are well worth tak-

A calf from the South Unit's herd of 400 bison

The Little Missouri winding through rugged badlands of the North Unit

ing. The **Ridgeline Nature Trail,** while only $^3/_5$ of a mile long, involves some strenuous climbing; a pamphlet at the trailhead provides a good introduction to the complex interaction of wind, fire, water, and vegetation in this harsh environment. The **Coal Vein Trail,** at the end of the short unpaved road branching off at mile 15.6 (there's a sign), is a full mile but less difficult; look for the manifold effects of a lignite bed that burned here from 1951 until early 1977. Between these two trails, pull off at the **North Dakota Badlands Overlook** for an exceptional view of the surroundings.

One-and-a-half miles past the turnoff for Coal Vein is the short road to **Buck Hill.** Take the 100-yard path to the summit for a 360-degree panorama of the eastern end of the park and beyond. Those oil wells on the horizon remind you that, although the badlands stretch for hundreds of miles, the park does not.

Return to the main road and turn right. The backstretch of the loop, running from Buck Hill to **Wind Canyon,** offers several possibilities for longer hikes. The **Talkington Trail** can be followed to the east or to the west, but even better is the **Jones Creek Trail** at mile 21. This trail follows a deeply eroded creek bed for about 3½ miles, bisecting the loop road and offering good opportunities to see wildlife (including prairie rattlesnakes, *so be careful*). Since this trail is not a loop, you'll want to turn back at the halfway point or arrange to be picked up at the other end.

Back in the car, continue to the **Wind Canyon Trail.** This short but steep path offers a double treat: Not only do you get a magnificent vista of a long oxbow curve in the Little Missouri River, you also get a glimpse of how wind plays a part in shaping this landscape. The prevailing winds pick up sand from the riverbed and elsewhere and blow it into the northwest-facing canyon to your left, sandblasting the rock into smooth, bizarre shapes.

Back on the road, you pass another prairie dog town and then the **Peaceful Valley Ranch** on your right. These historic buildings have had a number of incarnations over the years, from working cattle ranch to park headquarters. These days the ranch is a private saddle horse concession, so you can stop for a ride (May to October) before rejoining the entrance road back to the visitor center.

North Unit: Scenic Drive

30 miles round-trip; a half to full day

Many people regard the **North Unit** as the more attractive of the two major portions of the park. Certainly the canyons seem steeper here, the river bottomlands lusher, and the blue, black, red, and beige stripes on every butte more pronounced. Located about 52 miles north of I-94, the North Unit is also more isolated, and consequently even less visited. According to one ranger, there are times off-season when visitors can be almost alone in the North Unit.

Starting at the visitor center, take the **Scenic Drive** west into the park. Stop at the **Longhorn Pullout** to catch a glimpse of the park's demonstration herd of longhorn steers, kept here to commemorate the historic Long-X Trail, the major conduit for longhorns traveling from Texas to the Long-X Ranch just north of the park. If you hike the 11-mile **Buckhorn Trail Loop**, you'll travel along a part of this Old West "highway."

Stop at the **Slump Block Pullout** to see badlands erosion in action. The small hill to your right was once part of the higher cliff beyond—until unstable underlying sediments caused this piece to slump away. Try matching the diagonal layers of the slump block to the horizontal layers on the cliff to see how the block once fit in.

Pull off at the **Cannonball Concretions Pullout** to see how weathering agents have eroded out sandstone spheres formed by groundwater minerals cementing. Opposite the pullout, look for the **Squaw Creek Nature Trail**. This easy ½-mile loop takes you through typical river woodlands, and a guide leaflet (available at the trailhead) allows you to identify many native plants the Plains Indians used for medicine, food, and raw materials. Watch for beavers and white-tailed deer.

Returning to the car, follow the road to the **Caprock Coulee Pullout**, where you can pick up the nature trail of the same name. Take this easy trail ¾ of a mile up a dry canyon (a "coulee") to a grove of pedestal rocks ("caprocks"). The harder caprocks protect the sediments below while the surrounding sediments erode away, leaving the mushroom-shaped formations around you. At the end of the nature trail, you can either turn back or make a 5-mile loop by continuing to the **Upper Caprock Coulee Trail**, a choice which involves some steeper climbing but lots of opportunities to view wildlife.

Beyond the Caprock parking lot, the road climbs steeply to the level of the original prairie. At the top, the **River Bend Overlook** offers an absolutely stunning vista of the deep Little Missouri Valley and the extensive badlands on either side. The **Bentonitic Clay Overlook** a little farther on offers a less dramatic but perhaps

A caprock formation

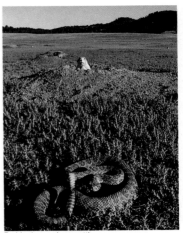
Prairie dog eyeing a rattler

more instructive view. The blue-colored bentonite layer visible for miles is composed of an extremely absorbent volcanic ash that flows when wet. The plasticity of this layer accounts for much of the dynamism of the badlands landscape.

The road now traces the edge of a grassy plateau. This is prime bison territory; you may even have to wait while a herd crosses the road in front of you. At the **Man and Grass Pullout** you can get some idea of the extensive grasslands that made this part of Dakota worth the trip up the Long-X Trail. Finally, the road ends—spectacularly—at the **Oxbow Overlook**. After enjoying the visual banquet of badlands, return along the same road to the visitor center.

Information & Activities

Headquarters
P.O. Box 7, Medora, North Dakota 58645. Phone (701) 623-4466.

Seasons & Accessibility
Park open all-year, but access may be limited in winter due to snow. The South Unit road from Medora Visitor Center through Wind Canyon to the north boundary is kept plowed, but not the Scenic Loop Drive. The North Unit road is plowed from the entrance to the Caprock Coulee Trailhead. Call headquarters for weather and road information.

Visitor & Information Centers
Medora Visitor Center and the Maltese Cross Cabin, at the entrance to the South Unit, open daily all year, except Thanksgiving, Christmas, and New Year's Day. Painted Canyon Visitor Center, in the southeastern part of the South Unit off I-94, open from April to October. North Unit Visitor Center, open daily May through mid-September, open weekends and limited weekday hours in winter. Call headquarters for visitor information.

Entrance Fee
$3 per vehicle per day, collected May through September only.

Pets & Horses
Pets are permitted on leashes except on trails and in buildings. Horses are prohibited in campgrounds, picnic areas, and on self-guided trails.

Facilities for Disabled
Visitor centers, rest rooms, and campground sites are wheelchair accessible.

Things to Do
Free naturalist-led activities: nature walks and talks, tours of Roosevelt's Maltese Cross Cabin (mid-June to mid-September), evening campfire programs. Also available, hiking, horseback riding (contact the Peaceful Valley Ranch in South Unit; phone 701-623-4496), interpretive exhibits, auto tours, limited canoeing and float trips, fishing (license needed), and cross-country skiing.

Special Advisories
☐View bison from a distance; they are known to attack if provoked.
☐Rattlesnakes and black widow spiders often live in prairie dog burrows; be alert for them when hiking.
☐Do not feed the prairie dogs; they bite and may carry disease.
☐Be prepared for extremes of temperatures and sudden violent thunderstorms.

Overnight Backpacking
Permits required. They are free and can be obtained at visitor centers.

Campgrounds
Two campgrounds, both with 14-day limit. **Cottonwood** and **Squaw Creek** open all year, first come, first served. Fees $7 per night, May through September (none the rest of the year when services are limited). No showers. Tent and RV sites; no hookups. Two group campgrounds, **Halliday Well** and **Squaw Creek**; reservations required; contact park headquarters.

Hotels, Motels, & Inns
(unless otherwise noted, rates are for 2 persons in a double room, high season)
OUTSIDE THE PARK:
In Dickinson, N. Dak. 58601:
Comfort Inn 493 Elk Dr. (800) 228-5150 or (701) 264-7300. 115 units. $37. AC, pool, jacuzzi. **Friendship Inn** (1000 W. Villerd St.) P.O. Box 690. (701) 225-6703. 35 units. $33-$41. AC, pool. **Hospitality Inn** P.O. Box 1778. (800) 344-2377 or (701) 227-1853. 149 units. $42-$46. AC, pool, rest.
In Medora, N. Dak. 58645:
Badlands Motel P.O. Box 198. (701) 623-4422. 115 units. $47-$63. AC, pool. Open May-Oct. **Medora Motel** P.O. Box 198. (701) 623-4422. 208 units. $40-$47. AC, pool. Open June-Labor Day. **Rough Riders Hotel** P.O. Box 198. (701) 623-4422. 10 units. $47-$57. AC, rest. Open June-Labor Day. **Sully Inn** P.O. Box 197. (701) 623-4455. 19 units. $30-$45. AC.
In Watford City, N. Dak. 58854:
Watford City Inn P.O. Box 1466. (701) 842-3686. 50 units. $30-$38. AC, restaurant.

Excursions

Little Missouri National Grassland

Dickinson & Watford City, North Dakota

Bighorn sheep, elk, pronghorn, eagles, hawks, and grouse live in the prairie and badlands around Theodore Roosevelt NP. 1,027,852 acres, administered by Custer NF. Facilities include 5 campgrounds, hiking, horseback riding, hunting. Open all year; campgrounds open late May-Labor Day. Info. in Dickinson, off I-94. (701) 225-5151 or (701) 842-2393.

Lake Ilo National Wildlife Refuge

Dunn Center, North Dakota

Waterfowl nest in the grasslands surrounding 1,240-acre Lake Ilo, which offers diverse water-based recreation not found on all refuges. 3,903 acres. Facilities include boating, boat ramp, fishing, picnic areas, scenic drives. Open year-round, dawn to dusk. Located on N. Dak. Hwy. 200, about 50 miles from Theodore Roosevelt NP's North Unit. (701) 548-8110.

Lostwood National Wildlife Refuge

Kenmare, North Dakota

Ducks, marsh birds, grouse, hawks, Baird's sparrows, and Sprague's pipits inhabit this stretch of prairie dotted with shallow glacial lakes, attracting birdwatchers from near and far. 26,747 acres. Facilities include hiking, hunting, scenic drives. Open all year, dawn to dusk. Located off N. Dak. Hwy. 8, about 135 miles northeast of Theodore Roosevelt NP's North Unit. (701) 848-2722.

Crosby Wetland Management District

Crosby, North Dakota

This prairie region comprises 92 waterfowl areas as well as Lake Zahl NWR. Features whooping cranes in migration, grouse on spring dancing grounds. 85,819 acres. Facilities: hunting. Permission required to use privately owned easement areas. Open all year. Lake Zahl NWR is off US 85, north of Theodore Roosevelt NP's North Unit. (701) 965-6488.

Prince of Wales Hotel on Waterton Lakes

Waterton-Glacier

Alberta, Canada, and Montana

Established June 18, 1932

Waterton Lakes, 73,800 acres

Glacier, 1,013,572 acres

Waterton-Glacier International Peace Park contains 2,000 square miles of what naturalist John Muir called "the best care-killing scenery on the continent." Many-hued summits—whittled by ancient glaciers into walls and horns—rise abruptly from gently rolling plains. Some 650 lakes, dozens of glaciers, and uncounted waterfalls glisten among stark cliffs and in forested valleys. A scenic highway crosses the park, making much of its beauty accessible to the casual visitor. More than 700 miles of trails await hikers and horseback riders.

In 1932 Canada and the United States declared Waterton Lakes National Park (founded in 1895) and neighboring Glacier National Park (founded in 1910) the world's first international peace park. While administered separately, the park's two sections cooperate in wildlife management, scientific research, and some visitor services.

The tremendous range of topography in Waterton-Glacier supports a rich variety of plants and wildlife. More than 1,000 plant species provide food and haven for 60 native species of mammals and more than 200 species of birds. Recently the gray wolf has settled into Glacier for the first time since the 1950s.

But now strip-mining and oil, gas, housing, and logging projects proposed or underway near the park's borders threaten the habitats of both water and land animals, including elk, bighorn sheep, and the endan-

outside the park at West Glacier
(Belton) and East Glacier Park; by
prior arrangement, buses take travelers into the park. Airports: Kalispell and Lethbridge, Alberta.

When to Go
Summer. All of Going-to-the-Sun
Road open about mid-June to mid-
October; Chief Mountain International Hwy., mid-May to mid-September. Trails at lower elevations
usually clear of snow by mid-June;
higher trails can remain snowed-in
until mid-July. Cross-country skiing
popular late December to April in
many areas of the park.

How to Visit
Spend your first day on and around
Going-to-the-Sun Road, considered by
many one of the world's most spectacular highways. On a second day,
travel the **Chief Mountain International
Highway** north to Waterton Lakes,
enjoying the contrast of peak and
prairie. Drive Waterton's **Akamina
Parkway** and **Red Rock Canyon Parkway.** Stay at least another day to visit
Many Glacier. For a longer visit, drive
to **Two Medicine** for a boat ride and
walk to an exquisite lake, then continue on to the **Walton Goat Lick Overlook.** If you have the stamina and
overnight reservations, hike or ride
horseback to one of the two remaining chalets built early in this century
by the Great Northern Railway.

Going-to-the-Sun Road
50 miles; a full day

Begin early at **Apgar** on Glacier's
west side. At the information center
pick up details about trails and, since
this is grizzly and black bear country, cautionary advice on avoiding
encounters. Then take time to admire **Lake McDonald** from an excellent vantage point a little farther
down the road. The park's largest
lake, McDonald is 10 miles long and
472 feet deep; a glacier more than
2,000 feet thick gouged out its basin.
Kutenai Indians, who performed
lakeshore ceremonies, called the waters Sacred Dancing Lake.
   Continue driving the Apgar loop
and turn left at **Going-to-the-Sun
Road.** Then pull over at **McDonald
Falls,** on your left after about 10

gered grizzly. Park officials and conservation groups are working with
the US Forest Service, the Canadian
government, the Blackfeet Indian
Reservation, and private companies
to try to protect critical habitats.
   Sheltered valleys and bountiful
food have lured people here for more
than 8,000 years. Ancient cultures
tracked buffalo across the plains,
fished the lakes, and traversed the
mountain passes. The Blackfeet controlled this land during the 18th and
much of the 19th century.

How to Get There
Approach West Glacier and East
Glacier Park from US 2. (From Kali-
spell, Mont., about 35 miles.) US 89
leads to Many Glacier and St. Mary
in the east; US 89 and Mont. Hwy. 17
(Chief Mountain International Hwy.)
form the shortest connection be-
tween Glacier and Waterton Lakes.
Coming from Canada, take Alberta
Hwy. 2, 5, or 6. Amtrak trains from
Chicago and Seattle stop year-round

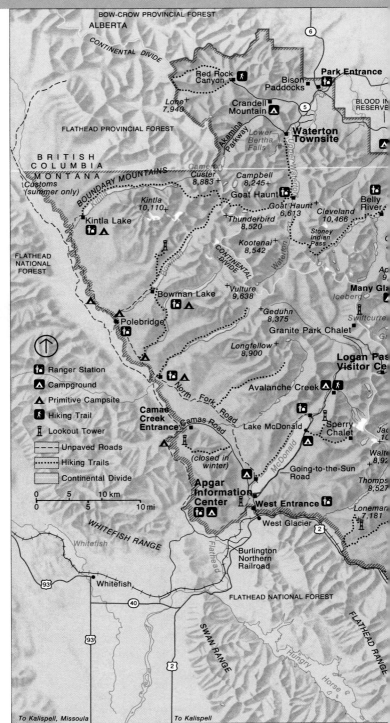

BOW-CROW PROVINCIAL FOREST
ALBERTA

CONTINENTAL DIVIDE

Red Rock
Canyon

Bison
Paddocks

Park Entrance

6

BLOOD IN
RESERVE

Lone +
7,940

Crandell
Mountain

FLATHEAD PROVINCIAL FOREST

5

**Waterton
Townsite**

Lower
Bertha
Falls

Akamina Parkway

Cameron

BRITISH
COLUMBIA

MONTANA
Customs
(summer only)

BOUNDARY MOUNTAINS

Custer
8,883 +

Campbell
8,245 +

Goat Haunt

Goat Haunt +
6,613

Belly
River

Kintla
10,110 +

+ Thunderbird
8,520

Cleveland
10,466

Stoney
Indian
Pass

Kintla Lake

Kootenai +
8,542

FLATHEAD
NATIONAL
FOREST

CONTINENTAL DIVIDE

Bowman

+ Vulture
9,638

Ap

Many Gla

Iceberg

Swiftcurre

Bowman Lake

+ Geduhn
8,375

Granite Park Chalet

Gr

Polebridge

Longfellow +
8,900

**Logan Pas
Visitor Ce**

↑

Ranger Station

Campground

Primitive Campsite

Hiking Trail

Lookout Tower

Unpaved Roads

Hiking Trails

Continental Divide

North Fork Road

Avalanche Creek

Sperry
Chalet

Jac
10

**Camas
Creek
Entrance**

Camas Road

Lake McDonald

McDonald

Walt
8,92

(closed in
winter)

Going-to-the-Sun
Road

Thomps
8,527

0   5   10 km
0   5   10 mi

**Apgar
Information
Center**

West Entrance

West Glacier

Loneman +
7,181

WHITEFISH RANGE

Whitefish

2

Flathead

Burlington
Northern
Railroad

93

Whitefish

40

FLATHEAD NATIONAL FOREST

FLATHEAD
RANGE

93

SWAN RANGE

2

Hungry

Horse R.

To Kalispell, Missoula

To Kalispell

miles. Stroll down to the viewpoint and note the layered rock. Waterton-Glacier's mountains are built mainly of sedimentary rock formed from mud and sand at the bottom of a sea that existed here for nearly a billion years. Over the eons, pressures in the earth uplifted, thrusted, and folded the seabed into mountains. The rock exposed at McDonald Falls is among the oldest in the park.

As you drive on, you may see moose, attracted to the vegetation in and around the beaver ponds. Pull over again near the campground at **Avalanche Creek** and start the self-guided **Trail of the Cedars** from the right side of the road. The easy $3/10$-mile nature stroll acquaints you with the cedar-hemlock forest through which you've been driving. Along the trail, Avalanche Creek tumbles through contoured walls of surprisingly red stone, formed during a period when the sea here retreated. In contact with oxygen, iron-bearing minerals in the mud formed the bright red mineral hematite that colors the rock. Extend your walk, if you wish, by taking the **Avalanche Lake Trail** from near the gorge up to glacier-fed **Avalanche Lake.** The gently climbing trail, about 4 miles round-trip, offers fine views of creek, lake, and waterfalls.

Return to your car. Directly ahead about 2 miles, you'll see the **Garden Wall**, part of the Continental Divide. West of the Divide, waters flow to the Pacific; east of it, to the Arctic and Atlantic. Two glaciers ground

On the Continental Divide

Hikers on Grinnell Glacier

down opposite sides of a mountain to form the knife-edged Garden Wall. At the **McDonald Valley** viewpoint (some 12 miles from the campground at Avalanche Creek), an exhibit illustrates how glaciers also carved this spectacular U-shaped valley. Glacier National Park takes its name from the huge rivers of ice that sculptured the landscape during ice ages of the last three million years.

At **Logan Pass,** atop the Continental Divide, the peaks crowd around as if nearly close enough to touch. Park and walk up the hill past the visitor center to take the **Hanging Garden Walk.** Be sure to buy or borrow a self-guiding pamphlet at the trailhead. The 3-mile round-trip on pavement and boardwalk offers vast displays of wildflowers framed by dramatic peaks. A breathtaking vista of **Hidden Lake** awaits you at the end. Watch for mountain goats grazing, marmots sunning, and golden eagles scanning for rodents. *Always stay on the trail:* Alpine plants, growing for short seasons in thin soil, are extremely fragile.

Return to your car and turn right onto the main road. Soon you'll be approaching **Going-to-the-Sun Mountain**—at 9,642 feet, the highest in this area of the park. The name comes,

depending on which story you believe, from a Blackfeet legend or an early explorer. The legend says that Napi, the creator, came to help the Blackfeet, then climbed this mountain to return to the sun.

Pull over again to view **Jackson Glacier,** one of the few glaciers visible from the road, about 4½ miles after Logan Pass. The turnoff for **Going-to-the-Sun Point** (or simply **Sun Point**) leads to picnic tables, fine vistas of **St. Mary Lake,** and a nature trail that introduces the ecology of the drier eastern portion of the park. Stop at the **Wild Goose Island Overlook,** another 3 miles down the road, and again at the display about **Triple Divide Peak,** less than 3 miles beyond. The road now crosses grasslands punctuated by groves of aspen and conifers. Going-to-the-Sun Road ends at **Divide Creek,** the border of the Blackfeet Indian Reservation.

Chief Mountain International Highway to Waterton Lakes

75 miles; at least a full day

Chief Mountain International Highway begins north of Babb off US 89. **Chief Mountain** (9,066 feet) dominates the

Rainbows on Swiftcurrent Lake

Mountain goat and kid

subalpine fir. *Do not continue past the end of the trail*—grizzlies are often sighted there.

Back in your car, return to Alberta Hwy. 5; turn left, then left again onto 10-mile-long **Red Rock Canyon Parkway**. The prairie here brims with flowers in May, June, and early July. Indians hunted bison along **Blakiston Creek**, driving them over the cliff to your left. In about 3 miles, near Crandell Mountain Campground, stop at the exhibit on ancient Indian life. Drive on to the road's end at **Red Rock Canyon**, where archaeologists found a camp dating from 8,400 years ago. Don't miss the ½-mile **Red Rock Canyon Loop Trail**.

Waterton Townsite, a village of about a hundred year-round residents, blossoms in summer with eateries and gift shops. From Red Rock Canyon Parkway head south on Hwy. 5 and turn left onto Mount View Road, which leads to town. On the lakeshore, near the road's end, a pavilion reviews the park's history.

Many Glacier & Swiftcurrent Valley

13 miles from Babb; at least a half day

Many Glacier, named for the six glaciers on surrounding mountains, is a hiker's Eden and a good place to see bighorn sheep and other wildlife. A dam a few miles outside the park created **Lake Sherburne**, on your left as you enter the park. The lake submerged much of Altyn, a boomtown built during the mining frenzy that started and fizzled out here at the turn of the century.

Just beyond the lake, to your left, is the **Many Glacier Hotel**. The Great Northern Railway built this hotel in 1915 to help promote tourism along its tracks. The company also built more than a dozen backcountry tent camps and chalets in Waterton-Glacier. Early tourists rode horses between the railway stations, hotels, and chalets. Park at the hotel and, for an easy walk and fine introduction to the area's plants, animals, peaks, and glaciers, take the **Swiftcurrent Lake Nature Trail**. This 2⅖-mile loop around the lake starts at the shore south of the hotel. The trail traverses both 400-year-old spruce-

horizon to your left, a solitary peak that commands awe. Blackfeet seeking spiritual guidance still tie a traditional offering of colored cloth to trees at its base.

Chief Mountain also represents the easternmost extension of the Lewis Overthrust, a major geological feature. About 8½ miles after the US-Canada customs station, an exhibit explains the overthrust. Pull over again in 1½ miles for a superb view of **Waterton Valley** and a display that identifies the summits.

Follow the signs for Waterton Lakes National Park. The park's main information center will be on your right, just before the town, about 4 miles past the entrance. On your left is the **Prince of Wales Hotel**, which commands a first-rate view of **Upper Waterton Lake** from its lobby. For a loftier panorama, climb the steep but gratifying **Bears Hump Trail**, 1½ miles round-trip. The path starts from the information center.

Back in your car, turn right onto **Akamina Parkway**, which traces **Cameron Valley** 10 miles to **Cameron Lake**. At the lake, which lies in a large glacier-carved basin, rent a boat, fish for trout, or stroll the 2-mile round-trip **Cameron Lakeshore Trail** through the forest of Englemann spruce and fir forest and 50-year-old lodgepole pine forest, planted in the aftermath of a great fire in 1936.

For an easy 2½-mile stroll through old-growth forest, go on the **Swiftcurrent** and **Josephine Lakes** boat tour and hike. With more time and plenty of stamina, join a naturalist-led hike (11 miles round-trip) to **Grinnell Glacier,** one of the largest and most accessible in the park. Check departure times in the park newspaper.

Other Sights & Trails

Before hiking, be sure to stop by a visitor center or ranger station to pick up maps and schedules—and check for trail closings due to bears.

Drive to **Two Medicine,** inside the park's southeastern border off Mont. Hwy. 49, and take the boat across **Two Medicine Lake.** Then walk past **Twin Falls** through huckleberry meadows to **Upper Two Medicine,** which is surrounded by brightly colored cliffs (4²⁄₅ miles round-trip). Back in your car, head south on US 2 to the **Walton Goat Lick Overlook.** A natural salt lick attracts mountain goats from miles around; more than 70 have been seen here at one time.

From Logan Pass, the **Highline Trail** offers splendid panoramic views on the way to **Granite Park Chalet** (7³⁄₅ miles), one of the Great Northern's two remaining chalets. Between July 1 and Labor Day, you can spend the night in rustic comfort—if you reserve months in advance. A part of the trail is cut into the cliff face, so it is not for the faint-hearted. The other chalet, **Sperry,** can be reached by riding or hiking from **Jackson Glacier Overlook** or Lake McDonald.

From Many Glacier, **Iceberg Lake Trail** leads you among wide panoramas to an iceberg-studded turquoise lake, a 10-mile round-trip. **Cracker Lake Trail,** 11 miles round-trip, parallels boulder-strewn **Canyon Creek** partway to this glacier-fed lake. Nearby lie remains of **Cracker Mine.**

From Waterton, **Rowe Meadow Lakes** (a moderately strenuous 6½-mile round-trip) offers a rainbow of wildflowers in early summer. Climb another ⁷⁄₁₀ mile to **Upper Rowe Lake** through an alpine larch forest. The **International Peace Park Hike,** Saturday mornings, leads from Waterton Townsite 8²⁄₅ miles to **Goat Haunt** in the United States. Return by boat.

The Grizzly

Blackfeet Indians called it Real Bear, this huge, intelligent, unpredictable animal we call the grizzly. An adult male may weigh 400 to 600 pounds, twice as much as a black bear, yet it can sprint up to 35 mph.

Tens of thousands of grizzlies roamed western North America in 1850; by 1975, the guns of settlers, hunters, and livestock owners, coupled with loss of habitat, had driven the bears close to extinction in the lower 48 states. While some 50,000 grizzlies may remain in Alaska and Canada, fewer than 900 now inhabit the rest of the United States, perhaps 300 of them in Waterton-Glacier and nearby wilderness lands.

Though mythologized as a ruthless predator, the grizzly eats mostly grass, berries, and roots. It will also consume insects and rodents and even larger animals if easy prey. Unless accustomed to human scent and food, most grizzlies will move on when they hear a human coming.

Grizzly

In Glacier they say that 90 percent of grizzly management is people management. And people management has changed greatly since 1967, when two Glacier campers were killed by grizzlies accustomed to eating garbage. (Before then at least one park lodge fed bears garbage to entertain visitors.) Today rangers carefully instruct visitors on sharing the wilderness with bears.

Information & Activities

Headquarters
Waterton: Waterton Park, Alberta, TOK 2MO, Canada. (403) 859-2224. *Glacier:* West Glacier, Montana 59936. (406) 888-5441.

Seasons & Accessibility
Parks open year-round; winter snows limit access and services.

Visitor & Information Centers
Waterton: Waterton Information Centre in Waterton Townsite. (403) 859-2445. Open May 15 to Sept. 30. *Glacier:* Apgar Information Center, inside West Entrance, open daily late May through Sept. (406) 888-5441 ext. 313. Logan Pass Visitor Center, open mid-June to mid-Sept. St. Mary Visitor Center at east entrance open late May to October.

Entrance Fees
Waterton: $5 daily per car valid until noon the next day, 4-day pass $10. *Glacier:* $5 per car valid for 7 days.

Facilities for Disabled
Waterton: International Peace Park Pavilion, Heritage Centre, Cameron Lake exhibit building wheelchair accessible. *Glacier:* Most visitor center facilities accessible; also, Trail of the Cedars and Apgar Nature Trail.

Things to Do
Waterton: Free naturalist-led activities: walks and hikes, canoe tours, puppet shows, junior workshops, slide shows, campfire programs. Also, swimming, fishing (license needed), boating, launch tours, nature courses, horseback rides, golf, fishing, cross-country skiing. *Glacier:* Free naturalist-led activities: walks and hikes, slide talks, campfire programs. Also, climbing, horseback rides, boating, fishing (no license required), bicycling, launch tours, nature courses, cross-country skiing.

Overnight Backpacking
Permits required. Obtainable free at parks, first come, first served.

Backcountry Chalets
For information and reservations at Granite Park and Sperry Chalets (see page 296), write or phone the concessioner, Belton Chalets, Inc., P.O. Box 188, West Glacier, Montana 59936, (406) 888-5511.

Campgrounds
Waterton: Three campgrounds, 14-day limit. Open mid-May to early Sept. (**Townsite** open to mid-Oct.). First come, first served. Fees Can. $7.25-$19 per night. Tent and RV sites; hookups at **Townsite**. Must reserve at **Belly River Group Campgrounds**; contact park. Food services in park.
Glacier: Eleven campgrounds, limit 7 days July-Aug., otherwise 14 days. **Apgar** and **St. Mary** open all year, others late spring to mid-fall. First come, first served. Fees $6-$8 per night. Tent and RV sites; no hookups. **Apgar Group Campground** first come, first served. Food in park.

Hotels, Motels, & Inns
(unless otherwise noted, rates are for 2 persons in a double room, high season)
INSIDE WATERTON, Alberta TOK 2MO:
Aspen Windflower Motels P.O. Box 100. (403) 859-2255. 50 units. Can. $67-$91. Open April to mid-October. **Bayshore Inn** P.O. Box 38. (403) 251-1441. 70 units. Can. $79-$125. Restaurant. Open May to Oct. **Crandell Mt. Lodge** P.O. Box 114. (403) 859-2288. 12 units. Can. $74-$118. Open April through Nov. **Kilmorey Lodge** P.O. Box 100. (403) 859-2334. 25 units. Can. $67-$96. Rest. **Prince of Wales Hotel** (in Waterton Townsite) Glacier Park, Inc., P.O. Box 146, East Glacier, Mont. 59434. (406) 226-5551. 82 units. Can. $90-$120. AC, rest. Open June to mid-September.
INSIDE GLACIER:
The following are open generally June to mid-Sept. They are operated by Glacier Park, Inc., Box 146, East Glacier, Mont. 59434. To reserve call (406) 226-5551 or (602) 248-6000: **Glacier Park Lodge** 155 units. $79-$145. AC, pool, rest. **Lake McDonald Lodge** 100 units, kitchenettes. $51-$91. AC, rest. **Many Glacier Hotel** 208 units. $78-$140. AC, rest. **Rising Sun Motor Inn** 72 units. Rooms $63; cabins $51. AC, rest. **Swiftcurrent Motor Inn** 26 cabins, central showers, $22; 62 rooms, $63. AC, pool. **The Village Inn** 36 units. $67-$92. AC.

Excursions

Flathead National Forest
Kalispell, Montana

Recreation opportunities abound here amid mountains, lakes, wild and scenic rivers, and more than 2,000 miles of trails. Contains parts of three wilderness areas, notably the Bob Marshall. 2,346,000 acres. Facilities include 400 campsites, hiking, boating, boat ramp, climbing, fishing, horseback riding, hunting, picnic areas, scenic drives, winter sports, water sports. Open all year; campsites open June to mid-September. Visitor center off US 89 at Hungry Horse Dam, about 7 miles from Waterton-Glacier NP. (406) 755-5401.

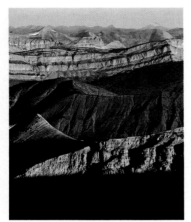

Lewis & Clark National Forest
Great Falls, Montana

This forest has two sections separated by plains: The Rockies section boasts steep terrain with parts of two wilderness areas; the Jefferson section contains gentler peaks and rolling hills with broad plateaus. Large bighorn herd. 1,843,000 acres. Facilities include 278 campsites, 5 winter cabins (reservations required), hiking, boating, boat ramp, climbing, fishing, horseback riding, hunting, winter sports, water sports, handicapped access. Open all year; campsites open late spring to fall. Adjoins Waterton-Glacier NP on south; information at 1101 15th St. North, Great Falls. (406) 791-7700.

Kootenai National Forest
Libby, Montana

With a climate closer to that of the Pacific coast than to the rest of Montana, Kootenai features virgin stands of western red cedar. Lake Koocanusa, 90 miles long, and many other streams and reservoirs offer abundant recreation. Contains Cabinet Mountains Wilderness. 2,250,000 acres, part in Idaho. Facilities include 520 campsites, hiking, boating, climbing, bicycling, fishing, hunting, picnic areas, scenic drives, winter sports. Open all year; most campsites open late spring to fall. Information at Libby on US 2, about 75 miles from Waterton-Glacier NP. (406) 293-6211.

Pine Butte Swamp Preserve
Choteau, Montana

Pine Butte, a 500-foot promontory, overlooks this Nature Conservancy refuge dedicated to maintaining the essential habitat of the grizzly. Also contains many other wildlife species, including lynx, cougar, sandhill crane, golden eagle, mink, and bighorn sheep. Features the Egg Mountain duckbill dinosaur nesting site; daily paleontological tours. Permission required to explore. 18,000 acres, along the Teton River. Facilities: hiking, climbing, and the Pine Butte Guest Ranch offering horseback riding, natural history tours (open May-October). Preserve open all year. Off US 89, about 60 miles southeast of Waterton-Glacier NP. (406) 466-2377.

Benton Lake
National Wildlife Refuge
Black Eagle, Montana

More than 200 species of birds find food, protection, and carefully maintained nesting areas on this large prairie marsh in the midst of Montana wheat fields and grasslands. Northern pintail, gadwall, shoveler, teal, mallard, lesser scaup, and Canada goose are among the species that nest in the ancient glacial lake bed that holds the marsh. 12,383 acres. Facilities include hunting, self-guided auto tour. Open March to November, dawn to dusk. Headquarters off US 87, about 100 miles from Waterton-Glacier NP. (406) 727-7400.

Evening light bathing prairie at Wind Cave

Wind Cave

South Dakota

Established January 9, 1903

28,292 acres

Too many visitors leave Wind Cave National Park knowing only half of its charms. Ironically, the half they know is the half that's not visible from the surface.

Above the spectacular underground labyrinth for which the park is named lies an unusual ecosystem, one that marks the boundary between the mixed-grass prairie of the western Great Plains and the ponderosa pine forests of the Black Hills. Thus, the park plays host to plant and animal species from several distinct geographical areas—prairie falcons and meadowlarks from the grasslands coexist here with nuthatches and wild turkeys from the forests.

Wildlife should be a major draw here. Because of the park's small size and relatively large bison population, the chances of seeing bison—the so-called American Buffalo—are probably better at this park than at almost any other; indeed it's often difficult to avoid the great (and notoriously unpredictable) beasts. Pronghorn antelope, mule deer, and prairie dogs are present in large numbers—and highly visible since 75 percent of the park is open grassland. Elk live in the forest fringes; you probably won't see many of them, but if you come in the autumn you'll hear their eerie bugling.

Below ground lies Wind Cave, where over 53 miles of explored passages make it the third longest cave in the United States and the seventh longest in the world. Because the cave is relatively dry, it contains few

east to Custer and 385 south from
there. Airport: Rapid City Regional.

When to Go
All-year park. Although the cave and
visitor center are open every day except Thanksgiving, Christmas, and
New Year's Day, the park offers far
fewer cave tours off-season (late
September to June). Late spring and
early summer are best for wildflowers. Mondays, Tuesdays, and
Wednesdays in summer are the days
most likely to be crowded. The campground is rarely, if ever, full.

How to Visit
A good plan of action for a single-day
visit would be to spend the morning
in **Wind Cave** on one of the shorter introductory tours and the afternoon
exploring the park's prairies and forests on the **Scenic Drive.** A second
day would be the time for one of the
longer **Candlelight** or **Caving Tours.** If
you arrive off-season, the longer
tours will no longer be offered, and
much of the territory covered in even
the introductory tours will be closed.

   People with physical limitations
will want to stick to the shorter, less
strenuous tours, although even the
shortest involves climbing up and
down about 450 steps. (If claustro-
phobia is a problem for you, you
might think twice about entering the
cave at all.) Wear good walking
shoes, and, since the cave temperature is a constant 53°F, take a jacket
even on hot summer days.

of the stalactites and stalagmites you
see in other caves. But it has many
unusual mineral formations, including perhaps the world's best
collection of boxwork, a calcite formation resembling irregular
honeycombs. The most distinctive
feature of the cave may be the strong
winds that alternately rush in and
out of its mouth, equalizing air pressure between the passages inside
and the atmosphere outside.

How to Get There
For the scenic route from Rapid City
(74 miles away), take US 16 to US
16A south, detouring for a glimpse of
Mount Rushmore, to S. Dak. Hwy.
87 south. This route—not open to
RVs and trailers—takes you along
the Needles Highway and through
Custer State Park to Wind Cave's
north entrance. The faster route is to
take S. Dak. Hwy. 79 south from
Rapid City to Hot Springs and then
turn north onto US 385 to the south
entrance. From the west, take US 16

Wind Cave:
Guided Tours
1¹/₄ hours to most of a day

All tours begin at the visitor center,
where several exhibits provide important background information. A
short slide show describes how the
cave began forming 60 million years
ago. The same forces that lifted the
nearby Black Hills created cracks
in the limestone layers beneath the
present-day park. Water seeped into
these cracks and, over millions of
years, gradually dissolved the rock,
creating the maze of passages and
tunnels we see today.

   Most first-timers will choose to
take either the **Natural Entrance Tour,**
which lasts about 1 hour, or else the

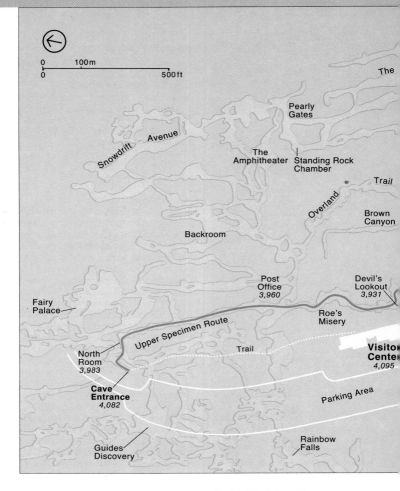

Fairgrounds Tour, which is 15 minutes longer. These tours introduce you to the underground world, stressing basic information about caves and cave formations; they take you through such colorfully named places as the Post Office (named for the extensive boxwork on the walls), the Devil's Lookout, and the Blue Grotto.

The Garden of Eden Tour is a loop around from the elevator to the Garden of Eden lasting only 45 minutes; it is recommended for people with time or physical limitations.

If you're a history buff, by all means take the Candlelight Tour (summer only). Conducted by the light of candle lanterns, this 2-hour tour harkens back to the 1890s, when Wind Cave was owned by the Wonderful Wind Cave Improvement Company and tours were measured by the number of candles needed to complete them. The tour goes up past the Fairgrounds to the Pearly Gates and beyond; it stresses the cave's ambience and exploration.

For those in good physical condition with a keen interest in caves, the park offers a 4-hour Caving Tour, designed to simulate a cave exploration trip. Rangers lead participants into the ghostly far reaches of the cave. You crawl through narrow openings, squeeze into tight passages, and make a glorious mess of yourself (take a change of clothes). The guide's commentary focuses on recreational caving and its impact on cave ecology.

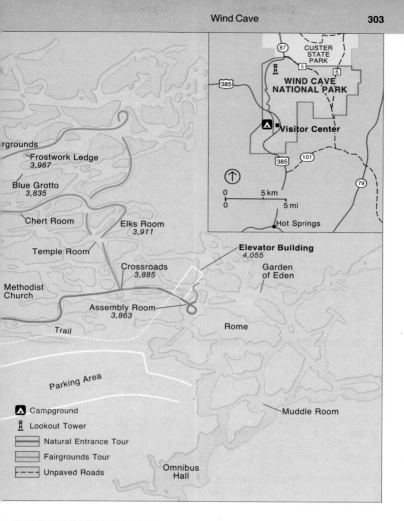

CUSTER
STATE
PARK

**WIND CAVE
NATIONAL PARK**

■ Visitor Center

Frostwork Ledge
3,967

Blue Grotto
3,835

Chert Room

Elks Room
3,911

Temple Room

Crossroads
3,885

Elevator Building
4,055

Garden
of Eden

Methodist
Church

Assembly Room
3,863

Rome

Trail

Parking Area

Muddle Room

▲ Campground

🏛 Lookout Tower

Natural Entrance Tour

Fairgrounds Tour

- - - Unpaved Roads

Omnibus
Hall

Hot Springs

0   5 km
0   5 mi

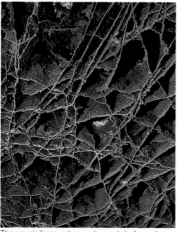

The cave's famous boxwork, a calcite formation

Scenic Drive

13 miles; at least a half day

Begin on US 385 at the southern
boundary of the park, about 11 miles
north of Hot Springs. At the **Buffalo
and Antelope Pullout** you get the first
of many excellent views of the prairie, much as it existed before the
plows of the white man drastically
changed it. You may see bison and
pronghorn grazing side by side on
the grassy hillsides. The **Concretions
Pullout** a little farther on overlooks a
large, dusty buffalo wallow.

From the visitor center, drive
out to the campground for the self-
guided **Elk Mountain Nature Trail**. This
easy 1-mile hike takes you through a

transitional prairie-and-pine-forest environment, where you'll see the grasses and trees encroaching on each other's domain. An accompanying trail guide points out some of the plant life around you, including prickly pear cactus and yucca.

Back on the road, continue to the junction with Route 87 and turn right, stopping at the **Prairie Dog Pullout** just after the turn. This is a good place to observe the behavior of these once abundant rodents, who survive the predation of many natural enemies by their efficient system of scanning territory and warning their fellows of approaching danger. Your approach will probably set off a cacophony of barks. If you stay in the car, you'll have more to watch; cars don't spook the prairie dogs but people do. At dawn or dusk, watch the outskirts of the prairie dog town for patrolling coyotes.

The road now climbs from the prairie into the higher ponderosa pine forests that cover much of the Black Hills. Stop at the **Pegmatite/Buffalo Gap Pullout** for a good view. Other pullouts show how various kinds of plants and animals coexist in this dynamic prairie-forest border area.

Turn right at the **Rankin Ridge Pullout** and follow the ½-mile road to the trailhead. The **Rankin Ridge Trail**, a 1-mile loop, climbs up among the pines to a fire tower. In summer, you can climb the tower for a great view and a chat with the ranger on duty.

Back at the car, return to the main road and continue to the north entrance of the park to complete the tour. Those with maneuverable vehicles may wish to make a loop by turning right on unpaved Route NPS-5. This road connects with Route NPS-6 and then County Road 101; it takes you through pronghorn and bison territory. Turn right on 101 to return to US 385 south of the park.

Information & Activities

Headquarters
Hot Springs, South Dakota 57747. Phone (605) 745-4600.

Seasons & Accessibility
Park open year-round. Winter moderately severe; call headquarters for weather and road conditions.

Visitor & Information Centers
Visitor Center located 11 miles from Hot Springs on US 385; both it and the cave open all year, except Thanksgiving, Christmas, and New Year's Day. Several tours offered daily Memorial Day to Labor Day; fewer the rest of the year. Call headquarters for information.

Entrance Fees
None. Fees for cave tours: $1-$6 adults; $1-$2.50 children ages 6-15.

Facilities for Disabled
The Visitor Center and a cave tour are wheelchair accessible.

Things to Do
Naturalist-led activities: a variety of cave tours, nature walks, campfire talks, night prowl. Also, interpretive exhibits, scenic drive, nature trails, hiking, bicycling.

Overnight Backpacking
Permits required; available free at Visitor Center.

Campgrounds
One campground; 14-day limit. Open all year, first come, first served. Fees $8 per night May 15 to Sept. 15. Tent and RV sites; no hookups. Food services in park in summer.

Hotels, Motels, & Inns
(unless otherwise noted, rates are for 2 persons in a double room, high season)
In Custer, S. Dak. 57730:
Bavarian Inn Motel P.O. Box 152. (800) 351-1477, ext. 459 or (605) 673-2802. 64 units. $56-$66. AC, pool, rest.
Dakota Cowboy Inn 208 W. Mt. Rushmore Rd. (605) 673-4659. 48 units. $67-$95. AC, pool, restaurant. Open May to early Oct.
In Hot Springs, S. Dak. 57747:
Best Western Inn by the River 602 W. River St. (800) 528-1234 or (605) 745-4292. 32 units. $74-$82. AC, pool.
Braun Motor Hotel 902 N. River St. (605) 745-3187. 12 units. $20-$60. AC.

Also, write or phone adjacent Custer State Park for information about its lodges: HCR 83 Box 70, Custer, S. Dak. 57730. Phone (800) 658-3530.

Excursions

Buffalo Gap National Grassland
Wall, South Dakota

This mixed-grass rangeland and badlands dotted with prairie dog towns offers superb rock hunting—including Fairburn agate, the state gem. 591,771 acres. Facilities include hiking, fishing, horseback riding, hunting, picnic areas. Open year-round. Information at Wall, off I-90, about 75 miles from Wind Cave National Park. Surrounds Badlands NP. (605) 279-2125.

Mount Rushmore National Memorial
Keystone, South Dakota

Colossal visages of Washington, Jefferson, Theodore Roosevelt, and Lincoln gaze out over the Black Hills NF. From May through September the sculptor's studio is open; a year-round evening program ends in the dramatic lighting of the memorial. 1,040 acres. Facilities: food services, handicapped access. Located on US 16A, about 25 miles north of Wind Cave NP. (605) 574-2523.

Jewel Cave National Monument
Custer, South Dakota

Sparkling crystals of calcite are the "jewels" of this more-than-79-mile-long cave. Scenic, historic, and spelunking (the most vigorous) tours offered. 1,275 acres. Facilities: hiking, picnic areas. Open all year (cave tours May-September). In Black Hills NF on US 16, about 35 miles NW of Wind Cave NP. (605) 673-2288.

Devils Tower National Monument
Devils Tower, Wyoming

Theodore Roosevelt established the first national monument in 1906 to preserve this 865-foot column of hardened magma—now a mecca for technical rock-climbers. 1,347 acres. Facilities also include 51 campsites, hiking, picnic areas, handicapped access. Open all year, but roads not plowed in winter; full facility open mid-April to mid-Oct. On Wyo. Hwy. 24, about 130 miles from Wind Cave NP. (307) 467-5370.

Summer morning along the Yellowstone River at Lower Falls

Yellowstone

Wyoming, Idaho, and Montana

Established March 1, 1872

2,221,766 acres

Yellowstone is a geological smoking gun that reminds us of how violent the earth can be. One event overshadows all others: Some 600,000 years ago, an area many miles square at what is now the center of the park suddenly exploded. In minutes the landscape was devastated. Fast-moving ash flows covered thousands of square miles. At the center there remained only a smoldering caldera, a collapsed crater 28 by 47 miles. At least two other cataclysmic events preceded this one. Boiling hot springs, fumaroles, and geysers serve as reminders that another could occur.

Yellowstone, however, is much more than hot ground and gushing steam. Located astride the Continental Divide, most of the park occupies a high plateau surrounded by mountains and drained by several rivers. Park boundaries enclose craggy peaks, alpine lakes, deep canyons, and vast forests. In 1872, Yellowstone became the world's first national park, the result of great foresight on the part of many people about our eventual need for the solace and beauty of wild places.

In early years, what made Yellowstone stand out was the extravaganza of geysers and hot springs. The wild landscape and the bison, elk, and bears were nice but, after all, America was still a pioneer country filled with scenic beauty and animals.

As the west was settled, however, Yellowstone's importance as a wildlife sanctuary grew. The list of park animals is a compendium of Rocky

planned geothermal development and oil and gas drilling. Cooperative management between the park and the seven forests that make up the greater Yellowstone ecosystem is essential if wildlife and thermal features are to survive.

How to Get There

There are five entrances: from the west, West Yellowstone (Montana); from the north and northeast, Gardiner and Cooke City (Montana); from the east, on US 14/16/20 from Cody (Wyoming); and from the south, at Flagg Ranch (Wyoming), which is north of Grand Teton National Park and Jackson (64 miles away). Airports are at West Yellowstone (summer only), Bozeman, and Billings in Montana; and at Cody and Jackson in Wyoming.

When to Go

More than half of the 2.9 million annual visitors come in July and August. In September and early October, the weather is good, the visitors few, and the wildlife abundant. In May and June, you can see newborn animals, but the weather may be cold, wet, and even snowy. Between about November 1 and May 1 most park roads are closed to vehicles.

Mountain fauna: elk, bison, mule deer, bighorn sheep, grizzly bear, black bear, moose, pronghorn, coyote, mountain lion, beaver, trumpeter swan, eagle, osprey, white pelican, and more.

During the summer of 1988, fire touched many sections of the park, in some areas dramatically changing the appearance of the landscape. Yet not one major feature was destroyed. The geysers, waterfalls, and herds of wildlife are still here. Many places show no impact at all; those that do will regenerate, benefiting both vegetation and animal life. Side by side, burned areas and nonburned areas provide an intriguing study in the causes and effects of fire in wild places. Yellowstone has witnessed bigger natural events than this and may well again.

Of far greater concern to environmentalists than the fires are the impact of increasing numbers of visitors, the dwindling grizzly bear population, and, on nearby lands, the

A bull moose wading in the Yellowstone

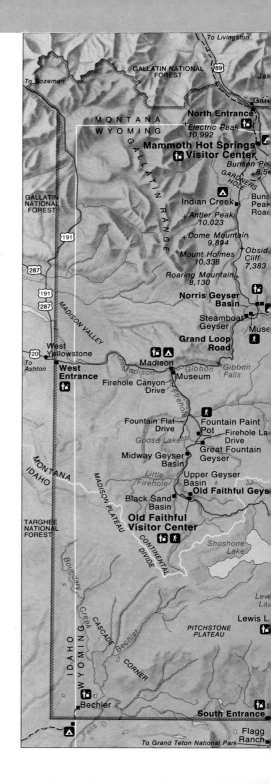

To Livingston

GALLATIN NATIONAL FOREST

89

To Bozeman

Ja

Gar

North Entrance

MONTANA
WYOMING

Electric Peak
10,992

Mammoth Hot Springs
Visitor Center

Bunsen Pe
+8,5

GARDNERS
HOLE

GALLATIN
NATIONAL
FOREST

Indian Creek

Buns
Peak
Road

Antler Peak
10,023

Dome Mountain
9,894

Mount Holmes
10,336

Obsid
Cliff
7,383

191

Roaring Mountain
8,130

287

191
287

Norris Geyser
Basin

Steamboat
Geyser

Muse

20

West
Yellowstone

Grand Loop
Road

MADISON VALLEY

To
Ashton

West
Entrance

Madison

Madison

Gibbon

Gibbon
Falls

Museum

Firehole Canyon
Drive

Firehole

Fountain Flat
Drive

Fountain Paint
Pot

Firehole La
Drive

Goose Lake

Great Fountain
Geyser

MONTANA
IDAHO

Midway Geyser
Basin

Little
Firehole

Upper Geyser
Basin

Old Faithful Geys

MADISON PLATEAU

Black Sand
Basin

TARGHEE
NATIONAL
FOREST

Old Faithful
Visitor Center

CONTINENTAL DIVIDE

Shoshone
Lake

Boundary

Creek

CASCADE

Bechler

CORNER

Lew
La

Lewis L

PITCHSTONE
PLATEAU

IDAHO
WYOMING

Bechler

South Entrance

Falls

Flagg
Ranch

To Grand Teton National Park

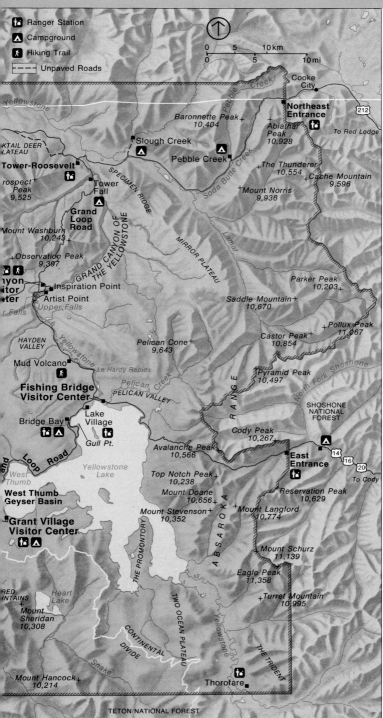

Ranger Station
Campground
Hiking Trail
Unpaved Roads

0 5 10 km
0 5 10 mi

Cooke City
Yellowstone
Northeast Entrance
212
To Red Lodge

Baronnette Peak
10,404
Abiathar Peak
10,928
Slough Creek
Pebble Creek
KTAIL DEER LATEAU
The Thunderer
10,554
Cache Mountain
9,596

Tower-Roosevelt
rospect Peak 9,525
Tower Fall
SPECIMEN RIDGE
Mount Norris
9,936

Grand Loop Road
Mount Washburn
10,243
Observation Peak
9,397
MIRROR PLATEAU

Parker Peak
10,203
nyon iter
Inspiration Point
Artist Point
r Falls Upper Falls
Saddle Mountain
10,670

Pollux Peak
11,067
Pelican Cone
9,643
Castor Peak
10,854

HAYDEN VALLEY
Yellowstone
Le Hardy Rapids
Pyramid Peak
10,497

Mud Volcano
Pelican Creek
PELICAN VALLEY
RANGE
North Fork Shoshone
SHOSHONE NATIONAL FOREST

Fishing Bridge Visitor Center
Lake Village
Gull Pt.
Cody Peak
10,267

Bridge Bay
Avalanche Peak
10,566
East Entrance
14
16
20
To Cody

Yellowstone Lake
Top Notch Peak
10,238
Mount Doane
10,656
Reservation Peak
10,629

West Thumb
West Thumb Geyser Basin
Mount Stevenson
10,352
A B S A R O K A
Mount Langford
10,774

Grant Village Visitor Center
Mount Schurz
11,139

THE PROMONTORY
Eagle Peak
11,358
Turret Mountain
10,995

RED NTAINS
Heart Lake
Mount Sheridan
10,308
TWO OCEAN PLATEAU
Yellowstone
THE TRIDENT

CONTINENTAL DIVIDE
Snake
Mount Hancock
10,214
Thorofare

TETON NATIONAL FOREST

Old Faithful blasting off at sunset

During the winter season, mid-December to mid-March, Yellowstone becomes a fantasy of steam and ice; facilities are limited but sufficient. Only the road between the North and Northeast Entrances stays open to cars, but snowmobiling is permitted on unplowed roads. Heated snow coaches offer tours and give cross-country skiers access to the 50 miles of groomed trails.

How to Visit

The 142-mile **Grand Loop Road** forms a figure eight, with connecting spurs to the five entrances. In early years, visitors took a week going around the loop—still a good idea. On any visit, start with the geyser basins and **Mammoth Hot Springs** to see wildlife and thermal features *(caution: both can be hazardous if approached too closely)*. On the second day, travel to **Grand Canyon of the Yellowstone, Hayden Valley,** and **Yellowstone Lake.** On a longer stay, visit the **Northern Range,** or consider getting away from pavement: a boating or fishing trip on Yellowstone Lake; a backcountry excursion on foot or horse; or any of the numerous easy nature trails throughout the park.

Your best chance of seeing wildlife is in early morning or evening.

The Geyser Basins: Old Faithful to Mammoth Hot Springs

51 miles; a full day

Begin by leaving your car in the parking lot at **Old Faithful.** Check at the visitor center for predicted eruption times of the major geysers. While there, pick up an **Upper Geyser Basin** map (also available from area dispensers). Wait on benches near the visitor center for the eruption of Old Faithful (named and celebrated for its steadiness rather than a predictable schedule of eruptions) or walk the path that circles it. Almost any point along the path offers a good view of the eruption so don't worry if you're not at the benches when it happens. You can see from here that Old Faithful is not alone. The mile-long Upper Geyser Basin

Morning Glory Pool, named for the flower

Mud pot near the Grand Canyon

Fumaroles in Norris Geyser Basin

contains the world's greatest concentration of hot springs and geysers.

Try to allow a minimum of two hours to see more of it. This must be done on foot, but trails are easy and diversions many. The best choice is to start from the back side of Old Faithful, on the trail that crosses the **Firehole River** to **Geyser Hill**, and follow the map (or your nose; you can't get lost here). You can cross the river at several points and return on the other side, making the walk as long or short as you like. You'll pass dozens of colorful boiling springs and delicate formations of geyserite, a silicate mineral deposited by hot water. Chances are good to see one or more geysers erupt at short range. Keep an eye out for elk and bison. **Morning Glory Pool**, named for its resemblance to the flower, marks the far end of the basin.

Back in your car, drive north. **Black Sand Basin** is worth a quick stop, but bypass **Biscuit Basin.** The road follows the Firehole River several miles to **Midway Geyser Basin,** where a 20-minute stroll on the boardwalk takes you past the enormous crater of **Excelsior Geyser.** Its last known eruptions, in 1890, blew to some 300 feet. Now it is a huge boiling vat producing about 4,000

Minerva Terraces at Mammoth Hot Springs

gallons of scalding water each minute. The boardwalk continues across the brightly colored and delicate terraces of **Grand Prismatic Spring**, 370 feet wide, the largest and most beautiful hot spring in the park. The colors are caused by algae and bacteria, different types of which thrive in different water temperatures.

Two miles farther, turn right on the one-way **Firehole Lake Drive** to **Great Fountain Geyser.** Check the prediction board for the estimated time of eruption. If you have time to wait — Great Fountain goes off every 11 hours or so — this eruption is one of the best. A bit farther along is **White Dome Geyser.** Its cone may be massive, but its eruption is a thin spray. Perhaps centuries ago it had more power. Yellowstone is always changing.

Rejoin the main road at **Fountain Paint Pot,** a cauldron of hot reddish-pinkish mud, blooping and spitting — always entertaining. Any hot spring could become a mud pot with the right balance of acidity, moisture, and clay; however, a constant flow of water keeps most springs clear.

For the next few miles, rest your eyes on meadows and forest. Look for bison on **Fountain Flat**; also for purple-colored western fringed gentian, the park flower. **Fountain Flat Drive** ends at **Goose Lake**, a peaceful picnic site. The Firehole River, warmed by hot water from springs and geysers along its course, flows through the meadows and along the main road before dropping into a canyon with nice waterfalls; to see them, turn left on **Firehole Canyon Drive** just before **Madison Junction.**

At Madison Junction, a left turn follows the **Madison River** to the **West Entrance,** but stay on the road to Norris. In this area, the fires of 1988 burned extensively. Their effects — the jagged sweeps of charred lodgepole pine forest — will be visible for a long time. Already, however, new lodgepole pines have sprouted amid the dead trees; the fires' heat released their seedlings from cones on the forest floor. And since the fires moved erratically, the burned areas are not far from unburned areas, another source of seeds for regrowth.

The road climbs beside the **Gibbon River** to **Gibbon Falls,** and continues through the **Gibbon Canyon** and large meadows, where elk are commonly seen, to Norris.

Norris Geyser Basin contains the hottest ground in the park, as well as the world's biggest geyser, **Steamboat.** Its eruptions are infrequent and

Bison grazing near Firehole River

Male elk in fall mating season

Storm Creek fire, near Northeast Entrance, 1988

Rust-colored cones that release seeds after fire

unpredictable; it may stay quiet for years at a time. **Echinus,** however, goes off about once an hour.

Highlights of the drive north include the steamy fumaroles of **Roaring Mountain** that snore rather than roar and **Obsidian Cliff,** an outcrop containing black volcanic glass that was valued for arrowpoints by Indians throughout the area. The road crosses **Gardners Hole,** with nice views of the **Gallatin Range** to the west, and drops toward Mammoth through **Golden Gate,** cliffs with bright yellow lichen growing on them. An optional and interesting route is the **Bunsen Peak Road,** a steep, dirt road not suitable for trailers; if you go this way, stop at the **Osprey Falls Overlook.** The falls are at the bottom of a dizzying canyon.

At **Mammoth Hot Springs** you can drive or walk around the dozens of colorful steaming terraces. They are made of travertine—calcium carbonate—which the hot water brings to the surface from beds of limestone. The formations look quite different from the silica-based geyserite deposits seen elsewhere in the park. The park's headquarters and largest visitor center are at Mammoth. The **North Entrance** is 5 miles down the **Gardner River Canyon.**

Landing a cutthroat trout on Slough Creek

Yellowstone Lake & River: Canyon to West Thumb

37 miles; at least a half day

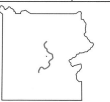

From the **Canyon Visitor Center**, follow the one-way **Canyon Rim Drive** to lookout points for great views of the canyon and the **Yellowstone River**'s 308-foot **Lower Falls**, nearly twice as high as Niagara. The bright yellow, orange, and red of the canyon walls are caused by heat and chemical action on gray or brown rhyolite rock.

Walk the rim trail from **Inspiration Point** to **Grandview Point** for the best look at the canyon's natural grandeur. Also consider the paved but strenuous **Brink of the Falls Trail,** which descends several hundred feet through steep forest. Standing beside the green river where it suddenly drops into space is one of the most exciting experiences in the park.

Continue south on the main road. The **Upper Falls** are, at 109 feet high, almost as impressive as the lower falls and easier to reach. A short trail leads to **Upper Falls View.** Half a mile farther south, a side road crosses the river to **Artist Point**, the best overall view of the canyon.

Upriver, the Yellowstone flows gently through the sage-covered hills of **Hayden Valley.** Go slowly and stop often in the roadside parking areas; this is prime wildlife country. American white pelicans and trumpeter swans share the river with Canada geese, gulls, and ducks. Bison are visible most of the year. *Keep your distance.* Use binoculars to check meadows across the river for grizzlies digging for roots or rodents. Grizzlies are often seen in the open; black bears, their smaller, shier relations, rarely. But be careful not to surprise one; both are dangerous.

Well-named **Mud Volcano** and **Black Dragon's Caldron** are not pretty to look at, but they are impressive. Springs in this area have been known to hurl football-sized blobs of mud tens of feet. From here to the lake, the Yellowstone River provides excellent catch-and-release fishing for cutthroat trout. At **Le Hardy Rapids** in June you can watch cutthroat jumping on their way to spawning grounds.

Look for trout also at **Fishing Bridge** (no fishing allowed) where the river flows out of the lake. Two miles farther east is **Pelican Valley**, a lush lakeside meadow where you might find moose or white pelicans.

Return to the loop road, following the shore of **Yellowstone Lake** most of the next 21 miles. This is the largest lake in North America above 7,000 feet. The **Absaroka Range**, visible across the blue waters, was

Petrified Forest on Specimen Ridge

named for the Absaroka, or Crow Indians. The volcanic peaks define the park's eastern boundary.

Bison frequent the meadows near **Bridge Bay,** while moose favor ponds along the **Gull Point Road. Gull Point** is a good picnic site.

West Thumb, almost a separate lake, is a water-filled caldera created by an eruption about 150,000 years ago, a smaller version of the great Yellowstone caldera. A boardwalk leads around the **West Thumb Geyser Basin,** a modest group of thermal features made charming by its location beside the lake.

Northern Range

Between Mammoth Hot Springs and Cooke City, Yellowstone is warmer and drier than the interior. Called the **Northern Range** for its importance as wintering ground for large animals, this area is characterized by sagebrush and grassy valleys. Open all year, the road from Mammoth stays high above the Yellowstone River, crosses it near **Tower-Roosevelt,** and follows the **Lamar River** and **Soda Butte Creek** to the **Northeast En-**

trance, a magnificent little-used gateway. A few miles past Tower, **Specimen Ridge** contains the world's largest fossil forest. Over 100 plant species, including redwoods, grow in 27 layers of volcanic ash from repeated eruptions 50 million years ago.

Hiking, Fishing, & Boating

More than a thousand miles of trails lead to wilderness valleys, mountaintops, lakes, and thermal basins. Take horses and a guide for a week-long trip, or go on foot for an hour or 2. Even a short walk can put you in a wilderness setting beyond roads and crowds. Ask at any visitor center for recommended hikes that match your time and energy.

Yellowstone offers fine trout fishing, especially for the fly-fisherman. A free license is required, available at visitor centers and ranger stations. Regulations are complicated, so read them carefully. Guide service is available at fishing shops in surrounding communities.

Motorboating is permitted on most of Yellowstone Lake and **Lewis Lake;** passenger boats operate from **Bridge Bay Marina** for sightseeing and fishing. Other lakes are limited to hand-propelled craft. Rivers and streams are closed to all boating to avoid disturbing wildlife; an exception is the channel between Lewis and **Shoshone Lakes,** where paddlers are permitted.

Information & Activities

Headquarters
P.O. Box 168, Yellowstone National Park, Wyoming 82190. Phone (307) 344-7381.

Seasons & Accessibility
Park open year-round. Road from North Entrance to Northeast Entrance open all year; most other park roads closed to cars November through April. Call headquarters for latest weather and road conditions.

Visitor & Information Centers
Mammoth Hot Springs Visitor Center open daily all year. Old Faithful Visitor Center open May through October and mid-December to mid-March, depending on weather. Canyon Visitor Center, near center of park, and Fishing Bridge and Grant Village Visitor Centers, on Yellowstone Lake, open May through September (reduced hours in Sept.). Phone headquarters number for visitor information.

Entrance Fees
$10 per motorized vehicle per week, good for multiple entries at both Yellowstone and Grand Teton. $4 per person on foot, bicycle, or bus.

Facilities for Disabled
Visitor centers, Madison and Fishing Bridge Campgrounds, most rest rooms, amphitheaters, numerous ranger-led activities, walks, and exhibits are wheelchair accessible. Free brochure available.

Things to Do
Free naturalist-led activities: nature walks, camera walks, evening programs. Also available, hiking, boating, fishing (permit required), horseback riding (stables at Roosevelt, Canyon, and Mammoth), bicycling, stagecoach rides, courses in natural history and photography, art exhibits, children's activities, bus and boat tours, snow-coach tours, cross-country skiing, ice-skating, snowshoeing, and snowmobiling.

Overnight Backpacking
Permits required. They are free and available at visitor centers and ranger stations; apply in person not more than 48 hours in advance of use.

Campgrounds
Thirteen campgrounds, all with 7-day limit from June 16 to August 25; other times 30-day limit. **Mammoth** open all year; others open late spring to mid-fall. Reservations accepted for **Fishing Bridge RV Park;** contact TW Services, Inc., Yellowstone NP, Wyo. 82190. (307) 344-7311. Mid-June to early Sept., reserve for **Bridge Bay** through MISTIX (see page 11). All others first come, first served. Fees $6-$10 per night; **Fishing Bridge RV Park** $17. Showers near several campgrounds. Both tent and RV sites at most campgrounds; at **Canyon** and **Fishing Bridge RV Park,** RV sites only. Hookups at **Fishing Bridge RV Park** only. Also, group campgrounds; reserve through headquarters. Food services in park.

Hotels, Motels, & Inns
(unless otherwise noted, rates are for 2 persons in a double room, high season)
INSIDE THE PARK:
The following are operated by TW Services, Inc., Yellowstone NP, Wyo. 82190. Open generally June to Sept. except where noted. For reservations call (307) 344-7311.
Canyon Lodge 572 cabins. $72. Rest. **Grant Village** 299 units. $56-$60. Rest. Open June through Sept. **Lake Lodge & Cabins** 186 cabins. $72. Rest. **Lake Yellowstone Hotel & Cabins** 296 units. Hotel $66-$260; cabins $49. Rest. Open mid-May through Sept. **Mammoth Hot Springs Hotel & Cabins** 126 cabins, 73 with private baths $24-$49; 94 rooms, 69 with private baths $50-$150. Rest. Hotel closes late Sept., reopens late Dec. to early March. **Old Faithful Inn** 327 units, 190 with private baths. $35-$170. Rest. Open early May to mid-Oct. **Old Faithful Lodge & Cabins** 132 cabins, 83 with private baths. $19-$31. Rest. **Old Faithful Snow Lodge & Cabins** 34 cabins; 31 rooms with shared baths. Cabins $49-$72; rooms $35. Rest. Open mid-May to mid-Oct. and mid-Dec. to mid-March. **Roosevelt Lodge & Cabins** 80 cabins, 10 private baths. $19-$49. Rest.

See also Grand Teton NP listings.

Excursions

Shoshone National Forest
Cody, Wyoming
Teddy Roosevelt dubbed this forest's
Wapiti Valley "the most scenic 52
miles in the United States." Wapiti
(elk) find a year-round home here in
the lee of the Absaroka and Bear-
tooth Ranges, as do bighorn sheep,
grizzlies, moose, and deer. Contains
three wilderness and two primitive
areas. 2,433,000 acres. Facilities include 374 campsites, food services,
hiking, boating, boat ramp, fishing,
horseback riding, hunting, picnic
areas, winter sports. Some parts
open year-round; campsites open
June-September. Adjoins Yellowstone NP on the east. (307) 527-6241.

Red Rock Lakes
National Wildlife Refuge
Lakeview, Montana
In this Centennial Valley refuge,
trumpeter swans and nesting sandhill cranes find shelter among grasslands, lakes, and marshes. Large
mammals include moose, mule deer,
pronghorn, and coyotes. 42,525
acres. Facilities: 10 campsites, hiking, boating, fishing, hunting, scenic
drives. Open all year, though snow
closes roads in winter. Off Hwy.
20/191, about 45 miles from Yellowstone NP. (406) 276-3347.

Bighorn Canyon
National Recreation Area
Fort Smith, Montana
Water-based recreation is the focus
of this 71-mile-long reservoir impounded from the Bighorn River by
the Yellowtail Dam. Fossils exposed
in steep canyon walls, wildlife from
four life zones, and historic and
archaeological sites also featured.
Surrounded by Crow Indian Reservation. 120,284 acres, part in
Wyoming. Facilities include 125
campsites, hiking, boating, boat
ramps, bicycling, fishing (and ice
fishing), hunting, picnic areas, scenic
drives, water sports, handicapped
access. Visitor center at Lovell on
US 310, about 100 miles from Yellowstone NP. (406) 666-2412.

PACIFIC OCEAN

North Cascades NP

SAN JUAN NWR

OKANO

OLYMPIC NF

DUNGENESS NWR

Olympic NP

OLYMPIC NF

OKANOGAN NF

9

104

5

20

SKAGIT RIVER BALD EAGLE NATURAL AREA

Seattle

101

Tacoma

MOUNT BAKER-SNOQUALMIE NF

Chelan

Colum

NISQUALLY NWR

7

169

410

90

97

WASHINGTON

Mount Rainier NP

410

12

MOUNT ST. HELENS NVM

12

Yakima

GIFFORD PINCHOT NF

RIDGEFIELD NWR

82

Portland

84

Columbia

101

5

97

OREGON DUNES NRA

OREGON

Crater Lake NP

KLAMATH FOREST NWR

SISKIYOU NF

62

Medford

199

UPPER KLAMATH NWR

ROGUE RIVER NF

Klamath Falls

OREGON CAVES NM

Redwood NP

BEAR VALLEY NWR

97

LOWER KLAMATH NWR

SIX RIVERS NF

TULE LAKE NWR

LAVA BEDS NM

CLEAR LAKE NWR

Goose Lake

WHISKEYTOWN-SHASTA-TRINITY NRA

Eureka

HUMBOLDT BAY NWR

299

89

LASSEN NF

Redding

44

Lassen Volcanic NP

36

Red Bluff

101

PLUMAS NF

Pyramid Lake

5

CALIFORNIA

Reno

NEVADA

Lake Tahoe

80

Sacramento

5

San Francisco

Walker Lake

Preceding pages: Sea stacks, Olympic Peninsula

The Pacific Northwest

In the late 19th and early 20th centuries, East Coast loggers pushed west, downing mile after mile of the continent's primeval forests. Today, almost all of the large ancient forests left in the lower 48 states grow in the Pacific Northwest, most of them in national forests and parks.

Visitors to Mt. Rainier, Olympic, and North Cascades can hike cathedral-like glades of Douglas-fir, western red cedar, and other conifers. The redwoods in the park named for them include trees in their second millennium, the tallest on earth. In Olympic, temperate rain forests soar near some of the nation's wildest coastline; in the US, only there and at Mt. Rainier do such forests still exist. All these ancient forests knit together the lives of hundreds of species of plants, animals, and microbes in a web we don't fully understand. Yet the web is increasingly threatened as trees in private, state, and national forests are cut down.

The Northwest is also known for its volcanoes, many of which, including Mt. Rainier and Mt. St. Helens, lie in the Pacific Ring of Fire, the great belt of crustal instability responsible for three-quarters of the world's active volcanoes. Visitors to Lassen Volcanic can see evidence of the planet's violence in broken mountains and boiling mud pots. At Crater Lake, they can imagine the titanic forces that collapsed a mountaintop, turning it into a lake bed 6 miles wide and the deepest in the nation. They can marvel at the majesty of cloud-swathed Mt. Rainier, which grew on a foundation of lava flows from extinct volcanoes, and now shoulders breathtaking wildflowers and more glaciers than any other US peak south of Alaska.

Each of the region's northernmost national parks is less than half a day's drive from Seattle. This group merits at least a week of touring, more if you want to visit other natural areas nearby. The more southern parks can each be seen in a day, but allow plenty of time for travel between them. Beautiful but winding Calif. Hwy. 299 that connects the Lassen Volcanic and Redwood areas can wash out in spring, so check conditions if that's when you plan to go.

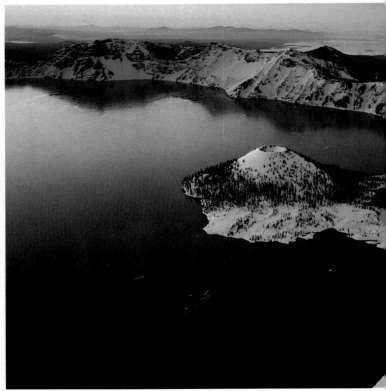

Wizard Island rising out of Crater Lake

Crater Lake

Oregon

Established May 22, 1902

183,227 acres

Few forget their first glimpse of Crater Lake on a clear summer's day— 21 square miles of water so intensely blue it looks like ink, ringed by cliffs towering up to 2,000 feet above its surface. The mountain bluebird, Indian legend says, was gray before dipping into Crater Lake's waters.

The tranquil Gem of the Cascades is set in a dormant volcano called Mt. Mazama, one in the chain of volcanoes that includes Mt. St. Helens. Mt. Mazama's final eruption occurred around 5700 BC. The explosion catapulted volcanic ash miles into the sky and expelled so much pumice and ash that soon Mt. Mazama's summit collapsed, creating a huge, smoldering caldera.

Over the centuries, rain and snowmelt accumulated in this caldera, forming a lake more than 1,900 feet deep, the deepest lake in the United States. Wildflowers, along with hemlock, fir, and pine, recolonized the lava-covered surroundings. Black bears and bobcats, deer and marmots, eagles and hawks returned.

Scientists have yet to understand completely Crater Lake's ecology. In 1988 and 1989, using a manned submarine, they discovered evidence that suggests hydrothermal venting exists on the lake's bottom and may play a role in the lake's character.

Crater Lake forms a superb setting for day hikes. Thanks to some of the cleanest air in the nation, you can see more than 100 miles from points along many of the park's 140 miles of trails. Forests of mountain hemlock and Shasta red fir predominate near

How to Visit

Spend at least ¹/₂ day touring the 33-mile **Rim Drive**, enjoying its many overlooks and several hiking trails. On a second day, consider a hike down to the shore for the 1³/₄-hour, narrated boat tour of the lake. The boat stops at **Wizard Island**; if time permits, climb to the top of it and catch a later boat back.

Rim Drive & Godfrey Glen Trail

33-38 miles; a half to full day

Rim Drive circles **Crater Lake**, providing more than 25 scenic overlooks and some good picnic areas. (Trailers and other oversize vehicles not recommended on east Rim Drive.) Begin your tour by parking in **Rim Village** and strolling to the **Sinnott Memorial Overlook**, a prime vantage point directly over the lake. Crater Lake's vivid color is a sign of purity and depth. The lake contains few minerals and impurities. Its only fish—rainbow trout and kokanee salmon—were introduced. As sunlight penetrates the deep, pure lake, water molecules absorb the colors of the spectrum except for blue, which is scattered back to the surface. Scientists have recently found green algae growing at a record 725 feet below the surface, indicating that sunlight may penetrate deeper here than in any other body of water in the world.

To begin your lake tour, set your car's odometer at zero (or note the setting) as you leave Rim Village parking lot. Head west or clockwise around the lake, and be careful: The road is narrow and has sharp curves. Watch out for bikers and pedestrians. Turn right at 0.1 mile for Rim Drive. The first stop (mile 1.3) brings you near **Discovery Point**, where, on June 12, 1853, a group of prospectors searching for a gold mine happened upon the lake, which they named Deep Blue Lake. Indians, believing the lake sacred, had told no outsiders about it. **Hillman Peak**, to the far left on the rim, is named for one of the prospectors. The peak is a 70,000-year-old volcano—one of the compact cluster of overlapping volcanic cones that formed Mt. Mazama. It was cleaved

the caldera rim. At the rim twisted whitebark pine testify to the harshness of the long winter, during which, on average, 45 feet of snow fall. Ponderosa pine, the park's largest tree, and lodgepole pine are common farther down from the rim.

How to Get There

Enter the park from the west (Medford, about 75 miles away) or the south (Klamath Falls, about 55 miles away) on Ore. Hwy. 62, or from the north on Ore. Hwy. 138. Airports: Medford and Klamath Falls.

When to Go

The lake best displays its dazzling color in summer. Ore. Hwy. 62 and the access road leading to Rim Village remain open during daylight in winter, and cross-country skiing is becoming increasingly popular. The drive around the lake usually closes in October because of snow; in some years, the drive may not reopen completely until late July.

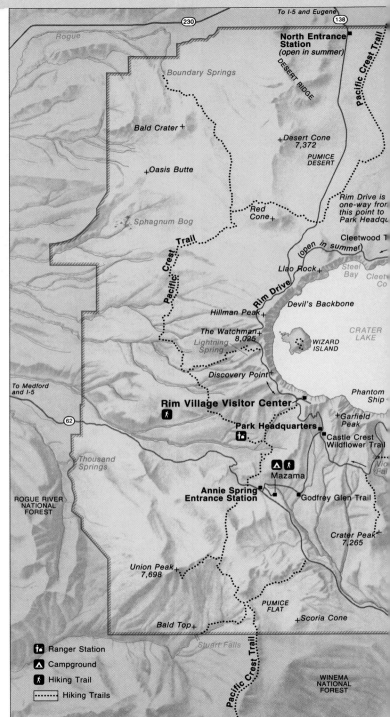

To I-5 and Eugene

230

138

North Entrance Station
(open in summer)

Rogue

DESERT RIDGE

Pacific Crest Trail

Boundary Springs

Bald Crater +

+*Desert Cone*
7,372

PUMICE DESERT

+*Oasis Butte*

Rim Drive is one-way from this point to Park Headqu...

Cleetwood T

Red Cone +

Sphagnum Bog

Pacific Crest Trail

Rim Drive

(open in summer)

Llao Rock +

Steel Bay

Cleet Co

Pacific Crest Trail

Hillman Peak +

Devil's Backbone

CRATER LAKE

The Watchman +
8,025

Lightning Spring

WIZARD ISLAND

Discovery Point +

Phantom Ship

To Medford and I-5

62

Rim Village Visitor Center

+*Garfield Peak*

Park Headquarters

Castle Crest Wildflower Trail

Vid Fal

Thousand Springs

Mazama

Annie Spring Entrance Station

Godfrey Glen Trail

ROGUE RIVER NATIONAL FOREST

Union Peak +
7,698

Crater Peak +
7,265

PUMICE FLAT

Bald Top +

+*Scoria Cone*

Stuart Falls

Pacific Crest Trail

WINEMA NATIONAL FOREST

Ranger Station

Campground

Hiking Trail

Hiking Trails

To US 97 and Bend

WINEMA
NATIONAL
FOREST

ber Crater
7,403

Sharp Peak +

Bear Butte +

ineglass

Drive (one-way)

+ Scout Hill

cap +

+ Mount Scott
8,929

Rim Drive
(open in summer)

Lost Creek

THE
PINNACLES

Maklaks Crater +

0 1 2 km
0 1 2 mi

o US 97 and Klamath Falls

SUN MOUNTAIN

Rabbit brush at Cleetwood Cove

in half when the summit collapsed. At 2,000 feet above the water, it forms the highest point on the rim.

The overlook at mile 4 offers a good view of **Wizard Island**, named for its resemblance to a sorcerer's hat. Rising over 700 feet above the surface of the lake, Wizard Island is a classic cinder cone—built of red-hot cinders ejected from the caldera floor sometime after Mt. Mazama collapsed. An Indian legend portrays the island as the head of Llao, Chief of the Below World. Skell, Chief of the Above World, killed and dismembered Llao in the final, literally earth-shattering battle waged on the mountaintop. Time and weather permitting, you'll enjoy superb views in every direction if you take the moderately steep $\frac{4}{5}$-mile trail that leads from here to the fire tower on **The Watchman** (8,025 feet) south of the overlook.

Back in your car, turn away from the lake at the **Mt. Thielsen Overview** on the left. A plaque identifies the major landmarks of the countryside. When the road forks at North Junction (mile 6.1), bear right to remain on Rim Drive. Straight, the road leads to the **North Entrance**.

Steel Bay (mile 8.8) commemorates William Gladstone Steel, who dedicated his fortune and career to making Crater Lake a national park. Steel became fascinated by the lake when he read about it in a newspaper used to wrap his school lunch. Seventeen years of lobbying, culminating in a personal appeal to President Theodore Roosevelt, succeeded in making it the country's sixth national park in 1902. The tireless Steel stocked the lake with fish and led the efforts to build Rim Drive and the Crater Lake Lodge.

The Pinnacles, southeast of Kerr Notch

Six miles farther on, pull off the road at **Skell Head** for another excellent view of the entire lake. **Mt. Scott**, highest point in the park, looms ahead as you drive on towards **Cloudcap**; it may have been the oldest of Mt. Mazama's volcanic cones. Bear right (mile 17.4) for the short spur road to Cloudcap, Rim Drive's highest overlook (8,070 feet). **Phantom Ship**, an island to the southwest, consists of an erosion-resistant dike of 400,000-year-old rock. Dwarfed by the surrounding cliffs, it nevertheless stands 160 feet above the water.

Circle back to Rim Drive and turn right. For a closer look at Phantom Ship, which in some lights seems to vanish and reappear, stop at **Kerr Notch** (mile 23.2), one of the U-shaped valleys carved by a glacier before Mt. Mazama exploded. A road here leads to **The Pinnacles**, spires of hardened volcanic ash. Just after Kerr Notch, bear right to stay on Rim Drive.

At mile 31.2 you can stretch your legs on the **Castle Crest Wildflower Trail**. This fragrant ½-mile loop begins in a forest of mountain hemlock and red fir, then enters a meadow run riot with flowers, many of them identified by plaques. Watch your step—the wet rocks can be slippery.

From here you can either proceed back to Rim Village or, if time permits, turn left toward Ore. Hwy. 62 and after 2⅓ miles park on the left for a final stroll through **Godfrey Glen Trail**, an easy, 1-mile-loop nature trail. The path leads through forest that developed on a flow of pumice and ash 250 feet thick. The fluted pinnacles on the walls of the gorges began as the same material, but hot gases seeped up from within the earth and hardened these areas. They defied erosion as the creeks formed canyons.

Boat Tour & Hikes

The mile-long **Cleetwood Trail**, at mile 10.7 by car from the visitor center, leads steeply down to the water and the landing for the boat tour. The hike back up is strenuous (and there's no other way), so only attempt the trail if you are in good physical condition, and take it slowly. Wear sturdy shoes and bring water, a snack, and a jacket. The boat tour shows you the lake from a different perspective; on it you can see waterfalls and geological features invisible from the rim, and a ranger-guide offers a detailed account of the lake and its environs.

The tour leaves every hour between 10 a.m. and 4 p.m. (July to early September). The relatively steep **Wizard Island Summit Trail** ($^9/_{10}$ of a mile one way) begins at the island's dock and winds through mountain hemlock, Shasta red fir, and wildflowers to the crater at the top. Awaiting you are superb views of bleached, contorted whitebark pines against the blue water.

Another good park hike is on the **Annie Creek Trail**, a $1^7/_{10}$-mile self-guided loop that wends through beds of wildflowers to the bottom of a canyon and back. It begins behind the amphitheater at the Mazama Campground. The **Mt. Scott Trail**, considered by many to be the most spectacular in the park, starts from the left side of Rim Drive just after mile 17. It ascends 2½ miles to the park's highest point. On this trail you might see falcons, hawks, and eagles, particularly in spring and fall.

Information & Activities

Headquarters
P.O. Box 7, Crater Lake, Oregon 97604. Phone (503) 594-2211.

Seasons & Accessibility
South and west entrances open year-round. North entrance open mid-June to mid-October, snow permitting. East side of Rim Drive, from Cleetwood Cove to park headquarters, may remain closed by snow until late July.

For weather and road reports, tune car radio to 1610 AM in the Crater Lake area. Signs along Hwy. 62 will indicate when you are in range.

Visitor & Information Centers
Rim Village Visitor Center, on rim overlooking the lake, 7 miles off Hwy. 62, open daily from early June to end of September. Closed rest of year. Steel Center, located at park headquarters, open daily all year except Christmas.

Entrance Fee
$5 from late May to early October only, good for 7 days.

Pets
Pets must be leashed at all times and are not permitted on the trails or in buildings.

Facilities for Disabled
Most viewpoints are accessible to wheelchairs. Also accessible are the visitor center, Rim Center, Mazama Campground, and the cafeteria/gift shop at Rim Village.

Things to Do
Free naturalist-led activities: nature walks, children's programs, campfire programs, historical tours. Fees for the 1¾-hour ranger-narrated boat tours. Also available, hiking, bicycling, fishing (license not required), snowshoeing, and cross-country skiing.

Special Advisory
☐Hiking inside the caldera rim permitted only on the Cleetwood Trail. Volcanic rock and soil are unstable and dangerous to climb on.

Overnight Backpacking
Permits required. They are free and can be obtained at the Steel Center, the visitor center, and on the Pacific Crest Trail where it enters the park.

Campgrounds
Two campgrounds, both with 14-day limit. **Lost Creek** open mid-July to late September. **Mazama** open late-June to mid-October. Both first come, first served. Fees $5-$10 per night. Showers at Mazama Village. Both tent and RV sites at **Mazama;** no hookups. Tent sites only at **Lost Creek.** Food services at Rim Village.

Hotels, Motels, & Inns
(unless otherwise noted, rates are for 2 persons in a double room, high season)
INSIDE THE PARK:
Mazama Village P.O. Box 128, Crater Lake, Oregon 97604. (503) 594-2511. 40 units. $70. Restaurant. Open late May to mid-Oct.
OUTSIDE THE PARK:
In Chiloquin, Oregon 97624:
Melita's Motel P.O. Box 470. (503) 783-2401. 13 units. $25-$45. Restaurant. **Sportsman Motel** HC 30, Box 27. (503) 783-2867. 10 units, 7 with kitchenettes. $22-$32. **Spring Creek Ranch Motel** HC 63, Box 440. (503) 783-2775. 10 units, 7 with kitchenettes. $24-$28. **Winema Rapids Motel** HC 30, Box 6. (503) 783-2271. 10 units. $22-$41. Restaurant.
In Diamond Lake, Oregon 97731:
Diamond Lake Resort (503) 793-3333. 92 units, 10 with kitchenettes. Rooms $51; cabins $81-$131; studios $56. Restaurant.
In Prospect, Oregon 97536:
Union Creek Resort (503) 560-3565. 14 cabins, 8 with kitchenettes; 9 rooms with shared baths. Cabins $40-$67; rooms $35-$44. Restaurant.

Ask the park for a complete list of accommodations within a 1-hour drive.

Excursions

Rogue River National Forest
Medford, Oregon

Sugar pines and Douglas-firs here cloak the slopes of the western Cascades where the Rogue River emerges from underground lava tubes. Forest contains parts of three wilderness areas, numerous lakes, and a stretch of the Pacific Crest Trail. 628,750 acres, part in Calif. Facilities include 30 rooms, 400 campsites, food services, hiking, boating, boat ramp, fishing, horseback riding, hunting, picnic areas, scenic drives, winter sports, water sports. Open all year; most campsites open May-September. In two sections; one adjoins Crater Lake NP on west and south, with entrance at Prospect on Oregon Hwy. 62. Lower section reached from I-5 south of Ashland, about 85 miles from the park. (503) 776-3600.

Oregon Caves National Monument
Cave Junction, Oregon

Guided tours take visitors age 6 and over through the "Marble Halls of Oregon," chambers and corridors formed by groundwater dissolving marble bedrock. 480 acres. Facilities include 29 rooms, food services, hiking, picnic areas, child care during tour. Open all year; lodge closed in winter. East on Oregon 46 from Cave Junction, about 125 miles from Crater Lake NP. (503) 592-2100.

Siskiyou National Forest
Grants Pass, Oregon

This coniferous forest boasts five wilderness areas, notably the Kalmiopsis, named for a flowering plant unique to the area. A section of the Wild and Scenic Rogue River offers white-water boating, fishing, and hiking along the river's National Scenic Trail. 1,092,302 acres, part in California. Facilities include 100 campsites, hiking, boating, boat ramp, fishing, horseback riding, hunting, picnic areas, scenic drives, water sports. Open year-round; most campsites open May-September. Headquarters at Grants Pass on I-5, about 100 miles southwest of Crater Lake NP. (503) 479-5301.

Oregon Dunes
National Recreation Area
Reedsport, Oregon
Forty-seven miles of towering
dunes—some as high as 400 feet—
stretch along the Pacific coast, inviting visitors to explore. Half of area
open to off-road vehicles. The 426
wildlife species include black bears,
black-tailed deer, and tundra swans.
32,000 acres. Facilities include 15
campgrounds, 30 miles of hiking
trails, boating, fishing, horseback
riding, picnic areas, swimming,
handicapped access. Open all year.
Headquarters at Reedsport on US
101, about 200 miles west of Crater
Lake NP. (503) 271-3611.

Lava Beds National Monument
Tulelake, California
Myriad lava-tube caves and cinder
cones mark this rugged terrain
where prehistoric Indians left glyphs
on the soft rock. Excellent spring
and fall birdwatching. 46,560 acres.
Facilities include 41 campsites, hiking, picnic areas. Open year-round.
Headquarters 30 miles south of Tulelake (26 miles off Calif. Hwy. 139),
about 120 miles south of Crater
Lake NP. (916) 667-2282.

Klamath Basin
National Wildlife Refuges
Tulelake, California
These six refuges protect diverse
habitats—marsh, open water, meadows, croplands, coniferous forest,
sagebrush and juniper uplands,
rocky slopes—and numerous waterfowl. The basin also provides a home
for the largest wintering bald eagle
population in the lower 48 states. Facilities include bicycling, hiking,
boating, fishing, hunting, handicapped access. Open all year, dawn
to dusk, except Bear Valley (closed
Nov.-April to protect eagles) and
Clear Lake (closed in spring-
summer). In Oregon: Klamath Forest, 16,376 acres; Upper Klamath,
14,886 acres; Bear Valley, 4,120
acres; Lower Klamath, 51,713 acres
(part in Calif.). In Calif.: Tule Lake,
38,908 acres; Clear Lake, 33,440
acres. Visitor center near Tulelake,
off Calif. 139, about 100 miles from
Crater Lake NP. (916) 667-2231.

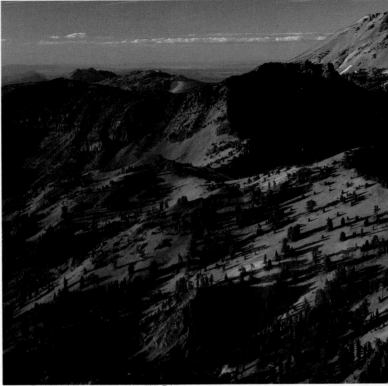

Lassen Peak looming over the remains of Mt. Tehama

Lassen Volcanic

California

Established August 9, 1916

106,000 acres

On June 14, 1914, three men climbed Lassen Peak to see why a seemingly dead volcano had started rumbling 16 days before. Now, peering into a newborn crater, they felt the ground tremble. As they turned and ran down the steep slope, the mountain erupted. Rocks hurtled through the ash-filled air. One struck a man, knocking him out. Ashes rained down on the men. They seemed doomed. But the eruption stopped as suddenly as it had begun, and the three men survived.

From May 1914 to early 1915, Lassen spewed steam and ashes in more than 150 eruptions. Finally, in May 1915, the mountaintop exploded. Lava crashed through the 1914 cra-

ter. A 20-foot-high wall of mud, ash, and melted snow roared down the mountain, snapping tree trunks. Three days later, a huge mass of ashes and gases shot out of the volcano, devastating a swath a mile wide and 3 miles long. Above the havoc a cloud of volcanic steam and ash rose 30,000 feet.

Since then, except for a small eruption in 1921, Lassen Peak has been quiet. But it is still a volcano, the centerpiece of a vast panorama, where volcanism displays its spectaculars—wrecked mountains, devastated land, bubbling cauldrons of mud. Until Mt. St. Helens blew in 1980, Lassen's eruption was the most recent volcanic explosion in the lower 48 states. Ecologists now study Lassen's landscape to see what the future may bring to the barren terrain around St. Helens.

Southwest and **Manzanita Lake Entrances,** encompasses the major volcanic features. Explore **Bumpass Hell** and other sites along the way. If you can stay longer, climb **Cinder Cone,** an outstanding example of the results of volcanism, and, if you have the stamina for a more demanding trek, try **Lassen Peak.**

Lassen Park Road & Bumpass Hell Trail

30 miles; a half to full day

If you start at the **Southwest Entrance,** your first stop on this twisting, climbing road will be the **Sulphur Works.** At a roadside exhibit you walk through sulphur fumes and see hissing fumaroles, sputtering mud, and gurgling clay tinted in pastels by minerals. Here was the heart of Mt. Tehama, the great volcano that spawned Lassen. The peaks around you once formed part of the rim of Tehama, created by lava oozing from the inner earth 600,000 to 200,000 years ago. Layer by layer, the lava built a mountain 11,500 feet high and 11 miles across.

Tehama gave birth to small volcanoes that emerged on its flanks. Repeated eruptions weakened the structure of the volcano, which collapsed, leaving behind a bowl-like caldera. Glaciers later scoured the caldera, wiping out the last remains of Tehama. **Lassen Peak,** born at least 11,500 years ago, was one of Tehama's offspring.

How to Get There

From Redding (about 45 miles away), take Calif. Hwy. 44 east to Manzanita Lake Entrance; from Red Bluff, take Calif. Hwy. 36 east to Mineral, turn north on Calif. Hwy. 89 to the Southwest Entrance. The three other entrances—at Warner Valley, Butte Lake, and Juniper Lake—are reached via unpaved roads. Airports: Redding and Chico; Reno, Nevada.

When to Go

The volcanic areas can be visited from spring through fall. Heavy snows close most of the main road in winter. But small sections at the southern and northern ends remain open for snowshoe hikes and downhill and cross-country skiing.

How to Visit

On a 1-day visit, drive the **Lassen Park Road,** linked to Calif. Hwy. 89. The road, snaking across the western side of the park between the

Thermal steam at Bumpass Hell

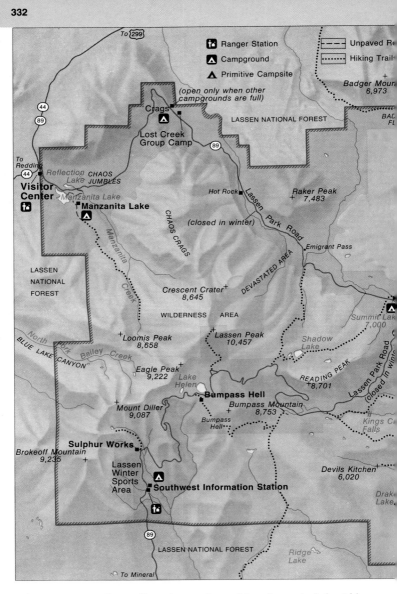

At **Bumpass Hell**, the road's next major stop, note a large balanced rock at the edge of the parking lot; it's a glacial erratic—a polished, glacier-borne boulder. Nearby begins the **Bumpass Hell Trail**, a fairly easy 3-mile hike that takes about 3 hours. Go on it if you have time.

The place is named after K. V. Bumpass, a local guide and promoter, who in the 1860s plunged a leg through the thin crust covering a seething mud pot. Though badly burned, he wisecracked about his easy descent into hell.

Sulphurous vapors drift over parts of the trail, which leads down to a railed boardwalk that winds past boiling mud pots, rumbling fumaroles, and hissing hot springs. At the springs' steamy pools look for floating golden flakes. They are crystals of iron pyrite—fool's gold—carried along in the superheated steam. The trail returns you to the parking lot.

Resume driving on the road, which

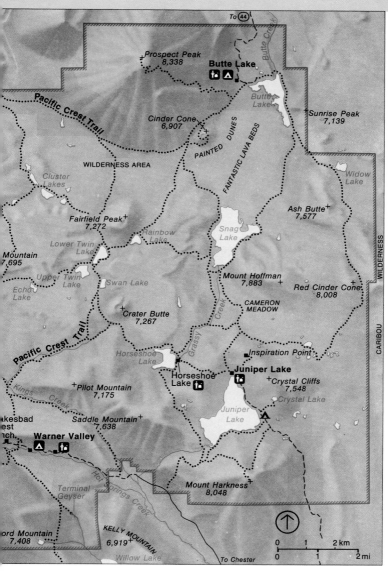

To 44

Prospect Peak
8,338

Butte Lake

Pacific Crest Trail

Butte
Lake

Cinder Cone
6,907

Sunrise Peak
7,139

PAINTED DUNES

FANTASTIC LAVA BEDS

WILDERNESS AREA

Cluster
Lakes

Widow
Lake

WILDERNESS

Fairfield Peak
7,272

Rainbow
Lake

Ash Butte
7,577

Snag
Lake

Lower Twin
Lake

Mountain
7,695

Upper Twin
Lake

Swan Lake

Mount Hoffman
7,883

Red Cinder Cone
8,008

Echo
Lake

CAMERON
MEADOW

Pacific Crest Trail

Crater Butte
7,267

Grassy Creek

CARIBOU

Inspiration Point

Horseshoe
Lake

Juniper Lake

Kings Creek

Horseshoe
Lake

Crystal Cliffs
7,548

Pilot Mountain
7,175

Crystal Lake

Juniper
Lake

kesbad
est
nch

Saddle Mountain
7,638

Warner Valley

Mount Harkness
8,048

Hot Springs Creek

Terminal
Geyser

ord Mountain
7,408

KELLY MOUNTAIN
6,919

Willow Lake

To Chester

0   1   2 km
0   1   2 mi

curves around Lassen Peak. Continue to the **Devastated Area**, wrecked by a massive May 1915 eruption. Amid the scarred and fallen trees notice the signs of renewal: Young trees and stubborn grasses are growing in a slow, natural comeback unaided by human hand. The road offers many turnoffs for viewing the crags and canyons that are Lassen's volcanic heritage.

You'll pass churned-up landscape dubbed **Chaos Crags** and **Chaos Jum-bles;** if space along the road permits, stop and walk around it. Here, about 300 years ago, a nearby volcanic dome suddenly collapsed, perhaps because of an earth tremor. Millions of tons of rock, riding a cushion of trapped air, sped across 2 miles of flat land. The horizontal avalanche smashed into a mountain and veered into a creek, damming it and forming **Manzanita Lake.** Just beyond, the road ends its course through the park and enters Lassen National Forest.

Cinder Cone Nature Trail

31-mile drive, 5-mile hike; a full day

Leave the park via the **Manzanita Lake Entrance.** Head north on Calif. Hwy. 44, which swings around the park for 26 miles toward the **Butte Lake Entrance.** From Hwy. 44 take the marked dirt road 6 miles to the Butte Lake Campground, where the trail begins. **Cinder Cone,** a nearly symmetrical, 755-foot-high mound of lava surrounded by multicolored cinders, stands black and solitary above a pine forest. Why all the cinders? This type of cone volcano ejects light lava that shatters in the air and falls back as cinders, which pile up around the volcanic vent. Don't expect to hurry on the cone trail, a round-trip of about 5 miles. Walking on loose cinders is like walking through sand. At the top (6,907 feet), you will see the craters of recent eruptions; the last was in 1851 and was seen more than 150 miles away.

Lassen Peak Trail

5 miles round-trip; a half to full day

The **Lassen Peak Trail** is a steep, arduous climb. The zigzagging trail begins at 8,463 feet, near the park road, and takes you to the 10,457-foot summit. The going can get tough for people used to breathing at sea level. Before you try the climb be sure you are acclimatized to the park's high elevations. Carry water, wear a hat, and bring a jacket. *Turn back if a storm threatens;* the peak is a lightning attractor. Lassen has scant vegetation. "A desert standing on end," a parched climber called it. But you can almost always spot a ground squirrel. And sometimes thousands of tortoiseshell butterflies suddenly flit by, their shadows cascading along the grayish volcanic rocks. At the summit, you can see the black, hardened vestige of the 1915 lava flow. And visible on a clear day, 75 miles away, is Mt. Shasta.

Information & Activities

Headquarters
Mineral, California 96063. Phone (916) 595-4444.

Seasons & Accessibility
Park and both its entrances open year-round. Lassen Park Road usually closed by snow from November to May. Ski area at Southwest Entrance open Thanksgiving to mid-April, weather permitting. For road conditions phone (916) 225-3028. For ski information call (916) 595-4464.

Visitor & Information Centers
Both the Visitor Center on Hwy. 89 at Manzanita Lake and the Southwest Information Station are open daily from mid-June to Labor Day. Call headquarters for information.

Entrance Fees
$5 per car in summer, good for 7 days; $1 per day in winter at the Southwest Entrance.

Facilities for Disabled
Visitor Center, information center, most rest rooms, the Devastated Area Nature Trail, and some picnic areas are wheelchair accessible.

Free brochures available.

Things to Do
Free naturalist-led activities: nature walks and hikes, talks, nature and history demonstrations, children's programs, evening programs (including stargazing and a "prowl" in summer), snowshoe walks, cross-country ski tours. Also, hiking, swimming, fishing, boating (no motors), cross-country and downhill skiing.

Overnight Backpacking
Permits required. They are free and can be obtained at headquarters, visitor centers, and ranger stations. No wood fires permitted.

Campgrounds
Six campgrounds, **Summit Lake-North** and **Summit Lake-South** have a 7-day limit; all others 14-day limit. Open late May through September, weather permitting. First come, first served. Fees: None to $8 per night. Showers at **Manzanita Lake.** RV sites except at **Juniper Lake** and **Southwest;** no hookups. Three group campgrounds; must reserve; contact headquarters. Food services in park.

Hotels, Motels, & Inns
(unless otherwise noted, rates are for 2 persons in a double room, high season)
INSIDE THE PARK:
Drakesbad Guest Ranch (47 miles SE of headquarters) Chester, Calif. 96020. Call long-distance operator and ask for the Susanville, Calif., operator; then ask for Drakesbad #2. 6 lodge rooms, 4 cabins, $152; 6 bungalows, $170; all meals included. Pool. Open mid-June to early October.

OUTSIDE THE PARK:
In Mineral, Calif. 96063:
Lassen Mineral Lodge (on Calif. 36, 8 miles from park gate) P.O. Box 160. (916) 595-4422. 20 units, 2 with kitchenettes. $42. Pool, restaurant.
In Redding, Calif. 96002:
Best Western Hilltop Inn 2300 Hilltop Drive. (800) 336-4880 or (916) 221-6100. 112 units. $76-$85. AC, pool, restaurant. **Holiday Inn** 1900 Hilltop Drive. (800) 465-4329 or (916) 221-7500. 165 units. $83. AC, pool, restaurant. **Red Lion Inn** 1830 Hilltop Drive. (800) 547-8010 or (916) 221-8700. 195 units, 2 with kitchenettes. $77-$117. AC, pool, restaurant. **Vagabond Inn** 536 E. Cypress Ave. (800) 522-1555 or (916) 223-1600. 71 units. $60-$65. AC, pool, restaurant.

For other accommodations in the area, contact the park or the Redding Chamber of Commerce, P.O. Box 1180, Redding, Calif. 96099. (916) 225-4433.

Excursions

Lassen National Forest
Susanville, California
Volcanic features dot this mountain forest surrounding the Lassen Volcanic NP. Also contains many lakes and streams. 1,100,000 acres. Facilities include 1,200 campsites, hiking, boating, boat ramp, fishing, horseback riding, hunting, picnic areas, winter sports, water sports, handicapped access. Open all year; most campsites open May 15-October 15. Information at Susanville on Calif. 36, about 70 miles from the park, or in Chester on Calif. 36, about 40 miles from the park. (916) 257-2151.

Whiskeytown-Shasta-Trinity National Recreation Area
Whiskeytown, California
Here in Gold Rush country, three impounded lakes provide unlimited opportunities for recreation on, in, and around water. Backcountry hiking and recreational gold panning also featured. 254,388 acres. Facilities include 1,156 campsites, cabins, houseboats (reservations required), food services, hiking, boat ramp, fishing, horseback riding, hunting, picnic areas, scenic drives, water sports, handicapped access. Open year-round. Whiskeytown headquarters on Calif. Hwy. 299, off I-5, about 60 miles west of Lassen Volcanic NP. (916) 241-6584. For Shasta and Trinity units call (916) 246-5222.

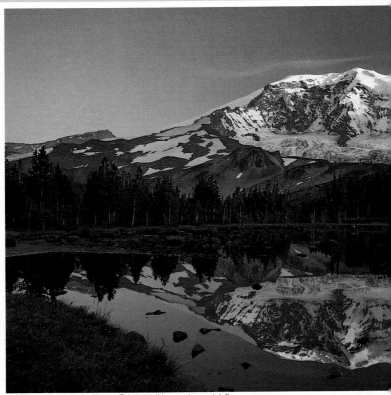

Mt. Rainier, known to Indians as Tahoma—"the great mountain"

Mount Rainier

Washington

Established March 2, 1899

235,404 acres

One of the world's most massive volcanoes, Mt. Rainier can dominate the skyline for 100 miles before you reach the park named after it. At nearly 3 miles in height, Mt. Rainier is the tallest peak in the Cascade Range; it dwarfs 6,000-foot surrounding summits, appearing to float alone among the clouds.

Mt. Rainier may be the centerpiece of the park, but it is hardly the only attraction. Here, less than 3 hours' drive from Seattle, you can stroll through seemingly endless fields of wildflowers, listen to a glacier flow, wander among trees nearly a thousand years old. The park's convenient location, however, also leads to weekend traffic jams, both summer and winter, and guarantees you company on popular trails.

Mt. Rainier is the offspring of fire and ice. Now dormant, it was probably born more than a half million years ago, on a base of lava spewed out by previous volcanoes. Lava and ash surged out of the young volcano's vent thousands of times, filling the neighboring canyons and building up a summit cone, layer by layer, to a height of some 16,000 feet.

Even while Mt. Rainier was growing, glaciers carved valleys on and around the mountain. The 25 major glaciers here form the largest collection of permanent ice on a single US peak south of Alaska.

Mt. Rainier's summit deteriorated over time, but eruptions in the last 2,000 years rebuilt it to its current height of 14,410 feet. The mountain last erupted about a century ago.

on to **Sunrise,** the highest point accessible by car. If you have 2 days, take the same route but do it more leisurely: Plan to explore as far as Paradise the first day, then tour **Stevens Canyon Road** and the route to Sunrise the next; arrive before 10 a.m. to catch the early light and wend your way back. For a longer stay, drive out and reenter the less known northwest corner at **Carbon River** for a look at a temperate rain forest and a hike to a dark, shiny glacier. Because **Mt. Rainier** creates its own clouds and can hide for days or weeks at a time, come prepared to focus on delights close at hand: waterfalls, woods, and wildflowers.

Nisqually to Paradise

18 miles; a half to full day

The pilgrimage to **Paradise** has been a classic for nearly a century. The first miles of your tour wind through a forest of giant Douglas-fir, western red cedar, and western hemlock. As you cross **Kautz Creek,** about 3 miles from the park entrance, look for flood debris and dead trees amidst the recovering forest. In 1947 the **Kautz Glacier** disgorged a flash flood of meltwater. The flood raged down the creek valley, carrying volcanic debris, trees, and boulders, and burying the road under 28 feet of mud. Similar, though mostly smaller, mudflows occur at least every few years at Mt. Rainier.

Park at **Longmire Museum,** 6 miles from the entrance. Pioneer James Longmire discovered mineral springs here in 1883 and built Mt. Rainier's first hotel; his ads for miraculous water cures helped generate early tourism and a constituency for the creation of the park. Take time for the easy $\frac{1}{2}$-mile **Trail of the Shadows** that starts on the opposite side of the main road. While in Longmire, also visit the **Hiker Information Center** for trail and weather information and backcountry permits.

Back in your car, continue east for about $6\frac{1}{2}$ miles, then take the spur road to the right to **Ricksecker Pt.** To the south loom the sawtoothed peaks of the **Tatoosh Range,** dramatic remains of lava flows that predated **Mt. Rainier** by some 25 to 35 million years. Glaciers that developed and

How to Get There

From Seattle (95 miles) or Tacoma (70 miles) to the Nisqually Entrance, take I-5 to Wash. Hwy. 7, then to Wash. Hwy. 706. From Yakima, take Wash. Hwy. 12 west to Hwy. 123 or 410, and enter from the east (Stevens Canyon or White River Entrances). For the northwest entrances (Carbon River and Mowich Lake), take Wash. Hwy. 410 to 169 to 165, then follow the signs. Airports: Seattle and Portland, Ore.

When to Go

All seasons. Wildflowers are at their best in July and August. High trails may remain snow covered until mid-July. Cross-country skiing and snowshoeing are popular in winter. Summer and winter, to miss the crowds, time your visit to midweek.

How to Visit

If you have only a day, drive from **Nisqually Entrance** in the southwest to the flowered fields of **Paradise,** then

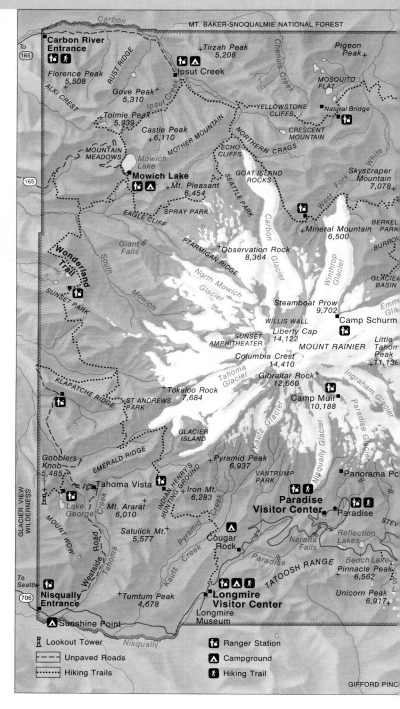

MT. BAKER-SNOQUALMIE NATIONAL FOREST

Carbon

To
165

**Carbon River
Entrance**

RUST RIDGE

ALKI CREST

Florence Peak
5,508

Gove Peak
5,310

Ipsut Creek

+Tolmie Peak
5,939

MOUNTAIN
MEADOWS

Castle Peak
+6,110

MOTHER MOUNTAIN

Mowich
Lake

165

Mowich Lake

EAGLE CLIFF

SPRAY PARK

+Mt. Pleasant
6,454

SEATTLE PARK

Giant
Falls

*Wonderland
Trail*

South

Mowich

SUNSET PARK

PTARMIGAN RIDGE

North Mowich
Glacier

+Observation Rock
8,364

+Tirzah Peak
5,208

Ipsut Creek

YELLOWSTONE
CLIFFS

ECHO
CLIFFS

NORTHERN CRAGS

GOAT ISLAND
ROCKS

Chenuis Creek

Pigeon
Peak+

MOSQUITO
FLAT

Natural Bridge

CRESCENT
MOUNTAIN

West Fork

White

Skyscraper
Mountain
7,078+

Carbon Glacier

Winthrop Glacier

BERKEL
PARK

+Mineral Mountain
6,500

BURRO

GLACIE
BASIN

Steamboat Prow
9,702

Emm
Gla

Camp Schurm

WILLIS WALL

KLAPATCHE RIDGE

ST ANDREWS
PARK

Liberty Cap
14,122

SUNSET
AMPHITHEATER

Columbia Crest
14,410

Tahoma
Glacier

+Tokaloo Rock
7,684

GLACIER
ISLAND

Gibraltar Rock+
12,660

MOUNT RAINIER

Little
Tahom
Peak
+11,138

Ingraham Glacier

Camp Muir
10,188

EMERALD RIDGE

Gobblers
Knob~
5,485+

INDIAN HENRY'S HUNTING GROUND

+Iron Mt.
6,283

Pyramid Creek

+Pyramid Peak
6,937

VANTRUMP
PARK

Paradise Glacier

Panorama Po

Tahoma Vista

Lake
George

+Mt. Ararat
6,010

Satulick Mt.+
5,577

Kautz Creek

Nisqually Glacier

**Paradise
Visitor Center**

Paradise

STEV

GLACIER VIEW
WILDERNESS

MOUNT WOW

Westside

Road

Tahoma

Cougar
Rock

Paradise

Narada
Falls

Reflection
Lakes

To
Seattle
706

**Nisqually
Entrance**

+Tumtum Peak
4,678

Kautz Creek

**Longmire
Visitor Center**

Longmire
Museum

TATOOSH RANGE

Bench Lake

Pinnacle Peak
6,562

Unicorn Peak
6,917+

S

Sunshine Point

Nisqually

Lookout Tower		Ranger Station
Unpaved Roads		Campground
Hiking Trails		Hiking Trail

GIFFORD PINC

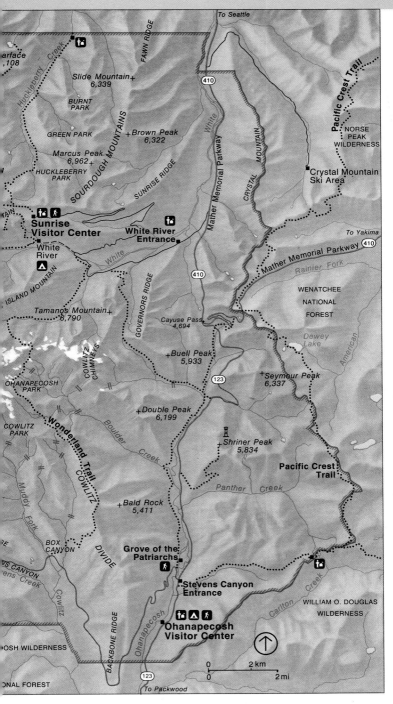

To Seattle

FAWN RIDGE

410

Pacific Crest Trail

NORSE
PEAK
WILDERNESS

arface
,108

Huckleberry Creek

Slide Mountain
6,339

BURNT
PARK

GREEN PARK

Brown Peak
6,322

SOURDOUGH MOUNTAINS

Marcus Peak
6,962

HUCKLEBERRY
PARK

SUNRISE RIDGE

White

Mather Memorial Parkway

CRYSTAL MOUNTAIN

Crystal Mountain
Ski Area

Sunrise
Visitor Center

White River
Entrance

To Yakima

410

Mather Memorial Parkway

Rainier Fork

WENATCHEE

NATIONAL

FOREST

White
River

AIN

ISLAND MOUNTAIN

GOVERNORS RIDGE

410

Tamanos Mountain
6,790

Cayuse Pass
4,694

Dewey
Lake

OHANAPECOSH
PARK

COWLITZ
CHIMNEYS

Buell Peak
5,933

123

Seymour Peak
6,337

American

COWLITZ
PARK

Wonderland Trail

COWLITZ

Double Peak
6,199

Boulder Creek

Shriner Peak
5,834

Pacific Crest
Trail

Muddy Fork

Bald Rock
5,411

Panther   Creek

BOX
CANYON

DIVIDE

Grove of the
Patriarchs

VS CANYON
ens Creek

Cowlitz

Stevens Canyon
Entrance

Carbon   Creek

WILLIAM O. DOUGLAS

WILDERNESS

Ohanapecosh

BACKBONE RIDGE

Ohanapecosh
Visitor Center

OSH WILDERNESS

123

NAL FOREST

To Packwood

0   2 km
0   2 mi

Paradise Valley and visitor center

receded during the last million years carved the sharp pinnacles and the steep-sided mountainside hollows called cirques. Below meanders the **Nisqually River,** which originates at the snout of the **Nisqually Glacier** that faces you on Mt. Rainier. This glacier is about 4 miles long and flows downhill a foot every summer's day.

Rejoin the highway. Another $1\frac{1}{2}$ miles brings you to the **Narada Falls** pullover. The shimmering, 168-foot plunge of the **Paradise River** is well worth the steep but short walk down to the viewing area below the bridge. Climb back up to your car and proceed; in less than 3 miles you'll reach the most popular part of the park.

"It looks just like paradise!" exclaimed Martha Longmire in 1885 on first sighting the rolling hills swathed in wildflowers and framed by Mt. Rainier's white dome. An average of 100 inches of precipitation falls here each year; as many as 40 species of flowers bloom on the thin, volcanic soil during July and August. Park near the **Henry M. Jackson Memorial Visitor Center,** or the **Paradise Inn,** built in 1917.

Begin your exploration of Paradise meadows on the **Nisqually Vista Trail** ($1\frac{1}{5}$ miles), especially if time is short. This easy, self-guided nature walk starts at the staircase to the west of the visitor center. Its booklet acquaints you with the geology and meadow life of Mt. Rainier.

Make sure you stay on the path, no matter how tempting a meadow stroll. Trampling by just a few peo-

Narada Falls in summer

ple can kill these fragile plants. Park staffers are still at work replanting old trails and other damaged areas. Only recently have the meadows recovered from the Camp of the Clouds, a tent city in operation here from 1898 to 1915. Be sure to view the startling before-and-after pictures of meadow repair at the visitor center before you leave Paradise. Not only people damage meadows, though. Elk, introduced in the first part of the century and now numbering some 2,000 inside the park, trample and graze the meadows. Researchers are seeking a solution to the problem.

If you're up to tackling some steep hills, try the 5-mile **Skyline Trail.** Start from the staircase west of the visitor center. The trail will take you to **Panorama Point** for spectacular views. Consider a $1\frac{1}{2}$-mile detour to **Paradise Glacier.** Listen to this river of ice squeak and groan as it flows; touch it, but don't walk on it.

Paradise to Sunrise

50 miles; a half to full day

Leaving Paradise, turn left at the sign for **Sunrise** and Yakima. You'll soon pass the glacier-carved **Reflection Lakes** on your left; on a calm day, the reflection looks as solid as the mountain. Continue a mile past the lakes' pullover and park on the right for a $2\frac{1}{2}$-mile, hilly, round-trip walk to **Snow** and **Bench Lakes,** gems surrounded by the steep headwalls of the Tatoosh Range.

Drive on and stop after about 3 miles at an overlook of **Stevens Canyon,** named for a climber who in 1870 became one of the first people to reach the summit of Mt. Rainier. Huge glaciers grating through this river gorge deepened and widened it into a classic U-shaped valley. Tributaries of **Stevens Creek** spill from the canyon's rim as waterfalls. Drive on another 3 miles, to **Box Canyon** (just past the picnic area). Park and cross the street for the nearly level $\frac{1}{2}$-mile **Canyon Stroll** and you'll see a 100-foot-deep gorge whose straight walls were carved by the **Muddy Fork** of the **Cowlitz River.**

Continue another $9\frac{1}{2}$ miles, then park to walk the **Grove of the Patriarchs** nature trail. This easy $1\frac{1}{3}$-mile loop leads to an island in the **Ohanapecosh River** dominated by grand Douglas-fir, western red cedar, and western hemlock, many of them 500 to 1,000 years old. After rejoining the road, turn left on Wash. Hwy. 123 for Sunrise.

At **Cayuse Pass,** continue north on Hwy. 410, then make a sharp left toward the **White River Entrance.** The road ends at Sunrise. Spire-shaped subalpine fir and whitebark pine grow here. Near tree line, harsh temperatures and winds stunt the trees into twisted shrubs called krummholz, or elfin timber; trees only inches in diameter may be 250 years old. Fragile wildflowers bloom among grass and sedge in terrain inhospitable to trees.

Grove of the Patriarchs

Marmot eating Indian paintbrush

Northern saw-whet owl in aspen tree

Four-mile-long Nisqually Glacier

At the visitor center ask about snow conditions on the higher trails. If time is short, take the self-guided **Sourdough Ridge Nature Trail** for $1\frac{1}{2}$ miles, then the **Emmons Vista Trail** for $\frac{1}{2}$ mile. The Sourdough Ridge trail, which starts with a climb, introduces plants and animals of the subalpine region. The Emmons Vista Trail offers an easy way to view **Emmons Glacier**, Mt. Rainier's largest, covering more than 4 square miles.

But if you have more time and energy, and the snow has melted (snow on the slopes can be dangerous if you're not equipped with an ice ax and trained to use it), take the **Burroughs Mountain Trail** (5 miles to **First Burroughs**, or 7 miles to **Second Burroughs**). Begin as for the nature trail, but turn left at the top of the hill and follow the signs. The trail soon enters tundra. Compact little plants sport lilliputian blossoms and leaves that are dull gray from the tiny hairs that protect them against drying winds. *Stay on the trail:* If trod on, these plants can take decades to heal. At Second Burroughs you feel you can almost touch Mt. Rainier's imposing peak. Return to your car by way of the **Sunrise Rim Trail**.

The Northwest Corner: Carbon River

5 miles inside park boundary; a half day

To beat the crowds, to visit a rare inland temperate rain forest, to peer at the glacier that comes farthest down the mountain: All are reasons to visit this corner of the park. The **Carbon River Road** forks left off Wash. Hwy. 165 about 6 miles past Wilkeson. Unpaved inside the park, the road is passable for ordinary cars. Stop at the entrance to take the self-guided **Carbon River Rain Forest Trail**, a $\frac{1}{2}$-mile loop among colossal Sitka spruce, Douglas-fir, and western red cedar, blanketed with moss. Drive to the parking lot at Ipsut Creek Campground. If you're up to a 7-mile round-trip hike with a short, moderately steep climb, take the **Carbon Glacier Trail**. Bear right at first fork, left at second, then cross the swinging bridge over the river and continue on. The glistening glacier has taken on the charcoal gray color of the scree and boulders caught in the ice. *Don't get close:* Boulders continually tumble off the glacier's snout.

Mountain Wildflowers

Giant red paintbrush and daisies along Tatoosh Range

Glacier lilies

Pink mountain heather

Fireweed

Western pasque flowers

Phlox

Shooting star

Information & Activities

Headquarters
Tahoma Woods, Star Route, Ashford, Washington 98304. Phone (206) 569-2211.

Seasons & Accessibility
Park open year-round. Many roads closed by snow from late November through May or June. Call (206) 569-2211 for recorded weather, road, trail, and facility information, or in the Nisqually area tune in to 1610 AM.

Visitor & Information Centers
Longmire Visitor (or Hiker Information) Center, open daily mid-June to Sept. 30. Henry M. Jackson Memorial Visitor Center, at Paradise, open daily from early May to mid-October, weekends the rest of the year. Ohanapecosh Visitor Center, at park's southeast entrance, open daily Memorial Day through mid-Oct. Sunrise Visitor Center open daily, July to third Sunday in Sept.

Entrance Fee
$5 per car allows unlimited access up to 7 days.

Pets
Permitted leashed on roads, on the Pacific Crest Trail, and in parts of Paradise and Sunrise.

Facilities for Disabled
Most public buildings and some rest rooms are wheelchair accessible. Portions of some trails may be accessible (assistance may be needed). Inquire at park for details.

Things to Do
Free naturalist-led activities: nature and history walks, hikes, campfire and children's programs, talks, films, slide shows. Also available, hiking, mountain climbing, fishing (license not needed), cross-country skiing, snowshoeing.

Special Advisories
☐Watch out for falling rocks, debris, and avalanches. Look up!
☐Some areas may be subject to flash floods, especially in late summer and fall. Inquire about current conditions before hiking.

Overnight Backpacking
Permit required. Available free from visitor centers, ranger stations, and the Longmire hiker center, where you can also get help with your trip planning. For information write to Backcountry Desk c/o park headquarters or call (206) 569-2211.

Campgrounds
Five campgrounds, all with 14-day limit. **Sunshine Point** open all year. Others open late spring to early fall. All campgrounds first come, first served. Fees $5-$8 per night. Showers available at the visitor center at Paradise. Both tent and RV sites; no hookups. Two group campgrounds; must reserve; contact headquarters. Food services in park.

Hotels, Motels, & Inns
(unless otherwise noted, rates are for 2 persons in a double room, high season)

INSIDE THE PARK:
National Park Inn (at 2,700 ft. level of Mt. Rainier) Mt. Rainier Guest Services, P.O. Box 108, Ashford, Wash. 98304. (206) 569-2275. 25 units, 18 with private baths. $52-$72. Restaurant. Open all year. **Paradise Inn** (at 5,400 ft. level of Mt. Rainier) Mt. Rainier Guest Services, see above. 126 units, 95 with private baths. $54-$77. Restaurant. Open mid-May to mid-October.

OUTSIDE THE PARK:
Alexander's Country Inn (1 mi. from park's main entrance) 37515 SR 706 East, Ashford, Wash. 98304. (800) 654-7615 or (206) 569-2300. 14 units, 9 with private baths. $65-$98. Restaurant. **Mountain View Lodge Motel** (12163 US Hwy. 12) P.O. Box 525, Packwood, Wash. 98361. (206) 494-5555. 23 units, 8 with kitchens. $31-$70. AC, pool. **Woodland Motel** (10 miles from park entrance) 11890 US Hwy. 12, Randle, Wash. 98377. (206) 494-6766. 8 units, 6 with kitchens. $38-$45.

Excursions

Gifford Pinchot National Forest
Vancouver, Washington
Dense coniferous forest encompassing the Mount St. Helens National Volcanic Monument (see below) offers superb views of the volcano and the recovering terrain. Also presents unlimited recreational opportunities in its lakes, streams, rivers, and waterfalls. Contains glaciers and seven wilderness areas. 1,251,000 acres. Facilities include 900 campsites, hiking, boating, boat ramp, climbing, fishing, horseback riding, hunting, picnic areas, winter sports, water sports, handicapped access. Open all year; most campsites open June-October. Adjoins Mount Rainier NP on south. Information at Packwood on Wash. Hwy. 12, about 10 miles from the park. (206) 494-5515.

Mount St. Helens
National Volcanic Monument
Amboy, Washington
This monument owes its existence to the day in May 1980 when Mount St. Helens erupted, blowing its top and laying waste to the surrounding forest. Visitors here witness the rebirth through interpretive programs and tours. 110,000 acres. Facilities include hiking, bicycling, climbing (reservations required), fishing, hunting, picnic areas, scenic drives, winter sports, handicapped access. Open year-round, but winter snows close many roads. Within Gifford Pinchot NF. Visitor center at Castle Rock on Wash. Hwy. 504, about 80 miles southwest of Mount Rainier NP. (206) 274-6644.

Ridgefield
National Wildlife Refuge
Ridgefield, Washington
Established to protect the winter habitat of the dusky Canada goose, this site on the floodplain of the Columbia River provides a winter haven for many waterfowl species. It also serves as a year-round home for great blue herons and a resting spot for migrating sandhill cranes. 4,615 acres. Facilities include hiking, boating, hunting, scenic drives. Open all year, dawn to dusk (winter best time). Off I-5, about 90 miles from Mount Rainier NP. (206) 887-4106.

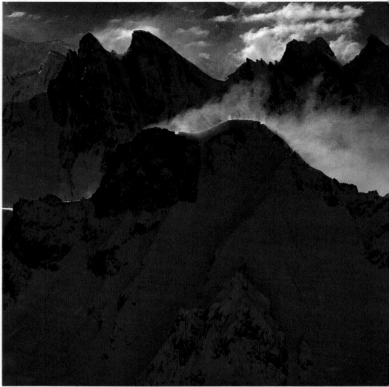

Glacier-carved peaks of the North Cascades

North Cascades

Washington

Established October 2, 1968

684,000 acres, includes two recreation areas

With glacier-clad peaks rising almost vertically from thickly forested valleys, the North Cascades are often called the American Alps. The national park forms two units, North and South, of the North Cascades National Park Service Complex. The two other units—Ross Lake National Recreation Area and Lake Chelan National Recreation Area—contain most visitor facilities and permit private land ownership and commercial activity.

The park complex preserves virgin forests, fragile subalpine meadows, and hundreds of glaciers. Mule deer and black-tailed deer graze the high meadows, where black bears gorge on berries and hoary marmots sunbathe. Mountain goats clamber on rock faces. Mountain lions and bobcats, seldom seen, help keep other wildlife populations in balance.

The wildness and ruggedness of the park especially lure hikers, backpackers, and mountaineers. "A more difficult route to travel never fell to man's lot," complained trapper Alexander Ross, who came here in 1814. But today the main road (through Ross Lake NRA) and easy access into the park—on some of its 360 miles of trails—also allow more casual visitors to experience the peaceful forests and the drama of the mountains.

The region forms part of the Cascade Range, named for its innumerable waterfalls. The range extends from British Columbia to northern California. A geological theory proposes that the mountains began as a

micro-continent several hundred miles out in the Pacific Ocean. Over the eons the island floated on its plate towards North America. About a hundred million years ago, it smashed into the North American continent, folding and crumpling into a mountain range as it lodged against the landmass. Those mountains eroded; the Cascades you see today rose only five or six million years ago.

The western part of the park differs markedly from the east. Moisture blows in from Puget Sound and the Strait of Juan de Fuca. It hits the western slopes and rises, condensing to rain and snow. Western red cedar, hemlock, and Douglas-fir luxuriate on slopes that receive 110 inches of precipitation a year. When the winds reach the east, they are mostly wrung dry: Only 35 inches of precipitation fall in Stehekin at the head of Lake Chelan. Arid-dwelling sagebrush and ponderosa pine grow in the peaks' rain shadow.

How to Get There

From Seattle (about 115 miles from the park), take I-5 to Wash. Hwy. 20, also called the North Cascades Highway. From the east, get on Wash. Hwy. 20 south of Mazama. To reach Stehekin Valley, either hike over Cascade Pass from the Cascade River Road or take a 4-hour ferry or chartered floatplane from Chelan, at the southern tip of Lake Chelan. Chelan is on US 97. Airports: Seattle and Bellingham.

When to Go

Summer gives the best access, though snow can block high trails into July. The North Cascades Highway, from Ross Dam to beyond Washington Pass, closes in winter, as do some areas in spring and fall. Stehekin, a year-round resort, offers winter cross-country skiing.

How to Visit

On a day trip, take the **North Cascades Highway** through the **Ross Lake National Recreation Area** for an overview of the recreation area's lakes and dams, the park's mountains, and the glacier-fed **Skagit River.** If you have 2 days, drive up the unpaved **Cascade River Road** and picnic and hike among the park's peaks and alpine meadows. On a longer stay, drive south to **Chelan,** and take the ferry or fly to **Stehekin** to overnight in a serene, isolated community or in the backcountry.

North Cascades Highway: Marblemount to Washington Pass

60 miles; a half to full day

The ease of driving the **North Cascades Highway** belies the terrain's ruggedness, although names supplied by explorers and climbers attest to it: Mt. Terror, Mt. Despair, Damnation Pk., Mt. Fury, Mt. Challenger. This transmountain road was completed only in 1972.

Enter the **Ross Lake National Recreation Area** after crossing **Bacon Creek,** $6\frac{1}{2}$ miles from the park information station at **Marblemount.** Parallel to the road, the **Skagit River** appears emerald in summer—evidence of the park's many glaciers. As they move, glaciers grind bedrock into a

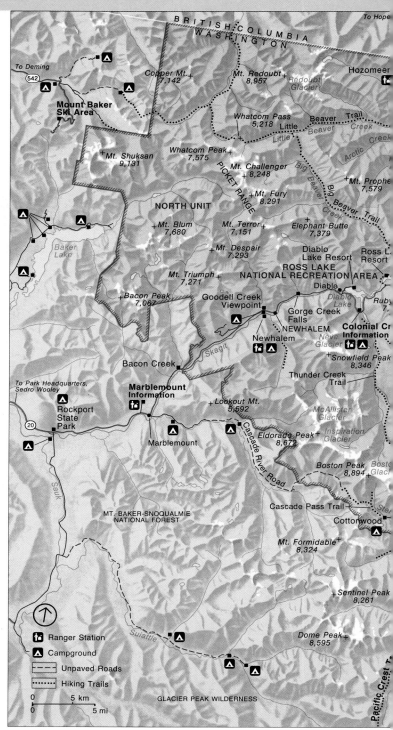

BRITISH COLUMBIA
WASHINGTON

To Hope

To Deming

542

Copper Mt. 7,142

Mt. Redoubt 8,957

Redoubt Glacier

Hozomeer

Mount Baker Ski Area

Whatcom Pass 5,218

Beaver Trail

Little Beaver Creek

Little

Arctic Creek

Mt. Shuksan 9,131

Whatcom Peak 7,575

Mt. Challenger 8,248

PICKET RANGE

Big Beaver Creek

Mt. Fury 8,291

Mt. Prophe 7,579

NORTH UNIT

Mt. Blum 7,680

Mt. Terror 7,151

Elephant Butte 7,379

Big Beaver Trail

Mt. Despair 7,293

Diablo Lake Resort

Ross L. Resort

Baker Lake

Mt. Triumph 7,271

ROSS LAKE NATIONAL RECREATION AREA

Bacon Peak 7,067

Goodell Creek Viewpoint

Diablo

Diablo Lake

Ruby 7,

Gorge Creek Falls

NEWHALEM

Colonial Cr Information

Bacon Creek

Newhalem

Skagit

Neve Glacier

Snowfield Peak 8,346

To Park Headquarters, Sedro Wooley

Marblemount Information

Thunder Creek Trail

Rockport State Park

20

Lookout Mt. 5,692

McAllister Glacier

Marblemount

Cascade River Road

Eldorado Peak 8,672

Inspiration Glacier

Sauk

Boston Peak 8,894

Bosto Glaci

MT. BAKER-SNOQUALMIE NATIONAL FOREST

Cascade Pass Trail

Ste

Cottonwood

Mt. Formidable 8,324

Sentinel Peak 8,261

Suiattle

Dome Peak 8,595

Ranger Station

Campground

Unpaved Roads

Hiking Trails

0   5 km
0   5 mi

GLACIER PEAK WILDERNESS

Pacific Crest T

fine "flour." Water carrying a high concentration of glacial flour reflects the green part of the light spectrum. In winter bald eagles feast on salmon running the Skagit.

At **Goodell Creek Bridge** (milepost 119), look left to catch a rare glimpse of the high, sawtoothed peaks of the **Picket Range.** Turn right onto Main Street at **Newhalem,** a town of Seattle City Light (milepost 121). The company's dams—Gorge, Diablo, and Ross—generate about a third of Seattle's peak-time electricity. The dams created both **Diablo** and **Ross Lakes.** To haul men and materials for construction, the company built a railway from Rockport to Diablo in the 1920s. Check at the Park Service-City Light information center to see if there is room on City Light's 4-hour Skagit Tour, which includes a cruise on Diablo Lake and a ride up a mountainside. (For reservations, see **Information & Activities.**) Or board a City Light tugboat plying between **Diablo** and **Ross Dams.** This enjoyable 1-hour round-trip begins near the **Diablo Lake Resort.**

For an easy walk before leaving Newhalem and an introduction to the towering, lush western red cedar and hemlock forest typical of the mountains' western slopes, stroll the $\frac{1}{2}$-mile, self-guided **Trail of the Cedars.** It starts at the suspension bridge at the end of Main Street.

Drive on to **Diablo,** another City Light settlement, by turning left at milepost 126. Near here in 1901, pioneer Lucinda Davis and her three children cleared land and put up a roadhouse to feed and house the miners who still trudged the mountains in the wake of two abortive gold rushes. The Davis family built the first hydroelectric project on the Skagit—a waterwheel that generated enough electricity to light three light bulbs. A replica of the waterwheel stands next to the modern Diablo powerhouse; the **Davis Museum** preserves mementos of the era.

Drive back to the highway and, if you are looking for an invigorating climb, turn right after about 4 miles at Colonial Creek Campground. Behind the amphitheater the **Thunder Woods Nature Trail** begins. This steep 1-mile loop rises among giant, fragrant cedar trees, some of them more than three centuries old. The

Backpackers on the trail to Cascade Pass

red cedar—characterized by ropy, cinnamon-colored bark and flat, fern-like foliage—provided Indians with wood for canoes and houses and fiber for mats, clothing, and baskets. To extend your walk, continue along the 19-mile **Thunder Creek Trail** for a while; the views are good and the hiking relatively easy at first. (Eventually it ascends 6,300 feet.)

When you're back in the car, don't miss the **Diablo Lake Overlook** (5,985 feet), milepost 132. Amid the splendid scenery are exhibits that honor Senator Henry M. Jackson, who helped create the park and to whom Congress dedicated it in 1987. The highest mountain visible here is **Colonial Peak** (7,776 feet) to the southwest; note the glacial cirque, or bowl-shaped depression, carved out of its side. North is **Sourdough Mountain**, site of a fire lookout tower.

Near milepost 134 you'll find an informative ⅓-mile boardwalk nature trail, the **Happy Creek Forest Walk**. A few miles farther on, the highway leaves the park complex and enters the Okanogan National Forest (milepost 140). For a superb overview of Cascades peaks, follow the road about 20 miles to **Washington Pass Overlook** (5,483 feet), the highest point on the North Cascades Hwy. Take the left exit at milepost 162, and walk to the lookout. Directly to the south is massive **Liberty Bell Mountain** (7,808 feet), south of that are **Early Winter Spires** (7,600 feet). With binoculars you might spot climbers on the solid granite faces.

Cascade River Road

45 miles round-trip; a half day

The **Cascade River Road,** the only road to enter the park proper from the west, passes through national forest for most of its length. The road starts in front of the Log House Inn in Marblemount. Before departing, pick up maps and check road conditions at the Marblemount information station. The road becomes progressively narrower, steeper, and bumpier, though passenger cars can travel it in an hour without difficulty (trailers should not attempt the last few miles). The drive ends at a parking lot and picnic area (3,660 feet) between the glacier-studded summits of **Johannesburg Mountain** (8,200 feet) to the west and **Boston Peak** (8,894 feet) to the east.

Hikers will enjoy the 3¾-mile trail to **Cascade Pass** (5,384 feet). The Skagit and Chelan Indians used the pass to and from **Lake Chelan** for hunting and trading. The trail leaves the lowland forest to enter woods of silver fir, mountain hemlock, and Alaska yellow-cedar, then flower-strewn subalpine meadows. Stay on the path; previous visitors have damaged the fragile meadow flora.

Park employees and volunteers grow native plants in a greenhouse in Marblemount, then backpack or airlift them in for planting in late summer to revegetate the pass. The greenhouse, near the information center, is open for visits.

Lake Chelan, a year-round resort

Stehekin Valley

an overnight or 2

Stehekin has been a tourist hideaway since hotels first opened here at the turn of the century and miners spread tales of magical scenery. On the northern shores of glacier-carved Lake Chelan and inaccessible by road, Stehekin is a community of hardy contemporary homesteaders, complete with one-room schoolhouse in use from 1921 to 1988. The valley offers numerous lodging alternatives as well as backcountry camping without backpacking: Simply fill out a permit after you get there, take a shuttle bus to any of eight backcountry sites, and stake your claim.

Even if you don't plan to camp, head for the **Golden West Visitor Center** when you arrive at Stehekin Landing to pick up hiking maps and schedules of tours and buses. Be sure to ask about trail conditions; high trails—and the last stretch of the shuttle bus route—can be blocked by snow until midsummer.

After lunch, tour the **Buckner Homestead**. Home of the Buckner family from 1911 to 1953, it offers a thought-provoking look at the challenges and joys of frontier living.

Next morning follow the nature trails near the landing. The informative ³⁄₄-mile **Imus Creek Nature Trail** starts near the visitor center, and the **McKellar Cabin Historical Trail** begins just past the post office. Or catch the early shuttle bus upvalley. The buses (8:00 a.m. and 2:00 p.m.) run 23 winding miles on the old mine-to-market road. The scenic round-trip to the terminus at Cottonwood Campground takes 2-5 hours and can be wearing. If you have the time, it may be better to get off at a trailhead, hike, and catch the later bus back. Another good bet is the **Horseshoe Basin Trail** (off the **Cascade Pass Trail**), a moderately steep 3³⁄₄-mile trail that passes more than 15 waterfalls among spectacular glacial and mountain views. At the trail's end, you can explore the old **Black Warrior Mine** with a flashlight. *Be careful!*

For an easier hike try the **Agnes Gorge Trail**, 5 miles round-trip and level. Get off the bus at **High Bridge** near the intersection with the Pacific Crest Trail and walk across the bridge, past the sign for **Agnes Creek**, to the trailhead for **Agnes Gorge**. The trail provides fine views of the 210-foot gorge and **Agnes Mountain** (8,115 feet). Be sure to keep a bus schedule with you to avoid being stranded.

Information & Activities

Headquarters
2105 Highway 20, Sedro Woolley, Wash. 98284. Phone (206) 856-5700.

Seasons & Accessibility
Park open year-round, but snow prevents access to much of it from mid-October to April.

Visitor & Information Centers
North Cascades Information Center, on Wash. Hwy. 20 (North Cascades Highway), in Sedro Woolley. Marblemount Ranger Station just west of park boundary off North Cascades Hwy. Both open all year, daily from April through summer, weekdays only the rest of year. Phone headquarters number for information. *Ross Lake NRA:* in Newhalem, joint Park Service-City Light information center open daily in summer. Information also at Newhalem and Colonial Creek Campgrounds. *Lake Chelan NRA:* Golden West Visitor Center (Stehekin), access by ferry, floatplane, or foot, open May 15 to Oct. 15. Ranger station open weekdays all year. For information call (509) 682-2549.

Pets
Prohibited in national park except on Pacific Crest Trail. Permitted on leashes in NRAs.

Facilities for Disabled
Most information facilities are wheelchair accessible. Also accessible are the Happy Creek Forest Walk and the Washington Pass Overlook.

Things to Do
Free naturalist-led activities: *Ross Lake NRA,* guided nature walks, evening campfire programs. *Lake Chelan NRA,* nature and Buckner Orchard walks, evening programs. Also available, hiking, boating, fishing, hunting (NRAs only, in season), horseback riding, rafting on upper Skagit, cross-country skiing.

In summer, Seattle City Light sponsors tours of Diablo Lake and Ross Dam. Reserve at least a month in advance through Seattle City Light's Skagit Tour Desk, 1015 Third Avenue, Seattle, Wash. 98104. Phone (206) 684-3030.

Overnight Backpacking
Permits required; available free at ranger stations and the Golden West Visitor Center.

Campgrounds
Ross Lake NRA: Five campgrounds, 14-day limit. **Colonial Creek** and **Hozomeen** open mid-spring to mid-fall. **Newhalem** open mid-June to Labor Day. **Goodell Creek** open all year. All first come, first served. Fees: None to $7 per night. No showers. Tent and RV sites; no hookups. **Goodell Creek Group Campground**, reservations required; contact Marblemount Ranger Station (206) 873-4590. *Lake Chelan NRA:* Three campgrounds, **Harlequin, Bullion,** and **Purple Point,** 14-day limit. Open mid-spring to mid-fall. First come, first served. No fees. Showers near **Purple Point.** Tent sites only. Reservations required at **Harlequin Group Campground;** contact Marblemount Ranger Station (see above). Food services in both NRAs.

Hotels, Motels, & Inns
(unless otherwise noted, rates are for 2 persons in a double room, high season)
In Ross Lake NRA:
Ross Lake Resort Rockport, Wash. 98283. (206) 386-4437. (Access by boat or foot.) 13 cabins floating on lake, kitchens. $36-$56. Open late June to late October.
In Lake Chelan NRA:
North Cascades Lodge P.O. Box 1779, Chelan, Wash. 98816. (509) 682-4711. (Access by boat, seaplane, or foot.) 25 units, 4 kitchenettes. $46-$68. Rest. **Silver Bay Inn** P.O. Box 43, Stehekin, Wash. 98852. (509) 682-2212. 2 cabins, kitchenettes, $120; 2 rooms, $75-$110, breakfast. **Stehekin Valley Ranch** P.O. Box 36, Stehekin, Wash. 98852. (509) 682-4677. 10 tent-cabins, shared showers. $55 per person, meals. Open late May to Sept. 30.
In Concrete, Wash. 98237:
Cascade Mountain Inn 3840 Pioneer Lane, Birdsview. (206) 826-4333. 6 units. $80-$90, includes breakfast. Open early May through October.

For accommodations in Chelan, contact the Chamber of Commerce, P.O. Box 216, Chelan, Wash. 98816. (509) 682-3503; in Wash. (800) 424-3526.

Excursions

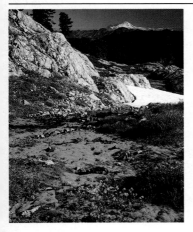

Mt. Baker-Snoqualmie National Forest
Seattle, Washington
The Cascades' evergreen-covered western slopes feature active and dormant volcanoes, 400 glaciers, lakes, streams, and waterfalls. Contains several wilderness areas. Long winter sports season. 1,724,011 acres. Facilities include 1,596 campsites, hiking, boating, boat ramp, climbing, fishing, horseback riding, hunting, picnic areas, scenic drives, winter sports, swimming, handicapped access. Open all year; campsites open May-October. Roads often impassable in winter. Adjoins North Cascades NP on west; also borders Mt. Rainier NP. (206) 442-0170.

Skagit River Bald Eagle Natural Area
Rockport, Washington
This Nature Conservancy refuge is the favored wintering ground of several hundred bald eagles that feed on spawning chum salmon on gravel bars along the Skagit River. Population peaks in mid-January. 924 acres. No visitor facilities. Marked viewing vistas with handicapped access located off Wash. 20 about 10 miles from North Cascades NP. (206) 728-9696.

Okanogan National Forest
Okanogan, Washington
Remote, rugged mountain area with evergreen forest and open woodlands features high peaks, mountain lakes, and meadows. Contains the Pasayten and Lake Chelan-Sawtooth Wilderness Areas. 1,706,000 acres. Facilities include 51 campsites, hiking, boating, boat ramp, climbing, fishing, horseback riding, hunting, picnic areas, scenic drives, winter sports, swimming, handicapped access. Open year-round; most campsites open May-October. Adjoins North Cascades NP on east. (509) 422-2704.

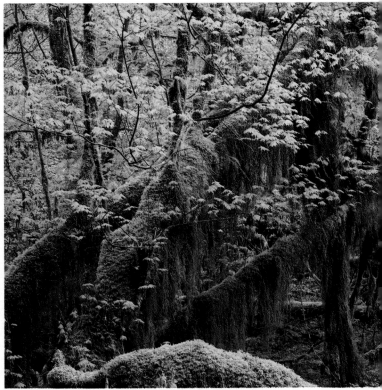

Club moss on vine maple and bigleaf maple in the Hoh Rain Forest

Olympic

Washington

Established June 29, 1938

922,000 acres

Encompassing 1,441 square miles of the Olympic Peninsula, Olympic National Park invites visitors to explore three distinct ecosystems: subalpine forest and wildflower meadow; temperate rain forest; and the rugged Pacific shore. Because of the park's relatively unspoiled condition and outstanding scenery, the United Nations has declared Olympic both an International Biosphere Reserve and a World Heritage site.

Inside the park, the Olympic mountain range is nearly circular, contoured by 13 rivers that radiate out like the spokes of a wheel. No road traverses the park, but a dozen spur roads lead into it from US 101.

Residents of the Olympic Peninsu-
la refer to it as a gift from the sea, and its features were indeed shaped by water and ice. The rock of the Olympics developed under the ocean—marine fossils are embedded in the mountain summits. About 30 million years ago, the plate carrying the Pacific Ocean floor collided with the plate supporting the North American continent. As the heavy oceanic plate slid beneath the lighter continental plate, the upper layers of seabed jammed against the coastline, crumpling into what would become the Olympic Mountains. Glaciers and streams sculptured the mountains into their current profiles.

Glaciers over 1-mile thick also gouged out Puget Sound and Hood Canal to the east, and the Strait of Juan de Fuca to the north, isolating the peninsula from the mainland.

The Ice Age isolation led to the

How to Get There
Approach the park from US 101,
which skirts three sides of the Olympic Peninsula. The main visitor center and entrance are in Port Angeles.
From Seattle, take the Washington
State Ferry to Winslow, then drive
north to Wash. 104 to join US 101
west to Port Angeles, a drive of
about 60 miles. Airports: Port Angeles, Seattle, Sequim, and Olympia.

When to Go
All-year park. Summer is the "dry"
season, but be prepared for cool temperatures, fog, and rain at any time.
Hurricane Ridge opens for skiing on
winter weekends and holidays,
weather permitting.

How to Visit
Plan to spend at least 2 days. On the
first day, stroll subalpine meadows
at **Hurricane Ridge** while admiring the
peaks and glaciers in the distance.
Savor the **Lake Crescent** area and, if
you're feeling energetic, wind up
with a dip at **Sol Duc Hot Springs.** On
the second day, drive to the **Hoh Rain
Forest** and sample its nature trails
before heading west for the Pacific
Ocean beaches and tide pools. If you
have more time, consider a trip to
Ozette in the northwest, or visit less
known **Quinault.**

Port Angeles to Hurricane Ridge, Lake Crescent, & Soleduck
76 miles; a very full day

Plan to spend the night in the area to
get an early start. At the **Olympic
Park Visitor Center** in Port Angeles,
inquire about the weather on **Hurricane Ridge** and pick up a tide table
for the next day. On a clear day, the
ridge offers spectacular views of the
Olympic Mountains and northward as
far as the Strait of Juan de Fuca and
Canada's Vancouver Island. The 18-
mile drive to Hurricane Ridge—so
named for the force of its winter

"endemic 16," as biologists refer to
the 16 species of wildflowers and animals that evolved nowhere else on
earth. They include the Olympic ma-
genta painted cup, Olympic marmot,
Olympic Mazama pocket gopher, and
Beardslee trout.

There are also the "missing 11,"
mammals common in the nearby
Cascades and Rockies that either
died out in the Olympics or never
found their way into the peninsula.
The missing include the grizzly bear,
porcupine, and mountain sheep.
Mountain goats, introduced in the
1920s, have so damaged alpine meadows in Olympic that in 1988 the park
staff began efforts to reduce the
population.

Moist winds from the Pacific con-
dense in the cool air of the Olympics
and drop rain or snow, bestowing on
the mountains' western slopes the
wettest climate in the lower 48
states. Mt. Olympus, which crowns
the park at 7,965 feet, receives 200
inches of precipitation a year.

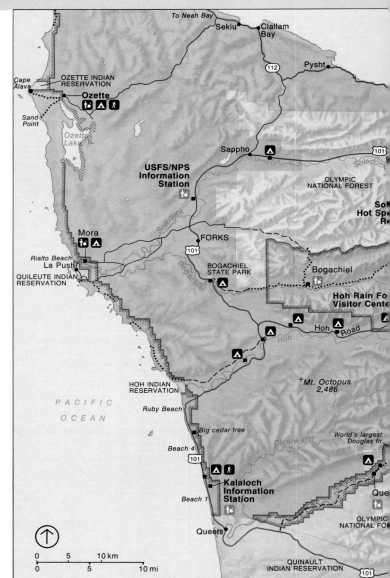

winds—takes you from lowland forest to timberline, nearly a mile above sea level, and reveals some of the remarkable geology of the peninsula.

After the tunnels, 11 miles in, stop at a pullover and look at the rock faces above the road. The bubbles of rock, called pillow basalt, are a clue that these mountains began under the ocean; when hot lava oozes into seawater, its surface cools and hardens quickly, often forming the globules you see here.

Drive on toward **Hurricane Ridge Visitor Center.** Plaques identify the peaks and glaciers of the inner Olympics. **Mt. Olympus** carries 7 of Olympic's 60 major glaciers. Its **Blue Glacier** receives some 500 inches of snow a year and flows downhill at the rate of 5 inches a day.

You will probably see black-tailed

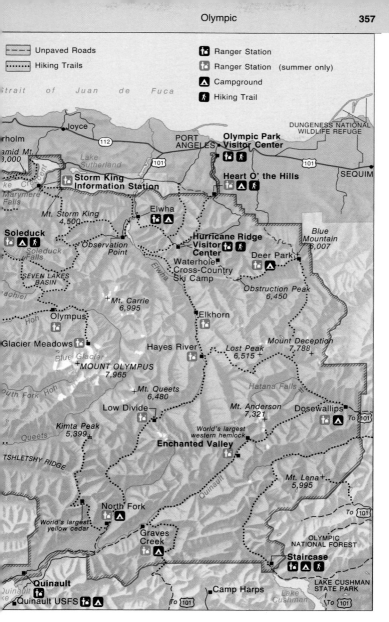

Unpaved Roads

Hiking Trails

Ranger Station

Ranger Station (summer only)

Campground

Hiking Trail

deer here, and possibly Olympic marmots that whistle when approached. Most of the trees are sub-alpine fir. Their distinctive steeple shape helps shed snow. Near timberline, a 3-foot-tall tree may be 100 years old; summer wildflowers thrive where no tree can take hold.

Fine picnic sites lie toward the end of the road, about a mile beyond Hurricane Ridge. Try the **Hurricane Hill Trail**, starting where the road ends, for 3 miles (round-trip) of wildflowers and stunning mountain views. Layers of sedimentary rock along the trail stand folded and tilted on end from the continental collision.

If you prefer to continue driving—some of it is tricky—take the 8-mile, unpaved road to **Obstruction Peak** from the east end of the Hurricane Ridge parking lot for the park's best

Fog-filled Elwha Valley at sunset, from Hurricane Ridge

Glacier-carved Lake Crescent

windshield view of Mt. Olympus and some of Olympic's most diverse wildflower displays. The road generally opens by July 4. **Grand Valley Trail** ($3\frac{1}{2}$ miles one way) starts at the parking lot at road's end. Take at least a stroll on it for grand ridgetop views. Then double back to Port Angeles and pick up US 101 west.

The highway passes **Lake Sutherland** before tracing the southern shore of **Lake Crescent**. Carved by a glacier, the two lakes began as one, but a great landslide created the dam that now divides them. Indian legend says that Mount Storm King, angered at the fighting between the Quileute and Clallam Indians, threw down a boulder, killing the combatants and splitting the lake in two. Lake Crescent, 600 feet deep, is known for its azure waters and trout.

Turn off at the **Storm King Information Station** to walk the **Marymere Falls Trail**, a $1\frac{3}{4}$-mile round-trip through lowland forest to a graceful, 90-foot waterfall. A quarter buys a guide booklet that will help you identify the trees—primarily Douglas-fir and western hemlock, with the occasional western red cedar. Back in the car, time permitting, turn left $1\frac{1}{2}$ miles west of Fairholm to take the 14-mile road to **Soleduck**. Indians, who named the springs Sol Duc, or "sparkling water," probably used the hot springs for medicinal treatments. Travelers have soothed tired muscles in pools here since a resort was first established in 1912. In case you want to stroll before you soak, the **Soleduck Falls Trail**, starting at the end of the road, leads through a mile of dense forest to a waterfall.

Marymere Falls

Hoh Rain Forest to the Pacific Beaches

45 miles; a full day

The **Hoh Rain Forest** is 2½ hours from Port Angeles. To see it and the coast, continue skirting the park as you drive west and south on US 101. Check the schedule of guided tide pool walks in your park newspaper and then decide whether to go first to the rain forest or to the beaches.

For the rain forest, take the **Hoh**

Road inland 19 miles to the visitor center. You'll pass large clear-cut areas on private, state, and national forest lands, but none in the park, where logging is prohibited. Still, environmentalists cite evidence of damage done to park wildlife—some of whose living area extends outside the park—by shrinking habitat.

Two nature trails start behind the visitor center and are well worth taking: the **Hall of Mosses Trail** (³/₄ mile) and the **Spruce Nature Trail** (1¼ miles). This is an enchanted land. Sitka spruce, western hemlock, and western red cedar, measuring up to 25 feet in circumference, tower 300 feet in the air. Club moss and licorice ferns drape the conifers and bigleaf maples, suffusing the air with green. Seedlings, unable to compete on the crowded forest floor, sprout luxuriantly on fallen trees, called nurse logs. Aged giants, lined up in colonnades, stand on huge roots called stilts where their nurse log rotted away. You may see Roosevelt elk—members of the largest herd in the nation—or hear their eerie bugle.

The Spruce Nature Trail shows how the forest develops. Where the **Hoh River** has shifted course in the last few decades, the first trees to move in needed full sunlight to grow —red alder, willow, and Douglas-fir. Later, shade-tolerant spruce and hemlock will succeed these pioneers to dominate the forest.

After your forest sojourn, rejoin US 101 south, stopping at **Ruby Beach**. Walk the trail down to the sand—and keep track of where you came out of the woods. It might be hard to find the trail again, and the tough, oval-leaved shrubs off the trail are virtually impenetrable.

Olympic preserves 57 miles of coastal wilderness: To the north, the beaches tend to have more pebbles and rocks; to the south, the beaches are broader and sandier. Rock outcroppings called sea stacks, isolated from the shoreline by erosion, have caused many a shipwreck.

The driftwood you might have to climb over once grew where you just were: upriver in the forest. Toppled by a winter storm or undercut by a flooding creek, trees tumbled downstream to the sea. *Beware:* Picturesque at low tide, driftwood can suddenly roll with lethal force at high.

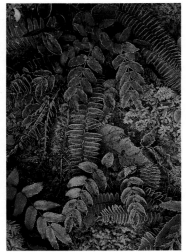
Frost-clad ferns and grape leaves

tures belonging to more than 20 species. Look closely to spot gooseneck and acorn barnacles, periwinkle snails, and rocks with holes drilled by piddock clams. Brightly colored sea stars, or starfish, prowl the rocky pools, preying on the mussels and other mollusks. Green sea anemones stun their tiny prey with stinging cells on their tentacles. Purple sea urchins dine on bits of kelp and other algae.

To view a third mood of Olympic beach, park near **Beach 1**, a stroller's delight, at milepost 155. Follow the sign to the **Spruce Burl Trail** for a brief detour before descending to the sand. Near the ocean, Sitka spruce commonly develop large, nobby growths that may be triggered by a virus, a bacterium, or some substance carried in the ocean spray.

You may see harbor seals, the most common marine mammal on this coast, swimming or lounging on the rocks. In the spring and winter, California gray whales dive and spout near land on their migration between Alaska and Baja California. Gulls and northwestern crows drop clams from 50 feet in the air to crack them open on the rocks. Bald eagles soar from their forest perches to nab fish. The possibility of offshore oil drilling worries conservationists concerned about the coast's delicate ecosystem. A government moratorium bans it at least until the year 2000.

Continue south on US 101 and turn left at the sign for the big cedar tree, one of the world's largest. Standing at the end of a short spur road, the tree looks like something conjured up from the land of Oz. Monstrous in scale, its girth exceeds 66 feet. Walk right inside and decide for yourself if it's one tree or several that grew together.

US 101 from here to the park's southwest border is dotted with overlooks and short access trails to the beaches. If it's low tide—and you missed the guided tide pool walk—try the trail at **Beach 4**, just north of milepost 160. A short, steep hike brings you to the shoreline and the rocky tide pools. Alternately battered by waves and dried out by the sun, tide pools nevertheless teem with life. An area 1 foot square may support 4,000 individual crea-

Ozette & Quinault

A hiking experience in Olympic can range from a paved $\frac{1}{4}$-mile nature walk to the ascent of Mt. Olympus. Of the more than 600 miles of trails, here are a few suggestions. Take US 101 to Sappho, head north to Wash. Hwy. 112 and take it into Sekiu. Then go southwest to **Ozette**. There trails lead on wooden walkways through lush coastal forest to the beach. Register at the ranger station first.

For a level $9\frac{1}{3}$-mile loop, take the **Cape Alava Trail**, walk south along the rocky beach, then return to your car along the **Sand Point Trail**. You'll pass **Cape Alava**, the westernmost point of the contiguous United States, stunning seacoast scenery, and rock etchings left by Indians who lived by whaling and fishing.

For a remote and peaceful visit to the rain forest, drive south to **Quinault** (32 miles from Kalaloch) and take the **North Fork** spur road. Walk the $\frac{1}{2}$-mile **Quinault Rain Forest Nature Trail** from near the **Quinault Ranger Station** or the $2\frac{1}{5}$-mile round-trip **Irely Lake Trail** from $\frac{1}{4}$ mile before the North Fork Campground. Look for beaver dams, herons, and ospreys, which often nest at the lake. Also in the Quinault district, the **Enchanted Valley Trail** starts $\frac{1}{2}$ mile past the **Graves Creek Ranger Station**. A $2\frac{1}{2}$-mile walk will take you to the scenic gorge at **Pony Bridge**.

Tide Pool Creatures

Olympic coast tide pools

Purple sea stars

Green sea anemone

Sea urchin

Chlamys scallop

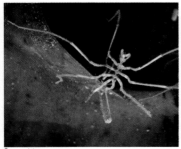
Sea spider

Sea slug

Information & Activities

Headquarters
600 E. Park Avenue, Port Angeles, Wash. 98362. Phone (206) 452-4501.

Seasons & Accessibility
Park open year-round. Some roads closed in winter.

Visitor & Information Centers
In Port Angeles, the Olympic Park Visitor Center, 3002 Mt. Angeles Road; call (206) 452-0330. The Hoh Rain Forest Visitor Center off 101 at western edge of park, (206) 374-6925. Both open daily all year. Hurricane Ridge Visitor Center also open all year, weather permitting.

In summer, information stations open at Storm King on Lake Crescent, Kalaloch, and other locations.

For park information, tune in to 530 AM in the Port Angeles and Lake Crescent areas.

Entrance Fee
$3 collected May to September, allows unlimited access for 7 days.

Pets
Allowed on leashes except on trails and in backcountry.

Facilities for Disabled
Visitor centers are accessible to wheelchairs. Also accessible are Hurricane Ridge's paved trails; a short loop trail into the Hoh Rain Forest; the Madison Falls Trail in the Elwha Valley.

Things to Do
Free naturalist-led activities: meadow, forest, beach, and tide pool walks; campfire programs. Also available, hiking, boating, fishing (no license needed), climbing, swimming, windsurfing, waterskiing, river rafting, cross-country and alpine skiing, snowshoeing.

Special Advisory
☐Be careful when hiking along the coast; rocks and logs can be slippery and unstable. Be aware of incoming tides (current tables posted at trailheads). Surf logs can kill.

Overnight Backpacking
Permits required. They are free and available at visitor centers, ranger stations, and trailheads. Ask for information on backcountry use.

Campgrounds
Fifteen campgrounds, all with a 14-day limit. Most open all year, except when snow is heavy. Four campgrounds—**Deer Park, Dosewallips, North Fork, Queets**—inaccessible to RVs. All first come, first served. Fees: None to $6 per night. No showers. Four group campgrounds; reservations required; contact headquarters. Food services in park.

Hotels, Motels, & Inns
(unless otherwise noted, rates are for 2 persons in a double room, high season)

INSIDE THE PARK:
Kalaloch Lodge (on US 101, 36 miles south of Forks) HC 80, Box 1100, Forks, Wash. 98331. (206) 962-2271. 18 rooms; 40 cabins, 34 with kitchenettes. Rooms $48-$90; cabins $78-$110. Restaurant. **Lake Crescent Lodge** (on US 101) HC 62, Box 11, Port Angeles, Wash. 98362. (206) 928-3211. 52 units, 47 with private bath. $69-$120. Restaurant. Open late April through October. **Log Cabin Resort** (on Lake Crescent) 6540 E. Beach Road, Port Angeles, Wash. 98362. (206) 928-3326 or 928-3245. 28 units, 3 with kitchenettes. $30-$70. Rest. Open April through Sept. **Sol Duc Hot Springs Resort** (12 miles off US 101) P.O. Box 2169, Port Angeles, Wash. 98362. (206) 327-3583. 32 cabins, 6 kitchens. $70-$78. Pool, rest. Open mid-May through September.

OUTSIDE THE PARK:
Lake Quinault Lodge (South Shore Road in Olympic NF) P.O. Box 7, Lake Quinault, Wash. 98575. (206) 288-2571; in Wash. (800) 562-6672. 89 units. $80-$105. Pool, restaurant.

In Port Angeles, Wash. 98362:
Red Lion Bayshore Inn 221 N. Lincoln. (800) 547-8010 or (206) 452-9215. 187 units. $120. Pool, rest. **The Tudor Inn** 1108 S. Oak St. (206) 452-3138. 5 rooms. $55-$90, includes breakfast.

For other area accommodations, contact the Chambers of Commerce in Port Angeles, 121 E. Railroad, zip 98362, (206) 452-2363; and Forks, P.O. Box 1249, zip 98331. (206) 374-2531.

Excursions

Olympic National Forest
Olympia, Washington

Nearly surrounding Olympic National Park, the forest offers the varied terrain of the Olympic Peninsula: lush rain forest, snowy peaks, dense stands of evergreens, alpine meadows. Roosevelt elk found here also. 631,514 acres. Facilities include 402 campsites, hiking, boating, boat ramp, fishing, horseback riding, hunting, picnic areas, scenic drives, swimming, handicapped access. Open year-round; most campsites open May-October. (206) 753-9534.

Nisqually National Wildlife Refuge
Olympia, Washington

Waterfowl, marsh and wading birds, and raptors visit this river delta on Puget Sound. Among them are western grebes, dunlins, and 19 duck species. 2,818 acres. Facilities include hiking, boating, fishing, photo blind. Open year-round, dawn to dusk. Off I-5, about 35 miles south of Olympic NP. (206) 753-9467.

Dungeness National Wildlife Refuge
Sequim, Washington

Excellent birdwatching from this finger of the Olympic Peninsula that reaches into the Strait of Juan de Fuca. Winter brings Brandt's cormorants, mew gulls, red-throated loons, and black turnstones. 572 acres. Facilities: hiking, boating, fishing, horseback riding; no vehicles permitted. Open all year, dawn to dusk. Off US 101, about 10 miles north of Olympic NP. (206) 457-8451.

San Juan Islands National Wildlife Refuge
Olympia, Washington

Myriad islands, reefs, and rocks in northern Puget Sound offer superb birdwatching with species such as tufted puffins, cormorants, and pigeon guillemots. Two refuge islands open to public all year. Facilities include primitive campsites (Turn Island), hiking, picnic areas. Birds easily visible from ferry out of Anacortes (off Wash. 20, about 50 miles from Olympic NP), but access by private boat only. (206) 753-9467.

Coast redwoods, a grove of giants

Redwood

California

Established October 2, 1968

108,400 acres, including 3 state parks

Sometimes, when the morning fog caresses the great trees, you can imagine the past flowing through the long, misty shadows . . . . Vast redwood forests flourishing across a lush and humid North America . . . . After the final ice age, a last stand here in the sustaining climate along the Pacific coast . . . . Tree after tree falling to the loggers. Then, in a windswept moment, the past vanishes and you stand beside other visitors, gazing up at the earth's tallest living things. That is the essence of Redwood National Park.

The park, near the northern limit of the coast redwood's narrow range, preserves the remnants of a forest that once covered two million acres

and, at the turn of the century, was badly threatened by logging. The state of California and the Save-the-Redwoods League came to the rescue by acquiring hundreds of groves and protecting them within 26 state parks. Three redwood state parks— Jedediah Smith, Del Norte Coast, and Prairie Creek—were encompassed by the national park when it was created in 1968.

Logging on surrounding private land, however, threatened the parks' protected redwoods. Soil and sediments from the logged-over tracts washed into the rivers and creeks, settling to the bottom downstream. Silt deposits can smother redwoods—for the giants are amazingly vulnerable. And the waterlogged soil weakens the trees' resistance to wind. Their roots are shallow, often only 10 feet deep.

park. From the south, take 101 to the information center near Orick, about 40 miles north of Eureka. From the north, enter through Crescent City, also an information center site. From the east, take US 199, another redwood-flanked highway, to Hiouchi. Airport: Arcata-Eureka at McKinleyville.

When to Go
All-year park. Summer draws highway-clogging crowds, so think about a visit in spring or fall. In both seasons, bird migrations enhance the redwood groves. Rhododendrons burst forth in spring; deciduous trees add color in fall. Rains, welcome to the redwoods but not to visitors, drench the park in winter.

How to Visit
US 101, with its many redwood sentinels, gives you a windshield-framed panorama of the trees. But to appreciate the redwoods, you must walk among them. If you have only a day to visit this 50-mile-long park, stop and see the **Lady Bird Johnson Grove** and **Big Tree.** Hike or just stretch your legs (depending on your time) along the **Coastal Trail** and savor the Pacific prospect of the park. For a longer stay, take the shuttle bus to **Tall Trees Grove,** drive **Howland Hill Road,** and end your visit with a splash in a kayak on the **Smith River** or a jouncy drive to **Fern Canyon** and **Gold Bluffs Beach.** If you are driving an RV or towing a trailer, some stretches of road may be closed to you; check at information centers.

In 1978 Congress added 48,000 acres to the national park's 58,000 acres, including about 36,000 that had been logged. The raw, clear-cut land, a park official wrote, had "the look of an active war zone." Today, in an epic earthmoving project—a redwood renaissance—crews are beginning to reclaim vast stretches of logged-over lands. Hillsides, carved away for logging roads, are being restored. Most of the 220 miles of roads are being erased. It will take at least 50 years for the scars of logging to disappear and another 250 or so years for the introduced redwood seedlings to grow to modest size.

The renaissance has added a new dimension to the traditional rite of staring up at redwoods. Today's visitor can look at hillsides shorn of giants and know that generations from now the trees will grow there again.

How to Get There
Tree-lined US 101, the Redwood Highway, runs the length of the

Lady Bird Johnson Grove & Big Tree
13 miles; 2 hours

Just before Orick, stop at the **Redwood Information Center** (once the site of a redwood-slicing lumber mill) to see the film and exhibits, and then continue north on US 101 to the Bald Hills Road sign. Turn right and drive 2 miles to **Lady Bird Johnson Grove,** a jewel that gives you an understanding of the entire park treasure. On the grove's mile-long trail you feel the cool, moist air that redwoods need. You see a hollowed-out tree that still lives. Such redwoods— "goose-pen" trees—once sheltered

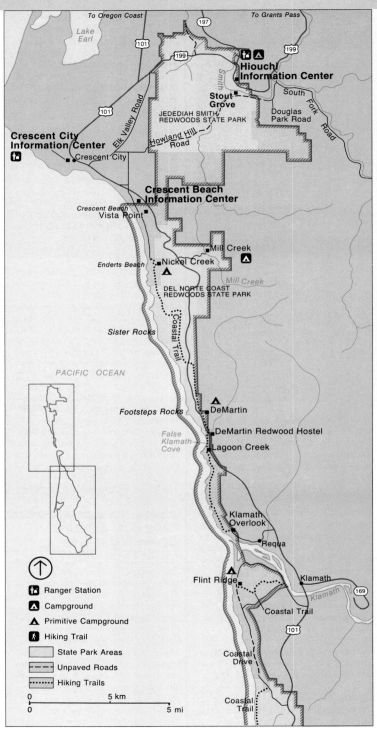

To Oregon Coast

To Grants Pass

Lake Earl

101

197

199

Hiouchi Information Center

Smith River

South Fork Road

199

199

Stout Grove

JEDEDIAH SMITH REDWOODS STATE PARK

Douglas Park Road

101

Elk Valley Road

Howland Hill Road

Crescent City Information Center

Crescent City

Crescent Beach Information Center

Crescent Beach Vista Point

Mill Creek

Nickel Creek

Enderts Beach

Mill Creek

DEL NORTE COAST REDWOODS STATE PARK

Sister Rocks

Coastal Trail

PACIFIC OCEAN

Footsteps Rocks

DeMartin

DeMartin Redwood Hostel

False Klamath Cove

Lagoon Creek

Klamath Overlook

Requa

Flint Ridge

Klamath

169

Coastal Trail

101

Coastal Drive

Coastal Trail

Ranger Station

Campground

Primitive Campground

Hiking Trail

State Park Areas

Unpaved Roads

Hiking Trails

0   5 km
0   5 mi

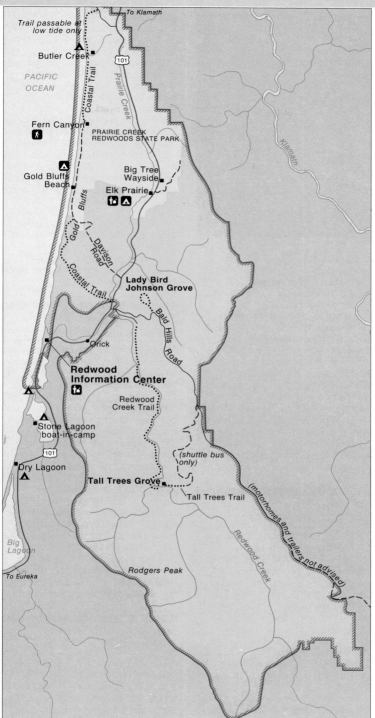

Trail passable at low tide only

To Klamath

Butler Creek

101

PACIFIC OCEAN

Prairie Creek

Coastal Trail

Fern Canyon

PRAIRIE CREEK REDWOODS STATE PARK

Gold Bluffs Beach

Big Tree Wayside

Elk Prairie

Gold Bluffs

Davison Road

Coastal Trail

Lady Bird Johnson Grove

Bald Hills Road

Orick

Redwood Information Center

Redwood Creek Trail

Stone Lagoon boat-in-camp

101

Dry Lagoon

(shuttle bus only)

Tall Trees Grove

Tall Trees Trail

(motorhomes and trailers not advised)

Big Lagoon

Redwood Creek

To Eureka

Rodgers Peak

Klamath

Lady Bird Johnson Grove

settlers' fowl and livestock. You smell and touch the many plants that share the redwoods' domain. Most of all, you feel the peace; visitors speak quietly in this pillared place.

Return to US 101 and continue north about 4 miles. Near the entrance to **Prairie Creek Redwoods State Park,** pull into the turnout to watch the free-roaming Roosevelt elk that live in the park. A mile ahead on the right is a wayside sign for **Big Tree.** A short trail from the parking lot leads to the aptly named tree. It's 304 feet tall, $21\frac{3}{5}$ feet in diameter, 66 feet in circumference, and about 1,500 years old. Here the experience is singular: you and one great tree.

Coastal Trail

4 miles one way; at least 2 hours

From Orick, drive north 20 miles on US 101, passing Klamath, and turn left onto Requa Road. Park and picnic at **Klamath Overlook,** a high hill. On a clear day you can see 65 miles down the bluff-guarded coast. The **Hidden Beach Section** of the **Coastal Trail** begins here, heads west, and then veers north along the wild, driftwood-decorated shore. Yurok Indians walked these shores, as did Jedediah Smith, the first white man to reach California's northern coast by land.

The trail, often bowered by branches of spruce and alder, sometimes seals you from the sight—though not the sounds—of the ocean. But there are many spots where you can sit and gaze out to sea. In spring and fall you may see migrating gray whales. Almost any time you will see gulls, cormorants, and ospreys.

A short side path leads down to **Hidden Beach.** Even on a day when the park is crowded yours may be the only footprints on the sand. Look at the ocean but don't swim: The undertow is dangerous all along the park's coast. The beach walk ends at a wall of gnarled black rocks. Follow your footprints back to the path and return to the trail, which heads north along the wild shore, then veers inland.

The north trailhead is at **Lagoon Creek,** where fresh water and forest meet ocean and high bluff. If you don't want to trudge the 4 miles back, have someone drive up to meet you at the parking lot.

Tall Trees Grove

2 ⅔ miles; a half day

If you're here between late May and mid-September, buy a ticket at the Redwood Information Center for the Tall Trees shuttle bus (tickets on first-come basis), which will take you the 12 miles to the grove's trailhead. No other vehicles are allowed on the rugged, unpaved road.

The trail is a very steep $2\frac{2}{3}$-mile round-trip. The hike down takes at least 30 minutes. Plan on another 30 to 45 minutes in the grove among the giants. The star is the **Tall Tree,** discovered in 1963 by Paul Zahl of the National Geographic Society. Towering $367\frac{4}{5}$ feet, this is one of the world's tallest known trees. Its circumference is 44 feet and its estimated age is more than 600 years. Time the 1-hour hike back up to the trailhead so that you catch a returning bus; daily schedules may vary.

Howland Hill Road & Smith River

8 miles dry and 3 miles wet; a full day

Just south of Crescent City, take Elk Valley Road northeast. Keep a sharp watch on your right for the turnoff to **Howland Hill Road,** once a miners' supply road partially redwood-planked

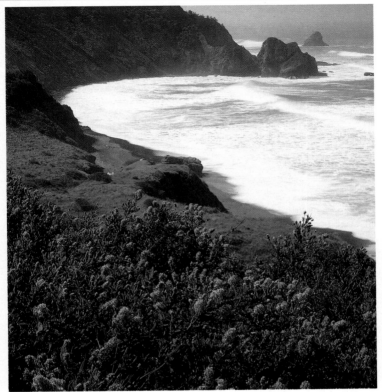

Blueblossom, Enderts Beach

for oxcarts and horse-drawn wagons. The 6-mile road, mostly unpaved, winds between redwoods that loom much closer than the ones along highways. Stop at **Stout Grove**, where you can see one of many preserves set aside, this one donated by the wife of a logging company owner. (In summer you can also reach the grove from the **Hiouchi Information Center** via a footbridge across the crystal-clear **Smith River**.)

Continue past the grove to Douglas Park Road, which ends at South Fork Road. Turn left to US 199 and drive west about 2½ miles to the Hiouchi Information Center. Park here and sign up for an interpretive walk with a ranger. If you make a reservation in person no more than 2 days ahead and pay a fee, you can take a guide-led Smith River kayak trip. This thrilling but safe ride takes you down the only major undammed river in California, a crystal stream that is part of the Wild and Scenic River System. You make arrange-

ments here for getting yourself and your car back together. Wear clothes to be dunked in, tie on your glasses, bring a waterproof lunch, and don't take anything you would not want to lose in the rapids.

Gold Bluffs Beach & Fern Canyon

20 miles; a half day

From the Redwood Information Center, head north for 4½ miles to Davison Road, on your left. This rough dirt road bounces you for about 4 miles down to **Gold Bluffs,** named for the gold found here. The road continues for 4 miles along the beach, ending near **Fern Canyon,** where a ¾-mile loop trail climbs to a prairie—site of a vanished mining camp. Back down the canyon, walk through elk-roamed grass to a beautiful, desolate beach sprinkled with driftwood and frequently grazed by fog. Return the way you came.

Information & Activities

Headquarters
1111 Second Street, Crescent City, Calif. 95531. Phone (707) 464-6101.

Seasons & Accessibility
Open year-round.

Visitor & Information Centers
Crescent City Information Center, at north end of park, open daily all year. For visitor information, phone (707) 464-6101. Redwood Information Center, at south end of park near Orick, also open all year. Hiouchi Information Center, at north end of park, open spring through fall. Crescent Beach Information Center (5 miles south of Crescent City) open spring through fall.

Pets
Permitted on leashes except on trails and in backcountry.

Facilities for Disabled
Information centers, the Hiouchi Ranger Station, Crescent Beach, Lagoon Creek picnic area, Klamath Overlook, the Tall Trees shuttle bus, and some trails are accessible to wheelchairs. Free brochure.

Things to Do
Free naturalist-led activities: tide pool and seashore walks, evening programs. Also available, hiking, shuttle bus to Tall Trees (May to September), canoeing, guided kayak trips, field seminars, horseback riding, freshwater and ocean fishing (need license), swimming (inland only), whale-watching.

Special Advisories
☐Be aware that ticks may transmit Lyme disease.
☐Ocean swimming is not advised due to extremely cold water and treacherous undertow.

Overnight Backpacking
Permit required; can be obtained free at trailheads and the Redwood Information Center. The Park Service operates three backcountry campsites—**DeMartin**, **Flint Ridge**, and **Nickel Creek**; 14-day limit. Open all year, first come, first served. No fees. Tent sites only. No showers.

Campgrounds
There are four state-run campgrounds inside the park—**Gold Bluffs Beach, Jedediah Smith, Mill Creek,** and **Elk Prairie**; 15-day limit. **Mill Creek** open April to October; others open all year; **Gold Bluffs Beach** may close in bad weather. Showers available nearby. Tent and RV sites; no hookups; large RVs not recommended at **Gold Bluffs Beach.** Fees $10 per night. Reservations required from mid-May through August and are available through MISTIX, P.O. Box 85705, San Diego, Calif. 92138. The reservations number for these state-run campgrounds is (800) 444-7275. No food services inside park.

Hotels, Motels, & Inns
(unless otherwise noted, rates are for 2 persons in a double room, high season)
In Crescent City, Calif. 95531:
Crescent City Travelodge 725 Highway 101 North. (800) 255-3050 or (707) 464-6106. 52 units. $57-$67.
Curly Redwood Lodge 701 Redwood Hwy. South. (707) 464-2137. 36 units. $50-$54.
Pacific Motor Hotel P.O. Box 595, 440 Highway 101 North. (707) 464-4141. 62 units. $58. Restaurant.
Royal Inn Motel 102 L Street. (800) 543-5326 or (707) 464-4113. 35 units. $40-$90. Restaurant. Closed Mon.-Wed. in winter.
In Eureka, Calif. 95501:
Eureka Inn 7th and F Streets. (800) 862-4906 or (707) 442-6441. 105 units. $95-$125. Pool, restaurant.
Hotel Carter 301 L Street. (707) 444-8062. 30 units. $69-$185, includes continental breakfast.
In Klamath, Calif. 95548:
Motel Trees (on US 101) P.O. Box 309. (707) 482-3152. 23 units. $40-$48. Restaurant.
Requa Inn 451 Requa Road. (707) 482-8205. 10 units. $55-$85, includes breakfast. Restaurant.

Excursions

Humboldt Bay
National Wildlife Refuge
Loleta, California
The islands and wetlands of Humboldt Bay provide critical habitat for the brant, a small, stocky sea goose. In late winter-early spring, thousands of brant use the refuge as a staging area enroute to northern nesting grounds. Other waterfowl and peregrine falcons also present. 2,085 acres. Refuge closed to public (expected opening 1990), but excellent birdwatching from the South Spit (access via Hookton Road). Off US 101, about 40 miles from Redwood NP. (707) 733-5406.

Six Rivers National Forest
Eureka, California
Six major rivers crisscross this fir-covered mountain forest, providing nearly 10 percent of the state's run-off and a wealth of recreational opportunities, including white-water rafting, kayaking, and excellent steelhead and salmon fishing. Contains parts of four wilderness areas. 957,590 acres. Facilities: 395 campsites, hiking, boating, boat ramp, fishing, horseback riding, hunting, picnic areas, scenic drives, winter sports, water sports, handicapped access. Open all year, though most off-highway areas closed in winter. Campsites open May-November. Information at Gasquet on US 199, about 15 miles from Redwood NP. (707) 442-1721.

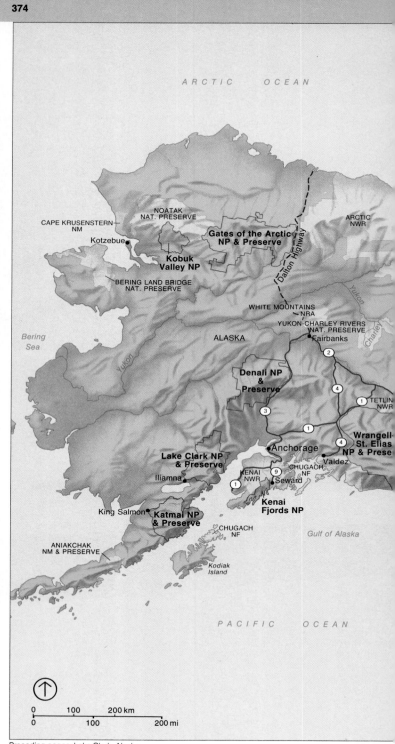

ARCTIC   OCEAN

NOATAK
NAT. PRESERVE

CAPE KRUSENSTERN
NM

Kotzebue

**Gates of the Arctic
NP & Preserve**

ARCTIC
NWR

**Kobuk
Valley NP**

BERING LAND BRIDGE
NAT. PRESERVE

Dalton Highway

WHITE MOUNTAINS
NRA

YUKON-CHARLEY RIVERS
NAT. PRESERVE

*Bering
Sea*

ALASKA

Yukon

Yukon

Charley

Fairbanks

②

**Denali NP
&
Preserve**

④

① TETLIN
NWR

③

①

④

**Wrangell-
St. Elias
NP & Prese**

**Lake Clark NP
& Preserve**

Anchorage

Iliamna

KENAI
NWR

⑨

CHUGACH
NF

Valdez

①

Seward

King Salmon

**Katmai NP
& Preserve**

**Kenai
Fjords NP**

CHUGACH
NF

Gulf of Alaska

ANIAKCHAK
NM & PRESERVE

*Kodiak
Island*

PACIFIC   OCEAN

↑

0   100   200 km
0   100   200 mi

Preceding pages: Lake Clark, Alaska

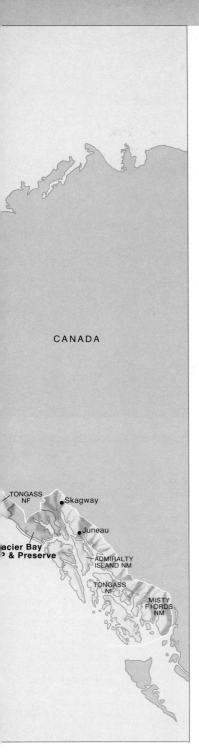

CANADA

TONGASS
NF
●Skagway

●Juneau

acier Bay
? & Preserve
ADMIRALTY
ISLAND NM

TONGASS
NF

MISTY
FJORDS
NM

Alaska

In 1867 Secretary of State William Seward bought Alaska from Russia for two cents an acre—and the public labeled the vast empty land Seward's Folly. Today, more than six billion barrels of oil have gushed through the Prudhoe Bay pipeline, and Alaska's wilderness and wildlife attract visitors by the thousands.

Eight national parks protect 41.5 million acres of these natural treasures. Katmai and Lake Clark lie along the Pacific Ring of Fire—a region of active volcanoes, earthquakes, giant brown bears, and salmon. Whales, sea lions, and flocks of seabirds seek out the cold, food-laden waters of Glacier Bay and Kenai Fjords. Huge Wrangell-St. Elias is a jumble of mountains and glaciers so rugged that many remain unnamed and untrodden by humans. Above the Arctic Circle, Gates of the Arctic and Kobuk Valley protect the tundra and migrant herds of caribou. Compared to these parks, Denali seems civilized with its nearby railroad and hotels; yet here the wildlife is so abundant and visible, the park is called a "subarctic Serengeti."

Alaska parks include national preserves that allow hunting, vast wilderness areas that prohibit buildings and roads, and native-owned lands still used for subsistence in a tradition thousands of years old.

In 1989 the *Exxon Valdez* ran aground in Prince William Sound, spilling nearly 11 million gallons of oil. The slick spread into the Gulf of Alaska and onto the beaches of Katmai and Kenai Fjords. It killed more than 3,500 sea otters and 350,000 seabirds, as well as unknown numbers of scavenging mammals. The visible oil slick is gone, but the damage to the area's ecological balance may well last forever.

Though most areas of Alaska's national parks are accessible only by plane or boat, you can drive to Denali and Wrangell-St. Elias, and to the edges of Kenai Fjords and Gates of the Arctic. The loop connecting Anchorage to Denali to Fairbanks to Wrangell-St. Elias, with a side trip to Kenai Fjords, is 1,100 miles. It's a 600-mile round-trip from Fairbanks to Gates of the Arctic on the unpaved Dalton Highway. Alaska parks are rugged, yet fragile; tread lightly.

Moose on an autumn landscape beneath Mt. McKinley

Denali

Alaska

Established February 26, 1917

6,028,091 acres

On any summer day in Denali, Alaska's most popular national park, hundreds of people see sights that will stay with them the rest of their lives. Perhaps a golden eagle will soar off the cliffs at Polychrome Pass, or 20 Dall's sheep will rest on a green shoulder of Primrose Ridge, or a grizzly will ramble over the tundra at Sable Pass. Maybe a caribou will pause on a ridgetop, silhouetted by the warm light of day's end, or a loon will call across Wonder Lake, or clouds will part to reveal the great massif of Mt. McKinley, 20,320 feet high, the roof of North America. The drama is always there. To see it, all you need to do is travel the 85-mile park road. The farther you go, the more you'll see, for the subarctic landscape will open up as big as the sky and the animals will move through it with wild, ancient poetry.

Other North American parks have their wildlife, but none has animals so visible or diverse as Denali. And other parks have their mountains, but none with a stature so stunning, a summit so towering as McKinley.

Denali's visitors have increased more than 30-fold in 25 years. More visitors come here—nearly 600,000 in 1991—than to Alaska's 7 other national parks combined. How to accommodate that many people without eroding the park's wilderness? A bus system has been designed that permits maximum wildlife viewing while holding down traffic. Campgrounds have been kept modest and unobtrusive. And the wilderness area has been divided into manage-

July and August. In late August or early September, the tundra turns rich tones of red, orange, and yellow. In winter, visitors can take the road 3 miles to park headquarters and cross-country ski from there.

May and early June are the best times to climb Mt. McKinley; after June, avalanches threaten. Most mountaineers fly by ski-plane from Talkeetna and land at 7,500 feet on the Kahiltna Glacier to begin a climb that will take 10 to 20 days.

How to Visit
The more time the better, but plan on at least 2 days. You can drive your car on the **park road** as far as the **Savage River Check Station** at mile 12.8 but no farther (except by special permit). Free shuttle buses and tour buses operate on the road by day and into evening, late May to mid-September; schedules vary. **Mt. McKinley** is often covered with clouds; you're most likely to get a clear view of it early or late in the long day.

Park campgrounds and buses are usually full, so plan on the possibility of staying a night or two in a hotel or nearby private campground if you must wait for a campsite or bus ticket. The 85-mile shuttle bus trip along the park road to **Wonder Lake** takes 11 hours round-trip, including many stops to watch wildlife; other buses go part way. Make the full trip if you can. Take a jacket, binoculars, and a lunch (available near the **Visitor Access Center** or outside the park; no food along the way). In the park, consider getting off the bus for a hike; buses will stop almost anywhere. To get on another bus, just wave one down. In busy times, you may have to wait a while.

ment units with strict visitation ceilings to prevent overcrowding and damage to the flora and fauna. You may not get campsite or bus reservations as soon as you arrive. But whatever the wait, it's worth it.

How to Get There
From Anchorage, take Alaska Hwy. 1 (Glenn Highway) 35 miles north to Alaska Hwy. 3 (George Parks Hwy.). Go north 205 miles. From Fairbanks, take Alaska Hwy. 3 west and south 120 miles. In summer, the Alaska Railroad runs between Anchorage and Fairbanks and stops daily at the Denali railroad station. In winter, the train runs on weekends only. Air service available in summer to the small park airstrip from Anchorage, Fairbanks, and Talkeetna.

When to Go
In summer, there are up to 24 hours of daylight. The park road is open from late May to mid-September. June is usually less crowded than

The Park Road
85 miles one way; 11 hours round-trip

Your bus journey begins at the **Visitor Access Center** or **VAC** (mile 0.7), surrounded by the spruce forest called taiga, a Russian word meaning "land of little sticks." Within minutes you'll see the railroad station used by the Alaska Railroad, and you'll pass park headquarters, where sled dogs are kept in their kennels for winter patrols and summer exhibitions.

Soon the road begins climbing out

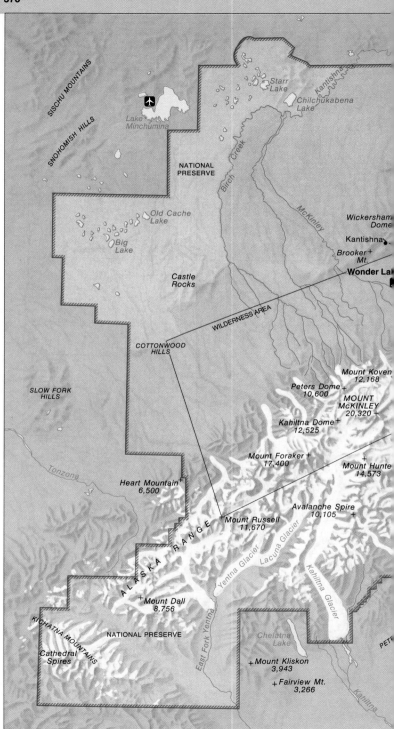

SISCHU MOUNTAINS

SNOHOMISH HILLS

Starr
Lake

Chilchukabena
Lake

Lake
Minchumina

Kantishna

Birch

Creek

McKinley

NATIONAL
PRESERVE

Wickersham
Dome

Kantishna

Old Cache
Lake

Brooker +
Mt.

Big
Lake

Wonder Lak

Castle
Rocks

WILDERNESS AREA

COTTONWOOD
HILLS

Mount Koven
12,168

SLOW FORK
HILLS

Peters Dome +
10,600

MOUNT
McKINLEY
20,320 +

Kahiltna Dome +
12,525

Tonzona

Mount Foraker +
17,400

+
Mount Hunte
14,573

Heart Mountain +
6,500

Avalanche Spire
10,105
+

+ Mount Russell
11,670

A L A S K A   R A N G E

Yentna Glacier

Lacuna Glacier

Kahiltna Glacier

KICHATNA MOUNTAINS

+ Mount Dall
8,756

East Fork Yentna

PET

NATIONAL PRESERVE

Chelatna
Lake

Cathedral
Spires

+ Mount Kliskon
3,943

+ Fairview Mt.
3,266

Kahiltna

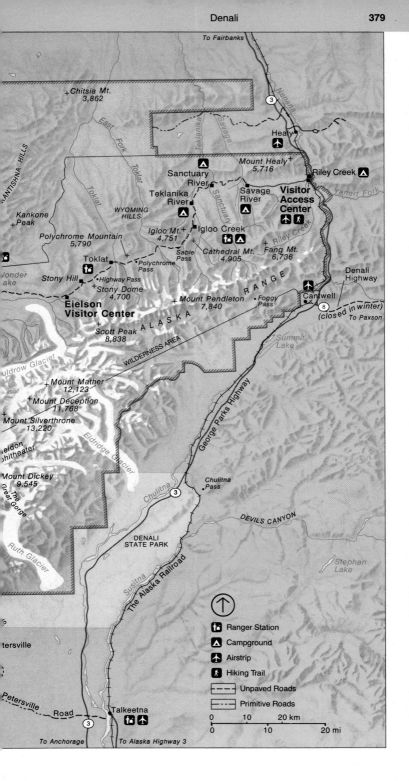

To Fairbanks

③ Nenana

+Chitsia Mt.
3,862

East Fork

Teklanika

Savage

Healy ✈

KANTISHNA HILLS

Toklat

Mount Healy +
5,716

Riley Creek ◩

Sanctuary
River ◲

Teklanika
River

WYOMING
HILLS

Sanctuary

Savage
River

**Visitor
Access
Center**
✈ 🚶

Yanert Fork

Kankone
+Peak

Igloo Mt.+
4,751

Igloo Creek

Riley Creek

Polychrome Mountain
5,790

Sable
Pass

Cathedral Mt.
4,905

Fang Mt.
6,736

Toklat 🏚

•Polychrome
Pass

R A N G E

Denali
Highway

Wonder
Lake

Stony Hill ▪

•Highway Pass

+Stony Dome
4,700

**Eielson
Visitor Center**

+Mount Pendleton
7,840

•Foggy
Pass

✈ Cantwell
⑧

A L A S K A

+Scott Peak
8,838

WILDERNESS AREA

(closed in winter)
To Paxson

Muldrow Glacier

Summit
Lake

+Mount Mather
12,123

+Mount Deception
11,768

+
Mount Silverthrone
13,220

Eldridge Glacier

George Parks Highway

Sheldon
Amphitheater

Mount Dickey
9,545

Chulitna

Chulitna
Pass

③

DEVILS CANYON

The
Great
Gorge

DENALI
STATE PARK

Stephan
Lake

Ruth Glacier

Susitna

The Alaska Railroad

⬆

🏚 Ranger Station

◩ Campground

✈ Airstrip

🚶 Hiking Trail

----- Unpaved Roads

—·—·— Primitive Roads

tersville

0   10   20 km
0   10   20 mi

Petersville

Road •Talkeetna
③ 🏚 ✈

To Anchorage   To Alaska Highway 3

Backpackers above tree line

of the taiga and into the treeless expanse of the tundra. Magnificent vistas open up; on clear days **Mt. McKinley** can be seen 70 miles to the southwest. As the bus crosses the **Savage River Bridge** (mile 14.8), note how the gentle, glacier-sculptured topography to the south meets the rugged river-cut canyon to the north; this spot marks the farthest advance of a glacier that flowed north out of the **Alaska Range** and across the valley thousands of years ago.

The road winds along **Primrose Ridge** before dropping into a marshy flat where spruce trees lean haphazardly in all directions. This "drunken forest" forms as permafrost thaws and the land slumps gradually downhill, tilting the trees. Watch for moose here and in other spruce forests, especially in areas with willow, their favorite browse.

Just beyond Teklanika River Campground (mile 29) is the **Teklanika River Bridge.** Like other rivers in Denali, the Teklanika is braided by channels. Its Athapaskan name means "middle water." The road passes Igloo Creek Campground and cuts between **Igloo** and **Cathedral Mountains,** favorite haunts of Dall's sheep, the world's only species of wild white sheep. Watch for them on the upper slopes.

If you want to see grizzly bears, there's no better place than just up the road at **Sable Pass** (3,895 feet). The grizzlies feed primarily on roots, berries, and other plant materials, and occasionally on arctic ground

squirrels, moose calves, injured or infirm caribou, and carrion. To protect the bears' habitat, the Sable Pass area is closed to foot traffic, except on the road.

About 5 miles farther the road climbs a steep slope to **Polychrome Pass** and a spectacular view of the Alaska Range to the south. Below see the **Plains of Murie,** where fast running water has created alluvial terraces. At mile 53.1 the **Toklat River** has special significance, for it was here (5 miles north of where the bridge crosses the river today) that the naturalist Charles Sheldon built a cabin and wintered in 1907-08. The area so inspired him that he moved back East and spent 9 years lobbying for legislation to create Alaska's first national park. Originally called Mt. McKinley, the park in 1980 was renamed Denali — a local name for the mountain meaning "the high one."

The road reaches its highest elevation at **Highway Pass** (3,980 feet) before descending to cross **Stony Creek** and climbing again to the **Stony Hill Overlook,** where, weather permitting, Mt. McKinley looms into view 40 miles away. Watch for caribou as they funnel through the Stony Hill area. Although the total Denali herd numbers about 2,700, the caribou usually move in small groups. They can appear almost any time of day anywhere in the lowlands between the park road and the Alaska Range.

Eielson Visitor Center (mile 66) is a comfortable, scenic rest stop 33 miles from Mt. McKinley. Arctic ground

Tussock grass

squirrels scamper about, begging for handouts they don't need and shouldn't have. Wildflowers splash the tundra with reds and yellows, and sometimes you'll see a grizzly on a distant ridge or on the road.

Continuing west, the road cuts along a steep cliff, then enters more gentle terrain as it comes within a mile of the dark, gravel-covered snout of the **Muldrow Glacier** to the south. Beginning just below the summit of Mt. McKinley, the Muldrow flows 35 miles through a granite gorge and across the tundra to its terminus. Twice in the last 100 years (and for reasons not fully understood) the Muldrow has surged forward, most recently in the winter of 1956-57, when it advanced 5 miles.

The road passes several ponds where chances improve for sighting beavers, moose, and waterfowl, and finally arrives at Wonder Lake Campground. Here the shuttle bus will turn around for the $5\frac{1}{2}$-hour trip back, after allowing you time to stroll and take pictures. Twenty-seven miles to the south is Mt. McKinley, its north face—the **Wickersham Wall**—rising more than 14,000 feet in a single precipice, one of the greatest mountain walls in the world. And just north of the campground lies **Wonder Lake**, 4 miles long, 280 feet deep, and home to lake trout, lingcod, burbot, and moose that occasionally wade in belly-deep to feed on aquatic vegetation near the shore. Loons, grebes, and mergansers also visit the lake.

Hikes

In a park larger than Massachusetts, the hiking opportunities are endless, but the only maintained trails are in the front country, beginning at the park hotel and railroad station, near the park entrance.

The **Horseshoe Lake Trail** winds gently through a handsome forest of aspen and spruce $1\frac{1}{4}$ miles to **Horseshoe Lake**, an old oxbow of the **Nenana River**. Interpretive signs introduce you to the flora along the way. Branching off this trail just past the stream-crossing is a more strenuous one, the **Mt. Healy Overlook Trail.** Climbing 1,700 feet in less than 3 miles, it breaks above timberline and arrives at the overlook among wildflowers, rock outcrops, arctic ground squirrels, and pikas. And if the weather is clear, Mt. McKinley is visible more than 80 miles to the southwest. The **Triple Lakes Trail** is a moderate all-day hike (9 miles round-trip) with excellent views of **Mt. Fellows, Pyramid Mountain,** and other peaks in the Alaska Range.

In the backcountry, hiking is a matter of taking whatever route you wish—down a drainage, up a ridge, across a valley. The object is to spread out and tread lightly, leaving no evidence of your visit. For the most part, trails are nonexistent or intermittent. There are trails down **Savage River Canyon** from the Savage River Bridge, down to the **Thorofare River** bar from Eielson Visitor Center, and down to the **McKinley River** bar from the park road near Wonder Lake Campground, but none are maintained.

Other popular backcountry hikes (without trails) include Primrose Ridge, Mt. Wright, Igloo Mountain, Cathedral Mountain, Calico Creek, Tattler Creek, the Polychrome Cliffs Loop, Stony Dome and Stony Hill, the Stony Creek Loop, the Sunrise Glacier Loop, Sunset Glacier, Eielson Visitor Center Ridge, and around Wonder Lake. Some of these hikes take an hour or more, some take several days. Find out more about these at the Visitor Access Center. And because a backcountry management unit might be closed or full, it's important to check at the VAC before choosing an overnight hike.

Float Trips

If you enjoy rafting through a mix of calm water and white water, don't miss a trip down the Nenana River, along the George Parks Highway and the park's eastern border. Several companies offer guided trips lasting 2 hours to 4 days. From McKinley Village, about 6 miles south of the park entrance, a 2-hour float takes you to the McKinley Chalet Resort, just outside the entrance. The next 2 hours, to Healy, offer a white-water experience. Allow an hour or 2 for travel and instruction.

Rafting along the Nenana River

Animals of Denali

Grizzly stretching in the sunshine

Dall's sheep

Willow ptarmigan

Caribou

Information & Activities

Headquarters
P.O. Box 9, Denali, Alaska 99755. Phone (907) 683-2294.

Seasons & Accessibility
Park open year-round. Park road open, weather permitting, Memorial Day to Sept. 10, but car travel is restricted beyond Savage River, 14 miles into the park. During snow season, the park road is not plowed beyond headquarters (mile 3.5), which limits access to skiers and dogsledders. Animal activity may temporarily close backcountry areas.

Visitor & Information Centers
Visitor Access Center (VAC), at east border of park, open daily late May to late September (reduced hours after mid-Sept.). Eielson Visitor Center open early June to mid-September. Off-season information available at headquarters, open daily all year. Call (907) 683-2686 for recording.

Entrance Fees
$3 fee per person, $5 per family per week, allows multiple entries.

Shuttle Bus Transportation
From the VAC, free buses operate regularly from 5:00 a.m. to 3:00 p.m. between late May and mid-Sept. Reserve in person. Trips not narrated, but buses stop for wildlife-watching. Also, twice daily campers bus.

Facilities for Disabled
Most buildings accessible to wheelchairs, as is shuttle bus. Pamphlet.

Things to Do
Free naturalist-led activities: nature walks and hikes, children's programs, sled-dog demonstrations, talks, slide shows, and films. Also, narrated bus tours, hiking, limited fishing, mountain climbing, rafting, canoeing, horseback riding, cross-country skiing, dogsledding. Ask the park for a list of guide services.

Overnight Backpacking
Backcountry divided into units with limits (2-12) on the number of campers. Permits required; available free at VAC, first come, first served. Must carry bear-proof containers.

Campgrounds
Seven campgrounds, 14-day limit from mid-May to mid-Sept.; other times, 30-day limit. **Riley Creek** open all year. Others open late spring to early fall. First come, first served. Fees $12 per night. Showers in park. RV sites except at **Igloo Creek, Morino,** and **Wonder Lake;** no hookups. **Morino** inaccessible to vehicles. Buses transport campers to **Igloo Creek** and **Wonder Lake** and farther. Must reserve for **Savage River Group Campground;** contact headquarters.

Hotels, Motels, & Inns
(unless otherwise noted, rates are for 2 persons in a double room, high season)

INSIDE THE PARK:
Camp Denali (3 miles west of Wonder Lake) and **North Face Lodge** (1 mile west of Wonder Lake) P.O. Box 67, Denali NP, Alas. 99775. (907) 683-2290 (summer); P.O. Box 216, Cornish, N.H. 03746. (603) 675-2248 (winter). Camp Denali: 18 cabins, central showers. North Face Lodge: 15 rooms. $210-$235 per person, all inclusive. Open mid-June to early Sept. **Denali Mtn. Lodge** (near Kantishna) P.O. Box 229, Denali NP, Alas. 99755. (907) 683-2643. 200 units. $150, with 2 meals. Open mid-May to Oct. **Denali National Park Hotel** (1 mile inside park) 825 W. 8th Ave., Suite 240, Anchorage, Alas. 99501. Res.: (907) 276-7234. Hotel: (907) 683-2215. 100 units. $119. Restaurant. Open mid-May to early Sept.

OUTSIDE THE PARK:
Denali Cabins (8 mi. so. of entrance) P.O. Box 229, Denali NP, Alas. 99755. (907) 683-2643. 49 cabins. $94. Rest. Open May to late Sept. **Harper Lodge Princess** ($\frac{1}{2}$ mile from entrance) P.O. Box 110, Denali NP, Alas. 99755. (800) 426-0500 or (907) 258-5993. 192 units. $145. Rest. Open late May through Sept. **McKinley Chalet Resort** (1 mile from entrance) 825 W. 8th Ave., Suite 240, Anchorage, Alas. 99501. (907) 276-7234. 290 units. $140. Pool, rest. Open mid-May to mid-Sept. **McKinley Village Lodge** (7 mi. from entrance) 825 W. 8th Ave., Suite 240, Anchorage, Alas. 99501. (907) 276-7234. 50 units. $109. Restaurant. Open late May to early Sept.

Excursions

Chugach National Forest
Anchorage, Alaska

The Chugach includes 3,550 miles of coastline, more than 200 bird species, and numerous glaciers, including one, the Portage, that is easily accessible from Anchorage. 5,936,000 acres. Facilities: 400 campsites, 36 cabins, hiking, boating, boat ramp, climbing, bicycling, fishing, horseback riding, hunting, picnic areas, scenic drives, winter sports, water sports, handicapped access. Open all year; most campsites open late May-early September. Visitor center at Portage on Seward-Anchorage Hwy., about 35 miles southeast of Anchorage. (907) 271-2500.

Tetlin National Wildlife Refuge
Tok, Alaska

Bounded by the Alaska Highway on the north and Wrangell-St. Elias National Park on the south, Tetlin offers a wilderness experience among marshes, lakes, ponds, rivers, forests, and hills abundant with waterfowl and fish. 930,000 acres. Facilities include 25 campsites, 3 rustic cabins (first come, first served), hiking, boating, boat ramp, fishing, hunting, picnic areas. Open all year. Visitor center on Alaska Hwy. (milepost 1229), about 200 miles southeast of Fairbanks. (907) 883-5312.

Tongass National Forest
Petersburg, Alaska

Stretching some 500 miles along the Alaska Panhandle, this largest US national forest features coastal rain forests, glaciers, mountains, islands, and nearly 11,000 miles of shoreline. 16,832,727 acres. Facilities include 171 campsites, 130 cabins (reservations required), food services, boating, fishing, hunting. Open all year; most campsites open May-October. Limited road access; can be reached by plane or boat. On Alaska Marine Highway with ferry service from Seattle, Wash., and Prince Rupert, British Columbia. (907) 772-3841. Offices also in Sitka, (907) 747-6671, and Ketchikan, (907) 225-3101.

Admiralty Island National Monument

Juneau, Alaska

Thousands of years ago, the Tlingit named the island Xootsnoowu — "fortress of bears." Today, Admiralty is still the domain of the brown bears; they share an ecosystem of coastal rain forest, muskeg, alpine meadows, and rocky peaks with a variety of wildlife and with the Tlingit village of Angoon. The nation's largest known population of bald eagles nests here. 955,810 acres. Facilities include primitive camping, rustic cabins (reservations needed), hiking, boating, fishing, hunting. Open all year. Within Tongass NF; access by charter boat or plane from Juneau, Petersburg, and Sitka, or by scheduled ferry to Angoon. (907) 789-3111.

Misty Fiords National Monument

Ketchikan, Alaska

The Behm Canal, an arm of the Pacific Ocean, leads into the rugged, brooding interior of this coastal monument with its massive rock-lined coves and bays. Wildlife of land, sea, and air abounds. One of the nation's largest concentrations of nesting bald eagles. 2,284,800 acres. Facilities include primitive camping, cabins (reservations required), hiking, boating, fishing, hunting. Open year-round. Within Tongass National Forest; access by boat or plane from several Panhandle towns. (907) 225-2148.

Kenai National Wildlife Refuge

Soldotna, Alaska

Large numbers of moose share this refuge with bears, mountain goats, Dall's sheep, loons, eagles, and 14 species of fish. 2,000,000 acres, includes some 4,000 lakes. Facilities: 300 campsites, hiking, boating, boat ramp, bicycling, fishing, hunting, picnic areas, scenic drives, winter sports, water sports, handicapped access. Open year-round. Adjacent to Kenai Fjords NP. Visitor center at Soldotna on Sterling Hwy., about 110 miles southwest of Anchorage. (907) 262-7021.

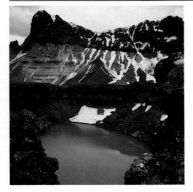

Aniakchak
National Monument & Preserve
King Salmon, Alaska

The 6-mile-wide Aniakchak caldera, dormant since 1931, is the focus of this section of the remote Alaska Peninsula. From Surprise Lake inside the caldera, the wild Aniakchak River flows 27 miles on its journey to the Pacific Ocean, offering class II-IV white water along the way. 603,000 acres. Facilities: primitive camping, hiking, rafting, fishing, and hunting in preserve. Open year-round. Access by plane from King Salmon. (907) 246-3305.

Arctic National Wildlife Refuge
Fairbanks, Alaska

This Brooks Range refuge contains the calving grounds for 170,000 caribou and serves as staging area for millions of migratory birds. Legislation would open 1.5 million acres to oil and gas exploration. 19,500,000 acres. Facilities: primitive camping, boating, fishing, hunting. Open all year. Access by foot or air charter; commercial service to Prudhoe Bay, Barter I., Ft. Yukon. (907) 456-0250.

Noatak National Preserve
Kotzebue, Alaska

The gentle Noatak River meanders 210 miles through a broad valley, abundant with wildlife, in this remote preserve ringed by the Brooks Range. 6,559,000 acres. Facilities include primitive camping, boating, fishing, hunting. Open all year but winter visiting discouraged. Access by charter boat or plane from Kotzebue. (907) 442-3890.

Cape Krusenstern
National Monument
Kotzebue, Alaska

For more than 6,000 years, Eskimos have forged a living on this stretch of gravel projecting into the Chukchi Sea; its 114 beach ridges, rich in artifacts, reveal their archaeological benchmarks. Today, the cape's large land and sea mammals are still crucial to local subsistence. 658,000 acres. Facilities: primitive camping, boating, fishing. Open year-round. Access by charter boat or plane from Kotzebue. (907) 442-3890.

White Mountains National Recreation Area
Fairbanks, Alaska

The jagged White Mountains preside over wild Beaver Creek and an extensive winter cabin/trail system, inviting a closeup look at the area by skiers, dog mushers, and snowmobile riders. A summer hiking trail traverses spruce forests and alpine ridges for 22 miles to reach the creek. 1,000,000 acres. Facilities include primitive camping, 5 cabins (must reserve), boating, climbing, fishing, horseback riding, hunting. Open all year. Trailheads on Steese and Elliot Hwys., 30 to 70 miles north of Fairbanks. (907) 474-2350.

Yukon-Charley Rivers National Preserve
Eagle, Alaska

For millennia, the Yukon corridor has seen passing boats and sleds and migrating herds of caribou, but humans have made little imprint. Breeding ground for large population of peregrine falcons. With its tributary, the Yukon offers superb boating and floating. 2,527,000 acres. Facilities include primitive camping, climbing, fishing, hunting. Open all year. Gateway towns of Circle and Eagle reached by Steese and Taylor Hwys. respectively. Access by boat or air charter. Info. and library at Eagle headquarters. (907) 547-2233.

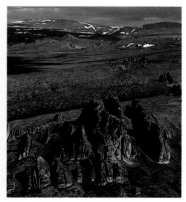

Bering Land Bridge National Preserve
Nome, Alaska

Part of the Bering Land Bridge, a 900-mile-wide landmass where people and animals passed between Asia and North America, survives today in this isolated preserve 80 miles from Siberia. Here, rolling uplands of tundra teem with wildlife and plants, and feature hot springs, lava beds, and archaeological sites. In summer, local Eskimos hunt, fish, herd reindeer (introduced from Siberia when native caribou population declined), and pursue arts and crafts. 2,784,960 acres. Facilities: primitive camping, hiking, boating, fishing, hunting. Open all year. Access by charter plane from Kotzebue or Nome. (907) 443-2522.

Autumn in August: Arrigetch Valley's poplar, spruce, and scrub

Gates of the Arctic

Alaska

Established December 2, 1980

8,500,000 acres

"The view from the top gave us an excellent idea of the jagged country toward which we were heading. The main Brooks Range divide was entirely covered with snow. Close at hand, only about ten miles to the north, was a precipitous pair of mountains, one on each side of the North Fork. I bestowed the name Gates of the Arctic on them . . . . "

It was the early 1930s, and Robert Marshall had found his wilderness home, an unpeopled, uncluttered source of inspiration that would make him one of America's greatest conservationists. Gates of the Arctic was the ultimate North American wilderness. Congress created the park to keep it that way.

Climb practically any ridge in the heart of the park and you'll see a dozen glacial cirques side by side; serrated mountains that scythe the sky; and storms that snap out of dark, brooding clouds. Six National Wild and Scenic Rivers—Alatna, John, Kobuk, Noatak, North Fork Koyukuk, and Tinayguk—tumble out of high alpine valleys into forested lowlands. The park lies entirely above the Arctic Circle, straddling the Brooks Range, one of the world's northernmost mountain chains.

With Kobuk Valley National Park and Noatak National Preserve, Gates of the Arctic protects much of the habitat of the western arctic caribou. Grizzlies, wolves, wolverines, and foxes also roam over the severe land in search of food. Ptarmigan nibble on willow, and gyrfalcons dive for ptarmigan. Shafts of cinnabar

sunlight pour through the mountains at 2 a.m. in June, setting the wild land ablaze. "No sight or sound or smell or feeling even remotely hinted of men or their creations," wrote Marshall. "It seemed as if time had dropped away a million years and we were back in a primordial world."

How to Get There

Bush pilots say that where the road ends, the real Alaska begins. And so it is in Gates of the Arctic. You can fly or walk in; most people fly. From Fairbanks (about 250 miles away), scheduled flights serve Anaktuvuk Pass, an Eskimo village within the park borders; Bettles/Evansville; and Ambler, to the west. From those points or from Fairbanks, you can air taxi into the park. Allow time for bad weather and delayed flights. From Anaktuvuk Pass, you can also hike into the park along the John River.

Or, you can drive up from Fairbanks on the unpaved Dalton Highway (pipeline haul road) and hike to the park from Wiseman or other points. But it's a long, hard walk into the interior. The road is open to the public as far as Dietrich Field Camp, about 40 miles north of Wiseman.

When to Go

Summer. It is short, but days are very long and for a while temperatures may be relatively mild. Weather is highly unpredictable. Expect snow or rain in any month. August can be very wet, with freezing temperatures by mid-month. Mosquitoes and gnats are bad in late June and July. Fall colors peak in mid-August at high elevations, late August to early September at low elevations.

How to Visit

Give yourself time to savor the subtle beauty of this vast wilderness. A combination river-hiking trip offers the best of both. Air taxis are equipped to land on lakes and gravel bars for drop-offs and pickups.

Plan carefully and bring everything you need; there are no visitor facilities in the park. This spare, harsh land is so fragile that a hiker's step can kill lichens that take 150 years to reach full growth. Certain areas were badly damaged by the increase in visitors after Gates of the Arctic became a park.

Write or call park headquarters in Fairbanks before planning a trip. Ask for suggestions about areas to visit and hiking routes, along with names of air taxis, guides, and outfitters who operate in the park.

Black granite peaks of the Arrigetch

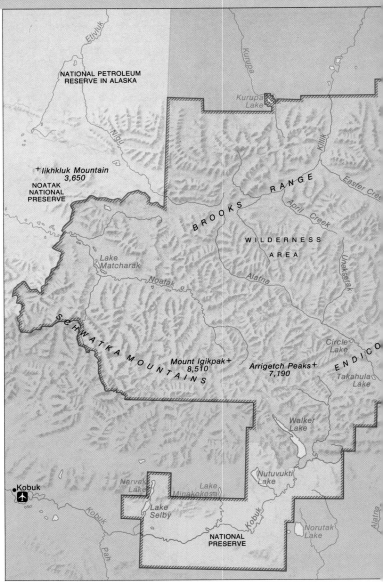

River Trips

Rivers are the main travel routes through Gates of the Arctic. Eskimos and caribou have followed them for centuries. Near some are lakes on which aircraft can land. Camping is good on the gravel bars, but be aware that summer rainstorms can quickly raise water levels. Most rivers are at their highest in May and June. Hiking is difficult but rewarding, especially in alpine areas. The following six rivers are only a sampling of what the park has to offer:

Alatna River is ideal for a first wilderness float trip. It takes 4 to 7 days, running gently down from the treeless Arctic Divide through beautiful tundra to the forested **Koyukuk River** lowlands. There are put-ins at

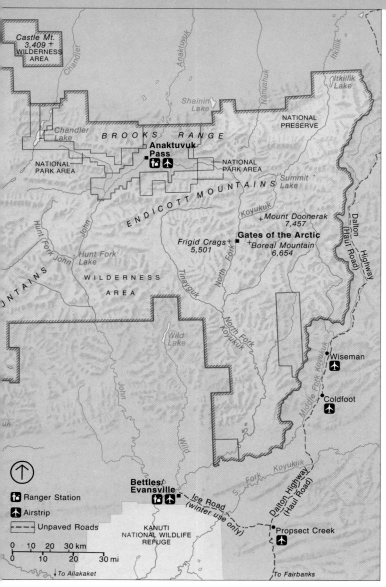

Castle Mt. 3,409 +
WILDERNESS
AREA

Chandler

BROOKS   RANGE

Anaktuvuk Pass

Shainin
Lake

Nanushuk

Anaktuvuk

Ikilllik

Oltkillik
Lake

NATIONAL
PRESERVE

Chandler
Lake

NATIONAL
PARK AREA

NATIONAL
PARK AREA

ENDICOTT MOUNTAINS

Summit
Lake

Koyukuk

+ Mount Doonerak
7,457

John

Frigid Crags +
5,501

Gates of the Arctic
+ **Boreal Mountain**
6,654

Dalton
(Haul)
Highway

Hunt Fork John

Hunt Fork
Lake

North Fork

Tinayguk

UNTAINS

WILDERNESS

AREA

North Fork
Koyukuk

Wild
Lake

Middle Fork Koyukuk

• **Wiseman**
✈

John

Wild

• **Coldfoot**
✈

↑

🏠 Ranger Station
✈ Airstrip
- - - Unpaved Roads

0   10   20   30 km
0   10   20   30 mi

uk

**Bettles/
Evansville**
🏠 ✈

Ice Road
(winter use only)

S. Fork   Koyukuk

Dalton Highway
(Haul Road)

KANUTI
NATIONAL WILDLIFE
REFUGE

• **Propsect Creek**
✈

↓ To Allakaket

To Fairbanks →

Takahula Lake, Circle Lake, or at a series of unnamed lakes farther upstream. Most boaters take-out at the village of Allakaket (75 and 85 miles from Takahula and Circle Lakes, respectively), where the Alatna meets the Koyukuk River.

John River is a mere stream at its headwater at Anaktuvuk Pass (the only remaining settlement of the inland Nunamiut Eskimo), but it gains

Tundra swan, a bird of summer

The North Fork Koyukuk near the Gates of the Arctic

Purple saxifrage

power and momentum as it flows south through the alpine heart of the park. **Hunt Fork Lake** is the best put-in; water levels above this point are usually too low. The John drops into lowland forest and joins the Koyukuk River just downstream of Bettles, a journey of a hundred miles.

Kobuk River begins at **Walker Lake** (a good put-in) and runs south and west through the mountains, canyons, foothills, and lowlands of Gates of the Arctic National Preserve. Kobuk village, 140 river miles from Walker Lake, is a popular take-out. Or you can continue downriver to Ambler and on through Kobuk Valley National Park to Kiana.

North Fork Koyukuk begins at **Summit Lake** and cuts between **Boreal Mountain** and **Frigid Crags**—the **Gates of the Arctic**—then flows past **Redstar Creek Lakes** (a good put-in) and continues south a hundred miles to Bettles.

One of the largest wilderness river basins in North America, the **Noatak** flows west 450 miles from Gates of the Arctic through Noatak National Preserve into the Chukchi Sea. From a put-in at **Lake Matcharak** to Noatak village is a 350-mile trip. The river, a major thoroughfare in a trackless realm, demands minimal boating skills but maximal planning. Give yourself a month for the trip.

The seldom visited **Tinayguk** flows through a broad glacier-cut valley before joining the Koyukuk below Boreal Mountain and Frigid Crags. Put in after landing on a gravel bar along the Tinayguk 35 miles north of where it joins the Koyukuk. (Consult local maps and outfitters for the exact location.) Float down to the Koyukuk, then continue on for another 80 miles to Bettles.

Information & Activities

Headquarters
P.O. Box 74680, Fairbanks, Alaska 99707. Phone (907) 456-0281.

Seasons & Accessibility
Park open year-round. Access by air or foot; there are no roads to or within the park. Contact park headquarters before planning a visit.

Dalton Highway, running parallel to the park's east boundary, is an unpaved pipeline haul road; it is closed to the public beyond Dietrich Field Camp (about 40 miles north of Wiseman). For information about permits to travel farther north, call the state Department of Transportation, (907) 451-2209.

Visitor & Information Centers
There are no visitor centers or facilities of any kind within the park. The only ranger stations are located in Bettles and Anaktuvuk Pass. An interagency visitor center is staffed in Coldfoot during the summer.

Gas & Supplies
Bring supplies with you (Fairbanks has a full selection); few available in communities of Bettles and Anaktuvuk Pass, which are not accessible by road. Gas stations on the Dalton Highway at milepost 56 (just north of the Yukon River) and at Coldfoot, milepost 173.6.

Pets
Only pack dogs allowed.

Facilities for Disabled
None.

Things to Do
Hiking (no established trails), backpacking, canoeing, kayaking and rafting, fishing (license required), hunting (in preserve only, with license), rock- and mountain climbing, wildlife-watching. Ask park for list of licensed guides and outfitters.

Special Advisories
☐This is a wilderness park; all visitors should be well skilled in the outdoors; firearms may be carried for protection.
☐Eskimos use the park for subsistence fishing and hunting; respect them and their property.
☐From mid-June through July, be prepared for plenty of mosquitoes and gnats; bring insect repellent, a head net, and an insect-proof tent.
☐Swift currents and freezing water make river crossings particularly hazardous.

Overnight Backpacking
No permit required, but get up-to-date bear information from ranger station. Food, stoves, and all equipment must be carried. Camp on gravel bars to avoid damaging fragile tundra.

Campgrounds
None; backcountry camping only.

Hotels, Motels, & Inns
INSIDE THE PARK:
Alatna Lodge (on the headwaters of the Alatna River) Alatna Guide Service, P.O. Box 80424, Fairbanks, Alas. 99708. (907) 479-6354. 3 rooms. $95-$200 per day, per person, depending on activities. Open July to early September. **Alatna River Wilderness Cabins** (on Alatna River near Arrigetch Peaks) Alatna Guide Service, P.O. Box 80424, Fairbanks, Alas. 99708. (907) 479-6354. 2 cabins. $95-$200 per day, per person, depending on activities. Open mid-June to early September.

OUTSIDE THE PARK:
Arctic Acres Inn Mile 175, Dalton Highway, Coldfoot, Alas. 99701. (907) 678-5201. 52 units. $108. Open May through Sept. **Coldfoot Services Motel** Mile 175, Dalton Highway, Coldfoot, Alas. 99701. (907) 678-5201. 50 units with shared bath. $85. Rest. Open late May to mid-Sept. **Iniakuk Lodge** (on Iniakuk Lake) Alatna Guide Service, P.O. Box 80424, Fairbanks, Alas. 99708. (907) 479-6354. 6 rooms with central bath. $250 per person, per day, includes all meals and activities. Open mid-June through mid-September.

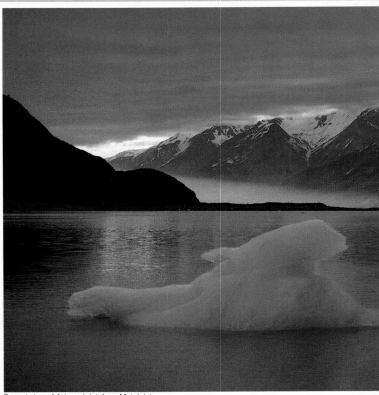

Sunset view of Adams Inlet, from Muir Inlet

Glacier Bay

Alaska

Established December 2, 1980

3,280,198 acres

When Capt. George Vancouver sailed the Alaska coast in 1794, Glacier Bay did not exist. It lay beneath a sheet of glacial ice several miles wide and thousands of feet thick. Since then, in the fastest glacial retreat on record, the ice has shrunk back 65 miles to unveil new land and a new bay, now returning to life after a long winter's sleep.

Scientists call Glacier Bay a living laboratory for the grand processes of glacial retreat, plant succession, and animal dynamics. It is an open book on the last ice age. At the southern end of the bay, where the ice departed 200 years ago, a spruce-hemlock rain forest has taken root. Farther north, in areas more recently degla-ciated, the land becomes rugged and thinly vegetated.

The bay branches into two major arms, the west arm and Muir Inlet, which themselves branch into small-er inlets. There, on slopes deglaciat-ed 50 to 100 years ago, alder and willow grow, while mosses, moun-tain avens, and dwarf fireweed pio-neer areas exposed within the last two or three decades.

The new vegetation creates habi-tats for wolves, moose, mountain goats, black bears, brown bears, ptarmigan, and other wildlife, and the sea supports a food chain that in-cludes salmon, bald eagles, harbor seals, harbor porpoises, humpback whales, and killer whales—all in an environment less than 200 years old.

Roughly 16 tidewater glaciers still flow into the park. Primarily because of variations in sea depths, most

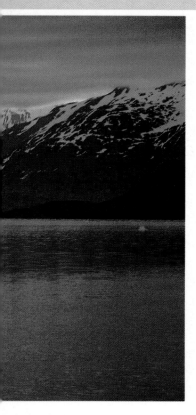

thick with icebergs then and the tide-water glaciers less approachable. September is often rainy.

How to Visit
Glacier Bay is a marine highway. Most visitors experience the park from the deck of a cruise ship, or a tour boat, or from the waterline of a sea kayak. Many of the large cruise ships that travel southeastern Alaska's Inside Passage go into Glacier Bay. Other tours offer accommodations at **Glacier Bay Lodge** (the park's center of activity) and a 1-day or overnight boat trip to the glaciers and back. Campers and kayakers can take the boat and be dropped off at one of several sites up the bay, either to be picked up at a later date or to paddle back to **Bartlett Cove.**

The Lower Bay

The lower bay reaches from **Bartlett Cove** north to **Tlingit Point,** where it separates into its two arms and continues north. Bartlett Cove has the only two maintained trails in the park. Beginning at the **Glacier Bay Lodge,** the **Forest Loop Trail** is a 1-mile, 1-hour round-trip through the young spruce-hemlock rain forest. A boardwalk covers the first part of the trail out to **Blackwater Pond.** For a $\frac{1}{2}$-day trip (and more rugged walking), the **Bartlett River Trail** begins at the roadside, a $\frac{1}{2}$ mile from the lodge, and winds another $1\frac{1}{2}$ miles through the rain forest to the **Bartlett River,** ending in a quiet meadow. It's not unusual to see red squirrels, blue grouse, and black bears along either of these trails.

If you want to kayak, the **Beardslee Islands** just north of Bartlett Cove offer a maze of shorelines and waterways—a quiet counterpoint to the buses and boats coming and going at Bartlett Cove. Reaching across the lower bay, **Sitakaday Narrows** is a shoal that creates strong and dangerous whirlpools and currents as the tides (rising and falling an average of 15 feet in 6 hours) rush over it. Watch for phalaropes, gulls, terns, and other birds feeding here as the swirling water flushes small fish to the surface. To the north, the **Marble Islands** rise abruptly out of the middle of the bay. The islands, deglaciated

glaciers in the eastern and southwestern areas of the bay are receding, while several on its west side are advancing. The glaciers calve icebergs that hit the water with a sound like cannon-shot. "White thunder," the Tlingit Indians called it, the awesome voice of ancient ice.

How to Get There
By boat or plane only. From Juneau, take a scheduled flight 53 miles to Gustavus. Catch the bus to Glacier Bay Lodge and Bartlett Cove Campground, 10 miles away at the park's southern end. Charter flights also service Gustavus from Juneau, Skagway, Haines, and Hoonah. Private boats can enter the bay with permits obtained by phone or mail from park headquarters at Bartlett Cove.

When to Go
Late May to mid-September. Summer days are long and temperatures cool. May and June have the most sunshine, but the upper inlets can be

Yakutat Glacier

Alsek

BRITISH COLUMBIA
ALASKA

SAINT ELIAS MOUNTAINS

Taishenshini

ALSEK

Melburn Glacier

Alsek

Dry Bay

 Cabin ■

NATIONAL PRESERVE

DECEPTION HILLS

Alsek Glacier

Grand Plateau Glacier

Grand Pacific Glacier

Mt. Lodge
10,530

CANADA
UNITED ST

Mt. Root
12,660

Margerie

Mt. Fairweather
15,300

Mt. Quincy Adams
13,650

Cape Fairweather

Mt. Salisbury
12,000

FAIRWEATHER

Johns Hopkins Glacier

Lituya Mountain
11,750

Mt. L
10,

Mt. Crillon
12,728

R A N

Lituya Bay

Mt. LaPerouse
10,728

PACIFIC OCEAN

Icy Point

GULF OF ALASKA

🛈 Ranger Station

🔺 Campground

✈ Airstrip

🚶 Hiking Trail

0   5   10   15 km
0   5   10   15 mi

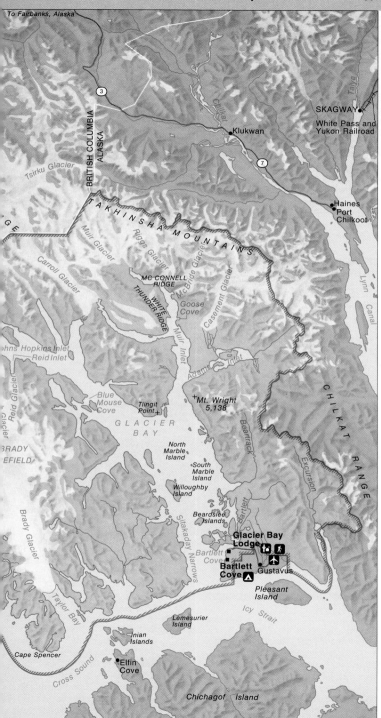

To Fairbanks, Alaska

3

BRITISH COLUMBIA
ALASKA

Chilkat

7

SKAGWAY

White Pass and
Yukon Railroad

Klukwan

Taiya

Tsirku Glacier

Haines
Port
Chilkoot

TAKHINSHA MOUNTAINS

Muir Glacier

Riggs Glacier

McBride Glacier

MC CONNELL
RIDGE

WHITE
THUNDER RIDGE

Casement Glacier

Goose
Cove

Carroll Glacier

Lynn Canal

Johns Hopkins Inlet
Reid Inlet

Muir Inlet

Adams Inlet

CHILKAT

Reid Glacier

Blue
Mouse
Cove

Tlingit
Point

Mt. Wright
5,138

GLACIER
BAY

BRADY
EFIELD

North
Marble
Island

South
Marble
Island

Willoughby
Island

Bearhtrack

Excursion

RANGE

Brady Glacier

Sitakaday Narrows

Beardslee
Islands

Bartlett

Glacier Bay
Lodge

Bartlett
Cove

Gustavus

Bartlett
Cove

Pleasant
Island

Taylor Bay

Icy Strait

Lemesurier
Island

Cape Spencer

Inian
Islands

Cross Sound

Elfin
Cove

Chichagof Island

Northern sea lions

around 1835, today support breeding colonies of gulls, cormorants, puffins, and murres (and are off-limits to visitors during the summer). Keep a lookout for northern sea lions on **South Marble Island.**

The West Arm

The bay's west arm contains the highest mountains and most active tidewater glaciers in the park. Clear days afford stunning views of the **Fairweather Range,** crowned by **Mt. Fairweather** at 15,300 feet; cloudy days lend a moody, rich blue cast to the tidewater faces of the **Margerie, Grand Pacific, Lamplugh,** and **Reid Glaciers.** In the wildest inlet, **Johns Hopkins,** 7 glaciers tumble down mountains, whose surrounding peaks reach 8,000 feet. Each June thousands of harbor seals give birth to their pups on icebergs in Johns Hopkins Inlet. **Blue Mouse Cove** and the northwest corner of **Reid Inlet** are the best anchorages. Good camping sites can be found almost anywhere (except in Johns Hopkins Inlet where the terrain is generally too steep). Hiking is a matter of going where the spirit and the topography take you. Brown bears are common throughout the area. *Be careful.*

Muir Inlet

Reaching 25 miles into the northeast corner of the park, **Muir Inlet** is a mecca for kayakers. Tour boats, cruise ships, and fishing boats seldom come in here. The camping is good, and so is the hiking, if you avoid thickets of alder. **Adams Inlet** branches east off lower Muir Inlet and is a favorite among kayakers. You can time your

An ice cave

entry and exit by the strong tides that flow in and out through the narrow opening. To the north, **Sealers Island** (closed to visitors) is a breeding site for arctic terns and black oystercatchers. Nearby is **Goose Cove,** the most protected anchorage in Muir Inlet. In contrast to the tidewater glaciers that are advancing in the west arm, most in Muir Inlet continue to retreat. The **McBride** and **Riggs Glaciers** separated from the retreating **Muir Glacier** in 1941 and 1960 respectively; since then, all three have retreated long distances. A journey up **White Thunder Ridge** or **McConnell Ridge** rewards hikers with spectacular views of upper Muir Inlet. Both hikes take a full day and climb about 1,500 feet. Also rewarding is a hike along **Wolf Creek** (beginning at the south end of White Thunder Ridge), where running water has exposed the remains of a forest buried by a glacier 4,000 to 7,000 years ago.

Information & Activities

Headquarters
Gustavus, Alaska 99826. Phone (907) 697-2230.

Seasons & Accessibility
Park open year-round, but late May to mid-September is visitor season; transportation and facilities limited rest of year. Call the park before going in the off-season.

There are no roads to or in the park; access by boat or airplane only. Visitors with private boats need a permit between June 1 and Aug. 30; phone (907) 697-2268.

Visitor & Information Centers
Information centers on the dock at Bartlett Cove and at Glacier Bay Lodge. Call (907) 697-2268 for visitor information.

Entrance Fee
None.

Pets
Permitted on leashes on Bartlett Cove roads and trails only. Prohibited in backcountry; boaters must keep pets aboard vessels.

Facilities for Disabled
Glacier Bay Lodge is accessible to wheelchairs. One trail, with a stretch of boardwalk, is also accessible.

Things to Do
Free naturalist-led activities (from Glacier Bay Lodge): nature walks, films, slide presentations, and evening programs. Also available, kayaking, fishing (license required), scheduled boat tours, glacier viewing, whale-watching and birdwatching, crabbing, hiking, berry picking, mountain and glacier climbing (for the experienced only), aerial sightseeing, cross-country skiing.

For information and reservations for naturalist-guided boat tours from Bartlett Cove, contact Glacier Bay Lodge, Inc., 523 Pine Street, Suite 203, Seattle, Wash. 98101 (phone 800-622-2042 or 206-623-2417). Ask the park for a list of other concessioners offering a variety of rental and guide services.

Special Advisories
☐ Do not get too close to icebergs when boating, and do not climb on the glaciers without a guide or plenty of experience.
☐ Carry plenty of insect repellent.

Overnight Backpacking
Permits not required, but registration recommended. Backcountry users must receive orientation from rangers before setting out. Use of Park Service food storage canisters required.

Campgrounds
One campground only; **Bartlett Cove** has 14-day limit. Open all year; first come, first served. No fees. Showers at lodge (within a mile) available only seasonally. Warming hut provided. Tent sites only. **Bartlett Cove Group Campground**; open all year; first come, first served.

Hotels, Motels, & Inns
(unless otherwise noted, rates are for 2 persons in a double room, high season)
INSIDE THE PARK:
Glacier Bay Lodge Gustavus, Alaska 99826. (800) 451-5952. 55 units. $138. Packages that include airfare available, $269-$1,500. Restaurant. Open mid-May to mid-September.

OUTSIDE THE PARK:
In Gustavus, Alaska 99826
Glacier Bay Country Inn P.O. Box 5. (907) 697-2288. 9 units, 8 with private baths. $129-$198, includes all meals and some activities. Open mid-April through September.
Gustavus Inn P.O. Box 60. (907) 697-2254. 13 units, 9 with private baths. $120 per person, includes all meals and some activities. Open May 15 to September 15.
Salmon River Cabins P.O. Box 13. (907) 697-2245. 10 rustic cabins with kitchenettes, 3 private baths. $40-$50. Open May through September.

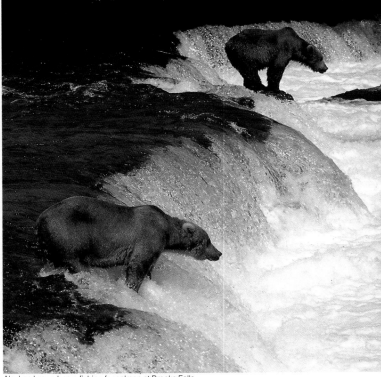

Alaskan brown bears fishing for salmon at Brooks Falls

Katmai

Alaska

Established December 2, 1980

4,090,000 acres

Volcanoes and bears—powerful, unpredictable, and awe inspiring—embody the wild heart of Katmai. Within the borders of the national park and preserve are 15 active volcanoes, some still steaming, and North America's largest population of protected brown bears—about 750 of them. You can hike, kayak, and canoe here. You can fish waist-deep in rivers as clear as glass. And you can watch the best fish catcher of all, the Alaskan brown bear, sometimes diving completely under the water, sometimes catching fish in midair. At the end of the day you can relax in a rustic yet sumptuous lodge on the shore of a sapphire lake.

In 1912 a volcano here erupted with a force ten times that of Mt. St. Helens in 1980. Suddenly Katmai, a place hardly anyone had heard of, was on front pages around the world. Ash filled the air, global temperatures cooled, acid rain burned clothing off lines in Vancouver, British Columbia, and on Kodiak Island, just across Shelikof Strait from Katmai, day became night.

Leading a 1916 expedition sponsored by the National Geographic Society, botanist Robert Griggs ascended Katmai Pass from Shelikof Strait. "The whole valley as far as the eye could reach was full of hundreds, no thousands—literally, tens of thousands—of smokes curling up from its fissured floor," he wrote. The smokes were fumaroles steaming 500 to 1,000 feet into the air. Griggs, who named the Valley of Ten Thousand Smokes, spearheaded the

lodges, cabins, and Brooks Camp Campground open. Bear watching, an increasingly popular pastime, is best in July when the sockeye salmon spawn. Fishing and hiking are good throughout summer, but come prepared for rain. Heavy snowpack may remain in the upper elevations into July. Summer daytime temperatures range from the mid-50s to mid-60s; the average low is 44°F.

How to Visit

If your time is short, get to **Brooks Camp.** People, fish, bears, boats, and planes concentrate here. Compared to the rest of the park, it's crowded. But the lodge and campground are comfortable (reservations essential) and the bear viewing unforgettable. You'll find good hiking and fishing.

If at all possible, take the bus or van tour 23 miles out from Brooks Camp to the **Valley of Ten Thousand Smokes.** Return the same day or hike into the valley and camp. You can extend your stay by boating or flying to the many other lakes, streams, rivers, and lodges in the park. Pick your area, make a safe plan, and go.

Brooks Camp & Valley of Ten Thousand Smokes

Some nice hikes begin near **Brooks Camp.** The trail you'll first want to take goes to the bear-viewing platform. The ½-mile trail starts between Brooks Camp and **Brooks Lake** and winds gently through the forest to **Brooks Falls,** ending at the viewing platform. Wooden steps ascend a balcony overlooking the spectacle of jumping fish and feeding bears. Averaging a thousand pounds in weight and measuring up to ten feet long, these Alaskan brown bears are the continent's largest land carnivores.

The hike up **Dumpling Mountain** is a good day trip. The trail begins at the campground and climbs to an 800-foot overlook in 1½ miles. From there you can continue another 2 miles over alpine tundra to the summit, elevation 2,440 feet. Both the overlook and summit afford tremendous views of **Naknek Lake** and the surrounding mountains.

The most popular and spectacular hiking in the park is in the **Valley of Ten Thousand Smokes.** There's no

campaign to include Katmai in the National Park System.

The smokes are gone from the valley. But steam vents still appear elsewhere in the park.

How to Get There

From Anchorage, scheduled jets fly the 290 miles to King Salmon, park headquarters; from there, June to September 10, daily floatplanes fly the last 33 miles to Brooks Camp, site of a summer visitor center and the center of activity. Air charters can be arranged into other areas. You can drive the 9 miles from King Salmon to Lake Camp, at the western end of the park on the Naknek River, then go by boat to Brooks Camp, the Bay of Islands, and other areas of Naknek Lake.

When to Go

June to early September. Only then, with transportation available between Brooks Camp and the Valley of Ten Thousand Smokes, are the

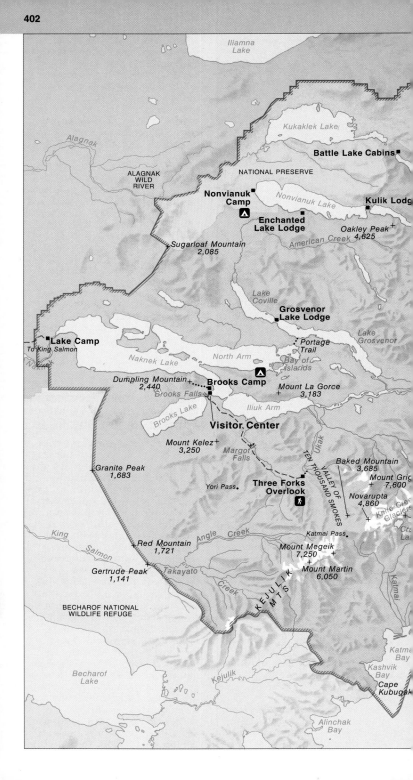

Iliamna Lake

Alagnak

Kukaklek Lake

Battle Lake Cabins ■

ALAGNAK
WILD
RIVER

NATIONAL PRESERVE

Nonvianuk Camp ■
⛺

Nonvianuk Lake

Kulik Lodge ■

Enchanted Lake Lodge ■

*Oakley Peak +
4,625*

*Sugarloaf Mountain
2,085*

American Creek

Lake Coville

Grosvenor Lake Lodge ■

Lake Grosvenor

Lake Camp ■
To King Salmon

Naknek Lake

North Arm

Portage Trail

Bay of Islands

⛺

*Dumpling Mountain
2,440* +

Brooks Camp ■

*Mount La Gorce
3,183* +

Brooks Falls

Brooks Lake

Iliuk Arm

Visitor Center

*Mount Kelez +
3,250*

Margot Falls

*Granite Peak
1,683*

Yori Pass

Three Forks Overlook
🚶

Ukak

VALLEY OF TEN THOUSAND SMOKES

*Baked Mountain
3,685*

*Mount Grig
7,600* +

*Novarupta
4,860* +

Knife Creek Glaciers

Ctl La

King

Salmon

Angle Creek

Katmai Pass ■

*Red Mountain
1,721* +

Takayato

*Mount Megeik
7,250* +

*Mount Martin
6,050* +

Katmai

*Gertrude Peak
1,141* +

Creek

KEJULIK MTS

BECHAROF NATIONAL
WILDLIFE REFUGE

Kejulik

Becharof Lake

Katmai Bay

Kashvik Bay

Cape Kubugak

Alinchak Bay

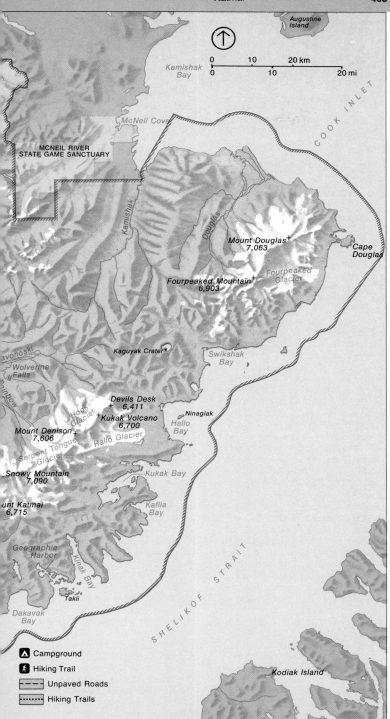

Campground

Hiking Trail

Unpaved Roads

Hiking Trails

Mt. Katolinat bordering the Valley of Ten Thousand Smokes

other landscape like it in the world. Daily tours connect Brooks Camp with the **Three Forks Overlook** and a cabin at the north end of the valley, where you can camp or picnic. A short trail descends 200 feet to where the **Ukak River** roars through a bedrock canyon crowned by cliffs of volcanic ash.

To hike into the valley, take the trail that begins $\frac{1}{2}$ mile back from the end of the road and plan to camp overnight. The trail crosses **Windy Creek,** passes the north end of the **Buttress Range,** follows the **River Lethe,** and finally climbs 1,000 feet to the Baked Mountain Cabin, a shelter available for overnights. The challenging 12-mile trip takes a full day; drinking water is scarce.

Due south $5\frac{1}{2}$ miles from the cabin is **Katmai Pass,** the place from which Robert Griggs first beheld the valley in 1916. Strong winds often funnel through here.

A fascinating side trip between **Baked Mountain** and Katmai Pass is to **Novarupta,** a 200-foot-high dome of volcanic rock that was the extrusion plug of the great eruption. Scientists believe most of the 1912 lava and ash spewed out through a fissure here, drawing magma from nearby **Mt. Katmai** and causing its summit to collapse into a caldera.

To reach the caldera (a strenuous 1- to 2-day trip), head east from Novarupta or Baked Mountain to the stagnant, ash-covered **Knife Creek Glaciers,** then climb 3,800 feet up ash and ice to the caldera rim, where, if you peer over the edge, you'll see what Robert Griggs saw: "a wonderful lake, of a weird vitriolic robin's-egg blue."

Water & Air Trips

Boaters, kayakers, and canoeists find no shortage of places to explore in Katmai. Guides and equipment are available for hire through Brooks Lodge or one of the other, smaller lodges catering mostly to fishermen. An especially popular and picturesque spot is the **Bay of Islands** in the **North Arm** of Naknek Lake, 22 miles from Brooks Camp.

For serious paddlers looking for the truly wild side of Katmai, the **Savonoski Loop** is an 85-mile round-trip from Brooks Camp that takes 4 to 8 days, depending on the weather. You paddle through the Bay of Islands, portage to **Lake Grosvenor,** and float the **Grosvenor** and **Savonoski Rivers** into the **Iliuk Arm** of Naknek Lake for the return to Brooks Camp. Follow the shorelines, for the wind can suddenly transform lakes from tranquil to tempestuous. If you'd like to take a river trip, inquire about the **Alagnak River,** a designated Wild and Scenic River, and the **Ukak River,** which, with class V rapids, is for the very experienced only.

Like the other national parks in Alaska, Katmai is spectacular from the air. Flight-seeing trips can be arranged in **King Salmon** or Brooks Camp. The grand tour might swing over the Valley of Ten Thousand Smokes, through Katmai Pass, up the coast from **Katmai Bay** to **Swikshak Bay,** over **Kaguyak Crater,** and down the Savonoski River back to Brooks Camp. Take plenty of film and a calm stomach.

Information & Activities

Headquarters
P.O. Box 7, King Salmon, Alaska 99613. Phone (907) 246-3305.

Seasons & Accessibility
Park open year-round, but scheduled flights from Anchorage to King Salmon (with connecting seaplane flights into the park) available June to mid-Sept. only. Reserve well in advance. Accessible by private or charter plane all year; the park has a list of licensed air charter companies.

Visitor & Information Centers
Brooks Camp Visitor Center and the concessions are open from June to mid-Sept. For visitor information contact park or Katmailand, Inc., the park's main concessioner, at 4700 Aircraft Drive, Anchorage 99502, or call (800) 544-0551 or (907) 243-5448.

Entrance Fee
None.

Facilities for Disabled
Brooks Lodge accessible with assistance.

Things to Do
Free naturalist-led activities: daily interpretive programs, evening programs, nature walks. Also available, bus trips to the Valley of Ten Thousand Smokes, bear-watching, hiking, kayaking, canoeing, boating, mountain climbing, aerial sightseeing, fishing (license required and available in park), float trips.

Katmailand, Inc. has guides and boating and fishing equipment available for hire at Brooks Lodge. Reserve ahead. Ask the park for a list of other outfitters and guides licensed within its borders.

Special Advisories
☐Alaskan brown bears are unpredictable and dangerous; stay far away from them unless at the bear-viewing platforms.
☐Be very careful when crossing glacial streams.
☐Carry plenty of insect repellent.

Overnight Backpacking
Camping allowed anywhere in park without reservations, except at Brooks Camp (see below). Backcountry permits not required, but registration strongly suggested. Information pamphlet available.

Campgrounds
One backcountry campground, **Brooks Camp,** with 7-day limit. Open year-round; reservations required June 1 to Sept. 1; contact park headquarters early. No fee. Showers at Brooks Lodge. Tent sites only. Three-sided shelters for cooking. Limited food services in park.

Hotels, Motels, & Inns
Katmailand, Inc. offers multiday package tours from Anchorage that can include airfare, lodging at Brooks Lodge, Grosvenor Lake Lodge, or Kulik Lodge, meals, guides, fishing tackle, rafts, licenses, and boats or planes to fishing spots. For information contact the company at 4700 Aircraft Drive, Anchorage, Alaska 99502, or call (800) 544-0551 or (907) 243-5448.

INSIDE THE PARK:
Brooks Lodge 16 cabins. Packages starting from $526 per person. Open June to mid-September.
Grosvenor Lake Lodge 9 cabins. Packages starting from $1,425 per person. Open June to late September.
Kulik Lodge 9 cabins. Packages starting from $2,250 per person. Open mid-June to late September.

Also, **Alaska's Enchanted Lake Lodge** P.O. Box 97, King Salmon, Alas. 99613. (907) 246-6878 (May to September); (206) 643-2172 (winter). 7 cabins. Fly-in sportfishing only. $4,500 per person per week, includes meals, lodging, tackle, fishing license, airfare from Anchorage. Open June to October.
Battle River Wilderness Retreat 8076 Caribbean Way, Sacramento, Calif. 95826. (916) 381-0250. 3 cabins, central showers. Packages start at $1,500 per person. Includes airfare from Anchorage, meals, and guides. Open June to October 1.

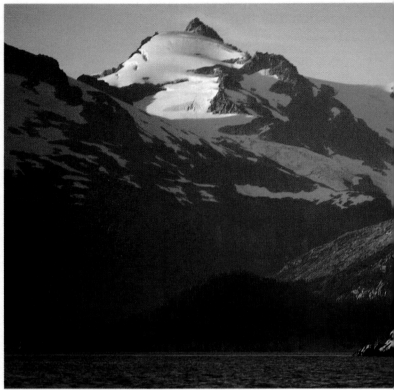

Granite Passage at the tip of Harris Peninsula

Kenai Fjords

Alaska

Established December 2, 1980

670,000 acres

Distill the essence of coastal Alaska into one place—wild, dynamic, and scenic, rich with the signatures of glaciers, light with the marks of people, unforgiving in stormy seas, unforgettable in warm sunshine—and you have Kenai Fjords, the smallest national park in Alaska. Here the south-central part of the state tumbles into the Gulf of Alaska; here the land challenges the sea with talonlike peninsulas and rocky headlands, while the sea itself reaches inland with long fjords and hundreds of quiet bays and coves.

Crowning the park is the Harding Icefield, almost 700 square miles of ice up to a mile thick. It feeds over 30 glaciers flowing out of the mountains, 8 of them to tidewater. The Harding Icefield is a vestige of the massive ice sheet that covered much of Alaska in the Pleistocene era.

The ancient ice gouged out Kenai's fjords, creating habitats for throngs of sea animals. About 20 species of seabirds nest along the rocky coastline; most of the birds are clownfaced puffins. Bald eagles swoop along the towering cliffs, and peregrine falcons hunt over the outer islands. Seabirds, by the tens of thousands, migrate or congregate here.

Twenty-three species of mammals, including harbor seals, northern sea lions, and sea otters, live here. Moose, black bears, wolverines, lynx, and marten roam narrow bands of forest between the coast and icefield. And just above them, on the treeless slopes, climb sure-footed mountain goats.

How to Get There

Seward is the gateway to Kenai Fjords. To get to Seward, take the Seward Highway (Alaska Hwy. 9) south from Anchorage. The 130-mile drive is spectacular. Buses and small commuter planes also connect Anchorage and Seward, and the Alaska Marine Highway (ferry) links Seward with Homer, Seldovia, Kodiak, Valdez, and Cordova. You can also charter a flight from Seward or Homer directly to the park. In summer, the Alaska Railroad serves Seward from Anchorage (with connections to Fairbanks and Whittier).

When to Go

Usually summer. The days lengthen, the seas calm down. The road to Exit Glacier generally opens in May and closes with the first snowfall, usually in October. Many winter visitors ski the road into Exit Glacier, or snowmobile in. Flight-seeing trips can be arranged in Seward any time of the year, subject to weather.

How to Visit

The most popular and accessible area in the park is **Exit Glacier**, 13 miles northwest of Seward. You can drive to it or take a tour bus. Trails offer $1/2$-hour hikes to the glacier and a full-day hike to the **Harding Icefield.**

Otherwise, hiking is a matter of exploring wilderness shores and ridges accessible only by boat and plane. From mid-May to late September, daily tour boats from Seward offer round-trip $1/2$-day and full-day excursions to the fjords and outlying islands. Charter boats take kayakers and campers to any fjord they wish (most often **Aialik Bay**) and pick them up the same day or days later. Kayaking, fishing, and backpacking guides are available. Ask the park for a list.

From Seward or Homer you can book a breathtaking 1-hour flight over the Harding Icefield and Kenai coast. For extended adventures, ski-planes drop off and pick up skiers on the icefield, and floatplanes do the same for kayakers in the fjords, weather permitting.

Exit Glacier & Harding Icefield

Exit Glacier is one of many rivers of ice that flow off the **Harding Icefield.** From Seward, follow the highway north to mile 3.7 where a gravel road leads 9 miles to a parking lot. There are three trails: The **Main Trail** is paved for $1/3$ of a mile to a viewing

Climber on Bear Glacier

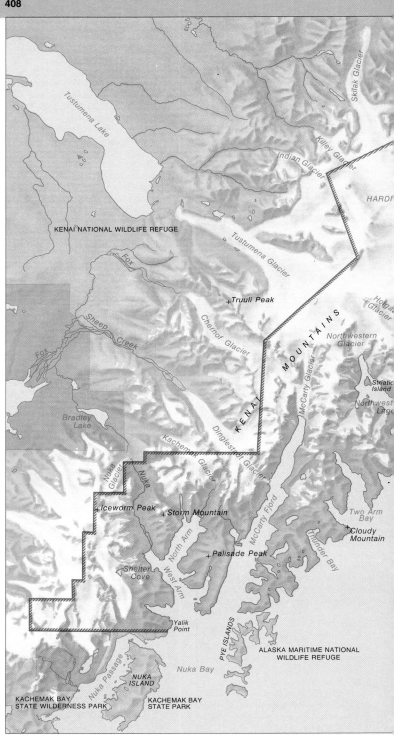

Tustumena Lake

Skilak Glacier

Killey Glacier

Indian Glacier

HARDI

KENAI NATIONAL WILDLIFE REFUGE

Tustumena Glacier

Fox

+Truuli Peak

Holga
Glacier

Chernof Glacier

Northwestern
Glacier

Sheep Creek

M
O
U
N
T
A
I
N
S

Fox

McCarty Glacier

Striatic
Island

Bradley
Lake

K
E
N
A
I

Northwest
Lago

Kachemak Glacier

Dinglestadt Glacier

Nuka Glacier

Nuka

+Iceworm Peak

•Storm Mountain

McCarty Fiord

Two Arm
Bay

North Arm

+Cloudy
Mountain

•Palisade Peak

Thunder Bay

Shelter
Cove

West Arm

Yalik
Point

PYE ISLANDS

ALASKA MARITIME NATIONAL
WILDLIFE REFUGE

Nuka Passage

Nuka Bay

NUKA
ISLAND

KACHEMAK BAY
STATE WILDERNESS PARK

KACHEMAK BAY
STATE PARK

area. The trail then separates into two loops. The lower loop continues to the outwash plain for a close view of the glacier terminus; the upper loop climbs $\frac{1}{3}$ of a mile for a view of deep crevasses and towering seracs along the glacier's flank.

A $\frac{1}{2}$-mile **Nature Trail** begins at the ranger station and winds over old moraines and through cottonwood, alder, and willow before following **Exit Creek** to connect with the Main Trail. The **Harding Icefield Trail** branches off the Main Trail and climbs 3,000 feet in $3\frac{1}{2}$ miles, ending on the icefield. The upper section of the trail is usually snow covered; the lower portion is slippery and muddy after rain. Ask a ranger about current conditions and sign in at the trail register. On the slopes you may see mountain goats and black bears.

The Fjords

Daily tour boats travel down **Resurrection Bay**, pass picturesque **Caines Head** and **Callisto Head**, then round rugged **Aialik Cape** and enter **Aialik Bay**, the most visited fjord in the park. The **Holgate** and **Aialik Glaciers** flow into this fjord. Tour boats usually visit the Holgate, then return to Seward via the **Chiswell Islands** (part of the Alaska Maritime NWR), an excellent place to see sea lions hauled out on rocks and nesting seabirds.

Endless exploring awaits boaters and hikers on the shores of Kenai Fjords. If you are without a guide, be sure to inquire at the visitor center about weather, landing sites, tides, and hazards. The farther down the coast to the southwest, the fewer the people. Narrow **Granite Passage** is an exciting entrance into **Harris Bay**. From 1910 to 1960, **Northwestern Glacier** retreated $9\frac{1}{2}$ miles and opened up **Northwestern Lagoon** at the head of Harris Bay. The lagoon should be entered on calm water (preferably in a kayak) and at high tide only. Once you are inside and on the shore, you will find excellent hiking, especially to **Northeastern, Southwestern**, and **Sunlight Glaciers**.

Down the coast, **Thunder Bay** is a welcome anchorage during inclement weather. A narrow waterway cuts between the mainland and the **Pye Islands**. From here, **McCarty Fjord** slices 23 miles into the coast, its steep walls rising more than 4,000 feet overhead on either side of **McCarty Glacier.** The **West** and **North Arms** of **Nuka Bay** offer a variety of terrain and wildlife. Watch for the craggy profile of **Palisade Peak,** a 900-foot waterfall, historic gold mine sites, and for black bears, moose, and river otters near the **Nuka River,** for shorebirds along the mud flats at **Shelter Cove,** and for black sand beaches around **Yalik Point,** at the park's southern end. Few people come here; travel to Nuka Bay and you might have it all to yourself.

Horned puffins

Red fox and pup

Northern sea lions

Humpback whale in Aialik Bay

Information & Activities

Headquarters
P.O. Box 1727, Seward, Alaska 99664. Phone (907) 224-3175.

Seasons & Accessibility
Park open year-round, but from about mid-October to May, the road to Exit Glacier may be closed by snow. Access then is by ski, snowmobile, dog team, or snowshoe only. Call headquarters for information about weather and road conditions.

Visitor & Information Centers
Visitor Center in Seward, on Hwy. 9 just outside the eastern border of the park, open daily from Memorial Day to Labor Day; weekdays only the rest of the year. Ranger Station at Exit Glacier open intermittently in summer only. Phone headquarters number for visitor information.

Entrance Fee
None.

Pets
Permitted leashed on the Exit Glacier Road and in parking areas. Prohibited on all trails.

Facilities for Disabled
Exit Glacier is the most accessible area. From the Ranger Station, wheelchairs can maneuver the glacier trail for the first $\frac{1}{3}$ mile, to an interpretive shelter offering exhibits and views of the glacier. Visitor Center is also wheelchair accessible.

Things to Do
Free naturalist-led activities: In summer (from the Exit Glacier Ranger Station), walks to the glacier's base, all-day hikes to the icefield, and evening programs. Also available, advanced mountain climbing, sailing, fishing (license required), wildlife-watching, cross-country skiing, dogsledding, snowshoeing.

Authorized commercial guides offer camping, fishing, kayaking, flight-seeing, and boat trips for exploring the fjords and watching seabirds, whales, porpoises, and other wildlife. Write or call park headquarters for a list of companies that do business in the park.

Special Advisories
☐If planning a backcountry trip without a guide, first check conditions with park staff.
☐Hypothermia is a danger on the icefield, even in summer.
☐Do not venture out in a boat unless well experienced in rough water.

Overnight Backpacking
Permit not required, but registration requested for Harding Icefield.

Campgrounds
One walk-in campground at **Exit Glacier.** Public use cabin at **Aialik Bay** available May through Sept. for overnight use by permit. Access by boat or plane only. In winter, a public use cabin is available at Exit Glacier. Write or phone the Visitor Center.

Hotels, Motels & Inns
(unless otherwise noted, rates are for 2 persons in a double room, high season)
In Seward, Alaska 99664:
Best Western Hotel-Seward (on 5th Ave.) P.O. Box 330. (800) 528-1234 or (907) 224-2378. 72 units. $72-$169. 4 condominiums, $175. AC, restaurant.
Breeze Inn (1311 4th Ave.) P.O. Box 2147.(907) 224-5237. 49 units, 1 with a kitchenette. $90. Restaurant.
Marina Motel (on Alaska Hwy. 9) P.O. Box 1134. (907) 224-5518. 18 units, 1 with a kitchenette. $80-$90.
Murphy's Motel (911 4th Ave.) P.O. Box 736. (907) 224-8090. 10 units. $74-$104.
Van Gilder Hotel (308 Adams St.) P.O. Box 2. (907) 224-3525 or (907) 224-3079. 28 units, 15 with private baths. $50-$95. Suites $125-$135. Restaurant.

The Great Kobuk Sand Dunes, encroaching on a spruce forest

Kobuk Valley

Alaska

Established December 2, 1980

1,750,000 acres

"Now we were alone between fringes of spruce by a clear stream where tundra went up the sides of mountains," wrote John McPhee in *Coming into the Country*. The Kobuk Valley, said McPhee, "was, in all likelihood, the most isolated wilderness I would ever see." Located entirely above the Arctic Circle, Kobuk Valley is the least visited of the national parks. Float a river here in late August and the only other humans you're likely to encounter are Inupiaq Eskimos hunting the caribou that migrate through each year.

Twelve thousand years ago, when continental glaciers covered much of North America and a land bridge connected Alaska and Asia, Kobuk Valley was an ice-free refuge with grassy tundra similar to that found in Siberia today. Bison, mastodons, and mammoths roamed the valley, along with the humans who hunted them. Since then, the climate has shifted, and sea level has risen to flood the land bridge; many of the early mammals have disappeared. But today's shrubby flora harbors relics of the preglacial steppe, and in the cold, hard ground lie the legacies of ancient animals and peoples.

Here in Kobuk Valley the boreal forest reaches its northern limit, and the North American and Asiatic flyways cross. Pockets of tundra blend into birch and spruce, dwarfed by blasts of freezing air. And along the Kobuk River stretch 25 square miles of rolling, active sand dunes, where summer temperatures can climb to 100°F.

can charter a boat or plane into the park, or hike.

When to Go

Summer. Days are long (from about June 6 to July 3 the sun doesn't set at all), and temperatures in many places can reach into the 80s or more. Ice breaks up on the Kobuk River in May, and begins to form again by mid-October. Ranger stations at Onion Portage and sometimes Kallarichuk are staffed from June to September. Middle to late June is best for wildflowers. August can bring rain and September snow. In late August, the aspens begin to turn yellow and the tundra red, and the caribou migration begins.

How to Visit

Take a combination river-hiking trip that alternates days on the water with days on the land. That way you can paddle through the country and hike without having to carry all your gear. Bring everything you need; no visitor facilities exist within the park. The **Kobuk River**, wide and placid, is a pleasant river to travel by canoe, kayak, or motorboat. Most people put in at Ambler and take out at Kiana, both outside the park. You can rent or charter a boat in Ambler. You can also float or paddle the **Salmon**, a Wild and Scenic River, but it has rougher water and is harder to reach. Hiking in most places is excellent, but the park maintains no trails or river crossings. So plan carefully.

While in the park, be respectful of Eskimo lands, most of which are along the Kobuk River. Ask the park for a map showing where they are.

How to Get There

Commercial planes fly daily from Anchorage and Fairbanks to Kotzebue, where the park's information center is located. Connecting flights serve the Eskimo villages of Kiana and Ambler, both on the Kobuk River, on the park's western and eastern sides respectively. From these you

Caribou migrating across the Kobuk River

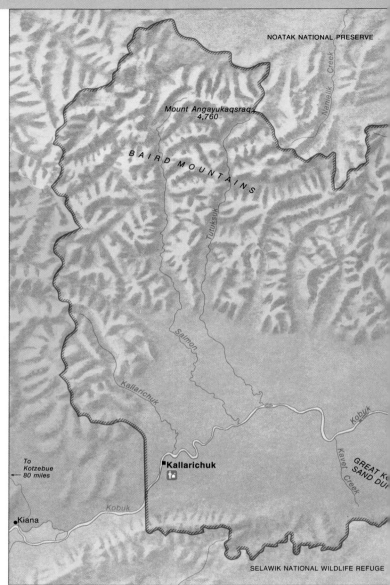

NOATAK NATIONAL PRESERVE

Namelik Creek

Mount Angayukaqsraq
4,760

B A I R D   M O U N T A I N S

Tutuksuk

Salmon

Kallarichuk

Kobuk

Kavet Creek

GREAT K
SAND DU

■ Kallarichuk

To
Kotzebue
← 80 miles

Kobuk

● Kiana

SELAWIK NATIONAL WILDLIFE REFUGE

Cranberries, club moss, and sphagnum in the tundra

A grizzly in a meadow

current that's hardly detectable.

Although steep bluffs sometimes rise above the riverbanks, hiking opportunities from the Kobuk are limitless. Park rangers will suggest routes. Both shores have forest, lakes, and tundra; the south shore has sand dunes also. Hike high ground to avoid swamps. In late August and early September you can sit on a bluff and watch caribou in striking autumn pelage as they swim across the river. Huge antlers and white ruffs mark the bulls.

A river trip through the park from Ambler to Kiana, with plenty of time for hiking, takes about a week. Or, if you want a more ambitious trip (requiring 2 to 3 weeks, depending on weather and river conditions), begin at **Walker Lake**, in Gates of the Arctic National Park, and paddle or motor all the way to Kiana.

On either trip you'll pass **Onion Portage**, a river bend, where for thousands of years migrating caribou have crossed the Kobuk. Here, in 1961, archaeologist J. Louis Giddings dug into the earth and could hardly believe his eyes. He had discovered what a Smithsonian Institution ethnologist would later call "the most important archaeological site ever found in the Arctic." Giddings' 2-acre plot yielded 30 artifact-bearing layers, reflecting 7 stages of flintworking technology, the oldest dating back at least 10,000 years.

Today, the archaeological site is inactive and largely overgrown. But in late summer and fall, Eskimos

Kobuk River

Beginning in the central Brooks Range, the **Kobuk** flows west 200 miles, winds slowly through the park for 50 miles, dropping only 2 to 3 inches per mile, and then continues west to drain into **Hotham Inlet**, off **Kotzebue Sound**. At times it seems more like a lake than a river, with a

Easily stowed inflatable craft for river runners

Hardy dune grass

hunt caribou here as they've done for millennia. During the summer, a backcountry ranger is stationed at Giddings' old cabin. Hiking is good at Onion Portage. The name comes from the wild chives that grow here.

Great Kobuk Sand Dunes

Farther downstream sprawls the **Great Kobuk Sand Dunes,** a 25-square-mile mini-Sahara. Visitors arrive by the river and leave their boats on shore for the short hike to the adventure of scaling the dunes. An Ice Age relic, the dunes formed from the windblown outwash of melting glaciers. A special combination of topography and eastern and northern winds keeps the dunes moving and inhospitable to vegetation. Some dunes measure 100 feet high. Older, thinly vegetated dunes surround this ever changing landscape 35 miles above the Arctic Circle.

Information & Activities

Headquarters
P.O. Box 1029, Kotzebue, Alaska 99752. Phone (907) 442-3760 or (907) 442-3890.

Seasons & Accessibility
Open year-round but access—by foot, boat, or charter aircraft from Kotzebue—generally June through September. (The Kobuk River usually thaws by June 1 and freezes by mid-October.) There are no roads to or in the park. Be prepared for severe arctic weather at any time. Contact park headquarters before visiting. If you plan to charter in by air, ask the park for a list of licensed companies.

Information Centers
In summer, the Kotzebue Headquarters and Information Center—80 miles from the park—is open daily, as are ranger stations at Onion Portage, and sometimes at Kallarichuk.

Entrance Fee
None.

Pets
Strongly discouraged.

Facilities for Disabled
Kotzebue information center accessible to wheelchairs; otherwise none.

Things to Do
Films at Kotzebue information center. The park organizes no activities, but rafting, kayaking, canoeing, hiking, sportfishing (license required), and aerial sightseeing are available. Commercial outfitters offer a variety of private guide services for floating, fishing, trekking trips. Call or write headquarters for a list of those licensed to work in the park.

Special Advisories
☐Take a guide along unless you are well experienced in the wilderness.
☐Mosquitoes and gnats can be brutal; bring plenty of repellent, a head net, and an insect-proof tent.
☐Eskimos own much of the land along the river and engage in subsistence hunting and fishing; be respectful of them and their property.

Overnight Backpacking
No permit required, but ask park for current information on weather, river conditions, bears, and Eskimo subsistence activities before venturing out. File a trip plan.

Campgrounds
None; backcountry camping only.

Hotels, Motels, & Inns
(unless otherwise noted, rates are for 2 persons in a double room, high season)
In Ambler, Alaska 99786:
Kobuk River Lodge (on the Kobuk River) P.O. Box 30. (907) 445-2150 or 445-2166. 6 rooms with a central bath, $125; 2 cabins with private baths and kitchenettes, $100. Restaurant.
In Kiana, Alaska 99749:
Blankenship Trading Post P.O. Box 1. (907) 475-2177. Rustic cabins with cots, propane and wood-burning stoves, no running water or electricity. Also, duplex with kitchen, water, electricity, private bath. $50 per person.
In Kotzebue, Alaska 99752:
Nullaġvik Hotel (308 Front St.) P.O. Box 336. (907) 442-3331. 75 units. $148. Restaurant.

Turquoise Lake, tinted by glacial silt

Lake Clark

Alaska

Established December 2, 1980

4,045,000 acres

"Think of all the splendors that be-speak Alaska," conservationist John Kauffmann has written, "glaciers, volcanoes, alpine spires, wild rivers, lakes with grayling on the rise. Picture coasts feathered with countless seabirds. Imagine dense forests and far-sweeping tundra, herds of caribou, great roving bears. Now concentrate all these and more into less than one percent of the state—and behold the Lake Clark region, Alaska's epitome."

Diversity is Lake Clark's hallmark. The Turquoise-Telaquana Plateau has tundra similar to Alaska's North Slope, while the coast has forests similar to the southeast panhandle. Black bears and Dall's sheep

reach their southern limits here, and Sitka spruce, Alaska's state tree, reaches its northern limit. Three rivers—the Mulchatna, Chilikadrotna, and Tlikakila—have been officially designated Wild and Scenic.

The Chigmit Mountains, spine of the park, are as rugged as mountains get. They lie on the edge of the North American plate where the oceanic plate slides under it, and their jumbled contours reflect centuries of geological violence. Two volcanoes here, Iliamna and Redoubt, are still active. Iliamna has erupted more than six times since 1768. Redoubt erupted in 1966, spewing clouds of ash 40,000 feet into the air. From 1972 to 1982 the park was shaken by 13 earthquakes that registered at least 5 on the Richter scale.

Archaeological finds show that humans, most recently Tanaina Indi-

ans, have lived in the area for centuries. The abundant salmon and game made possible a settled existence.

How to Get There

Take a plane into the heart of the park, or travel by boat or plane to the coast. Bush pilots in Anchorage say, "Lake Clark is just out the back-door"—a 1-hour flight. From Anchorage you can charter a plane to Port Alsworth, a small community on the southeast shore of Lake Clark. The flight through Lake Clark Pass takes you over immense blue glaciers, winding rivers, and snow-capped mountains. Planes also land on the coast for salmon fishing.

A less expensive alternative is to take a scheduled flight from Anchorage to Iliamna, 30 miles outside the park, and an air taxi from there into the park. Air taxis fly in from Homer and Kenai, too. To reach the park by boat, you must travel down Cook Inlet from Anchorage or across the inlet from the Kenai Peninsula.

When to Go

Summer. Wildflowers are best in late June. Autumn colors peak in early September in upper elevations, in mid-September lower down. June through August daytime temperatures usually stay in the 50s and low 60s in the eastern part of the park, and climb as high as 80°F in the western part and the interior.

How to Visit

Most visitors fly into the interior lake region of the park. Air taxis can make drop-offs and pickups at prearranged times and places. The smaller lakes offer excellent kayaking, and several rivers give kayakers and rafters great white-water experiences. Hiking is good around the lakes and from lake to lake. Fishing is usually first class. Write to park headquarters in Anchorage for information about guide services and lodges. Reserve early. If you don't plan to be completely self-sufficient, make thorough arrangements long before going.

On the Lakes & Rivers

Fishing is superb on the lakes and rivers of this fly-in park. Dolly Varden trout, northern pike, and five kinds of salmon—king, chum, coho, humpback, and, especially, sockeye—lure fishermen, many of whom take off from Port Alsworth, site of the park's field headquarters. Visitors can find lodgings at **Lake Clark** and other lakes.

As in many Alaska parks, a kayak in Lake Clark is an invitation to freedom. You can explore large areas, carry a lot of gear, and take intermittent hikes. Be aware that sudden winds can stir up large waves in minutes. Good lakes for paddling are **Telaquana, Turquoise, Twin,** Lake Clark, **Kontrashibuna,** and **Tazimina.**

Another way to see the country is to let a river take you through it. Your options are long trips (averaging 3 to 4 days) on the Wild and Scenic **Mulchatna, Chilikadrotna,** and **Tlikakila,** or short trips (averaging 1 to 2 days) on the **Kijik, Tanalian,** and the **Tazimina.** Hire a guide or check with rangers on water conditions, places to put in and take out, and what to look out for along the way.

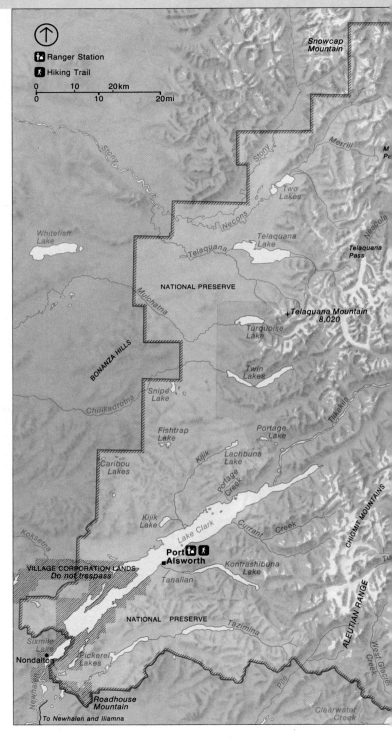

 Ranger Station

Hiking Trail

0　　10　　20km
0　　10　　　20mi

Snowcap
Mountain

Merrill

M
Pa

Stony

Two
Lakes

Necons

Neacola

Telaquana
Lake

Telaquana
Pass

Whitefish
Lake

Telaquana

NATIONAL PRESERVE

Mulchatna

+ Telaquana Mountain
8,020

Turquoise
Lake

BONANZA HILLS

Twin
Lakes

Chilikadrotna

Snipe
Lake

Tlikakila

Fishtrap
Lake

Portage
Lake

Caribou
Lakes

Kijik

Lachbuna
Lake

Portage Creek

CHIGMIT MOUNTAINS

Kijik
Lake

Koksetna

Lake Clark

Currant Creek

Port
Alsworth

Kontrashibuna
Lake

VILLAGE CORPORATION LANDS
Do not trespass

Tanalian

Tu

NATIONAL PRESERVE

Tazimina

ALEUTIAN RANGE

Sixmile
Lake

Nondalton

Pickerel
Lakes

Pile

West Glacier
Creek

Newhalen

Roadhouse
Mountain

Clearwater
Creek

To Newhalen and Iliamna

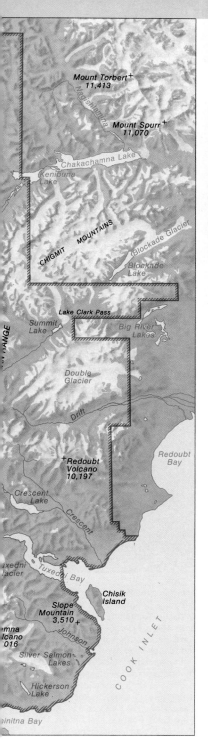

Autumn rainbow over Stony River

Hiking

In a park with no trail system and only one maintained hiking trail, route selection is critical. So is being prepared: wind and rain gear for swift changes in the weather and repellent for mosquitoes. If you intend to hike without a guide, consult with a park ranger before starting out and take a good map with you. Some general rules for hikers are: Stay as long as possible on dry tundra where footing is good, avoid heavy brush, and choose your river crossings carefully. Hiking is generally best above 2,000 feet in the interior (where the dry tundra begins), and above 700 feet along the coast (where the grassy areas begin). Below these elevations the vegetation can be thick and nearly impenetrable, especially the alder.

The 2-mile **Tanalian Falls Trail** is the only developed trail in the park. Beginning in Port Alsworth, this easy hike takes you through a forest of black spruce and birch, past bogs and ponds, and up along the tumbling Tanalian River. Watch for moose in the ponds, Arctic grayling in the river, Dall's sheep on **Tanalian Mountain**, and bears everywhere.

Another hike from Port Alsworth is the strenuous 3,600-foot climb up Tanalian Mountain. You can begin the climb off the Tanalian Falls Trail, or by hiking the shore of Lake Clark

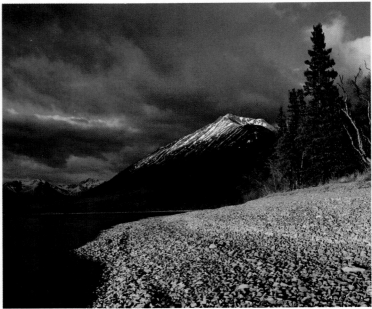

Tanalian Mountain rising from Lake Clark shores

Alpine bearberry and lichens

Arctic ground squirrel

and heading up a ridge where the walking is easier, a round-trip of about 7 miles.

North of Lake Clark are several lakes that offer excellent hiking. You can take an air taxi to one and hike to another, or stay at one lake—a world in itself—and go on day hikes along the shore and up the ridges. If a lake-to-lake trek appeals to you, try the 16 miles from Telaquana Lake south to Turquoise Lake, or from Turquoise Lake 13 miles south to Twin Lakes. From Twin Lakes you can hike 17 miles to **Portage Lake**, a beautiful tarn in an alpine valley, and from there 11 miles to **Lachbuna Lake**, over a ridge and down the **Portage Creek** drainage to Lake Clark.

For a longer, wilder, and more demanding hike through spectacular country, try the 50-mile trek from Telaquana Lake east over **Telaquana Pass**, along the **Neacola River** to **Kenibuna Lake**. From there, hike to the huge rock spire called **The Tusk**.

Information & Activities

Headquarters
4230 University Dr. #311, Anchorage, Alaska 99508. (907) 271-3751.

Seasons & Accessibility
Park open and accessible by small aircraft from Anchorage, Kenai, Homer, and Illiamna year-round. There are no roads to or in the park.

Weather changes rapidly. Call Port Alsworth at (907) 781-2218 for up-to-date conditions.

Visitor & Information Centers
Field headquarters station in Port Alsworth, on the south shore of Lake Clark. Call Anchorage headquarters at (907) 271-3751, or Port Alsworth at (907) 781-2218 for visitor information.

Gas & Supplies
Bring everything you will need.

Entrance Fee
None.

Pets
Park recommends that you leave your pets at home because they can attract bears.

Facilities for Disabled
None.

Things to Do
No park-organized activities, but the following are available: hiking, backpacking, climbing, rafting, kayaking, fishing (license required), boating, birdwatching and wildlife-watching, aerial sightseeing, hunting (in preserve).

Call or write headquarters for a list of concessioners offering a variety of guide services in the park.

Special Advisories
☐ You must possess good wilderness skills if you intend to hike, camp, or fish without a guide.
☐ Do not trespass onto or in any way disturb the property of local residents.
☐ Don't fail to bring insect repellent. A head net and insect-proof tent are also desirable.

Overnight Backpacking
No permit required, but campers are encouraged to contact field station before setting out.

Campgrounds
None. Backcountry camping only. No rest rooms, showers, or other visitor amenities except in lodges.

Hotels, Motels, & Inns
INSIDE THE PARK:
Alaska's Wilderness Lodge (on southern shore of Lake Clark) 1 Lang Road, Port Alsworth, Alaska 99653. (907) 781-2223. (from mid-May through Sept.), or 7320 Sixth Ave., Suite 1, Tacoma, Wash. 98406. (800) 835-8032 (year-round). 7 cabins. $1,600 per person, per week. 7-day sportfishing packages starting at $3,850 per person, per week. All inclusive. Open June 1 to October 1.
Lakeside Lodge (on southern shore of Lake Clark) Port Alsworth, Alaska 99653. (907) 781-2202. (from mid-May through Sept.); P.O. Box 1047, Soldotna, Alaska 99669 (907) 262-5245 (rest of year) 3 cabins, 2 with kitchenettes. Sportfishing packages. Open June to mid-Sept. **Silver Salmon Creek Lodge** (10 miles south of Tuxedni Bay on Silver Salmon Creek) P.O. Box 3234, Soldotna, Alaska 99669. (907) 262-4839. 3 lodge rooms; 3 cabins, shared baths. Sportfishing packages. $2,098 per person, per week, all inclusive. 1 tent-camp, $995 per week. Open mid-May through September.

OUTSIDE THE PARK:
Newhalen Lodge (near Nondalton) P.O. Box 102521, Anchorage, Alaska 99510. (907) 294-2233 (lodge) or (907) 522-3355 (all year). 6 units. Sportfishing packages. $3,800 per week, all inclusive. Open June to October.

Contact park headquarters for additional accommodations in and near the park.

Flowing Kennicott Glacier; Mt. Blackburn at left

Wrangell-St. Elias

Alaska

Established December 2, 1980

13,188,000 acres

Even in a state famous for its size, Wrangell-St. Elias stands out. It is by far the largest national park in the United States—almost six times the size of Yellowstone. You fly over it and see mountains beyond mountains, glaciers after glaciers, rivers upon rivers. You float a river and watch the moods and mountains change by the minute. As you walk the tundra slopes, you find Dall's sheep and mountain goats grazing.

Three major mountain ranges converge here: the volcanic Wrangells, the St. Elias—tallest coastal mountains in the world—and the Chugach. Together they contain 9 of the 16 highest peaks in the United States, 4 of them above 16,000 feet. There are more than 150 glaciers; one, the Malaspina, is larger than Rhode Island. In 1980 Wrangell-St. Elias and adjoining Kluane National Park in Canada were designated a United Nations World Heritage site.

Vast and rugged as it is, the park is not a fortress. Two roads lead into small communities, remnants of the gold and copper mining towns that thrived in the early days of this century. Today not mining but the nearly limitless hiking, rafting, kayaking, and climbing opportunities beckon.

How to Get There

Drive or charter a plane. By car from Anchorage, take Alaska Hwy. 1 (Glenn Hwy.) 189 miles northeast to Glennallen. Continue northeast 74 miles along the Copper River and the park's western boundary to Slana, where an unpaved road branches

When to Go

Summer. Lodges and guide services operate in the park from about mid-May to the end of September. June is best for wildflowers; July has the warmest days; berries ripen in August. Be prepared for cloudy skies, but September can be beautiful with clear skies, autumn colors, no mosquitoes, and a dusting of new snow on the mountain peaks. March and April offer excellent cross-country skiing for those of stout heart and strong will.

How to Visit

Take one of the two good, unpaved roads into the park. The **McCarthy Road** is maintained and usually passable in summer; four-wheel drive may be required at other times. The **Slana-Nabesna Road** is also maintained. Both roads end at colorful, historic mining towns and get you to trailheads for many hikes into the backcountry.

Or, charter a plane into a remote part of the park and hike or run a river. Several commercial companies offer guided rafting or kayaking trips on the rivers and in the spectacular coastal bays. You can get a full listing of them from the park.

into the park for 46 miles, ending at the old mining town of Nabesna.

Or, head toward the town of McCarthy by taking Alaska Hwy. 4 (Richardson Hwy.) from Glennallen 32 miles southeast to the Edgerton cutoff (Hwy. 10), then turning left and continuing 33 miles to Chitina. There the pavement ends and a road follows an old railroad bed about 60 miles into the park. These same roads can be reached from Fairbanks via Delta Junction, and from Haines, Skagway, and Whitehorse (along the Alaska-Canada Hwy.) via Haines Junction and Tok. Buses run regularly in summer from Anchorage to Valdez with stops in Glennallen.

Air charters into the park operate out of Anchorage, Fairbanks, Yakutat, Cordova, Glennallen, Gulkana, Tok, and Northway. Commercial jets service Yakutat and Cordova year-round. In summer, the Alaska State Ferry serves Valdez from Whittier (reachable by train from Anchorage).

The McCarthy Road to Kennicott

62 miles one way; a half day

From the town of Chitina and the confluence of the **Chitina** and **Copper Rivers,** the road follows the abandoned Copper River and Northwest Railroad bed. At mile 17 the road crosses the **Kuskulana River Bridge.** It spans 525 feet, crossing 260 feet above the river. Another abandoned railroad trestle spans the **Gilahina River** at mile 28.5. At the end of the road is a parking lot and the **Kennicott River.** To reach the old mining town of **McCarthy** on the other side of the river you pull yourself across on two cable trams—moderately hard work, but a great adventure. Today a tiny community of hardy individualists, McCarthy had a population of more than 2,000 in mining days.

From McCarthy, a dirt road climbs 500 feet in 5 miles to the former town and millsite of **Kennicott.** You can take a taxi or rent a bike in

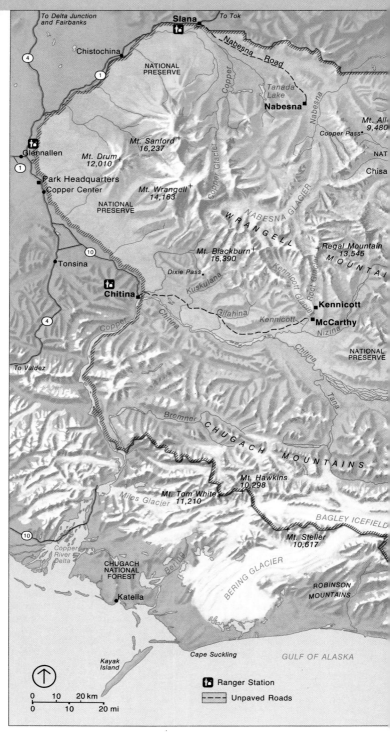

To Delta Junction
and Fairbanks

Slana

To Tok

Chistochina

Nabesna Road

NATIONAL
PRESERVE

Tanada
Lake

Nabesna

Mt. All
9,480

Cooper Pass

Mt. Sanford
16,237

Glennallen

Mt. Drum
12,010

NAT

Chisa

Park Headquarters
Copper Center

Mt. Wrangell
14,163

NATIONAL
PRESERVE

WRANGELL

NABESNA GLACIER

MOUNTAI

Regal Mountain
13,545

Tonsina

Mt. Blackburn
16,390

Dixie Pass

Kuskulana

Copper Glacier

Kennicott Glacier

Root Glacier

Kennicott

Chitina

Gilahina

Kennicott

McCarthy

Nizina

Copper

Chitina

Chitina

Tana

NATIONAL
PRESERVE

To Valdez

Bremner

CHUGACH

MOUNTAINS

Mt. Hawkins
10,298

Mt. Tom White
11,210

Miles Glacier

BAGLEY ICEFIELD

Mt. Steller
10,617

Copper
River
Delta

CHUGACH
NATIONAL
FOREST

Bering

BERING GLACIER

ROBINSON
MOUNTAINS

Katella

Kayak
Island

Cape Suckling

GULF OF ALASKA

0   10   20 km
0   10   20 mi

🏠 Ranger Station

- - - Unpaved Roads

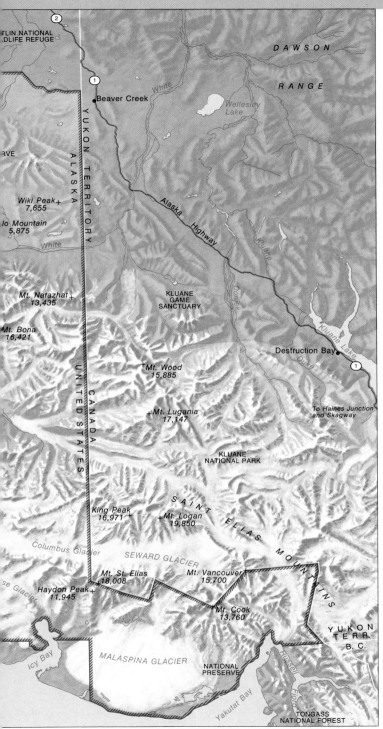

TLIN NATIONAL
DLIFE REFUGE

②

DAWSON

RANGE

① White

● Beaver Creek

Wellesley
Lake

YUKON TERRITORY

ALASKA

RVE

Alaska Highway

Kluane

Wiki Peak +
7,655

Io Mountain
5,875

White

Mt. Natazhat +
13,435

KLUANE
GAME
SANCTUARY

Donjek

Kluane Lake

Mt. Bona
16,421

UNITED STATES

CANADA

Mt. Wood
15,885

● Destruction Bay

①

Duke

+Mt. Lugania
17,147

To Haines Junction
and Skagway

KLUANE
NATIONAL PARK

SAINT

King Peak
16,971 +

+Mt. Logan
19,850

ELIAS

Columbus Glacier

SEWARD GLACIER

MOUNTAINS

se Glacier

Mt. St. Elias
18,008

Mt. Vancouver
15,700

Haydon Peak +
11,945

+Mt. Cook
13,760

YUKON
TERR.
B.C.

Icy Bay

MALASPINA GLACIER

NATIONAL
PRESERVE

Russell Fiord

Yakutat Bay

TONGASS
NATIONAL FOREST

Kennicott's copper mill, silent since 1938

McCarthy if you prefer not to walk. Kennicott was once the site of the world's richest copper mine. From 1906 to 1938, when the mine closed, it yielded 591,000 tons of copper and 900,000 ounces of silver. Today, the silent 13-story mill and other Kennicott buildings are still dressed in mineral oxide red with white trim. Though deteriorating, they form one of Alaska's most photogenic collections of historic structures and are, since 1986, on the National Register of Historic Places.

After exploring Kennicott, you can hike the trail north of town for spectacular views of the **Kennicott** and **Root Glaciers** and **Mt. Blackburn.**

The Nabesna Road

46 miles one way; a half day

Since parts of this road into the **Wrangell Mountains** are subject to washouts, be sure to check conditions with the Park Service before you set out. The road passes homesteads and fishing camps on privately owned land and then climbs over the watershed divide (mile 25) between the Copper River, which drains into the Gulf of Alaska, and the **Nabesna River,** which drains into the **Tanana River,** the Yukon River, and finally the Bering Sea. There are excellent views of **Mt. Sanford** and the **Copper Glacier** to the southwest. The final 4 miles, from **Devil's Mountain Lodge** to the quaint old mining town of **Nabesna,** are the most rugged.

Other Hikes & Water Trips

At mile 13.5 on the **McCarthy Road,** the **Nugget Creek-Kotsina Road** branches northeast 2½ miles to the **Nugget Creek Trail.** Sixteen miles later and 1,000 feet higher, the trail arrives at a public-use cabin beneath Mt. Blackburn, where you can picnic and camp. A dozen good day hikes can be taken from here. Watch for Dall's sheep. A little more than a mile past the Nugget Creek trailhead begins the **Dixie Pass Trail.** Climbing 3,600 feet in 10 miles, it's a strenuous hike, but worth it if the weather is clear.

Off the **Nabesna Road, Trail Creek** at mile 29.4 and **Lost Creek** at mile 31.2 offer good hiking routes. There are no defined trails, simply follow the creek bed northward as far as you like. Though the hiking is not generally difficult, you will run into rocky patches and may have to hop or wade the creek. But you will be rewarded with excellent views of the upper Copper River basin. Talk to a ranger and fill out a backcountry itinerary before any overnight stays.

Commercial outfitters offer rafting trips down the Nabesna, Kennicott, Copper, Chitina, and **Nizina Rivers.** Short trips last 3 hours, extended ones 2 weeks; there are all classes of water. It's an adventuresome way to see Wrangell-St. Elias. Contact the park for a full listing of the outfitters that operate there.

Information & Activities

Headquarters
P.O. Box 29, Glennallen, Alaska
99588. Phone (907) 822-5234.

Seasons & Accessibility
Park open year-round, but best time
is mid-May through September.
Snow limits winter access.

Call headquarters for road conditions before attempting to drive to
the park.

Visitor & Information Centers
Park headquarters at mile 105.5 Old
Richardson Hwy. (just off Alaska
Hwy. 4) at western edge of park.
Open daily Memorial Day through
Labor Day, weekdays the rest of
year. Information also available at
Yakutat, Slana, and Chitina ranger
stations, all outside park boundaries.
Chitina closed October through May.
Call headquarters for information.

Entrance Fee
None.

Pets
Permitted on leashes except in public
buildings; permitted off leashes in
the backcountry.

Facilities for Disabled
None.

Things to Do
No park-organized activities, but the
following are available: hiking,
horseback riding (rentals in McCarthy), pack trips, river running,
kayaking, jet boat rentals, lake fishing, mountain climbing, air tours,
cross-country skiing. Ask park for
list of companies that offer guide and
outfitting services.

Special Advisories
☐This is a wilderness park; hikers
and backpackers must be wholly self-
sufficient; do not attempt the backcountry without a guide unless
you're experienced and equipped.
☐Choose your river crossings carefully; many rivers are impassable.
☐Be respectful of native camps, fish-
nets, and other private property.
☐Mosquitoes can be brutal in July
and August; bring repellent, a

head net, and an insect-proof tent.

Overnight Backpacking
Permit not required, but best to reg-
ister before going into backcountry.
Let the park help plan your trip.

Campgrounds
Two private campgrounds within
park: **Silver Lake Campground** (milepost 9.3 on McCarthy Road) camping
and limited services. **Nelson's Lakeside Campground** (milepost 10.9 on
McCarthy Road) camping, boat rentals, and limited services.

Hotels, Motels, & Inns
*(unless otherwise noted, rates are for 2
persons in a double room, high season)*
INSIDE THE PARK:
Kennicott Glacier Lodge (in Kennicott)
P.O. Box 103940, Anchorage, Alaska
99510. (907) 258-2350. 12 rooms,
shared baths. $105 per person, in-
cludes meals. **McCarthy Wilderness
Bed & Breakfast** (in McCarthy) P.O.
Box 111241, Anchorage, Alaska
99511. (907) 277-6867. 3 rooms, $60,
includes breakfast; 1 cabin with
kitchenette, $150. No phones, elec-
tricity, running water. Open mid-
May to Oct. 1. **Tanada Lake Lodge** (on
Tanada Lake) P.O. Box 258, Fairbanks, Alaska 99707. (907) 452-1247.
6 cabins, shared baths, 3 kitchenettes. $250 per person, includes
meals and use of boats. Open July to
September 1.

OUTSIDE THE PARK:
Copper Center Lodge Drawer J, Copper Center, Alaska 99573. (907) 822-
3245. 18 rooms, 8 with private baths.
$50. Restaurant. **Gakona Lodge** (on
Alas. Hwy. 1, north of Glennallen)
P.O. Box 285, Gakona, Alaska 99586.
(907) 822-3482. 3 cabins, private
baths $100; 10 rooms, shared baths
$45. Restaurant. Open all year;
weekends only from Nov. to April.

*Contact headquarters for additional ac-
commodations in and near the park.*

Acknowledgments

We are indebted to the many individuals and the federal, state, and private agencies that helped prepare this guide, especially to the National Park Service and the superintendents and chiefs of interpretation and their staffs at each park. Our thanks go also to the National Parks and Conservation Association for its cooperation and to Frances Kennedy, who offered wise counsel.

For assistance at the National Geographic, we are particularly grateful to Dennis Collins and the Pre-Press/Typographic Division. Other divisions that deserve special thanks are Administrative Services, the Illustrations Library, Library/News Collection, Messenger Service, Photographic Laboratory, and Travel Office.

Illustrations Credits

Abbreviations for terms appearing below:
(t)-top; (b)-bottom; (l)-left; (r)-right;
(c)-center; BPS-Biological Photo Service;
DRK-DRK Photo; NGP-National Geographic
Photographer; NGS-National Geographic
Staff. P/A-Photographers/Aspen.

Cover, Tom Danielsen. 2-3, Gary Moon. 6-7, Pat O'Hara. 8, Frank S. Balthis. 9 (t), Lowell Georgia. (b), Tom Bean.

The East
12-13, James Valentine. 18-19, Glenn Van Nimwegen. 19, John Netherton. 20, Sonja Bullaty. 23 (t), Stephen J. Krasemann. (b), John Netherton. 24, Glenn Van Nimwegen. 25 (t), Alan Nyiri. (b), Clyde Smith. 27 (t), Bates Littlehales. (c), John Netherton. (b), Stephen J. Krasemann, DRK. 28-29, Stephen Frink, Waterhouse. 29, Robert Holland. 31 (t), James Valentine. (b), Doug Perrine, DRK. 32, Bruce Mounier. 33 (t), Doug Perrine, DRK. (cl), Larry Lipsky, DRK. (cr), (bl), (br), Stephen Frink, Waterhouse. 35 (t), James Valentine. (tc), C.C. Lockwood. (bc), Caulion Singletary. (b), R.J. Erwin, DRK. 36-37, Stephen J. Krasemann, DRK. 40 (t), Stephen J. Krasemann, Peter Arnold. (c), James A. Kern. (b), Ron Sanford. 41, David Hiser, P/A. 42 (t), Otis Imboden. (b), Bianca Lavies. 43 (t) Glenn Van Nimwegen. (b), Fred Hirschmann. 44 (t), Stephen J. Krasemann, DRK. (cl), Ronny Paille. (cr), Caulion Singletary. (bl), David Smart, DRK. (br), Grant Haist. 46 (t), James Valentine. (c), Farrell Grehan. (b), Glenn Van Nimwegen. 47 (t), Stephen J. Krasemann, DRK. (c), James P. Blair, NGP. (b), Matt Bradley. 48-49, John Netherton. 51-52, James P. Blair, NGP. 53, Tim Black. 54 (t), Tim Thompson. (bl), Tim Black. (br), John Netherton. 56 (t), Larry Ulrich. (c), Bill Peane. (b), Dick Durrance II. 57 (t), Pat O'Hara. (c), Larry Ulrich. (b), James Valentine. 58-59, Declan Haun. 59, Matt Bradley. 61, Declan Haun. 63 (t), Matt Bradley. (ct), Stephen J. Krasemann. (cb & b), Matt Bradley. 64-65, Daniel J. Cox. 65 & 67, John & Ann Mahan. 68, Jim Brandenburg. 70 (t) & (b), John & Ann Mahan. (c), C.C. Lockwood, Bruce Coleman Inc. 71 (t), John & Ann Mahan. (c), Carl R. Sams II. (b), Stephen J. Krasemann, DRK. 72-77, Chip Clark. 74 (b)-77 (b), Richard Schlecht. 79 (t), Dan Dry. (b), David

Muench. 80-81, Jeff Gnass. 84, David Muench. 85 (t) & (b), Stephen J. Krasemann. 87 (t) & (c), Carr Clifton. (b), Stephen J. Krasemann, DRK. 88-89, Tom Bean, DRK. 91-93, Jodi Cobb, NGP. 93 (r), Bruce Nyden. 95, Stephen Frink, Waterhouse. 96-97, John & Ann Mahan. 97, Erwin & Peggy Bauer. 99, Jeff Gnass. 100 (t), Erwin & Peggy Bauer. (b), R. Stottlemyer, Michigan Technological Univ./BPS. 101, Stephen J. Krasemann, DRK. 103 (t), John & Ann Mahan. (c), Stephen J. Krasemann, DRK. (b), David Hiser.

The Southwest
104-105, David Muench. 108-109, Tom Bean. 109-112, Matt Bradley. 113 (t), Tom Bean. (b), Larry Ulrich. 114, George Mobley, NGP. 115 (t), Larry Ulrich. (b), Tom Bean. 116 (t), Bruce Dale, NGP. (b), Stephen J. Krasemann. 117, David Muench. 118-119, Danny Lehman. 120-121, Tibor Toth. 122, David S. Boyer, NGS. 123, Stephen J. Krasemann. 125 (t) & (b), Shattil/Rozinski. (c), Lewis Kemper. 126-130, Matt Bradley.

The Colorado Plateau
132-133, W.M. Edwards. 136-137, Tom & Pat Leeson. 139, Ron Sanford. 141 (t), Farrell Grehan. (c), Larry Ulrich. (b), Jeff Gnass. 142-143, Larry Ulrich. 144, Fred Hirschmann. 145, Grant Haist. 147 (t), Fred Hirschmann. (c), Larry Ulrich. (b), Pat O'Hara. 148-149, George Mobley, NGP. 149, David Muench. 151, Becky & Gary Vestal. 152 (t), W.M. Edwards. (b), Becky & Gary Vestal. 153 (t), Pat O'Hara. (b), David Hiser, P/A. 154, Becky & Gary Vestal. 156 (t), Tom Till. (c), Farrell Grehan. (b), John Gerlach, DRK. 157, David Hiser, P/A. 158-159, Gordon Anderson. 159, Larry Ulrich. 161 (t), Charlie Borland. (b), Galen Rowell. 162 (t), Kerrick James. (b), Joel Grimes. 164-165, Larry Ulrich. 167, Ron Sanford. 168, Tom & Pat Leeson. 169, Jack W. Dykinga. 170, W. E. Garrett, NGS. 171, Ned Seidler, NGS. 173, Larry Ulrich. 174 (t), Jeff Gnass. (c & b), Larry Ulrich. 175 (t), Larry Ulrich. (c & b), Jeff Gnass. 176-177, Jeff Gnass. 177, David Muench. 179, Larry Ulrich. 180, Richard Olsenius. 181, Phil Schofield, Aperture. 183 (t), Jack Olson. (c), Gary Brettnacher. (b), Pat O'Hara. 184-185, David Muench. 188 (l), Dewitt Jones. (r), Richard Alexander Cooke III. 189, William Belknap, Jr. 191, Tom Till. (t), Larry Ulrich. 192-193, Tom Algire. 195, Larry Ulrich. 197 (t), Charles Krebs. (c & b), Fred Hirschmann. 198-199, Tom Algire. 199, James Randklev. 201, Fred Hirschmann. 202 (t), John Telford. (c), Fred Hirschmann. (b), George Mobley, NGP. 203 (t), Larry Ulrich. (b), David Muench. 204 (t), Pat O'Hara. (b), Stephen J. Krasemann, DRK.

The Pacific Southwest
206-207, Galen Rowell. 210-211, Thomas Nebbia. 212-213, Jeff Gnass. 215, James P. Blair, NGP. 216, Nicholas DeVore III, P/A. 217 (t), Caroline Sheen. (b), Pat O'Hara. 218-219, B.F. Molnia, Terraphotographics/BPS. 221, Stephen J. Krasemann. 222 (t), David Muench. (b), Robert J. Western. 223, David Muench. 225 (t), Jeff Gnass. (b), Steve Raymer, NGS. 226-227, David Muench. 227, James A. Sugar. 229, David Muench. 230, C.F. Miescke, Foto 64/BPS. 231 (t), Scott Rutherford. (b), Jeff Gnass. 233 (t), Scott Rutherford. (c), Jeff Gnass.

234-235, Larry Ulrich. 235, Angelo Lomeo.
238, David Muench. 241 (t & c), Pat O'Hara.
(b), Richard Frear, National Park Service.
242-243, Dewitt Jones. 245, David Muench.
246 (t), Pat O'Hara. (b), Jim Brandenburg.
247, Gordon Wiltsie, Bruce Coleman Inc.
248, Farrell Grehan. 248-9, Glenn Van Nimwegen. 249, Steve Raymer, NGS. 251 (t),
Pat O'Hara. (c), Lewis Kemper. (b), Larry
Ulrich.

The Rocky Mountains
252-253, Paul Chesley. 256-257, Jim Brandenburg. 259, Tom Bean/DRK. 260 (t), Fred
Hirschmann. (b), Don & Pat Valenti, DRK.
262-263, Tom Danielsen. 263, Erwin & Peggy Bauer. 265, James P. Blair, NGP. 266, Pat
O'Hara. 267 (t), David Hiser. (b), Virginia
Karrels. 268 (c), Ken McGraw. (b), Scott
Rutherford. 268-269, Erwin & Peggy Bauer.
271 (t), Jeff Foott, DRK. (ct), Pat O'Hara.
(cb), Charles Gurche. (b), James Amos. 272-
273, David Hiser, P/A. 275 (t), Linde Waid-
hofer. 276-277, Shattil/Rozinski. 278, Leon-
ard Lee Rue IV. 280 (t), Jeff Gnass. (c), John
Ward. (b), Shattil/Rozinski. 281 (t), John
Fielder. (c), Shattil/Rozinski. (b), David
Hiser. 282-285, Steve Kaufman. 286, Tom
Bean, DRK. 287 (t), Tom Till, DRK. (b), Jim
Brandenburg. 289 (t), David Muench. (ct),
Stephen J. Krasemann. (cb & b), Wayne
Lankinen, DRK. 290-291, Lowell Georgia.
293, Paul Chesley, P/A. 294, Steve Kaufman.
295, Janis Miglavs. 296, Erwin A. Bauer. 298
(t), Lowell Georgia. (c), Pat O'Hara. (b),
James P. Blair, NGP. 299 (t), Stephen J. Kra-
semann. (b), Wayne Lankinen, DRK. 300-
301, Gary Moon. 303, Tom Bean, DRK. 305
(t), Gary R. Zahm, DRK. (ct), Jeff Gnass.
(cb), Joel Strasser, South Dakota Division of
Tourism. (b), R. Stottlemyer, Michigan
Technological Univ./BPS. 306-307, Larry
Ulrich. 307, Dean Krakel II. 310, Jeff Henry.
311 (t), Jim Brandenburg. (c), Steven Fuller.
(b), Tom Danielsen. 312-13, Jim Brandenburg. 313 (t), Pat O'Hara. (cr), Farrell Grehan. (cl), Craig Fujii/The Seattle Times. (b),
Jeff Vanuga, OVIS. 314, Larry Auippy. 315,
Larry Ulrich. 317 (t), Pat O'Hara. (c), Wayne
Lankinen. (b), Randy Ury.

The Pacific Northwest
318-319, Pat O'Hara. 322-323, James A.
Sugar, Black Star. 325-326, Steve Terrill.
328 (t & b), Steve Terrill. (c), Larry Ulrich.
329 (t), Steve Terrill. (c), Jeff Gnass. (b),
Farrell Grehan. 330-331, Jeff Gnass. 331,
Frank S. Balthis. 335 (t), Pat O'Hara. (c &
b), Jeff Gnass. 336-337, Art Wolfe. 340 (t),
Charles A. Mauzy. (b), Steve Terrill. 341 (t),
David M. Seager, NGS. (c), Stephen J.
Krasemann, Art Wolfe. 342, David
Muench. 343 (t, ctl, ctr), Pat O'Hara. (cbl),
George F. Mobley, NGP. (cbr & br), Farrell
Grehan. (bl), Charles A. Mauzy. 345 (t & c),
Pat O'Hara. (b), Stephen J. Krasemann. 346-
347, Pat O'Hara. 350, David Hiser. 351,
Bruce Dale, NGP. 353 (t & b), Pat O'Hara.
(c), Art Wolfe. 354-355, Pat O'Hara. 358, Da-
vid M. Seager, NGS. 358-359, Charles A.
Mauzy. 359, Steve Terrill. 360, Pat O'Hara.
361 (t), Charles A. Mauzy. (ctl), Thomas Kit-
chin. (ctr), Wayne Lynch, DRK. (cbl, bl, &
br), David Denning, Earth Images. (cbr),
Jeff Foott. 363 (t), Jeff Gnass. (ct & b), Pat
O'Hara. (cb), Stephen J. Krasemann. 364-
365, David Muench. 368, Bob Clemenz. 369,
Larry Ulrich. 371 (t), Wayne Lynch, DRK.
(b), Lewis Kemper, DRK.

Alaska
372-373, Jim Brandenburg. 376-377, Michio
Hoshino. 380, Bruce Dale, NGP. 381, Ken-
nan Ward, DRK. 382 (t), Clark Mishler. (ct),
Helen Rhode. (cl), Tom Bean. (bl), Erwin &
Peggy Bauer. (br), Becky & Gary Vestal. 384
(t), Chris Johns. (c), Stephen J. Krasemann.
(b), Fred Hirschmann. 385 (t), Carr Clifton.
(c), Tom Bean. (b), Stephen J. Krasemann,
DRK. 386 (t), James A. Sugar. (ct), Lowell
Georgia. (cb), Stephen J. Krasemann, DRK.
(b), M. Woodbridge Williams. 387 (t), Ron-
ald Levy. (c), Stephen J. Krasemann, DRK.
(b), Tim Thompson. 388-389, J. & M. Ibbot-
son/Alaska Photo. 389, John Milton. 391,
Stephen J. Krasemann, DRK. 392 (t), Bob
Waldrop. (b), Fred Hirschmann. 394-395,
Tom Bean. 398 (t), Steve Kaufman. (b), Kim
Heacox, Earth Images. 400-401, Fred
Hirschmann. 404, Win Parks. 406-407, Boyd
Norton. 407, George Wuerthner. 410 (tl),
Johnny Johnson, DRK. (c), Stephen J.
Krasemann, DRK. (r), Boyd Norton. (b),
George Herben. 412-413, John Milton. 413,
Michio Hoshino. 414, Larry Ulrich. 415, Ste-
phen J. Krasemann, DRK. 416 (t), Tim
Thompson. (b), Stephen J. Krasemann,
DRK. 418-419, Will Troyer/Alaska Photo.
421, Fred Hirschmann. 422 (t & bl), Fred
Hirschmann. (br), Stephen J. Krasemann,
DRK. 424-425, Kim Heacox. 428, Tom
Bean/DRK.

Index of Excursions

(For national parks list see Contents)

Admiralty Island NM, Alas. 385
Agassiz NWR, Minn. 103
Akaka Falls State Park, Hawaii 233
Aniakchak NM & Preserve, Alas. 386
Apache-Sitgreaves NFs, Ariz. 173
Apostle Is. National Lakeshore, Wis. 71
Arapaho NF, Colo. 281
Arapaho NWR, Colo. 280
Arctic NWR, Alas. 386
Aztec Ruins NM, N. Mex. 191

Benton Lake NWR, Mont. 299
Bering Land Bridge National Preserve, Alas. 387
Big Cypress National Preserve, Fla. 48
Big South Fork National River & Recreation
   Area, Tenn. 57
Bighorn Canyon NRA, Mont. 317
Black Canyon of the Gunnison NM, Colo. 141
Bosque del Apache NWR, N. Mex. 125
Breaks Interstate Park, Va. 56
Bridger-Teton NF, Wyo. 271
Buck Island Reef NM, V. I. 95
Buffalo Gap National Grassland, S. Dak. 305
Buffalo National River, Ark. 63

Canyon de Chelly NM, Ariz. 175
Cape Krusenstern NM, Alas. 386
Cedar Breaks NM, Utah 147
Chattahoochee NF, Ga. 57
Cherokee NF, Tenn. 57
Chippewa NF, Minn. 103
Chugach NF, Alas. 384
Coconino NF, Ariz. 173
Colorado NM, Colo. 141
Corkscrew Swamp Sanctuary, Fla. 46
Crosby Wetland, N. Dak. 289
Cumberland Gap National Historical Park, Ky. 79

Daniel Boone NF, Ky. 79
Death Valley NM, Calif. 183
Desert National Wildlife Range, Nev. 183
Devils Postpile NM, Calif. 251
Devils Tower NM, Wyo. 305
Dinosaur NM, Colo. 281

Dixie NF, Utah 147
Dungeness NWR, Wash. 363

El Malpais NM, N. Mex. 197
El Morro NM, N. Mex. 197

Fishlake NF, Utah 147
Flathead NF, Mont. 298
Florissant Fossil Beds NM, Colo. 281
Fort Jefferson NM, Fla. 47
Fossil Butte NM, Wyo. 271

George Washington NF, Va. 87
Gifford Pinchot NF, Wash. 345
Glen Canyon NRA, Ariz. 157
Grand Portage NM, Minn. 70
Great White Heron NWR, Fla. 35

Henry Mts. Buffalo Herd, Utah 156
Hiawatha NF, Mich. 70
Hobe Sound NF, Fla. 47
Holla Bend NWR, Ark. 63
Horseshoe Harbor Preserve, Mich. 70
Hovenweep NM, Colo. 191
Humboldt Bay NWR, Calif. 371
Humboldt NF, Nev. 183

Iao Valley State Park, Hawaii 225
Inyo NF, Calif. 241

J. N. "Ding" Darling NWR, Fla. 46
Jefferson NF, Va. 87
Jewel Cave NM, S. Dak. 305
John Pennekamp Coral Reef State Park, Fla. 35
Joshua Tree NM, Calif. 217

Kaibab NF, Ariz. 173
Kenai NWR, Alas. 385
Key West NWR, Fla. 35
Klamath Basin NWR, Calif. 329
Kootenai NF, Mont. 298

Lake Ilo NWR, N. Dak. 289
Lake Mead NRA, Nev. 174
Lassen NF, Calif. 335
Lava Beds NM, Calif. 329
Lewis & Clark NF, Mont. 298
Lincoln NF, N. Mex. 125
Little Missouri National Grassland,
    N. Dak. 289
Lostwood NWR, N. Dak. 289
Loxahatchee NWR, Fla. 47

Manti-LaSal NF, Utah 141
Mason Neck NWR, Va. 87
Mauna Kea Observatory, Hawaii 233
Misty Fiords NM, Alas. 385
Montezuma Castle NM, Ariz. 175
Mooshorn NWR, Me. 27
Mt. Baker-Snoqualmie NF, Wash. 353
Mt. Rushmore National Mem., S. Dak. 305
Mt. St. Helens National Volcanic Monument,
    Wash. 345

Nantahala NF, N. C. 56
National Elk Refuge, Wyo. 271
National Key Deer Refuge, Fla. 35
Natural Bridges NM, Utah 156
Navajo NM, Ariz. 175
Nisqually NWR, Wash. 363
Noatak National Preserve, Alas. 386

Okanogan NF, Wash. 353
Olympic NF, Wash. 363
Oregon Caves NM, Oreg. 328
Oregon Dunes NRA, Oreg. 329
Ottawa NF, Mich. 71
Ouachita NF, Ark. 63
Ozark NF, Ark. 63

Petit Manan NWR, Me. 27
Pictured Rocks National Lakeshore, Mich. 71
Pine Butte Swamp Preserve, Mont. 299
Pinnacles NM, Calif. 241
Pisgah NF, N. C. 56

Rachel Carson NWR, Me. 27
Rainbow Bridge NM, Ariz. 157
Red Rock Lakes NWR, Mont. 317
Ridgefield NWR, Wash. 345

Rio Grande Wild and Scenic River, Big Bend NP,
    Tex. 117
Rogue River NF, Oreg. 328
Roosevelt NF, Colo. 280
Routt NF, Colo. 280

Saguaro NM, Ariz. 197
San Juan Islands NWR, Wash. 363
San Juan NF, Colo. 191
Santa Monica Mts. NRA, Calif. 217
Sequoia NF, Calif. 241
Shoshone NF, Wyo. 317
Sierra NF, Calif. 251
Siskiyou NF, Oreg. 328
Six Rivers NF, Calif. 371
Skagit River Bald Eagle Natural Area, Wash. 353
Stanislaus NF, Calif. 251
Sunset Crater NM, Ariz. 174
Superior NF, Minn. 103

Targhee NF, Idaho 271
Tetlin NWR, Alas. 384
Tongass NF, Alas. 384

Waianapanapa State Park, Hawaii 225
Westwater Canyon, Utah 156
Whiskeytown-Shasta-Trinity NRA, Calif. 335
White Mountains NRA, Alas. 387
White Sands NM, N. Mex. 125
Wupatki NM, Ariz. 174

Yukon-Charley Rivers National Preserve, Alas.
    387

Type composition by the Typographic section of National Geographic Production Services, Pre-Press Division. Maps by R. R. Donnelley & Sons Co., Cartographic Services, Lancaster, Pa. Color separations by The Lanman Companies, Washington, D. C.; Printed and bound by Ringier America, Inc., New Berlin, Wisconsin. Paper by Mead Paper Co., New York, N. Y.

Library of Congress ℭℐℙ Data

National geographic's guide to the national parks of the United States. — Rev. ed.
    p.   cm.
    Includes index.
    ISBN 0-87044-885-4
    1. National parks and reserves — United States — Guidebooks.   2. United States — Guidebooks.   3. Outdoor recreation — United States — Guidebooks.   I. National Geographic Society   (U. S.)
E160.N244 1992
917.304'928 — dc20   92-5851
                                          CIP